7.82 Russell + Russell 1162 (Swearingen)

MISSIONARY AND MANDARIN

C. N. Cochin eques. del.

C. S. Gaucher inc. 1780

The imperial Spring Plowing ceremony. An eighteenth-century
interpretation of paternalistic monarchy in China
(From Roucher's poem *Les Mois*)

MISSIONARY AND MANDARIN

The Jesuits at the Court of China

By

ARNOLD H. ROWBOTHAM

NEW YORK / RUSSELL & RUSSELL

1966

TO
MY WIFE

PREFACE

THIS VOLUME *is an attempt to relate for English-speaking readers a chapter in the history of cultural relations between East and West—a dramatic episode in which the predominant parts are played by members of the Society of Jesus.*

In the whole record of cultural contacts it would be difficult to find a period so definitely circumscribed and at the same time so rich in its influence. Jesuit history is not lacking in dramatic chapters—as the story of the communal experiment in Paraguay well attests—but no contribution of the order is more significant, none has a more important place in the account of human progress than the China mission. Here, in a unique and powerful way, the Jesuit was the voice of the East to the West and also the interpreter of the Occident to the Orient. In this field he stands without a peer, almost without a rival. It may be argued that the Jesuit contribution has not been indispensable to modern cultural relations between China and the West, but it is certainly true that what we know of the Far Eastern country today, and particularly what we value of its civilization, has its source in the traditions which the Jesuits established in the seventeenth and eighteenth centuries.

Such a story would be incomplete without a discussion of the Rites controversy, which intrudes itself like a skeleton at the feast. Experience has shown that, in dealing with any phase of the history of the Society, complete impartiality is an ideal difficult to attain. When it is a question of theological controversy, this impartiality is well-nigh impossible. In attempting the difficult task the author has approached his subject from the standpoint of a sympathetic non-Catholic who cannot be expected adequately to appreciate the high seriousness of distinctions of dogma or of ecclesiastical hierarchy. He must be pardoned if he judges history in the light of effects rather than of causes.

In such a discussion the problem of evidence is important. It is apparent that the bulk of the anti-Jesuit literature, as well as that of much of the Society, is biased and at times venomous but it cannot be completely ignored for that reason. The best that the critic can do is to review the clash of arguments and draw his own conclusions.

The story deals with China of the seventeenth and eighteenth centuries. Any statements or generalizations concerning the social or political life of the country have to do with that period and are not necessarily true for modern China where the process of Westernization has brought new and startling changes. In the same way the discussion of the Jesuits is limited to the Society as it appeared before the suppression in 1773. The old name of the capital has been retained in preference to the modern form Peiping. An attempt has been made at consistency in the romanization of Chinese names, but this consistency has been broken when general usage has seemed to demand it. Furthermore, many of the foreign names have been given in the French form, although the priest in question may have been of another nationality, because the greater part of the literature is in French and the name is to be found most frequently in that form.

The author wishes to express his grateful appreciation to those who have aided him in this work: To the authorities of the British Museum and the Bibliothèque Nationale, whose courtesies made easily available the documentary material from which some of these pages were written; to the late Père Planchet of the Catholic Mission of Peking, in whose small but precious library the idea of this work took shape; to Professor Harley F. MacNair of the University of Chicago, whose careful study of the manuscript and whose wise criticism and kindly encouragement have been invaluable; to Father George H. Dunne, S.J., of Chicago; to Professor Sha Chih-pei and Professor Woodbridge Bingham, both of the University of California, and others. Although they must be dissociated from errors of fact or interpretation, these friendly critics have, the author hopes, helped to reduce such errors to a respectable minimum.

A. H. R.

Berkeley, 1940

CONTENTS

ILLUSTRATIONS

THE FORERUNNERS OF THE JESUITS

Chapter I

CHRISTENDOM AND THE MONGOLS

HE HISTORY of the earliest days of Christianity in the Far East, obscured though it often is by uncertainty and legend, glows, nevertheless, with color and action. The deeds of the missionaries, Nestorian and Catholic, give to the story the romance of high spiritual achievement. Across its passages run the names of great men: T'ai Tsung of the brilliant T'ang dynasty, the mythical potentate Prester John, the mighty Kublai Khan and the apostle Thomas whose first resting place on the Coromandel Coast of India has for centuries been a shrine visited by thousands of devout Christians.

Saint Thomas is thought to have accepted the task of converting the Indies at the time of the dispersion of the apostles. Tradition says that, after preaching for some time in Arabia, he passed to the island of Socotra and thence to the Malabar Coast. He appears to have been called to India and to have been martyred there in 52 A.D. "The Syriac and Oriental versions of the martyrdom," says Sir Wallis Budge, "state that the Indian king whom he converted was called 'Gondaphorus' and as coins and inscriptions of this king have been found, there can no longer be any doubt that Thomas *did* preach in India."[1] That he pushed on eastward and reached China is much more doubtful. It is to an ancient breviary of the church of Malabar that the West owes the earliest reference to this legend. The document, written in Chaldean, says:

By Saint Thomas were the errors of idolatry banished from among the Indians.
By Saint Thomas were the Chinese and the Ethiopians converted to the truth.[2]

Arnobius, at the end of the third century, speaks of "the Christian deeds done in India and among the Seres, Persians and Medes."[3]

[1] For notes to chap. i, see pp. 305–306.

Since the word "Seres" is the term by which the Chinese were supposed to have been known to the ancient world, this statement might
seem to imply that Saint Thomas the Apostle actually did reach
China. There is, however, practically no other evidence to support
this contention and the theory has been held untenable by the great
majority of modern scholars.' It is probable that the error may have
arisen from a misconception of the word "Seres," which in the early
days of the Christian era may have had a vague geographical con-
notation and may have been used not so much for the Chinese themselves as for the peoples on the eastern rim of the Roman empire.

The first important evidence of the entrance of Christian missionaries into China comes seven centuries later (781), when the Nestorians raised a monument to celebrate the coming of their priests to
the T'ang capital of Ch'ang An in the year 635 A.D.

The Eastern or Assyrian Christian church had been cut off from
communion with the Roman and the Greek Catholic churches since
the fifth century. From its habitat in the Tigris-Euphrates Valley
it had gradually developed the power and intelligence of a great
evangelizing organization. While the Western church was becoming
steeped in Greek philosophy and taking on the color of a Western
religion, Nestorian Christianity acquired and retained many of the
outer and inner marks of an Oriental creed. Its spiritual outlook was
toward the East and eastward it continued to move. As with other
religions, persecution helped to foster its growth. The bigotry of Jus-
tinian had driven these pious and industrious subjects into the arms
of Rome's foe, the Persians, just as a thousand years later the revoca-
tion of the Edict of Nantes in France drove Huguenot artisans to
enrich the economic life of Holland and England and surrounding
countries. By the end of the fifth century Nestorianism had established itself in Persia, Mesopotamia, and surrounding countries.' From
Persia the persecutions of Shapur again scattered them throughout
Arabia and farther east. Cosmas, a Christian merchant of the sixth
century, says that "among the Bactrians, Huns, Persians, Persarme-

nians, Elamites and the whole country of Persia the churches are without number,"[6] and legend says that in the same century Nestorian monks brought silkworm eggs, for the first time, to Constantinople. If we can trust the meager evidence we possess, it would seem that Nestorian converts had penetrated to the Far East by this date, for Cosmas speaks of them as being in Siam and Tonking.

Mohammedanism was the final cause of the decline of Nestorianism in the West, but eastward the faith continued to expand. From its new center in Bagdad, which under the Abbaside caliphs was the greatest city of its time, the Syrian Christians continued to press eastward. Their progress was fostered by a system of monasticism and a kind of bible school, which trained its members for the work of proselytism. Following the paths of invasion, they carried on their nomad trade; commerce made the Assyrian merchant the pilgrim of the highroad, the disseminator of news, and even the banker of western and central Asia. The Nestorian Christians seem, too, to have translated the Greek classics into Arabic and so helped to preserve them for medieval Europe. They were often merchants rather than missionaries but, says Mingana, "whatever means were employed by those early pioneers of Christianity, there is no reason for denying the important fact that, in an amazingly short space of time, they introduced their religious convictions literally into the remote confines of ancient Asia."[7] A recent historian pays tribute to their zeal:

They pitched their tents in the camps of the wandering Tartar, the Lama of Thibet trembled at their words, they stood in the rice fields of the Punjab, and taught fishermen by the sea of Aral; they struggled through the vast deserts of Mongolia; the memorable inscription of Sianfu attests to their victories in China. In India the Zamorin (of Calicut) himself respected their spiritual, and courted their temporal, authority. They braved alike pagan and fire worshipper, the burning suns of Tiflis and the feverish swamps of Imeretia. They subjugated the border lands of Europe and Asia and planted a colony half way up the great mountain of Ararat.[8]

The period from the fourth to the ninth century was the golden age of the Faith in central Asia. By the end of this period there seems to have been a large number of churches within this area, with scattered mission stations on its perimeter. The Church exercised a marked cultural influence. It introduced letters and learning to the Turks, the Uigurs, and the Mongols, all of whom are supposed to have obtained their alphabet from the Nestorians. It is not surprising, then, to find the patriarch, in 858, referring to the metropolitan of China and India in conjunction with that of Samarkand. In fact, Mingana, after examining the evidence of Syriac writers, concludes that China was the seat of a metropolitan much earlier than the eighth century.[9]

About the year 1625 some workmen, digging near the ancient capital of China, the modern Sianfu, unearthed a large tablet of the kind called by the Chinese *pei* and used for various commemorative purposes. Among the many curious people who examined the stone was a local Chinese scholar, a friend of the learned Jesuit convert, the scholar-official Léon Li, and he immediately notified the latter of the discovery. When Li and his Jesuit teachers at Peking received the news, they were overjoyed, for the legend on the tablet purported to tell of the introduction into the empire, nearly a thousand years previously, of the "illustrious religion" (*ch'ing chiao*), a cult which had all the earmarks of a debased form of Christianity. The discovery was of inestimable value to the spread of Christianity since it gave to the Faith an aura of antiquity in a land where ancient tradition was the basis of all respect and ability. The Jesuit Father Trigault hastened to examine the monument, and his study confirmed first impressions of its value.[10]

The inscription bears the title "Tablet eulogizing the propagation of the Illustrious Religion (*ch'ing chiao*) in China, with a preface composed by Ching Ch'ing, a priest of the Syrian church." The legend begins with a summary of the tenets of the Church and the rules regarding neophytes. It then tells the history of the Church in China:

In the time of the accomplished emperor T'ai Tsung the illustrious and magnificent founder of the dynasty, among the enlightened and holy men who arrived was the most virtuous Olopên from the country of Syria. Observing the azure clouds he bore the true sacred books; beholding the direction of the winds he braved the difficulties and dangers. In the year 635 he arrived at Ch'ang An ...

The inscription then relates the story of Olopên's favorable reception by the emperor and of the honors bestowed on him by the succeeding monarch, Kao Tsung; of the persecutions of 699 and 713; of the emperor Hsuan Tsung's gifts; of the rebuilding of the "illustrious" churches at Ling Wu and four other places; and of the friendship of the Buddhist priest-official, I Sze—an interesting piece of evidence of the early relations of Nestorianism and Buddhism. The inscription then gives a list of priests and officials of the Church and the date of the erection of the tablet, A.D. 781.

The Nestorian monument has been the basis of extravagant claims on the one hand and of bitter attacks on the other. Led by the priest-hating Voltaire, some critics have seen in it a pious fraud. Bishop Horne in England, Neumann in Germany and Stanislas Julien in France joined the ranks of the doubters. On the other hand, several Jesuit apologists, notably Boym, Du Halde, and Lecomte, have tried to prove that it is a monument to Roman rather than to Nestorian Christianity, a theory which has not found much favor outside the Jesuit ranks. The Japanese scholar Saeki uses the monument as the basis of a claim that the Nestorians occupied an important place in the court life. He says:

They stood before the emperors of China as the apostles stood before the Roman governors and, like the Hebrew prophet Daniel or the monks of the West in the sub-apostolic age, they were the trusted advisers of Chinese and even of Japanese sovereigns.[11]

This optimism is probably as exaggerated as the pessimism of the skeptics is unwarranted. Scholars today have rendered their verdict and have, by a large majority, accepted the Nestorian tablet as authentic. Thus we can safely look upon it as one of the great monuments of the Faith, a landmark of the history of Christianity in the Far East.[12]

It was, indeed, an auspicious moment for the introduction of the

Christian religion into the Middle Kingdom. China was the mighti-
est empire in the world. The capital city of Ch'ang An was at the
height of its magnificence. T'ai Tsung, the representative of the T'ang
dynasty in 635, was in every respect a great monarch. In addition to
being a warrior he was an able administrator, a lover of arts, and a
liberal patron of learning. His munificence and liberal spirit opened
the doors to foreign learning and built a cultural bridge between
China and the West. Representatives of foreign nations, whose strange
air, appearance, and habits were a source of wonder and delight to the
Chinese, were received at his court with distinction. In matters of
religion the monarch showed that catholicity of interest which has
been a remarkable characteristic of the Chinese mind through the
ages. In 628 a Mohammedan mission was welcomed, and among the
responsible officials at court were a number of Turks. At this time
the Manichaeans penetrated into the empire, bringing with them
their books on astronomy and establishing their temples in many
towns. The Nestorians flourished with the other foreign sects, and
when in 845 the emperor Wu Tsung, an ardent Taoist, abolished the
mission, there seem to have been some two thousand Manichaean,
Mazdean, and Nestorian priests in the empire. There is little doubt,
however, that from this date Taoism, first, and then Buddhism began
to gain a permanent victory over the rival cults. Gradually the purity
of the Christian religious heritage was defiled until it became merged
in the stronger faiths around it, thus losing its identity.[18]

The curtain falls, and for some three hundred years little or nothing
is heard of Christianity in the Middle Kingdom. But, checked in
China proper, the Faith continued to make new conquests in the vast
plains and plateaus of central and northern Asia. Adequate evidence
is lacking, but there is sufficient to show that Eastern Christianity
during these centuries gained a powerful hold on the Turko-Mongol
tribes that peopled this part of Asia. These nomads provided an excellent medium for the propagation of the Faith since their wandering
existence permitted merchants, scholar-priests, and doctors, accom-

panying the tribe, to cover a great deal of territory and to expand this influence geographically in a short time. So successful were these missionaries that, at the beginning of the twelfth century, the authority of the Nestorian patriarch extended from China to the Tigris and from Lake Baikal to Cape Comorin.

The focal points of this Christianity are to be found in two tribes, the Uigurs and the Keraits. The former were converted at an early date and there is ample evidence to show that for some time many important members of the tribe were Christians. As late as the thirteenth century William of Rubruck notes that there were Nestorians in all the Uigur towns. This tribe, of Turkish origin, held a position of great importance in north-central Asia during the later Middle Ages, as is evidenced by the fact that its power, and the fear inspired by it, have given to our language the word "ogre." Among the stories of Christianity in the East none is more colorful than the story of two of these Uigur Christians,[14] Mar Jaballaha and the vicar Bar Sauma, who established direct communication with Europe in the Middle Ages. An old Syriac manuscript relates this story.[15]

There lived in the city of Khanbaliq a believer, a freeman, rich in the things of the world as well as in strength of character, and his wife named Kyamtha. The latter, like Hannah of old, faced with the threat of barrenness, prayed to the Lord and was at length blessed with a son whom the devoted couple named Sauma, "the son of fasting." The boy grew up pious and good. From his early years he showed signs of aspiring to the religious life though not, like Samuel, to the joy of his parents. Finally he assumed the habit of the monk, embraced the ascetic life and, retiring from the world, gained for himself a great reputation as a saintly hermit.

Now in the city of Koshang,[16] some hundred miles from Khanbaliq there lived a faithful and righteous man, an archdeacon, who had a son named Marcos, the Benjamin of the family. Hearing of the saintly hermit of Khanbaliq, the youth Marcos was seized with a desire to visit the man and he set out on the arduous fifteen-day jour-

ney to the capital. Sauma received him kindly and at first tried to
restrain his youthful enthusiasm to become a monk, but without
success, for after three years as a neophyte the young Marcos received
the tonsure at the hands of the metropolitan, Mar Nestorius. But the
adventurous spirit of the pioneer was in the young priest, and we soon
find him urging the hermit to give up his retirement and make with
him the great journey across Asia to the holy city, Jerusalem. In vain
Bar Sauma dwelt upon the dangers of the journey and the obstacles
to be found in a foreign land. The enthusiasm of Marcos was con-
tagious, and finally the older man agreed to accompany him. Inspired
by courage and stimulated by the friendly encouragement of the local
Ongut chieftains, they started off on that long road which passed
through Tangut, Khotan, Kashgar, Khorassan, and by the shores of
the Caspian Sea. They underwent the "vexation and trouble of the cold
desert." They crossed the traces of war. They came to a Khotan filled
with starving people and a Kashgar from whence all the inhabitants
had fled. They visited the court of the lesser khan Kaidu at Almaliq
and finally arrived at Bagdad, the center of the Eastern church at that
time. From there they made visits to many of the sacred shrines of
Nestorianism in Persia. For a while they rested from their arduous
journey at the monastery of St. Michael of Tar'el near Arbel, but they
were not left there long in obscurity.

A metropolitan was needed for the distant see of Cathay and what
more logical choice could there be than the young Marcos, the ardent
pilgrim who had come from those obscure regions and whose saintly
qualities and evangelical fervor so fitted him for the post? So in the
thirty-fifth year of his age Rabban Marcos became Mar Yaballaha III,
metropolitan of Cathay. But Marcos was never to visit his new see,
for the road to Cathay was again cut. The two priests remained for
two years at Arbel, and before they could start on the homeward journey, the head of the Nestorian church, the patriarch Mar Denha, died.
Who should succeed him? It was realized that a man was needed who,
in addition to possessing the qualities of leadership, could establish

and maintain political relations with the ruling Mongols, whose protection was so necessary for the well-being of the Church. But a priest who spoke the Mongol tongue was hard to find. Then they thought of the young metropolitan of Cathay at Arbel. Here was a man sent by God for their needs. And so it came about that the young priest of North China, though he was little versed in the Syrian books, was ordained head of the Oriental church in the great temple of Bagdad.

It was the year 1281. The Mongol chief Abaga, who showed favor to the Nestorians, died the following year, and his successor, Achmed Khan, was murdered two years later. Arghun Khan, who succeeded to the khanate in 1284, appears to have been a man of political sagacity. He saw the advantage of keeping the good will of the Western princes while he was fighting the Mohammedans. It is probable, too, that he dreamed of invading Syria and taking Jerusalem. For this reason he was desirous of keeping in touch with the European monarchs by means of an exchange of envoys. It is here that Bar Sauma comes into the story to give eloquent testimony concerning Mongol contact with the West, for Arghun chose him in 1287 to go to the courts of the Western princes.[17]

The Syriac manuscript goes on to relate the travels of the priestly envoy into medieval Europe. Armed with letters to the kings of the Greeks and the Franks, "two thousand pounds of gold, thirty good steeds and a tablet,"[18] Bar Sauma embarked at Trebizond for the Byzantine capital. At Constantinople the Basileus, Andronikos II, greeted him courteously and showed him the treasures of the city; the great church of Sophia containing a picture of the Virgin "which Luke the evangelist painted," the hand of John the Baptist, the relics of Lazarus and Mary Magdalene, and many other holy relics. From Constantinople he crossed the sea to Naples and Rome. At Naples he witnessed a sea battle between the forces of the ruler of that city and those of the king of Aragon. At the Holy City, Pope Honorius IV had just died, but the College of Cardinals received him joyfully, eagerly listening to the news from the East, for Bar Sauma seems to have given them the impression that the Mongols were almost a Christian nation. As he expounded to them the tenets of the Nestorian church, they expressed surprise at the similarity with their own. They took him on a tour of Rome and once more he gazed reverently on holy relics and sacred places.

Passing, then, through Tuscany and Genoa, Sauma traveled to Paris, to the court of Philippe le Bel, and to this monarch he preached an alliance with the Mongols for a concerted attack upon Jerusalem, a project to which the French king listened with sympathy. The envoy spent a month in Paris. He visited the university and was awed at its thirty thousand students, supported by the king's bounty. He saw Saint Denis, "where the coffins of the kings lie," and he greatly admired the lovely Sainte Chapelle with its crystal casket containing the Crown of Thorns. Philippe gave him gifts and fine garments and promised him "one of the principal amirs of my palace" to take back to Arghun the French reply.[19] Then Bar Sauma traveled south to Aquitaine, where the English king Edward I was at that moment visiting his French fiefs. Here he officiated at a Mass in the presence of the king and his court, and Edward assured him that Arghun's plan to capture Jerusalem coincided with his own wishes.

Then Sauma returned to Rome where Nicholas IV had just been installed as Pope. Once again he celebrated Mass in the Nestorian manner, and the papal attendants rejoiced, saying, "the language is different but the rite is one." On Palm Sunday he received absolution at the hands of the Pope himself and took part in all the ceremonies of the Passion week. Then, craving to return, he was given by the Holy Father for himself some relics and, for the patriarch at Bagdad, "a crown of pure gold adorned with very precious stones and vestments for his priestly office," together with a bull authorizing the patriarch to rule the Eastern church. In addition, he received one thousand five hundred pounds of red gold for his return journey and gifts for Arghun. Arriving back at the court of the khan "in soundness of body and preservation of soul," he related the marvels he had seen and the might of the empires he had visited. Arghun rejoiced and thanked him: "We have put thee to great trouble seeing thou art an old man. Therefore we will not let thee be separated from us. But we will establish a church in our own royal court and thou shalt serve and pray in it."[20] The aged Nestorian remained in Persia until his death in 1293. Two years earlier his benefactor, Khan Arghun, had died, just missing the young bride whom Marco Polo was bringing him from farthest Tartary.

The other center of Christianity in northern Asia was the tribe of the Keraits. They occupied the land bordering on the Chinese province of Kansu, and their chief city was Karakorum. When William of Rubruck visited this city in 1254, he officiated at the Nestorian church there. It is apparent that this region was a strong center of Christianity during the twelfth and thirteenth centuries. Together with the Naimans and the Merkites the leading families of this tribe contained many converts, some of whom intermarried with the families of the ruling khans. The influence of these people at court was undoubtedly useful to the Christian envoys who arrived there from the West, while on the western borders of the Mongol empire they so penetrated the entourage of the Khan Arghun that for a time there was really a possibility of the Persian Mongols accepting Christianity as a state cult.

But the Uigurs and the Keraits are chiefly interesting to us for their connection with the story of Prester John, one of the most fascinating and widespread of the great medieval legends.[21] Like most tales of its kind, it consists of a mass of tradition, grossly exaggerated and distorted, surrounding a tiny nucleus of fact. Who was the original Prester, or Priest, John? Where did he live? The authorities, of course, differ. Howorth[22] thinks he was king of the Keraits and, indeed, Bar Hebraeus, who wrote during the reign of Arghun Khan, identifies him with that tribe. Bishop Otto of Freisinger, the greatest scholar of medieval Germany, identifies him with the Karakitai or Black Tartars. Marco Polo has told us how these Karakitai were destroyed by Genghis Khan in 1206. The testimony of William of Rubruck is interesting.[23] He tells us that about the year 1098 A.D. there were certain Cathayans known as Kara or Black Cathayans living in the mountains and that in these mountains there was a Nestorian shepherd, who was the ruler of a tribe called the Naimans. They lived in the neighborhood of Lake Baikal and their prince was called "Con Cham." At his death he was succeeded by this shepherd, whom the Nestorians called Prester John.[24] Marco Polo says that Tenduc was the seat of Prester John, and, corroborating a statement of John of Montecorvino, he asserts that this region, in his time, was still ruled by a descendant, George, the same Prince George whom the Franciscan bishop converted to the Catholic faith.[25] In this way the legend is transferred to the Ongut tribe.

The story is bewildering in its ramifications. In the Middle Ages the habitat of Prester John was generally conceded to be central Asia. In the fifteenth century the legend was moved to Abyssinia, where it remained until well into the sixteenth century. So persistent was the legend that Henry the Navigator, of Portugal, dreamed of an alliance with the Christian ruler of Asia to crush the Moslem, and Vasco da Gama, sailing on his epoch-making trip around Africa in 1498, carried a letter to this mythical king.

So for centuries the shadow of this legendary monarch is thrown across the world. He is clothed in all the panoply and pomp of an Oriental potentate; his court is magnificent and his power dominates half the universe. This colorful story had its repercussions on Western life. It was the chief cause of the attempt during the later Middle Ages at a rapprochement between the Tartar empire and Christendom.

There seems to have been an undercurrent running through Europe [says Sir Henry Yule] that these Barbarians (the Tartars) were in some way ripe for conversion ... The heavy blows dealt at the Mohammedan enemy by the Tartars, then the old stories of Prester John with whom early rumor had confounded Genghis Khan, the vagueness of religious professions in the Khans and their captains, attributing to them the profession of that Christianity which was really professed by some of the tribes under them; the tolerance

and patronage extended to the Christians in the conquered countries in some
cases; all these circumstances perhaps contributed to create or augment in
Europe this impression . . ."[26]

The incentives for this attempt at contact are to be found in two
political movements which were occupying the attention of the world
at that time: namely, the world conquests of Genghis Khan and the
struggle between Christendom and Islam in the West.

About the year 1155[27] there was born in a little *yurt* of eastern Mongolia, in an obscure Tartar tribe, a child who was destined to shake
the foundations of civilization. The boy was given the name of Temuchin. He grew up amidst the dangerous and constantly moving surroundings of a Mongol tribe fighting for its life against powerful
neighbors. The struggle for existence led him early to fratricide. Often
his life hung by a hair. By the year 1206 he had made himself the
master of all northern Mongolia and had taken the title of khan. Then
began his work as administrator. While maintaining to a great degree
the nomadic character essential to the life of his people, he built up
a feudal system based upon an aristocracy of which he was the center.
He gave his people a religious faith and organized his army into
groups of hundreds and thousands, placing at the head of each unit
a commander whom he could trust. He organized a civil government
and encouraged learning (though he himself was illiterate). Last, but
most important of all, he created a system of communications and
post routes which, as he moved westward, opened a great highway
across Asia.

Then, continuing his career of conquest, he struck southward until
all the land north of the Yellow River was in his hands. The civilizing
influence of the Sons of Han was not long in making itself felt, however; with a Chinese scholar as mentor and guide, Genghis turned the
humble Mongal yurt into a court of truly magnificent splendor.

Dreams of world conquest haunted him and he turned his face to
the West, where Islam was at the zenith of its power. In 1219, with
an army of two hundred thousand men, he attacked the Khwarezm

Turks, after a stupendous march across the mid-Asian plateau from Lake Baikal. One by one he assaulted the cities in his path and left them smoldering ruins: Otrar, Kashgent, Bokhara, the city of schools and mosques, and lovely Samarkand, the fairest of them all.

One branch of the Mongol forces entered Russia and defeated the Russians on the banks of the Dnieper while, with his main army, Genghis turned south and, on the Indus, broke the back of Moslem resistance. It was the autumn of 1221.

Returning home, Genghis spent several years in consolidating his position in eastern Asia, then again turned southward, where the Sung emperors were ruling the rich land of southern China. He had actually crossed the Yellow River when death overtook him, in August, 1227. He died at the age of seventy-two, and his son Ogotai was chosen to succeed him.

For a time the spirit of Genghis lived on in his warrior sons and grandsons. Years were spent in plotting and planning; then, in 1235, Batu, son of Genghis' favorite child, Juchi, was sent to conquer the countries north of the Caucasus, with Subotai, who had invaded those regions twelve years earlier.

The Mongol forces descended like a thunderbolt on eastern Europe. In less than two months they had defeated three large armies and a dozen smaller ones. Boleslas of Poland was overwhelmed in March, 1241. At Leignitz, in Silesia, an army of Poles, Bavarians, Teutonic knights, and Templars was almost annihilated. Bela and his Hungarians were beaten on the Oder with a loss of forty thousand men, and Louis IX learned that France herself would soon be in the direct path of the conquerors.

Not since the days of Attila had Christendom been in such grave peril. Europe, exhausted by the crusades and weakened by the quarrel between the Papacy and the Empire, seemed incapable of strong, unified resistance. Then suddenly, almost miraculously, the Mongol wave receded. Ogotai had died at Karakorum and the Mongol chieftains had struck camp to hasten home for the election of the new khan. For the moment, Europe was saved. Kuyuk, the patron of the Nestorians, whom John of Plano Carpini visited, was elected khan. He was followed in 1248 by Mangu, who was succeeded nine years later by Marco Polo's patron, Kublai, the Mongol conqueror of China.

The Europe which faced the Mongols had just passed the zenith of the medieval Renaissance. France was the center of Western culture with Norman England as its support and ally. The glory of the Gothic was unfolding in France, England, and elsewhere. Chartres and Notre Dame de Paris, Salisbury and Canterbury were lifting their slender spires to the sky. The crusades were bringing from Asia Minor the wisdom of the Orient. Christian culture was at its flowering.

But against the unity of the Church appeared the disunity of the feudal system and the papal vision of temporal power. Fredrick II was dreaming of himself as a second Charlemagne. His plans fell athwart the ambitions of the Papacy and, in 1246, Innocent IV was expelled from Italy by the Hohenstaufen. Fifty years earlier the third crusade, the greatest military effort of medieval Europe, had failed. The mystical dream of a Holy Sepulchre regained had been dissipated by the genius of Saladin. The enthusiasm for the way of the Cross had ended in the tragic fanaticism of the Children's Crusade. Saint Louis alone continued to hold the vision, but he was soon to meet his death in Africa because his religious ardor was inferior to his knowledge of the art of war. Chivalry had spent its force, and in its place was rising the spirit of mercantilism. The great ports of Pisa, Genoa, and Venice were laying the foundations of international trade.

The military efficiency of the knight, also, was proving inadequate. The crusades were teaching that animal courage alone, even when stimulated by fanatical zeal, was no match for cunning in strategy and mobility in tactics. The bow had proved more effective than the mace or the sword, and burning naphtha and Greek fire more terrible than battering ram or catapult. It needed only the introduction of gunpowder to complete the ruin of medieval military science.

When the Mongols began to batter at the gates of Europe, the

West was aghast at the new horror. News of the conquerors was slow in reaching western Europe, but for some time rumors spread of terrible, swift purveyors of death, men with heads of dogs, who lived on human flesh. These stories had their basis in the sack of a score of fair cities and the slaughter of hundreds of thousands of their inhabitants. Already, in 1238, the Ismaelians had appealed to England and France for aid against the terrible foe. Then, at the council of Lyons, called by Innocent IV in 1245, Russian bishops brought firsthand information of the Mongol conquests in Russia. Plans were discussed for meeting the new menace. It was decided to open negotiations not only with the Ilkhans of the Near East but also with the Great Khan himself. Christendom resolved to send an embassy to Karakorum.

It is not easy to picture the terrors which such a trip into the unknown must have had for the medieval mind. It was a voyage into the land of Gog and Magog, the country of cannibals and half-human beasts. To undertake such a journey needed courage and devotion, men of stout hearts and spiritual vision. The need of the moment, however, produced men suitable and willing for the task. Contemporary with the rise of Genghis Khan, Europe had seen the development of the two great religious orders, the Dominicans and the Franciscans. These monks, fired with the vision of the glory of the Faith and the ideal of the conversion of the whole world to Christianity, were willing to undergo hardship and suffering and the uncertainties and dangers of a voyage into dark and unknown lands. Four Dominicans were chosen, therefore, to go to Persia where Hulagu, whose mother and wife were both Christians, was ruling. John of Plano Carpini, a Franciscan friar, was chosen to go to the court of the Great Khan.[28]

Chapter II

THE MISSIONARIES OF THE
MEDIEVAL PERIOD

FRIAR JOHN of Plano Carpini, a native of Perugia, had been a companion of the saintly founder of his order. An ardent Franciscan, he had spent a number of years devoted to the cause of his order in several countries of Europe. Further than this we know little of his life. Starting from Lyons in April, 1245, with another monk, Stephen of Bohemia, he traveled through Bohemia and Poland, where he was joined by Friar Benedict.

The most important barrier to his progress was the leader of the Golden Horde, Batu Khan of western Asia, who controlled the caravan routes eastward, having his camp on the Volga near the Caspian. Batu received the Western envoys with a haughty boorishness but, after retaining them for some time, finally allowed them to proceed. Then followed a terrible journey of several months, during which the dangers of the road were accentuated by the rigors of winter; the priestly travelers at times were exposed to death by starvation. From the depths of winter they were plunged suddenly into the devastating heat of summer as they came down to the great Gobi desert. Finally they arrived at the court of the Great Khan at Sira Ordu, near the Mongol capital of Karakorum. It was the month of August, 1246. Ogotai, the successor of Genghis Khan, had just died. The slow task of choosing his successor was being accomplished, and the envoys spent dreary days lingering in the Mongol camp, awaiting the new ruler's pleasure. The impatience of Friar John must doubtless have been tempered by the news he received of converts in the royal entourage. He tells us that he met several Christians of the khan's family who told him that the khan was about to become a Christian, showing as evidence of this statement certain "clergymen of the Christian faith" that Kuyuk kept near him and a "chapel of the Christians near his great tent."[1] This assertion must have been far from the truth, however, for in the same chapter of his narrative Friar John says: "The said Cuyne (Kuyuk) being emperor new elect, together with all his princes, erected a flag of defiance against the Church of God and the Roman empire and against all Christian kingdoms and nations of the West."

The history of Christian missions in the Orient is filled with prophecies and promises of the conversion of an Oriental chieftain or monarch. The optimism was rarely justified, but it served to sustain the interest of the people of Europe in the mission and to stimulate the efforts made to extend missionary work. From Carpini's narrative we get a profound impression of the might of the Mongols. In the course of their stay the priestly visitors were greatly surprised at the barbaric splendor of the court and the large amount of tribute presented by vassal states.[2] Friar John describes the great tent of the khan, erected on pillars covered with plates of gold, joined together with nails of the same metal, and roofed with costly Baldakan cloth. The interview with the khan, who received him on his throne of ivory inwrought with gold and precious stones, was, however, most unsatisfactory. The "ruler of the world" doubtless looked upon the Pope's admonition "to give over the bloudie slaughter of mankinde and to receive the Christian faith" as a piece of impertinence. It was evident that he considered the Franciscan as the representative of a vassal paying homage rather than as the envoy of a great Western power. Moreover, the practical Oriental mind could not understand why ambassadors with such lordly pretensions should bear such niggardly gifts. The envoys were quickly disillusioned with respect to Kuyuk's ripeness for conversion. Asking him whether he was a Christian, John received the insolent reply: "God knows, and if His Holiness wishes to find out, he has only to consult Him."

Finally, with little accomplished, the mission started home in November, 1246, bearing a letter from Kuyuk to the Pope. With the

---

[1] For notes to chap. ii, see pp. 307–308.

coming of winter the terrors of the journey had increased, and the old man of sixty-five and his companion suffered untold hardships before reaching their homeland. They arrived in Europe in the autumn of 1247, after an absence of some eighteen months. At Kiev in Russia the populace, turning out to meet them, greeted them as people returning from the dead.

John of Plano Carpini's account, written in Latin, was first published by Vincent of Beauvais and later printed in English by Hakluyt in his *Voyages*. It ranks among the greatest of travel stories, for, as the geographer Beazley says, "In John of Plano Carpini Christian Europe had at last a real explorer, a real historian, a genuine man of science in the service of the Church and discovery."[3] Carpini had blazed the trail across Asia which was soon to become a well-beaten path. The first direct official contacts between the Far East and medieval Europe had been made.

What had Friar John accomplished? As far as Christianity is concerned, very little. But if he had not found the Christian nation of the Prester John tradition, he had at least found traces of a definite interest in Christianity on the part of certain Mongol tribes and officials. Friar John never penetrated as far south as China proper and his account is limited therefore to the Mongol tribes of the North. Of the men of Cathay he gives this illuminating description:

They are pagans, having a special kind of writing by themselves and (it is reported) the Scriptures of the olde and newe Testament. They also have recorded in hystories the lives of their forefathers; and they have Eremites made after the manner of our Churches, which in those days they greatly resorted unto ... They love Christians and bestowe much almes, and are very courteous and gentle people.[4]

In a political way John of Plano Carpini had accomplished much more. His embassy had evidently had for its chief purpose the task of spying out the land. This was effectively accomplished. He gained among other things a healthy respect for the power and efficiency of the Mongols. He must have been aware of the relative weakness of the

Christian military power for, when friendly Tartar chieftains suggested that he ask for a Mongol embassy to accompany him on his
return, he ignored the suggestion, fearing that the picture of internecine strife presented by Europe at that time would encourage a
Mongol attack on Christendom.[5] His account of Mongol military
equipment and tactics should have been illuminating to medieval
knights. A hundred years later, the English yeomen at Crécy and
Poitiers were to defeat the flower of French chivalry by applying
John's admonitions concerning the importance of archery in warfare.

The road hewn out by Genghis Khan across Asia became, in the
latter half of the thirteenth century, a veritable highway. In his
triumphal march the Mongol conqueror had wiped out boundaries
which separated tribe from tribe. Behind him as he went westward
he left an excellent system of posts and couriers, which kept the road
open. Traffic was encouraged, and priests, physicians, and learned men
were exempted from taxes. Accordingly, along this highway went
many a pilgrim with his staff, many an official doing business for the
Great Khan, many a merchant with his caravan. This *pax tartarorum*
encouraged trade. For more than a century, conditions were created
favorable for a real world market as the growing commercial cities of
the Levant glimpsed the vast opportunities for commerce. Luxury
increased rapidly at the court of the Great Khan. Uigur and Mohammedan merchants took to Khanbaliq the products of the West.

In the chronicles of the time we get glimpses of Europeans who
had braved the dangers of the unknown to ply their craft or to trade
in the Far East. The name of Marco Polo the Venetian is known to
all. At Karakorum, William of Rubruck met a woman named Pa-
quette, from Metz in Lorraine, whose Russian husband was a carpen-
ter of the khan; and a jeweler named William Boucher.[6] We read of
a Lombard surgeon at Kublai Khan's court, and, a little later, of a
hermit from Mt. Sinai who had established a great reputation for
holiness. Friar Odoric, speaking of the greatness of Hangchow, says:
"I have found many persons in Venice who have been there."

One of these travelers, Pegolotti, an agent of the great commercial house of the Bardi of Florence has left us, in a little work entitled *La practica della mercatura,* a veritable guidebook for this three-hundred-day journey from the Caspian to Cathay. Not only does he tell us of the condition of the roads, which are "as safe to travel by night as by day," but he sums up the cost of the journey and the kind of goods the merchant should carry for trade.[7]

With the gradual dispelling of the mists of geographical uncertainty, it is not surprising that the Great Khan should begin to loom up as a potential ally. The third wave of Mongol invasion had definitely removed the Khwarezm Moslems as a menace to the peace of Europe. Cairo had displaced Bagdad as the center of Moslem power and there remained only the Mamelukes of Egypt as a common enemy of Christendom and Mongol Asia. Moreover, Saint Louis' two campaigns against the Mamelukes in Africa had ended in disaster, and a decade later the Moslems had gained a decided victory over Khan Hulagu at Ain Jalut and had followed this with other victories.

At the end of the thirteenth century, about the time that Andrew of Longjumeau was crossing the Mongolian plains to Karakorum, a mission from Khan Iltchigatai, successor to Baidu in Persia, had visited Louis at Cyprus and suggested that the French monarch cooperate with the Mongols, who were attacking Bagdad, by creating a diversion in Egypt. Evidence of the friendliness of the Near Eastern khans to the religion of the West is to be found in the fact that at the sack of Bagdad in 1258 the Mongols spared the Christians of the city. The Mongol khans of Persia had Christian wives. Abaga Khan had married a natural daughter of Michael Paleologus, the Greek conqueror of Constantinople. Armenian Christians served the Mongols as ministers, and crusaders sometimes fought in the Mongol ranks. It was logical, therefore, that the two opponents of the Moslems should try to find a basis for an alliance against their common foe.

The khan proposed that the Christian king of Armenia attack the Moslems in conjunction with the Mongols and, to further this diplomacy, Louis IX of France, at that time champion of Christendom, determined to send another embassy to the Great Khan.

The man chosen for the mission was a Franciscan, William of Rubruck (often referred to under his Latin name Rubruquis). He was born in northern France and was for some time with the armies of King Louis. He was with the king at Tripoli and may have been present at Cyprus when Louis received the mission from Iltchigatai. It is possible, too, that he may have met John of Plano Carpini in Paris when the latter returned from the Far East in 1247. William of Rubruck seems to have had a reputation as a geographer, for he is credited with having been the first to circumnavigate the Caspian Sea. Apart from these details, however, we know almost nothing of his life.

He started off on his long journey accompanied by Friar Bartholomew of Cremona, a member of his order. Leaving France in the winter of 1252, he made a long stay at Constantinople; then, crossing the Black Sea, he visited the camp of the Mongol chief, Sartach, with whom he obtained an interview through the mediation of a Nestorian official named Coiat. William of Rubruck announced that King Louis had heard of the conversion of the Mongol khan and had sent him to preach the gospel at his court. Sartach was mildly curious about the religion which William represented. He questioned him and then sent him on to his father Batu, who was encamped on the Volga. Coming into the presence of the latter, William threw himself on his knees saying,

"Sire, we beseech the Lord from whom all things good doe proceed and who hath given you these earthly benefits, that it would please him hereafter to make you partaker of his heavenly blessings; because the former without these are vain and unprofitable. Be it known unto you of a certainty that you shall not obtain the joys of heaven unless you become a Christian, for God saith: 'Whosoever believeth and is baptized shall be saved, but he that believeth not shall be condemned.' " At these words [says the priest] he (Batu) modestly smiled but the Moals (Mongols) began to clap their hands and to deride us.[8]

Here as elsewhere European presumption was met by Mongol arrogance. It is easy to understand why these men, who had reason to look upon themselves as world conquerors, should have treated with scorn bold and threatening admonitions coming from the head of a church of which they knew little and cared less. The tolerance of the Mongols in matters of religion could not be expected to extend itself to an acceptance of the temporal or even of the spiritual power of the head of an alien creed. Hence the missions to the Mongol courts were often received with boorish scorn or thinly veiled hostility.

Batu, however, gave permission to continue the journey. Friar William traveled for five weeks along the Volga and then started across the Mongolian plateau, a journey of four months, during which "of hunger and thirst, cold and weariness there was no end." Traveling over roads that were often no more than trails, sleeping in the open air, existing on cooked millet and melted snow, they finally reached the court of Mangu Khan, in December, 1253.

The first interview with the Great Khan was unsatisfactory, owing to the fact that the interpreter (and probably Mangu himself) was drunk with *kourmiss,* that national beverage of the Mongols made from mare's milk, so often spoken of by the travelers of the time. The priest followed the court to Karakorum, and once again a Western envoy had occasion to be astonished at the size and magnificence of the Oriental court. Here the Christian priest was able to celebrate the Mass with a crowd of Hungarian, Georgian, and Armenian Christian captives, who received the sacrament from his hands with great joy. Here also was staged one of those parliaments of religions in which the Asiatic mind seems to have delighted and which supplied interesting testimony of the tolerance of the Orientals in religious matters. Representatives of the different religions were called together so that, by public argument and dispute, they might show which faith was the true one. Friar William was chosen to represent Christianity—striking evidence of the state of Nestorianism at Mangu's court! With a naïve complaisance he tells us how he first decided to confound the Buddhists, attacking them with such eloquence and logic that they were overwhelmed. Thereupon the Mohammedans, seeing with what a doughty opponent they had to do, gracefully gave up the contest by admitting the truth of the learned friar's arguments.[9]

An Armenian priest whom he met at the court had told him that the khan was on the point of being baptized, but he soon found that this was not so. Mangu met his attempts at conversion with the statement that "like the five fingers of the hand, so are the several ways to Paradise" and he refused to express his preference for any one of these ways. The envoys were equally unsuccessful in their request to be allowed to dwell in the khan's territories, and after a stay of five months at Karakorum, they were sent back with a letter from Mangu Khan to King Louis. They arrived at Saint Jean d'Acre on the fifteenth of August, 1255. Saint Louis had already returned to France after the failure of his first crusade.[10]

It can be clearly seen that these early envoys were not missionaries in the strict sense of the term. They did indeed make use of their opportunities to try to convert the khans to Christianity, but whether they were hopeful of doing so is doubtful. Their purpose was to open avenues of communication between Europe and the Far East. They were ambassadors rather than missionaries, political agents as well as representatives of the Church.

In the meantime the little clan of the petty chieftain Temuchin had grown into a great and powerful nation, and simplicity had given way to Oriental magnificence. Mangu had died in 1259, and his successor had set about the complete subjugation of China. He had established his capital of Khanbaliq or Taidu (Ta Tu) on the site of the old imperial city of the Kin dynasty, where now stands the modern city of Peking. The great trans-Asian highway now had a worthy terminal in the capital of the Yuan dynasty, and, with the founding of Khanbaliq, the history of Christianity in the Far East deals once more with events taking place in China proper.

Among the travelers along the trans-Asian highway there were doubtless not a few wandering monks, adventurous spirits willing to brave the hardships of the road for the glory of God. For the most part their voices are mute, but we have the record of one of these preaching friars who for thirteen years trod the highways of Asia preaching the gospel—the Franciscan Odoric of Pordenone.

Odoric was born at Pordenone, in northern Italy, in 1286. He took the Franciscan vows in his early years and became a monk at the monastery of Udine. In April, 1318, he started from Padua on his long journey to the Far East and he did not return to his native city until 1330. Going first to Constantinople, he there entered upon the combined land-and-sea route which Marco Polo had taken on his return, by way of Trebizond, Erzerum, and Tabriz across Persia, through Sultanyeh, Yezd, and Persepolis to Ormuz on the Persian Gulf. There he embarked for India, arriving at Tana in Salsetta in 1321. He then traveled along the Malabar Coast to the supposed tomb of Saint Thomas at Meliapur. From there he sailed by junk to Sumatra, visited Java and the coast of Borneo, and finally reached China. Here he visited the great towns of Zaitun, Canton, Fuchow, Hangchow, Nanking, and Yangchow, and at length arrived at Khanbaliq. After living at the capital for three years he returned to Europe by the trans-Asian route, traversing Marco Polo's Tenduc (Kansu and Shensi) and on through Tibet, through the Hindu Kush to Kabul, Khorassan, Persia, and Venice.

Odoric's account contains little concerning the fortunes of Christianity in the Far East. It is a typical medieval travel account, in which the author interests himself in the marvelous, things "which I have seen with mine own eyes or heard the same reported by credible and substantial witnesses." He tells of the Old Man of the Mountain and his Earthly Paradise, of the Valley of Terror, of the Land of the Dog-Faced Men and other marvels—all of which gave the book a bad reputation for veracity and caused it for centuries to be accepted as the offspring of that medieval monument of mendacity, the *Travels of Sir John Mandeville*.[11]

Odoric was greatly astonished at the splendors of Khanbaliq and attempts to describe the imperial palace with its fourteen pillars of gold, its halls hung with red skins, "the costliest in the world," its great drinking fountains of precious jade with vessels of gold, and the golden peacocks which rise as if by magic when the guests clap their hands. He tells of the fourteen thousand "barons" in the train of the Great Khan, who wear apparel of gold and precious stones, each garment worth ten thousand florins; of the khan's chariot, made of aloe wood and beaten gold and drawn by four elephants; of the great feasts of the khan and other details testifying to the magnificence of the court and the beauty of the capital.[12] He is at times led to exaggeration by the Oriental custom of using numbers as symbols. It is impossible to take him seriously when he speaks of the eighteen *thuman* of actors or the fifteen *thuman* (one hundred and fifty thousand) of keepers of hounds and animals. His description, however, succeeds in impressing us with the distance which the Mongols had traveled since the time when they followed their yurts across the Mongolian plains.

In Khanbaliq Odoric found that tolerance in religious matters which made evangelism a somewhat easy, though by no means successful, task. At times he would go forth with others "to bless the king's meat" and he seems to have come closely in touch with the life of the court and frequently to have met the Great Khan himself. Friar Marchesino of Bassano, a contemporary, has preserved for us one of the interesting incidents in the life of this man.

Once upon a time, when the great Khan was on his journey from Sandu [Shang tu, the summer capital north of Khanbaliq] to Cambalech he (Odoric) was sitting under the shade of a tree by the side of the road along which the Khan was to pass, with four other minor friars, and one of the brethren was a bishop. So when the Khan began to draw near the bishop put on his episcopal robes and took a cross, and fastened it to the end of a staff, so as to raise it aloft; and then these four men began to chaunt with loud voices the hymn *Veni Creator Spiritus*. And then the great Khan, hearing the sound thereof, asked what it meant. And those four barons who were beside him replied that it was four of the Frank rabbans (i.e., of the Christian monks). So the

Khan called them to him and the bishop thereupon, taking the cross from the staff, presented it for the Khan to kiss. Now at the time he was lying down but as soon as he saw the Cross he sat up, and, doffing the cap that he wore, he kissed the Cross in a most reverent and humble manner.[13]

The bishop mentioned here was probably John of Montecorvino.

The early biographers of Odoric attribute to him wonderful success in preaching the gospel, claiming that he had baptized more than twelve thousand "saracens" alone. Sir Henry Yule, after studying the evidence with care, finds very little of an ascetic in Odoric and wonders why he was picked out for sainthood. The doughty friar was one of those freelances who were fairly common on the highroads in the Middle Ages, men filled with the spirit of adventure and a courage to face the perils of the unknown. That the success of his evangelical labors is exaggerated detracts no more from the value of the work than does the fact that he stressed a little too strongly the marvelous and the legendary. His account still remains one of the most enlightening of the time, a useful complement to the work of Marco Polo.

The book of Ser Marco Polo, dictated to Rusticiano of Pisa in a prison at Genoa at the turn of the thirteenth century, stands unequaled in the literature of travel. Over two hundred years later the people of Venice still remembered the sensation which the traveler had created when, in 1295, he arrived in their midst, like a man returned from the grave, clad in strange, exotic garb and recounting marvels and adventures passing all belief. For the first time the great spaces of eastern Asia were described by a man who had explored them, and Europe gained from one who had lived there a score of years its first intimate knowledge of the richness and wonders of Cathay.

But to those who seek information about Christianity in China at that time the great work of the Venetian traveler is as disappointing as is the book of Odoric. He tells of the interest of the Great Khan in religious matters and of his desire to have at his court learned priests skilled in the arguments concerning their faith and in a knowl-

edge of the seven arts. He describes the khan's reverence for the four
great teachers, Jesus, Mohammed, Moses, and Buddha. He mentions
the presence of Nestorian communities in the western provinces of
Kansu and Yunnan, and particularly in the cities of Ho Chien Fu,
Chen Chiang Fu (Chinkiang), Hangchow and other places. Interesting evidence of the Christian community of Chen Chiang Fu
has come down to us in a document which tells of the establishment
of the Ta hsing kuo monastery in 1281 by the official Ma-hsieh-li-
chi-ssu, who seems to have acquired favor at court by skill in making
sherbets.[14] The document gives the number and names of Christian
officials attached to the monastery. How many such communities
were scattered through the empire it is impossible to determine, but
they must have been numerous.

Marco Polo's references seem to imply that Nestorianism was
widespread, particularly in western Cathay. We have the evidence
of John of Montecorvino that the Nestorians had influence at the
court of Kublai Khan. It is difficult, then, to understand why Nestorianism, established in the entourage of the emperor and scattered
throughout the empire, disappeared completely, as it did from the
Middle Kingdom and the Orient generally. There is no doubt that
by the end of the thirteenth century it had lost a good many of the
dogmas of Christianity and had become debased. From the beginning a much more Oriental religion than the Roman cult, it had
doubtless shown that resiliency in matters of doctrine which is typi-
cally Oriental, and this tolerance (combined with the fact that it
was thousands of miles from the western source of Christian inspiration) gradually developed into an acceptance of the tenets of other
creeds, notably the Buddhist, until it completely lost its identity.[15]

Roman Christianity, which refused to lose contact with the Mother
Church, also disappeared when that contact was broken, but before
it disappeared, it gave us one of those splendid figures which stand
out as a bright light in Church history, the figure of the great Franciscan archbishop, John of Montecorvino.

Little is known of the archbishop's early life. He was born in Apulia in the little town of Monte Corvino, in 1246 or 1247. After joining the Franciscan order he was sent by Michael Paleologus, in 1272, on a mission to Pope Nicholas IV concerning the union of the Greek and Roman churches. About 1281 Bonogratia, the minister-general of his order, sent him to the Near East for the purpose of attempting the conversion of the Persians and Mongols. He remained here for nearly a decade and was then sent by Khan Arghun with a letter to Rome. The Pope listened to his eloquent appeals to be allowed to return and spread the Faith in the Orient and he once more started eastward provided with letters to Arghun and also to the Great Khan. He left Tauris in 1291, accompanied by Nicholas of Pistoia, a Dominican. Friar Nicholas died in India, where John spent about a year before entering China. He reached Khanbaliq not earlier than 1294, probably shortly after the death of Kublai Khan.

The account of his work in the Mongol capital is given in two letters from him, the first dated January 8, 1305. He tells of the violent opposition he met at the hands of the Nestorians, who were firmly established at the Mongol court. He describes them as follows:

... a certain body who profess to bear the Christian name but who deviate sadly from the Christian religion, have grown so powerful in these parts that they will not allow a Christian of another ritual to have ever so small a chapel or to publish any doctrine different from their own.[16]

The intrigues against him continued for five years. He was accused of being a spy, a sorcerer, and a magician and was several times haled before a magistrate, in danger of his life. Finally, however, he won his battle and by the end of the fifth year he had built a church, including a bell tower with three bells. He also acquired by purchase forty boys, ranging in age from seven to eleven, baptized them, and taught them "Greek and Latin after our manner." From these he chose eleven, whom he taught to help him with the offices of the church. He wrote his own psalters, hymnaries, and breviaries. John taught his neophytes to copy the psalter, but he lacked books for the ritual and in his letter he pleads for "an Antiphonary, a Legend of the Saints, a Gradual and a Psalter with music for a copy."[17] One of his first victories was the conversion of the Ongut Prince George and most of his tribe.[18]

For eleven years he had been a solitary exile in a strange land, before he was joined by Father Arnold of Cologne. He missed the beauty and glory of the ritual as it was performed in the churches of his order in far-off Italy but at times his heart beat with joy as he listened to the bells of his own little church, which were "rung at all canonical hours," within the hearing of the Great Khan. In the second letter, written in 1306, he says: "I am now old and grey, more from toil and trouble than from age, for I am fifty-eight years old." He tells of baptizing "several thousands," of building a second church within the city, two miles and a half from the first, and of decorating the churches with pictures of Old and New Testament scenes containing explanations in Latin, Tarsic, and Persian. The land for the second church had been bought by his friend Peter of Lucalongo, a merchant who had accompanied him to Tartary. By this time he must have gained a position of honor at court for he says: "I have a place in his [the Khan's] court, and a regular right of entrance, and of sitting, as legate of the lord Pope; and he honors me above all other prelates, whatever may be their titles."[19]

News of his success was received with enthusiasm in Rome, and the Pope forthwith created the archepiscopal see of Khanbaliq, making John the first archbishop. In response to his pleas for help other minorites were sent out to help him, with the title of bishop. Of these only three appear to have reached Cathay: Andrew of Perugia, Gerard, and Peregrine. They received the title of papal legate and were given an *alafa* or royal stipend, thus living on the bounty of the emperor. It was not long before they had developed a mission at Zaitun in South China, at that time one of the world's greatest ports.[20] In a letter written when bishop of that city Andrew tells of a rich Armenian lady who had built and endowed a cathedral there.[21] This was the second church in Zaitun. The letter states that Gerard had been installed there as bishop in 1313, that he had been followed by Peregrine, who died in 1322, and then by Andrew. The latter seems to have held his post only four years. When Odoric passed through in 1315, there were four Franciscans assisting Gerard. A third church was built later, according to Marignolli, who visited the town in 1346.

John of Montecorvino died in 1328. He was the first and last effective archbishop of Khanbaliq. When he died, it is estimated there were a hundred thousand Christians in the empire.

Archbishop John stands out as one of the greatest figures in the Catholic missionary field. A man of extraordinary intelligence, his abilities and education might well have carried him to a high post in the church at home but he chose to exile himself in a "heathen" city at the other end of the world; a great sacrifice on his part, for he loved the Church and all the physical manifestations of the glory and beauty of his religion. His gifts of statesmanship and devotion were, however, brilliantly used at the court of the khan. His achievements, brought about in the face of extraordinary obstacles of all kinds, mark him as the outstanding representative of the Faith in eastern Asia until the coming of Saint Francis Xavier.

Many efforts were made to replace him. Nicholas of Bentia, a Franciscan professor of theology from Paris, was sent out with a large group of priests, but neither they, nor others sent later, were ever heard from. The same uncertainty hangs over the fate of William of Prato, who journeyed eastward as late as 1370, and of Francis of Podio and his twelve companions, who left for the empire of the Great Khan the following year. James of Florence, the fifth bishop of Zaitun, was martyred somewhere in central Asia in 1362, and the mission in that city, like that of Khanbaliq, soon ceased to exist.[22]

The last papal legate who lived to bring back news of the mission was John of Marignolli, sent to the Far East in 1341 in answer to the pleas of the Christian Alans that they had been without spiritual guidance since the death of Archbishop John. He arrived in Khan-

baliq in 1342 and was given an impressive reception. From the head
of the Church he brought the papal benediction, together with a beautiful war horse, which the Chinese greatly admired, and other gifts.
He seems to have remained three years in the Chinese capital, living
on the khan's bounty and "making a great harvest of souls."

The visit of Marignolli rings down the curtain for the medieval
mission to China. Twenty-five years later the Mongol dynasty itself
was forced to give way to the native Ming emperors, and it is probable that the newcomers would not have looked with favor on any
sect encouraged by their predecessors. Mohammedanism displaced
Christianity as the chief foreign cult, and the Buddhists later replaced
them both. In Europe the dark days of the fifteenth century had
followed the medieval "renaissance," and the Black Death and the
Hundred Years' War were spreading ruin throughout western Christendom. In the Near East the ruthless exploits of Tamerlane were to
complete the separation of East and West by the breaking of the
trans-Asian highway and the trans-Persian routes. Europe for over
a hundred years lost all direct contact with the Chinese empire.

The great work of the Franciscan archbishop and his confreres left
no traceable impress on Chinese culture or thought. Unlike the Jesuits,
these men were either political envoys or evangelical laborers. They
gave little thought to the bridging of the gulf which divided the cultures of East and West. They were the representatives of a monotheistic civilization in a country where all religions were acceptable
and where tolerance was almost unconsciously practiced. It is easy to
understand, therefore, that when the foreign representatives of Christendom disappeared, their religion disappeared with them, merged in
the amorphous mass of Oriental religious thought. In some parts of
China evidences have been discovered to show that the Christian doctrines were not immediately forgotten,[23] but as a whole China, for
nearly two hundred years, was ignorant of the great religion of the
West and the culture of which Christianity has been the inspiration
and guide.

THE JESUITS IN CHINA

Chapter III

FRANCIS XAVIER, APOSTLE TO
THE INDIES

T HE DAWN of the sixteenth century, in many respects, marked the beginning of the new world. As the fifteenth century drew to a close, deeds were being done, tasks were being achieved, which were to establish the characteristic elements of Western history for nearly three hundred years. Amerigo Vespucci, Christopher Columbus, Bartholomew Diaz, and Vasco da Gama were on the high seas and a new world was in the making. Geographically, as well as mentally, old barriers were broken down and new horizons established.[1] Men pushed bravely into the unknown. Many were lost, but others returned to tell of strange lands and of unheard-of riches beyond the seas. Even the economic balance of Europe was disturbed as the great Italian trading ports of Venice and Genoa, which had risen to greatness on the trans-Asian trade, were displaced by new routes and new commercial rivals.

The internationalism of medieval Christendom was giving place to new and lusty nations clamoring for preëminence and a place in the new world trade. Before the century was over, Spain, Portugal, England, and the Netherlands were to engage in a vital struggle for the mastery of the seas and the right to exploit the new markets. The age of discovery had heralded an age of commercial opportunity.

It was the two nations of the Iberian peninsula which first saw the vision of the New World and followed it. Early in the movement there was an attempt at a gentlemen's agreement between these two powers to divide the world between them, Spain to take the northern road to the Indies and Portugal the southern. Since Spain pushed east and north following Columbus, her story does not come within the scope of our study. It is Portugal we must follow.

[1] For notes to chap. iii, see pp. 308–309.

It was Prince Henry, called the Navigator, who established the foundations of Portugal's colonial glory. Under the urge of his pioneer spirit his mariners in their frail caravels of two hundred tons felt their way slowly along the African coast southward. When Henry died in 1460, his nephew, John II, took up the task and under his practical genius the day soon arrived when Bartholomew Diaz turned the southern end of the continent and unwittingly faced the Orient with its strangeness and its richness. Diaz by this act changed the foundations of world commerce. Henceforth, Lisbon was to take the place of Venice as the center of Oriental trade.

After the explorer came the conqueror. Cabral followed Vasco da Gama, and two years later came Alfonso de Albuquerque. Socotra and Ormuz were captured in 1507; four years later Goa was taken and was made the capital of this Eastern empire. Goa is chiefly important to this study as the center of the Church in the Orient for nearly three centuries. Most of the religious orders in the mission field had establishments there. It was the seat of the first Catholic bishop having jurisdiction over the whole of Far Eastern Asia—the bishopric being established in 1534. It was also the center of Portuguese authority in the Extreme Orient.

The Portuguese progress around the Indian Ocean was not an easy one. The Arabs, through the sultan of Egypt, had grown rich on this Oriental trade and were not disposed to give it up without a struggle. The backbone of Moslem resistance was broken at Diu in 1509, however, when their fleet was defeated by the Portuguese. By their victory the latter became the masters of the Indian Ocean.

But the Portuguese were not satisfied with India. They had not forgotten the description of Oriental riches given by Marco Polo, the silks of Cathay, the gold and pearls of Japan, and the spices of Java and Sumatra. In 1508, De Sequeira was sent to Malacca and was given orders to obtain information. In 1511, Albuquerque established friendly relations with Chinese merchants. A trade mission went to China in 1514 and in the following year Raphael Perestrello traveled in a Chinese junk to South China and returned with a valuable cargo. Definite trade relations were now established. Perez de Andrade followed Perestrello in 1517, sailed up the river to Canton, and returned after making contact with the local mandarins. Thomas Perez, the first official envoy of Portugal, reached Peking in 1520 or 1521 but was almost immediately sent back to Canton as a prisoner, and it was nearly a century before another European penetrated to the emperor's court. In 1542, three Portuguese were driven by storms off the course and were shipwrecked on a strange island kingdom. They had discovered Japan—the first Europeans to visit that country, mentioned more than two centuries earlier by Marco Polo.

These adventures into unknown seas were directed by men who had something of the spirit of the medieval knight. The search for new lands acquired some of the mystical ardor of the quest for the Grail. Columbus, in undertaking his voyage into the unknown, thought little, if at all, of trade or conquest, but he had an enthusiastic belief in his divinely appointed mission to bring fresh souls to the knowledge of God and to the Holy Church.[2] Henry the Navigator, by his crusading zeal, belonged to the Middle Ages, though his critical mind and practical genius linked him with the modern world.[3] In his ardor for the cause of the Cross he is a pre-Renaissance Saint Louis, with administrative talents which the French king lacked. This enthusiasm was also shared by John II. The latter made the crushing of Islam one of his chief aims.

So, in these great voyages and voyagers, the romanticism of high adventure was coupled with a medieval love of the Church. It is not surprising, then, to find that in these explorations the Cross accompanied the Sword. At first it was the Franciscans and Dominicans who took up the arduous task, but soon there arose another order whose aim, purpose, and structure seem to have made it an instrument specially sent by Providence for the purpose. This order was the Society of Jesus, whose members are perhaps best known as the Jesuits. So ardently and so efficiently did this new order take up the work of evangelization that within a remarkably short space of time it had outposts in all the lonely corners of the world and a representative of the Christian cause among the people of nearly every nation.

About the time when Columbus was pleading his cause at the court of Isabella and Vasco da Gama was preparing to follow the trail of Diaz around the Cape, a child was born in the little province of Guipuzcoa in northern Spain who was destined to have as vital an influence on ecclesiastical history as any figure, probably, since Augustine. Iñigo de Loyola, born in a feudal castle and given the usual meager education of the noble youth of his time, seems to have shown little promise of worth or achievement in his youth. His intellectual desires were satisfied with the perusal of the romances: the story of Amadis of Gaul, of Tirante the White, of the Cid, of the Knight of the Green Sword, and of Montalvo's "Sir Love of God." His youth was divided between carefree pleasures and romantic dreams of chivalry. In early manhood he took up the only occupation possible for a man of his station outside the Church, the profession of arms. Then suddenly the fateful event occurred which changed the whole course of his life. In the attack on Pamplona he was struck by a cannon ball, which shattered one of his legs. The enforced idleness of the sick room drove him to the consolation of books. Lacking his old favorites, the romances, he turned to the *exempla* of the Church, to the *Flos Sanctorum* and the other edifying literature of its kind. The chivalric longings of the young noble took a religious turn and he dreamed of knight errantry in the service of his Lady, the Virgin. He saw himself as a new Sir Galahad, fighting the diabolic hosts that war on truth. He dreamed of a crusade to the Holy Land and the spiritual, as well as the temporal, conquest of that country. In this chivalric, idealistic mind, then, was born the germ of a society which throughout its history was to bear the stamp of a mystic militarism, of a fortitude in service combined with a strict devotion to duty and the Faith. Bearing the stamp of its founder, the Society of Jesus, in its highest moods, remained always a religious order of chivalry.

The transformed young Loyola passed his days in meditation, study, and penance. At the monastery of Montserrat he performed the vigil of the virgin knight. Then, his period of preparation over, he started out to convince his fellow men. Ignatius de Loyola possessed another great gift, that of making converts. Through Spain he traveled, stopping now and then to study and to preach, and writing his *Spiritual Exercises*, the astounding guidebook of the order he was to found. At Salamanca the Dominicans gave the first evidence of what was to be an endless opposition to Loyola and to the policies of his Society by condemning his methods and causing the young man to spend thirty-two days in prison on a charge of heresy.

On his release he continued his way to Paris. There the number of his personal followers grew to ten and there, in a chapel on Montmartre, the holy hill of Saint Denis' martyrdom, on the Feast of the Assumption in the year 1534, the little group formally dedicated themselves to the service of their Faith.

The youthful members of the group at first dreamed of a new crusade, a spiritual conquest of the Holy Land under the banner of Christ. But nothing could be done to carry out their purpose until the consent of the papal see had been obtained. The group dispersed to meet in Rome in 1538. By this time they had learned that, owing to war conditions prevailing in the Near East, they would be unable to reach the Holy Land. In Rome they occupied themselves in works of charity, visiting the sick and begging funds for the poor. Gradually in their minds the germ developed of a more ambitious plan. They began to dream of an organization which should carry reform and spiritual enlightenment to all Catholic countries and even beyond, to the newly discovered lands of the Orient and the New World. For this purpose they determined to form a permanent organization, and thus the Society of Jesus came into being.

In Rome the time was ripe for the foundation of the order. Reform was in the air. The thunderings of Luther at the gates of Wittenberg were having their repercussions in the center of Christendom. Pope

Paul III had already appointed a commission to consider ecclesiastical abuses. True, with the common fate of commissions, its report was accepted and neglected, but the necessity for reform was none the less keenly felt. Loyola's request for permission to found a new order was at first unsympathetically received. The Church had orders aplenty and was apparently none the better off for them, but perseverance finally brought its rewards and, in 1540, Paul III issued the bull which officially created the Society.[4] It is possible that he was finally persuaded to do this by the fact that the constitution for the new order contained, besides the threefold vow of poverty, chastity, and obedience, a clause making its professed members definitely henchmen of the papal see. Loyola was elected first general of the new order. Then followed a period of remarkable and astonishingly rapid expansion. At the beginning the Jesuits adopted methods which quickly brought to them a reputation for piety and saintliness. They begged their bread in the streets, slept in the poorhouse, cared for the prisoners in the jails, and indulged in other acts of charity.[5] The excess of their piety seems to have aroused criticism within the Church itself, where they were not long in creating enemies.

But these tactics were not long to remain the distinguishing mark of the order. From the beginning Loyola and his followers had close contact with the nobility, as well as with other people of influence in church and state. As the Society developed, this cult of the men and women in positions of importance became one of the central points in its diplomacy. From the latter half of the sixteenth century there was scarcely an outstanding figure in Europe with whom the Jesuits did not come in contact and whose good will they did not strive to gain. They revived the importance of the confessional and, when they had succeeded in establishing members of their order as confessors of kings and princes, they had reached a position of power which had a vital influence on the history of Europe.

In its inception and in its early years the Society was predominantly Spanish. Its most powerful patrons, such as John II, were in Spain and its first generals were Spaniards. It continued to spread, however, in other countries; in the Spanish Netherlands, in Italy and, to a lesser extent, in France. It opened colleges in the lands it penetrated, and its members were trained in the peculiar and difficult discipline of the Spiritual Exercises. Under the influence of this discipline its members, at a time when the Church was suffering bitter blows from Protestant rebels, brought a new vitality, a new enthusiasm, new methods, perhaps even a new spiritual outlook, to Christianity.

So, by the beginning of the seventeenth century, the Society found itself settled in most of the countries of Europe and had become a power in the political and ecclesiastical history of the time.

In the meantime, while the Society was extending its influence in Europe, the great New World beyond the seas was not neglected. When Rodriguez went to Portugal, he was accompanied by Francis Xavier, who had the ambition to be sent by King John to the Indies. Xavier and Rodriguez were doing a remarkable work in Portugal. They were fighting the immoral effects of the luxury which had resulted from the flow of wealth into the peninsula from the New World.[6] Therefore, when the call came for the men to go to the Orient, John did not wish to give them up. A compromise was effected, however, whereby Rodriguez should stay in Portugal while his companion took up the work of missionary, of spiritual conqueror of Albuquerque's new empire. So, on April 7, 1541, Xavier set sail from Lisbon with the fullest powers from Rome to establish Christianity in the Orient.[7]

A fun-loving, free-living young student, Francis Xavier had come under the influence of Loyola while studying in Paris. With admirable patience and no small degree of cleverness the latter had gradually won him over to listen to the voice of conscience so that he gave up his gay life and devoted himself to the cause of Christ. He was Loyola's greatest convert, the highest exemplification of the lofty ideals and mystic devotion of the founder of the order. So completely did Xavier devote himself to the new life and so striking was his success that he became known as the Apostle to the Indies.

His voyage across the world was a veritable triumph for the Faith, a triumph in which the Christian virtues of humility, charity, and self-abnegation bore remarkable fruit in rich harvests of conversion. The annals of the Church glow with his astounding accomplishments; even the ecclesiastical enemies of his order speak of him with reverence. At Mozambique, on the isle of Socotra, in the godless city of Goa, Xavier brought spiritual inspiration and healing. In all these places people turned to him for light and under his persuasion gave up their sinful ways. He visited the poverty-stricken fishermen, the Paravas, who had been nominally converted years before in one of those mass conversions which came to be characteristic of the Portuguese, and he brought them a renewed religious faith. He came to grips with the Brahmins in their own country and, in spite of their opposition, he baptized—in a single day, according to his assertion—ten thousand converts. At Travancor legend credits him with the miracle of raising from the dead a man who had been for many hours in the tomb.[8] A restless spirit, always under the urge of pushing farther afield, Xavier continued across southeastern Asia. In September, 1545, he was in Malacca, using the children of the place to fight the sensuous, tropic putrefaction of morals. At the island of Amboyna he found the pestilence among the Spanish fleet and he went among the sailors left to die on the sands, nursing them, breathing the miasma of their fever-infected surroundings, and going from place to place begging funds with which to buy them the necessities of life. In the Moluccas he opposed himself once more to the immorality in those places. After a startling success in these islands, he visited the isles of the cannibals where his kindness, his humanity, and his irresistible powers of persuasion turned the degraded savages to the gentleness of the gospel.

As a result of six years in India Xavier was able to report to his superiors that there were four Jesuit centers in the Moluccas, six at Cape Comorin, two in Cochin, two at Bassein, and four in Socotra.[9] The fire of his enthusiasm carried him from victory to victory. Despite the ardors of his work, his body seems to have supported the task well. With boundless vitality himself, he required the same standards from those around him. He secured the dismissal of the morally easy-going viceroy at Goa, Alphonse de Souza, and he unhesitatingly dismissed from the Company another Jesuit who refused to give up a fertile field to follow him into unknown lands. Gradually he seems to have been forced into the position of intermediary between the Portuguese and the native chiefs who wished to obtain the political support of the Europeans, a task which suited not only his own talents but also the genius of the Society he represented. At Malacca he called to the aid of the Christians the power of the Portuguese fleet and, in the face of apparent disaster, his enthusiasm made him the inspirer of victory. Then one day he met a renegade named Anjiro, who had fled from justice in Japan, and from him he learned of the isles of Nippon.

Anjiro must have given Xavier an optimistic picture of his people and of their ripeness for conversion, for the restless soldier of Christ immediately began planning the conversion of the kingdom. On April 15, 1549, he set sail for the islands and landed in Kagoshima four months later.[10] Here as elsewhere his linguistic ability apparently stood him in good stead. In a short time he had gained an elementary knowledge of Japanese and was ready for the conquest. "God has brought us to the land of our heart's desire," he triumphantly writes to his superiors at home, but he was doomed to much disillusionment before his task was done.

In Japan Xavier came into contact for the first time with another great religion, Buddhism. At first he hoped to convert the bonzes, but they, seeing their interests threatened, soon turned from curious inquiries to downright hostility. By busying himself in healing and in miracles, Xavier gradually made a place for himself and was soon able to claim the conversion of Kagoshima, though in the neighboring town of Yamaguchi he met with temporary defeat. With the Jesuit policy of reaching always to the top and working down, Xavier felt that to win Japan he must first win the ear of the emperor, that august head of the kingdom who was reverenced as a deity. So, barefoot and in rags, nourished on a little dried rice, he made the arduous journey across the country to Miyako (Kyoto), the capital. Here bitter disappointment awaited him. Miyako was a city of silent streets through which flitted the ghost of past imperial greatness. The emperor himself was a mere husk of royalty. The feudal barons, whose quarrels created discord and disaster for the empire, had deprived him of everything but traditional reverence. Xavier retraced his steps to Yamaguchi, where he finally succeeded in establishing a flourishing mission; then he passed on to the province of Bungo. By this time he and the Portuguese had found they could be of mutual assistance: the latter by paying him the ostentatious honors necessary for his status as a representative of a great religion, and Xavier by furthering their plans for commercial penetration into the empire. It must have been about this time that Xavier threw off the torn robe of the pilgrim and adorned himself with the rich dress befitting his rank, for he appeared before the ruler of Bungo amid the brilliant splendor of a Portuguese embassy. Here, as elsewhere, he was sorely annoyed by the persistent curiosity of the natives, who plied him with questions of a theological nature capable of testing the ingenuity of the most brilliant medieval rhetorician. At Bungo he gained an apparently striking success, but he failed to win the friendship of the Buddhist bonzes.

One of the most persistent objections made to his religion was the query: "If yours is the true faith why have not the Chinese, from whom comes all wisdom, heard of it?" This oft-repeated question turned his thoughts to the Middle Kingdom, and gradually he became convinced that the highest point of achievement, that which alone would secure ultimate success, was the spiritual conquest of China. From then on his mind dwelt constantly on this difficult task.

Leaving Japan, the great missionary returned to India. On the way he fell in with a Portuguese captain, who suggested that they should combine forces, the captain, Pereira, going to China as ambassador and Xavier as spiritual envoy. At Goa the viceroy gave his approval to the scheme, which seemed ripe for success. Disaster came, however, when the port captain of Malacca, evidently thinking that he should play some role in such an important adventure, refused to allow them to proceed. Undaunted, Xavier cast around for some other method of ingress into the Middle Kingdom.

He sailed to the island of Shang Ch'uan, off the Kwangtung coast, and there tried to enlist the aid of Chinese shipowners. Fearing official displeasure if they should introduce the forbidden foreigner into China, the shipowners received his plan with coldness, but finally Xavier found the captain of a junk, who, for two hundred *cruzados,* seemed willing to take the risk. Again Xavier's hopes ran high, but they were destined to be once more disappointed, for the Chinese failed to arrive at the appointed hour. Week after week the missionary waited on the rocky little island. He seems even to have tried to get to Siam in order to join the embassy from that place which, every three years, went to Peking.[11] The Portuguese, either through fear of offending the Chinese and thus imperiling their chances of trade or through a genuine skepticism regarding the possibility of the enterprise, refused assistance. As days went by, hope began to wane, and the ardent soldier of the Cross, in a little hovel by the sea, fell victim to ague and fever. Attended only by his faithful Chinese servant, Antonio, he grew worse and, after twenty-four days of delirium, on the second of December, 1552, he died. Today his tomb on the little rocky island off the coast of Canton is a shrine visited by hundreds of devout Catholics.

Xavier's place in the evangelization of the Orient is an enormously important one. He is credited with bringing a million souls to the Church. Although it is difficult to believe all the marvelous achievements accredited to him, there is no doubt that he was the greatest, as well as the most successful, product of an organization which set out to achieve the spiritual rejuvenation of the world. Not without reason has he been called the Alexander of missionary history. All the talents of the Jesuit Order seem to have centered in him. Besides those virtues of humility, modesty, and self-abnegation which he practiced throughout his mature life, he displayed those gifts of foresight, diplomacy, and courage which took the Jesuit into the courts of princes and made him the counselor of the great. When necessary, he became "all things to all men that he might gain all." His inexhaustible energy carried him from one adventure to another. His impatience to push beyond the frontiers of heathendom urged him ever on and on. No task was too humble or too revolting; no plan too grandiose or too sublime. With the poorer classes his methods were simple. Landing at an unknown port, he would walk through the streets clad in ragged garments. Ringing a bell to attract attention, he would proclaim the news that he had good tidings for all. Having gathered a crowd around him, he would preach to them, in their language. It is inconceivable that Xavier possessed the divine gift of tongues which the devout have ascribed to him, but there seems little doubt that he possessed to an extraordinary degree the facility of gaining a working knowledge of foreign languages, which, with true Jesuitical ability, he used to the greatest possible advantage. That his labors were vast and his success striking there is no doubt. He carried to the lands of the Orient the religion of the Occident. For this reason he must stand in the foremost ranks of those who have attempted to bridge the gulf between the East and the West.

When Xavier died, his spirit lived on. In Europe his fellow churchmen seem to have been set afire by the vision of the martyr. The spiritual conquest of the East appealed to the fervent Catholics of the West with the force of a new crusade, though there was never apparently any unified plan to accomplish the great task. A number of ardent spirits, however, attempted to follow in the footsteps of the Apostle to the Indies.

In the years following Xavier's death, several other priests tried to break through the barriers which Chinese conservatism had built around the empire. To succeed Xavier as provincial of the Indies and Japan came a Flemish Jesuit, Gaspard Barzei, who died in 1553. He was followed by Melchior Nuñez Barreto, a Portuguese who, in 1553, had started on an unsuccessful effort to evangelize Japan. Nuñez seems to have been the first Jesuit to reach the mainland. He visited Canton on two occasions for the purpose of seeking the release of Mathio di Brito and two other fellow countrymen, who were held in chains by a local magistrate. He is interesting to us principally, not because his fifteen-hundred-ducats bribe achieved its object, but mainly because he left a short account of the country and its institutions which is perhaps the first book on China to have been composed by a European since the fantastic work of Fernand Mendez Pinto.[12]

In the next year (1556) a Dominican, Gaspar da Cruz, attempted the task, but, although he was allowed to stay a few weeks on the mainland and seems to have made several conversions, he was soon expelled by hostile officials. A more pretentious mission, led by Juan Batista de Ribeira, sailed from Goa in 1565 but was shipwrecked in a typhoon and lost in April of the following year.[13]

The starting-point of these attempted spiritual invasions of China was the little Portuguese settlement at Macao, which for some time had been growing in size and importance. Its history goes back to the earliest days of Sino-Portuguese relations. According to one account the European seamen had been instrumental in administering a stunning defeat to the pirates who infested that part of the China seas, and, as a reward for their help, the local authorities had allowed them to use Macao as a base for their commerce with the mainland. Actually it was a bare rock, forming a kind of isthmus to the larger island of Hsiang Shan. Nieuhoff, who saw it in 1655, describes it as "a little hanging island, fixed to a greater, built on a very high rock ... whose wall is washed round about by the sea, except on the north side."[14] From the beginning the Portuguese had been there only on sufferance, and they paid a sum of money annually as rental. In 1575 the Chinese built a barrier on the neck of the isthmus, leaving only a small door which was constantly guarded. As, two centuries later, the Western nations raised on the marshes near the mouth of the Yangtze the great city of Shanghai so, on this little rock, the Portuguese built a town which, by the middle of the seventeenth century, had grown so important commercially that Nieuhoff refers to it as "the greatest trading city in all Asia." It soon became the center of the foreign commerce of China, not only with Europe but also with India and the Moluccas, a trade which brought to it people from all the neighboring countries. Threatened for a time with extinction on account of the xenophobia of the Ming government, Macao resumed relations with the officials of the mainland after 1554 and in the subsequent history of Oriental commerce it developed an importance out of all proportion to its size. By 1563 there were seven hundred Portuguese there, some of whom had intermarried with the Chinese. In view of its prosperous condition, it is not surprising that the Dutch cast jealous eyes on the settlement and, in 1622, made a valiant effort to take it by storm.

The Portuguese seem to have looked with favor on the conversion of the natives and must have encouraged the development of a Jesuit mission on the island, though they opposed all Spanish efforts at evangelization emanating from the Philippines.[15] When the order built its first residence there in 1565, the community already had five thousand Christians, including many native converts. The Jesuit mission at Macao grew rapidly. From an establishment which in 1581 had some fourscore workers the mission of the Society developed into a great center from which priests were sent, not only to various parts of China, but also to Japan and to other countries of the Eastern seas. The Jesuit house at Macao was always subservient juridically to the authority of Goa but, as time went on, this dependence became more and more a matter of form.

With the foundation of Catholic missions at Macao the stage was set for the China venture and it needed only the impetus of a personality with the faith and courage to start it. Providence supplied such a man in the person of Alexander Valignani, who had been appointed Jesuit visitor to the Indies in 1573 and had reached Macao on October

19, 1577. Seeing the possibilities of the new field, he immediately demanded recruits, and in 1578 Michael Ruggieri was sent from Goa to help him.

It was Valignani who, more than any other man, was responsible for the nature of the Jesuit work in China, for he planned the strategy which in later years proved its wisdom by its extraordinary success. Before he arrived, the Jesuits at Macao had based their tactics on the experience acquired in other mission fields, like the Americas and the Philippines, where they had proved successful. These methods, suitable to lands inhabited by backward and uncivilized peoples, were totally unfitted to a country of such ancient and widespread culture as that of China. It is probable, therefore, that the failure to make Chinese contacts during the early days was due chiefly to this error of judgment. When Valignani arrived and wished to change the Jesuit strategy, he had to overcome the opposition of those members within the order whose narrow and uncompromising methods had made China appear to be a land impenetrable to Christian propaganda.

Valignani at once set about changing this state of things. Realizing from the first that a knowledge of the traditions and culture of the empire was essential before the work of evangelization could be begun, he urged on Father Ruggieri the necessity of mastering the Chinese language. It was at first difficult to find a teacher, but the Jesuit overcame this and other obstacles and gradually acquired a knowledge of the written language, although he seems to have had less success with the vernacular. Other recruits soon began to arrive, among them Francisco Pasio and Matteo Ricci.

Chapter IV

RICCI, THE PIONEER

IF XAVIER may be looked upon as the Moses of the Jesuits' China mission, their Joshua, the man who led them into the Promised Land, was Matteo Ricci. When Ricci arrived in the Orient, nothing had been accomplished; when he died, in 1615, the Jesuits were definitely established in Peking and throughout the empire.

Born in a little town in the Papal States in the very year that Xavier died, Matteo Ricci entered the Society of Jesus in 1571. After seven years of study in his native town of Macerata, he went to Rome to study law. Here he worked under the scholar Clavius, from whom he acquired that love of mathematics which was later to be so useful to him. His training and all his instincts were scholarly and, like the majority of his fellow Jesuits, he dedicated all his personal gifts to the cause for which the Society stood. At last the China mission had a man who could stand before Chinese scholars, talk with them of scholarly things, and not be put to shame.

Ricci followed Valignani, with whom he had taken his novitiate, to Goa; thence he went to the Jesuit house in Cochin China, where he finished his studies. He arrived at Macao in 1582.

To some extent the way had been prepared for him. Ruggieri, guided by the wise counsel of his superior, Valignani, had made contacts with the officials on the mainland, with the result that they were invited to Chao Ch'ing, the capital of Kwangtung, in December, 1582, and given lodgings in a local temple. Everything seemed favorable to their stay. They adopted the dress of Buddhist bonzes and gained the ear of the local mandarin. Then suddenly the friendly official was displaced and the two Jesuits were forced to beat a retreat to Macao. Here, with Valignani's assistance, they renewed their efforts to return.

The history of the next seventeen years is the story of a hard struggle to strike roots in several of the cities of southern and central China.

Facing the conservatism of an official class which for centuries had believed that the outside world contained nothing that could contribute to Chinese culture, and the hostility of the populace which, in a more unenlightened way, reflected the mental attitude of its officials, the task was an enormously difficult one.[1] Semedo, the chronicler of those early days, comments on the problem:

It seems from the difficulties and persecutions they survived, as if the prince of darkness had employed all his powers to prevent the enterprise. So true was this that Father Valignani, the visitor, seeing the great opposition which was springing up on all sides; the almost unsurmountable difficulties which closed the gates of the Middle Kingdom and made the ports inaccessible to foreigners; the danger that had to be run to get a foothold in the country and the little profit gained by so much toil, had resolved to recall the fathers to Macao in order to employ them in missions where there was less difficulty and more profit for the souls of men and had even written several letters to that effect.[2]

From the beginning the mission suffered from the national rivalries of Portugal and Spain. It has been shown how the Jesuit Order had allied itself with, or followed closely in the path of, Portuguese conquest. The result was that, although many of the leading Jesuits, like Ricci, Verbiest, and Schall, were not of Portuguese nationality, the Society of Jesus was for many years the unofficial representative in many Oriental lands of the small Iberian monarchy which had just become the head of a great colonial empire. From their center at Goa, the Jesuits claimed the whole of the Far East as their spiritual empire just as the followers of Albuquerque had the ambition of making this part of the world their temporal empire.

The center of Spanish activities was in the Philippines, where the Dominicans and, to a lesser extent, the Franciscans were firmly established. Several attempts, notably in 1575, 1579, and 1583, were made by missionaries from Manila to gain footing in the mainland in China. These attempts were looked upon with disfavor by the Portuguese of Macao, who did not hesitate to spread the rumor that the

---

[1] For notes to chap. iv, see pp. 309–311.

Spaniards were seeking temporal, rather than spiritual, conquest. Apart from feelings of national rivalry there seems to have been reason for this hostility. The Spanish priests believed that the missionaries should enter the empire as mendicants pledged to the vow of poverty and that they should travel through the country begging their way and striving to gain the ear of the masses—a system of evangelization from the bottom up which was absolutely contrary to the policy adopted by the Society of Jesus. The Dominican plan condemned compromise with local prejudices or any attempt to make the path of evangelization easier by a surrender of even the least important principles. The Jesuits rightly feared that this policy would lead to imprudences and misunderstandings which would have repercussions on the work of the Society. This was probably the reason why they accepted the decision of the Council of the Indies whereby no priest was to be permitted to enter the Middle Kingdom except by way of Lisbon and Goa, that is, by the Jesuit route. This arrangement was confirmed by the papal brief, *Ex pastoralis officio,* in 1585.[8]

Events seemed to prove the wisdom of the Jesuit position. Whether it was the result of hostile propaganda or not, it is clear that the Spanish monks failed to make headway and sometimes found themselves in embarrassing situations. Ruggieri was forced, on one occasion, to rescue a group of Spanish Franciscans from prison, where their tactics had landed them, while on other occasions Jesuit priests are reported to have aided members of other orders who were in difficulties.

Ruggieri and his confreres, on the other hand, bent all their efforts to placate the local officials. The Jesuits soon found that they could arouse in the latter the spirit of curiosity, and they used this fact to the greatest advantage. They brought to their aid the attraction of mechanical things. In the early days we find Ruggieri promising the viceroy of Kwangtung "a clock with wheels marking and sounding all the hours," which he had, for this purpose, begged from the provincial at Goa. Bribery by this form of gift soon came to be a common Jesuit practice.

The use of these tactics brought results, and in December, 1582, Ruggieri and Pasio were received in audience by the viceroy at Chao Ch'ing. They immediately petitioned for a permanent residence and were granted a piece of land there, as well as permission to travel throughout the province. The officials were surprised when they refused the loan of a handsome temple building and chose rather to build their own mission outside the city, near a large tower called the Flowery Pagoda.

The building operations were witnessed by a crowd of curious natives, many of whom came from a distance to see the foreigners who worshipped a strange god. The priests were forced at this time to give up the idea of building a church in Western style, partly on account of lack of funds since, from the beginning, the members of the Society had been hampered by financial difficulties. When the buildings were finished, they obtained from the viceroy a document strengthening their hold on the property, a copy of which, according to Chinese custom, was posted at the front gate of the mission. In the meantime they went quietly on with their work of preparation, studying the language and preparing for the time when they might preach openly to the people. Ruggieri was writing a catechism in the native tongue while Ricci was composing an explanation of the Decalogue. For a while the hopes of their friends in Europe ran high, but we find Ricci writing to the general of the order in 1583, warning him not to give too much credence to optimistic reports from the East.[4]

This skepticism was justified, for they were not long allowed to remain in peace. From the first the ignorance of the populace had showed itself in acts of hostility. On Ruggieri had been bestowed the abusive term *yang kwei* ("foreign devil"), an epithet which, in spite of changing times, is still hurled at the foreigner in some parts of China. On several occasions the Jesuit building was attacked by the mob, which shouted imprecations and threw stones. Once the Jesuit property was almost demolished. One of the priests caught and rebuked a child who had insulted one of the servants and this was

made the basis of a charge of kidnapping, the priests being accused
of taking the child to be sold as a slave at Macao. The ignorant hostility of the natives resulted in accusations against the foreigners of
various crimes: Ruggieri was thought to be practicing magic and
adultery; the missionaries were blamed for a flood which imperiled
the city; a story was spread abroad that the pagoda in the vicinity had
been built by the foreigners to dominate the country with a view to
invasion; Father Cattaneo, on account of his stature, was suspected
of being a military leader.

In spite of opposition, however, the Jesuits continued to work,
using their talents for tact and diplomacy with the Chinese officials
who came to visit them, even though at times they were sorely tried
by the latter's embarrassing curiosity. To such an extent did they
adopt this practice of discretion that they refrained at first from men-
tioning the subject of religion. As a result of these tactics, their house
became increasingly popular. Encouraged by the friendship of the
viceroy for them, the local gentry soon came to talk with these gentle
and courteous foreign scholars, whose bearing bespoke wisdom to
men who held culture to be the highest attainment of life.

They displayed the treasures of their small European library—
tomes on astronomy, cosmography, and other learned subjects, beautifully printed and exquisitely bound—to men who all their lives had
lived under the influence of books.[5] From the first the Jesuits realized
the value and influence of the printed page; the picture, the engraving, the map, and the textbook were throughout the history of the
mission a powerful aid to propaganda. To satisfy the curiosity of the
local official Ricci was soon thrust into the role of cartographer. He
had in his room a map of the world (probably the "Typus orbis ter-
rarum" from the *Theatrum mundi* of Ortelius). This attracted the
attention of the local prefect and Ricci was forced to explain why the
all-important land of China appeared in an inconspicuous corner of
the map. This he did, apparently to the satisfaction of the official, who
asked him to reproduce the map with Chinese characters. Ricci did

so but altered the original by placing the meridian of China in the center. The result was engraved on wood and printed, the official insisting on keeping the copies in his possession so that he could give them as gifts to his friends. In the years following, Ricci made many other maps of the earth and the heavens with Chinese characters and distributed them to Chinese officials.[6]

Then, when everything seemed to be going favorably with the mission, a change of officials took place and the new viceroy immediately showed himself hostile to the foreigners. In August, 1586, he ordered Ricci and D'Almeida, who had been added to the mission, to leave the country. Evidently, however, the viceroy had some misgivings concerning his conduct toward men who had such a favorable reputation, for he offered to reimburse them for their property. The matter was finally settled by permission being granted the Jesuits to settle in the city of Ch'ao Chou, in the same province.

Their years at Chao Ch'ing (1583–1589) had been a period of preparation. At Ch'ao Chou they began to reap some of the rewards of their labors. The local gentry appeared sympathetic, even interested, and a number of conversions were made. Here again Ricci found the scholars intelligently inquisitive as they flocked to hear him and to see the wonders of the West which he possessed. The harvest, however, was lamentably scanty and there were moments of discouragement for some of the workers, as witness the complaints of Sebastian Fernandez, a Chinese Jesuit and one of the earliest martyrs of the China mission, who wrote to Ricci at this time: "We ought to abandon China and go to Japan . . . there to finish our life gloriously."[7] Ricci himself soon saw that the indifference which they encountered from the masses of people was a force which could be met only with the weapon of imperial favor.

From the beginning he had cast his eyes longingly to the North, in the direction of the great capital of which he had heard so much and which was just beginning to be associated in his mind with the stately Cambaluc of Marco Polo.[8] The Jesuit missionary had learned that any favor he might gain with provincial officials was at best local and temporary; that unless some more stable support was provided, the Church in China was doomed to a stormy and vicissitudinous existence, if not to ultimate failure. Stability could be established only from Peking, where the emperor, as representative of Heaven, directed with a more or less arbitrary will the destinies of his people.[9] To Peking therefore Ricci determined to go, and he kept his determination with a steadfast courage which finally gained him access to the throne of the Son of Heaven.

In May, 1595, an opportunity was given Ricci to travel north in the train of an official whose sick son was being tended by the priest, but after an accident on the Kan River, Ricci was forced to abandon the party and return to Nanking. Here he hoped to find refuge in the house of an official with whom he had been on friendly terms at Ch'ao Chou. The latter, however, was afraid of compromising himself, and the missionary moved on to Nanchang, the capital of Kiangsi, where, through friendly officials, he got in touch with the local gentry and was permitted to lay the foundations of a mission. Father Soerio and Brother Martinez (Huang Ming-sha), a Chinese Jesuit,[10] arrived shortly afterward; a house was bought, and thus the second Jesuit establishment in China was founded.[11]

At this time Ricci was made superior general of the mission in China, a post which his experience and tact well fitted him to fill. Valignani at Macao still continued to give Ricci and his confreres active support. Gradually funds available for the mission increased, and many objects such as watches, clocks, scientific instruments, paintings, engravings, maps, and prisms came to the missionaries to help them smooth the way to Peking.

In 1598 Ricci again started north from Nanchang with Father Cattaneo, traveling with a friendly official named Kuang who had been appointed president of one of the six boards, or administrative departments, of the government, and was returning from a mission in the provinces. Arriving at the capital, the missionary was entertained by friends, and efforts were made to introduce him into court circles. It was rumored that he possessed the power to transmute the baser metals into gold, a metal which was badly needed at this time to carry on the war with Japan. The cupidity of the court eunuchs was aroused and, when they found that Ricci did not possess this gift of magic, they turned against him and refused him access to the emperor. To make matters worse, a rumor spread that he and his companion were in Japanese pay. After a stay of two months, therefore, they were forced to return.

Ricci was severely ill en route but finally arrived back in Nanking on February 6, 1599. Here he was accorded a friendly reception by his friend Wang and other officials. Ricci was much impressed by the great city of Nanking, a former capital of the empire. He saw three things, in particular, which interested him: fireworks finer than anything to be seen in Europe; a magnificent temple built in a large pine wood; and an observatory containing instruments two hundred and fifty years old, similar, probably, to those to be seen today in the observatory on the walls of Peking. At Nanking he was once more the center of a coterie of scholars. He spent his days discoursing on religious matters and explaining his scientific instruments and charts to his curious visitors. Father Cattaneo had returned south by the sea route for additional gifts and he soon appeared bringing magnificent presents for the emperor. Fortified with these and with official letters of recommendation to scholars in the capital and accompanied by the newly arrived Spanish Jesuit Pantoja, Ricci turned north again in May, 1600.[12] Their traveling companion, a friendly eunuch, left them at Lin Ch'ing and they were unfortunate enough to fall into the hands of a customs official named Ma Ts'ang. Whether Ma wished to steal the imperial presents is not certain, but at any rate, he showed from the first a venomous dislike of the priests and in his dealings with them he exemplified Chinese officialdom at its worst. After vilifying the missionaries in a way typical of hostile Chinese magistrates in their dealings with accused persons, he seized their presents, sent an unfavorable report to court, conducted them to Tientsin, and started such a campaign of lies and abuse against them that friends tried to persuade Ricci to flee for his life. Thrown into prison, he and his companions began to despair of ever reaching the imperial court, when suddenly their fortunes took a turn for the better. The Son of Heaven appears to have remembered that certain gifts had come to him from foreign lands. He made inquiries and commanded that the foreigners be brought to the capital. So, after twenty years of constant effort, of courage and perseverance in the face of tremendous obstacles, the chief representatives of the Jesuits in China at last reached the foot of the imperial throne.

Ricci had now attained the height of his ambition and, at the same time, had made his greatest contribution to the cause of evangelism in the empire. The next ten years were devoted to the strengthening of the missionaries' position at court and the development of a reputation which should be proof against official jealousy, court intrigue, and the latent xenophobia of the people. That Ricci was successful in this is proved by the records of the next two hundred years for, although the missionaries at Peking were at times subjected to severe persecution, never were they irrevocably banished from the empire.

The emperor of China was not, as Westerners have often believed, an absolute monarch. His actions were modified, and often dictated, by six boards or departments, supervised (during the Ming dynasty) by the *Nei Ko* or "Grand Secretariat." These controlled the details of government and acted as intermediary between the sacred person of the emperor and the officials of the provinces. At times the boards did not hesitate to oppose firmly the monarch's will. One of these, the Board of Rites (*Li Pu*), had control of matters of official etiquette and deportment, so important in the Chinese system. Unfortunately, Ricci had been introduced to the capital by eunuchs of the imperial entourage and not through the official and proper channel, the Board of Rites, and this had aroused the antagonism of the board, whose members were jealous of their prerogatives. They immediately showed hostility by endeavoring to seize the foreigners and deport them. To the throne they sent a report which contains the quintessence of Chinese conservatism:

Europe has no connection with us and does not receive our laws. The image of the God of Heaven and of the Virgin which Li Ma T'ou (Ricci) offers as tribute is of no value. He also has presented a bag which contains some bones of genii, without remembering that the *hsien,* when ascending on high, take their bones with them. Let no such novelties be introduced to the palace, lest some evil might befall, and let Li Ma T'ou be sent back to his country.[13]

The sunshine of imperial favor had, however, fallen on the missionaries and, although the board tried on three occasions to get rid of them, they were henceforth not to lack friends.

The first task was the presentation of their gifts. Tradition forbade the emperor himself to meet the foreigners, therefore all communication had to be made through court eunuchs as intermediaries.[14] To satisfy the curiosity of the monarch, however, the court painter was commanded to paint their portraits, and the artist, influenced by hostile officials, made them as ugly as possible. Nevertheless, the presents were offered with elaborate ceremony, the priests making the customary three bows and nine prostrations before the empty throne. The emperor showed an almost childlike pleasure in the gifts, particularly in a clock which chimed the hours. Concerning this clock, an amusing story is related by the Jesuit chroniclers. The news of the wonderful "time-machine" came to the ears of the empress-mother who asked to see it. Filial duty forbade the denial of such a request, but the emperor feared to lose his newly acquired toy. He solved the problem neatly. Sending for a workman, he caused the mechanism which worked the bell to be disconnected before sending it to the empress dowager. The latter, failing to hear the chiming of the hours, thought the toy much overrated and sent it back to her imperial son. Shortly afterwards it became dirty and refused to run, resulting in great consternation among the officials until Ricci, hastily summoned, discovered the source of the trouble and remedied it.

One of the first acts of the missionaries after becoming established was to petition for permission to reside in the capital. Their request was granted. In addition, they were given from the imperial treasury a sum sufficient to support them and their establishment of four servants. Visitors soon began to arrive, curious to converse with the learned foreigners, and Ricci gradually dared to talk with them about the truths of the Christian faith. As elsewhere his learning, coupled with his gracious and dignified bearing, gained him friends. His fame gradually spread through the empire so that, years afterwards, missionaries claimed that they had only to mention his name when in trouble to have their difficulties eased. Ricci's ten years in the capital were filled with endless labors: everything depended on him, not only in Peking but also in the provinces. He had to play the role of host to curious visitors who had no conception of the value of time, talking with them for hours over the teacups concerning problems of science and philosophy. He was called upon to give lessons to scholars who wished to know more of Western learning. It was his task, also, to look after the affairs of the Jesuit property, to visit the sick, and to carry on endless negotiations with officials concerning a multitude of little matters in which the mission needed their protection or support. Manuel Diaz was later sent to relieve him of some of his onerous duties, but Ricci, nevertheless, was overworked and his remarkable vitality finally gave way. In May, 1610, he was forced to take to his bed and a week later he died. His last act was to appoint Father Longobardi as superior general and to hand over the affairs of the Peking residence to Father de Ursis.

Ricci's work has met with both glowing praise and bitter condemnation. His Jesuit brethren have rightfully looked upon him as one of the greatest of their Society. His ecclesiastical enemies, because of his attitude toward the Chinese rites, have seen in him an opportunist of the most flagrant sort.

Ricci was a pioneer. He had to blaze the trail leading to the reception of Christian doctrines. If he seemed more ready than others to accept compromises which made the path of evangelical progress smoother, it is only fair to admit, as he himself firmly believed, that without these compromises he would probably have left the Christian cause in China no further advanced than had Xavier. Ricci spent many hours in earnest conversation with Chinese scholars before he even attempted to broach the subject of religion. He went through a real apprenticeship, during which he became deeply imbued with the Chinese point of view. He must have been honestly convinced that in Confucian and ancestor worship there was, in essence, nothing fundamentally in opposition to the Christian ideas of God and the immortality of the soul, and with this conviction it would have been easy for him to accept certain ceremonies which wounded the suscep-tibilities of his less expert brethren.

Furthermore, it must be argued in his favor that his methods of compromise and conciliation were rather a part of the policy of his order than a matter of his personal predilection. Similar controversies over native ceremonies had appeared elsewhere. In the seventeenth century the question of the Malabar Rites divided the Church in India, and later the same problem appeared in Siam. In China the Society had decided from the beginning that the only way to ensure success was to keep the good will of the officials and literati. Granted the correctness of this premise, the policy of conciliating the Confu-cianists was a sound one. The Protestant churches in China in the last century used much the same weapons as the Jesuits. They intro-duced Western culture through the channels of schools and hospitals in order to obtain a *point d'appui* for their religious propaganda. What success they had certainly did not come through truckling to officials. But the Protestants had behind them the forceful and organized sup-port of their governments. The Jesuits were pioneers and had to rely upon themselves alone to establish their position in the empire.

Ricci's methods have been graphically described by Abbé Huc.

Ricci adopted for his neophytes a method of preaching which was simple, instructive and yet capable of attracting the attention of his auditors. He told them in what way Christianity was practiced in the West and the influence it exerted on Society and in the Family. He spoke to them of the number of the churches, of their great size and magnificence, of the splendor of the ceremonies, of the great crowds of the faithful who gathered there on feast-days—rich and poor, princes, magistrates and common people mingled together before the altars. He explained to them the ecclesiastical hierarchy, the organization of dioceses and parishes, the life of the monks and the nuns in the monasteries, the care of the sick and the needy in the hospitals. All these points were dwelt upon in turn in a manner to instruct and interest the new converts. It was, in a way, Christianity in *action* that Father Ricci placed before his auditors, in a series of pictures in which the Christian life was revealed to them in its many phases.[15]

The Jesuits emphasized the ritualism of the Church to auditors who were accustomed to the ceremonies of Buddhism. In his theology, however, Ricci's greatest efforts were made to harmonize the teachings of Christian dogma with those of Confucianism. His most famous work of Christian apologetics, "The Teaching of the Lord of Heaven" (*T'ien Chu shih I*), cited passages from the six Chinese classics which harmonize with Christian tenets. It will be shown later, in reviewing the events of the quarrel over the Rites, that it was on the ancient lore of Confucius, as distinct from its contemporary interpretations, that the Jesuits built their theories of compromise.

Following the same methods, Ricci opposed Buddhism, dwelling upon the natural opposition between the "doctrine of Fo" and that of Confucius in such matters as metempsychosis and prohibitions to marry and to kill animals for food. Like the Jesuits in Japan, Ricci made strenuous efforts to controvert Buddhist propaganda. He himself had a public debate at Hangchow with a noted Buddhist priest, Chu Hung of the Lien Tsung sect; and Ricci's most powerful convert, Hsü Kuang-ch'i, wrote a treatise, *P'i shih she shu wang*, attacking the Buddhists—provoking a response from the famous scholar Yu Chun-hsi.

The main strategy of the Jesuits who followed Ricci, then, resolved itself into a kind of dualistic conception of Chinese religious thought, with Confucianism in its pristine purity on the one hand, and all the other sects and beliefs classed as idolatrous, on the other. This division gave them a distinct advantage in their missionary work. It permitted an alliance with the sect which had vital official relations with the government. Through their acceptance of Confucianism as a civil and political cult the members of the Society were able to make contacts with great officials and so gained access to the men who ruled the empire.

The lines of strategy having been determined, it remained to carry them out, and this required an intelligence and a personality above the ordinary. These Ricci possessed, to an extent which justifies the praise of a fellow Jesuit, Alexandre de Rhodes, who says:

The zeal of Ricci, courageous and indefatigable, but also wise, patient, circumspect, slow in order to be more efficacious and well timed in order to be more daring, was befitting to the character of one whom God had destined to be the apostle of a nation delicate, suspicious and naturally inimical to all that is foreign.[16]

The Society of Jesus was a by-product of the Renaissance, some of the evils of which it tried to cure. In place of medieval asceticism it substituted a deep knowledge of, and a sympathy with, the nature of mankind. To his knowledge of his fellow men Ricci brought also knowledge of books and learning. He was a scholar as well as a priest. Thrust into an environment which was fundamentally intellectual, he was well fitted by nature to pursue that search for a compromise between faith and learning which the scholars of the early Renaissance had sought. The greatness of Chinese letters and civilization impressed him as had the glories of Greek culture the minds of fifteenth-century Italian scholars. Like many of the latter, Ricci became a Christian humanist. It is this fundamental humanism in the character and work of the brilliant Jesuit missionary which makes him a significant figure in the history of the great seventeenth-century attempt to bridge the gulf between East and West.[17]

Ricci was buried with honor in ground given by the emperor. This little spot outside the city gate, Ping Tze Men—known as the Chala cemetery—served later as the burying ground for other members of his order. There their funeral monuments may still be seen.[18]

Ricci left the cause he served so well in a favorable position. His reputed last words to his colleagues, "I leave you facing an open door," serve as his best epitaph, for it was his genius which opened the way for successful missionary effort. Among the great officials of the empire he left a number of notable converts, chief of whom were Paul Hsü (Hsü Kuang-ch'i), Michael Yang, and Léon Li. Men of influence and power, they were frequently able to use their position to protect the Christian cause and to further its propagation.[19]

Chapter V

CHRISTIANITY UNDER THE MINGS

THE HISTORY of all great enterprises is, in part, the sum of the histories of their chief proponents. After the death of Ricci the history of Christianity in China is chiefly concerned with the work of his two great successors, Adam Schall von Bell[1] and Ferdinand Verbiest.[2]

It was the role of Ricci chiefly to accustom the native scholars and officials to the presence of such a curiosity as a foreign scholar and to such an anomaly as excellence in foreign learning; it was the role of his two greatest successors to put their learning to practical use in the service of the Faith. This was done through their entrance into one of the great departments of the Chinese government, the Bureau of Mathematics or Astronomy (*ch'in t'ien chien*).

For some time it had been realized that this bureau had become inefficient and was in need of reform. In 1629 the Christian official, Hsü Kuang-ch'i, now one of the chief officials (*Ko lao*) of the empire, memorialized the throne, protesting against the outworn methods of the astronomers, which had been in use for centuries. In conjunction with another Christian official, Li Chih-tsao, Hsü suggested that the foreign scholars be summoned to help in the work of the bureau. Ricci and others had already aided the government with mathematical observations and experiments. Before de Ursis had been driven from the capital in 1611 he, aided by Pantoja, had been busy preparing data for the bureau while a Swiss,[3] Jean Terrenz (d. 1630) a friend of Galileo, had also been engaged in the work. The idea of giving the priests a permanent post in the Bureau was not, therefore, entirely new.

In September, 1629, when an imperial decree gave to Hsü and his Jesuit teacher, Schall, the task of reforming the calendar, a new chapter was opened in the history of Chinese astronomy.

---

[1] For notes to chap. v, see pp. 311–312.

Back in that dim borderland where Chinese history is inextricably mixed with legend can be traced an intelligent study of the stars and their influence on human destinies. The semimythical Huang Ti is said to have built an observatory and to have founded a bureau of astronomy for the purpose of compiling a calendar, and since very early times eclipses had been noted by scholars as memorable events. With such a corps of ancient traditions it is disappointing to discover that Chinese astronomy had made almost no development as a science, in the sense in which we understand the term today. It had contented itself merely with the practice of observation and the accumulation of isolated facts rather than with the continuous development of theories culminating, now and then, in the work of a Kepler or a Galileo.

In view of the native apathy, therefore, it is not surprising to find that foreign influence had always been important in the bureau. As was true in Europe, the contribution of the Arabs to the subject, though often indirect, had been considerable, their methods being used by the Mohammedan bureau when the Jesuits were called in. In the sixteenth year of his reign Kublai Khan had erected in the southeastern corner of Khanbaliq the observatory which is in existence today. He summoned a famous Chinese astronomer to cast for him instruments in bronze, two of which are still to be seen there. This observatory was put into the hands of Mohammedan scholars who had received their knowledge from Arabic sources. Gradually, however, their tables had become out of date, errors had crept in, and their science had turned to ignorance. "They saw things," scornfully comments a Jesuit contemporary, "that one would scarcely pardon in the most savage American Indian."

It was at this juncture that the missionaries were commanded to help with the work of the bureau. Longobardi and Terrenz, the former summoned from the provinces to the capital in 1629, were given the task. Later James Rho and Adam Schall, two priests skilled in astronomy, were called in to assist.

Because of their position as Christian missionaries their task in the bureau was a delicate one. It must be remembered that the purpose of the study of the stars in China, as in medieval Europe generally, was not to accumulate data to be used for the development of a system of scientific laws but to try to determine the influence of planets on human destiny. The immediate purpose was the compilation of the imperial calendar, which from the earliest times had been a document of the highest importance. The publication of this work was attended by solemn ceremonies. The first copies were distributed by the emperor himself to the chief ministers of the court, who received it on their knees. Wrapped in imperial yellow, it was dispatched broadcast throughout the empire to Mongol princes and tributary kings. A refusal to accept it was equivalent to a declaration of war.[4]

As a document it is without parallel in the history of the printed page. Its influence penetrated to the hut of the lowliest peasant as well as to the palace of the viceroy. Not a birth or marriage took place, not a journey was undertaken, not a building was erected without its being consulted. It was the arbiter of the destinies of the people—the time-schedule of the nation.[5] It can, therefore, be clearly appreciated that the summons to Western missionaries to work in this bureau was an event of the highest importance. Nevertheless, the appointment of Schall as director of the Bureau of Astronomy gave the enemies of the priests and of their order, both in Europe and in China, an opportunity to attack him. Not even all his Jesuit colleagues were convinced of the rectitude of his position. Aleni, in 1648, openly expressed doubt of the propriety of a Jesuit holding such a position and in the following year Maghalaens, in a formidable document of some eight hundred pages, presented the case against the missionary, following this with a challenge to him to resign his post. The news of the Jesuit's activities spread abroad, and from the Philippines Vittorio Ricci wrote to Rome condemning them. Schall replied in 1652 with a defense of his actions, and he was supported in his stand by several of his colleagues.[6]

The matter under dispute was a delicate one. The question involved was: At what point did the information in the calendar cease to be "scientific" and become superstition? This brought up the more general question, that of the divine intervention in the course of natural phenomena. Schall pointed out that the study of the heavens had been used frequently to interpret the will of God. He showed that the Bible was full of instances where the course of nature was changed or arrested by Jehovah.[7] His arguments renewed the whole question of miracles, a subject which was receiving much attention at that time from the English Deists and was therefore of timely interest. Furthermore, it must be remembered that even in Europe the line of demarcation between astronomy and astrology had not yet been definitely drawn; it was considered eminently proper to seek, in the actions of the natural world, the will of Providence. Three decades later Pierre Bayle, in his *Diverse Thoughts on the Comet,*[8] was to write a stinging protest against unscientific interpretation of such phenomena, condemning the superstitious idea that the Creator was wont to give notice of His wrath or His pleasure through unusual events in the world of nature. Schall and his colleagues themselves had not been averse to using this kind of argument to further the interests of their religion. At the moment when the Jesuits and the Buddhists were striving for the soul of the emperor Shun Chih, Schall interpreted certain sunspots as representing Buddhist priests who were trying to obscure the glory of the emperor.[9] In 1730, when a severe earthquake shook the capital, Parennin told an official sent to him to inquire about the cause of the quake, that these occurrences, though due to natural causes, were often sent by God to punish the sins of the people.[10] If the Jesuits were accustomed, on occasion, to make use of this kind of argument to further their cause, it can be seen that Schall was able to present many reasons for his acceptance of a position in the bureau.

The Holy See rendered its decision in August, 1655, but, since the document was vague and inconclusive, it served only to reopen the controversy. In the meantime the opponents of the Jesuits in Europe were accusing the members of the order of being dabblers in astrology and magic—of having, indeed, direct dealings with the devil.[11]

Verbiest, who reached China in 1659, came to the aid of Schall. In 1662 the two priests wrote a treatise on the calendar in Chinese, a Latin copy of which was sent to Rome. Four professors of the Roman college were then entrusted with the task of reëxamining the question. In the meantime Father Grueber arrived in the Eternal City after an epoch-making journey by land from China and it was probably his arguments that caused a final and favorable decision, which was approved by Pope Alexander VII early in 1664. This settled the controversy. Henceforth the Jesuits were to be permitted to hold their posts in the bureau, always with the understanding that they should have nothing to do with the "superstitious excrescence" of the calendar but should try to bring the document in line with Christian science and Christian doctrine. It was agreed that Schall should devote his energies to that part of the task which had to do with the course of the stars, the eclipses, and the vicissitudes of the seasons. So another danger to the mission was successfully passed, and the Jesuits were able to retain a position which gave them enormous prestige and aided wonderfully their evangelizing efforts.

The importance of the Jesuit work at the Bureau of Astronomy must not be exaggerated. The head was a prince of the imperial blood and the Jesuit was an assistant director, a post which he held conjointly with a native official.[12] The Jesuits seem to have worked in an annex to the main bureau, their work being that of technical advisers, arranging and computing statistics and attending to scientific details. Even these duties were performed under difficulty, for the conservatism of the officials was constantly hampering their efforts at scientific reform. The priests, then, were by no means autocrats in one of the main divisions of the government, as some have tried to assert, but humble servants of the emperor in a fairly exalted position at court.

If there is danger of misunderstanding the nature of their work at the Bureau of Astronomy, however, there is no doubt about the important effect which their position had upon their evangelical labors and their reputation throughout the empire. When Schall came to Peking, it was with a keen realization of the prestige connected with the task. It is true that for a short period the new labors of the Jesuits worked to their disadvantage; their task brought upon them the intense hatred of the Uigur officials whom they displaced, which resulted in several years of bitter persecution. In 1662, however, on the accession of the emperor K'ang Hsi, they were able to use their position with great benefit to the propaganda of their religion, and in the subsequent history of the order in China, a period of nearly one hundred and seventy years, they were able, amidst all changes of fortune, to hold on to their official posts.

In the meantime the Ming dynasty was rapidly going the way of most dynasties, through corruption to ruin. There were rebel movements in several of the provinces; disorder was rife throughout the whole empire. The first imperial patron of the Jesuits, Wan Li, was succeeded in 1621 by the debauched and incompetent Hsi Tsung, during whose six years of rule the country sank lower and lower under the pernicious influence of the eunuchs.

The expenses of the court ran into fantastic figures. To heighten their charms the ladies of the imperial harem spent ten millions in ceruse and cinnabar alone. The great K'ang Hsi later testified that in his whole entourage the number of servants was no greater than was to be found in the "household" of a single concubine of the last Ming emperor.[18] Ch'ung Chang, ascending the Dragon Throne in 1627, tried to get rid of these vicious parasites but, like Louis XVI of France under similar circumstances, he lacked the force to choose and support wise councilors, who alone could have undone the work of his unworthy predecessor. In the end tradition and custom became too strong for him, and he was forced to call in the eunuchs again. Of a mild and studious temperament, he was unable to cope with the forces of disintegration swirling around him. Revolt had broken out in Szechuan and Kweichow, while in Shantung the dreaded White Lotus Sect (*Pai Lien Kuo*) was spreading disaster and death.

In the North a cloud had arisen which soon gave evidences of the deluge which was to destroy the empire. The Tartar tribe known to Westerners as the Manchus had been accumulating territory by conquest until they were the possessors of the whole of the Liaotung Peninsula and adjacent territory. In 1618, under their leader Tai Tsung, they had advanced south and, gaining a brilliant victory, had threatened the capital to such a degree that the emperor was almost persuaded to abandon the city.

Alarmed at the menace, the Ming emperor was, in 1620, advised by the Christian officials, Paul Hsü and Michael Yang, to seek aid from foreign science. Portuguese cannoneers, with four guns, were summoned from Macao, but, when they reached the capital, they were met by the irresistible forces of conservatism and political intrigue and were obliged to return. In 1630 the government again appealed to Macao. The Portuguese captain, Gonsalez Texeira Correa, now organized a force of four hundred men—two hundred Portuguese and two hundred Chinese—with ten cannons. Semedo tells us that the troops were richly dressed and accoutered, each soldier bringing his own servant.[14] The troops started north under the leadership of Correa and del Capo, but once more intrigue killed the enterprise. The merchants of Canton, fearing that their profitable role as go-betweens in the Sino-Portuguese trade would be ruined if Peking began to deal directly with the foreigners, successfully used secret means to cause the emperor to rescind the order, although the soldiers had actually reached Peking.[15] Discouraged at the failure of the expedition, the Portuguese did not renew their attempt at rendering assistance to the corrupt and vacillating Mings.

The Manchu menace became increasingly threatening. By the exercise of stupid diplomacy the Chinese court had ignored the enemy's proffers of peace, the third of which was made in 1634, and the Manchu leader, Tai Tsung, then openly proclaimed himself the first ruler of a new dynasty, Ta Ts'ing, or "Great Pure," dynasty. The situation was critical: Shensi, Hukuang, Honan, Kiangsi, and Szechuan were in a state of revolt and there seemed to be no leader strong enough to oppose the rebels.

At this juncture the court decided to call in the Jesuits to increase the supply of those foreign arms, a few of which they seem already to have possessed. In 1636 Schall was ordered by imperial rescript to start a foundry for the making of cannon and, in spite of his protestations that he was ignorant of the art of this unpriestly occupation, he finally found it politic to obey. In two years he had made a score of pieces capable of throwing forty-pound shot, besides a number of smaller cannon. In order, probably, to prevent them from being dedicated to the heathen God of Fire, Schall gave to each cannon the name of a female saint.[16] These large guns were mounted on the walls of the capital and of smaller cities. Some of them can still be found, rusty and archaic by the side of the artillery with which most modern Chinese armies are supplied, but in their time they were immensely superior to the native armament and they did considerable damage to the invaders.[17]

The guns of the foreigner, however, availed the decaying dynasty but little. Grave danger soon arose within the empire itself. The unruly elements which years of corrupt government had fostered in the provinces found a leader in the bandit, Li Tze-ch'eng, whose early successes had gathered around him a huge army. He attacked the ancient city of Kaifeng in 1640, and again in 1642, without success, but in the following year he returned, and the action of the Chinese general, who cut the dykes of the Yellow River to stop the invaders, caused the whole city to be flooded, with a loss of two hundred thousand inhabitants.[18] Soon Li was master of Honan, Shensi, and Hukuang. Dreaming of empire, he then decided to attack Peking. In his conquering march to the capital he was opposed at Ning Wu, and the terrible fate of this town, where the whole population was slaughtered, won over the other cities in his path. From Ta T'ung and Hsuan

Fu he sprang suddenly on Peking. The emperor transferred the defense of the capital to the eunuchs, and seventy thousand picked troops were placed under their command. But they revenged themselves for the emperor's former attempt to dismiss them by opening the gates to the enemy. Ch'ung Cheng, seeing from an eminence in the imperial city the fires which marked the pillaging of the capital, exterminated his harem, mounted the historic Coal Hill, and committed suicide.

But the Ta Shun dynasty, which Li hoped to found, turned out to be nothing but the phantom of an imagination overheated with success. The valiant captain Wu San-kwei, watching the Manchu force in the northern marches, saw the threatened ruin of the empire and in desperation made a bargain with his enemies against the usurper. Romance here intrudes upon history for it was Wu's infatuation for a little Peking singing girl, Chen Yuan-yuan, and his anger at her seizure by the Chinese rebel, that hastened this decision to deal with his enemy.[19] Near Yung P'ing fu the new allies met the troops of Li and, in a fierce all-day battle, defeated them. Li retreated to Peking, burned the palace after looting it, and fled west, scarcely stopping until he reached his native Shensi, while his disappointed troops rapidly deserted his banner. His dream of imperial power ended in an obscure death in Hupeh.

Wu had naïvely expected the Manchus to retire after defeating Li, but he was soon bitterly disillusioned. They marched into the capital as conquerors, greeted by the shouts of *Wan sui* (literally "ten thousand years"—*ad multos annos*) from the populace, and another dynasty had begun. A boy of six ascended the Dragon Throne with the reign-title of Shun Chih.

The Ming dynasty, defeated in the North, dragged on a long and precarious existence in the southern provinces. Two pretenders to the throne had had short careers and ignominious deaths when the succession fell in 1647 to Yung Li. With the aid, possibly, of some Portuguese troops Yung Li was able to gain control of several provinces.

He established his court at Chao Ch'ing fu in Kwangtung, the first residence of the Jesuits in China, and here the two priests of the Society, Fathers Koffler and Boym, appear to have gained positions of great influence. The pretender's wife and mother were converted and openly professed the Faith and, although Yung Li himself found his harem an insuperable obstacle to conversion, some hundred members of the imperial clan and forty high officials became Christians.

The power behind the throne, the eunuch P'an Achilles (*P'an T'ienshou*), was an ardent Christian, and his fervor was matched by that of the Empress Helen. A mission from Yung Li's court was sent to Macao to ask for aid, without much result. Finally, it was decided to send an embassy to Rome, to the head of the Church himself, and Father Boym was chosen envoy. The letter of the Empress Helen to the Pope is still preserved in the archives of the Propaganda.[20] In spite of opposition at Macao, where the Portuguese had become pessimistic concerning Ming chances of success, the embassy started. At Goa there was further hostility, and Boym decided to take the route by way of India, Persia, and Smyrna. At Venice he was received with cold politeness but was allowed to present a letter from P'an Achilles to the Doge. Arriving finally in Rome, the Ming ambassador again met with opposition. He was caught in the vortex of political and nationalistic squabbles and it was some three years before he could get a hearing. Finally the Pope consented to answer the letter, and a guarded reply was sent to the Ming empress. Rome probably felt that the chance of success in China through the patronage of the Mings was very slight.

While Father Boym was arguing the cause of the pretender in Rome, the victorious Manchus were pressing the deposed Mings hard in the field. Fleeing from one stronghold to another, Yung Li came finally to Burma, whose ruler surrendered him to his foes, and the pretender met his death somewhere on the southwestern frontiers of the empire. The fate of the other actors in this tragedy is obscure. The Empress Helen appears to have died either in Kuangsi or in Yunnan.

P'an Achilles disappeared, no one knows exactly when, and Father Koffler died on a Manchu sword.[21] Boym returned to the Orient and was attempting to enter the empire when he died in August, 1659.

Thus ended an interesting interlude in the history of the Jesuits in China. Had the Mings succeeded in recapturing their empire, the foreign scholars would undoubtedly have had an outstanding position at court. The Jesuit efforts were foredoomed to failure, but their struggle to keep open this back door to success is characteristic of the efficiency and skill of their methods.

In these troubled times when, to quote a native chronicler, "all China was in the throes of famine and revolution and cannibalism became rather the rule than the exception," the Jesuit missions naturally suffered. At Kaifeng the priest Rodriguez de Figuerado, was involved in the common fate of the townspeople. At Ch'ien Ning, where three hundred thousand were put to the sword, the Jesuit property was destroyed, and at Nanchang two priests and a lay brother lost their lives when the large church in that city was burned. At Ch'eng Tu in Szechuan, where the Jesuits had a flourishing mission, Fathers Buglio and Magalhaens underwent terrible experiences at the hands of the rebel Chang Hsien-chung. This man, "one of the most murderous ruffians who have disgraced the history of China,"[22] caused the street of the provincial capital to run red with the blood of his victims, whom he slaughtered in thousands. Chinese historians relate that this bloodthirsty tyrant on one occasion had a savory dish made of one of his wives who had incurred his displeasure. The monster had dreams of empire and set up a temporary court at which he forced the Jesuits to accept the post of court astronomers. They were given high official rank, but their lives were constantly in danger and they were justified in considering their escape as nothing short of miraculous.[23] Finally the tyrant was killed by Manchu troops, and the two Jesuits were taken as prisoners to Peking. When they arrived at the capital, Schall had difficulty in persuading the authorities that their intentions had been innocent and that they were victims of force.[24]

In the capital Schall had stuck to his post, in spite of the entreaties of friends to retire to his old mission at Sianfu. His faithfulness was rewarded for, during the thirty days of terror of Li Tze-ch'eng and the ensuing interregnum, he succeeded, not only in protecting the Catholic property, with its library of three thousand European books, and a large number of Christian converts, but also in saving the observatory and his astronomical instruments.[25] He also made valiant efforts to save many of the women of the capital, who at such times were wont to find in suicide the only way of escape. On one occasion the rabble broke down the front door of his residence to be met by the tall bearded priest, a Japanese sword in his hand, which he brandished with such good effect that the intruders prudently withdrew.[26]

Schall was now fifty-three years of age. Under the last of the Ming monarchs he had gained for himself a reputation which at the time must have seemed proof against disaster. The emperor Ch'ung Cheng had developed a real friendship for the missionary and had shown him many favors. In the thirteenth year of his reign an old spinet had been discovered at the palace, probably a relic of Ricci's time, and Schall, who was credited with a mild form of omniscience, was called upon to repair it. The versatile priest not only did this but he pleased the monarch by composing some Chinese airs for the instrument. The emperor was delighted, too, with the foreign books presented to him and had them carefully explained by the priest. Schall also presented to the emperor a model in tinted wax of the Adoration of the Magi, which was put in a place of honor in the palace.

In the meantime the Jesuits had not been idle in the performance of their spiritual duties; the records tell of many conversions. Among them were three imperial concubines of the first rank, converted through Christian eunuchs, and several others from among the two thousand members of the imperial harem. There seems to have been a carefully devised Jesuit plan to insinuate themselves in the palace by way of the female entourage of the emperor with the hope that eventually the Son of Heaven himself might be won over to the Faith.[27]

Chapter VI

SCHALL AND VERBIEST

THE MANCHUS set about their task of ruling with seriousness and dignity. One of the first acts of the new government was an order which made it impossible for any official post to be held by a eunuch. Gradually chaos gave way to ordered government throughout the empire. The new dynasty appeared at first favorable to the foreign scholars. The regent, Ama Wang, whose political sagacity and administrative genius largely helped to consolidate the empire for the young Shun Chih, allowed Schall to retain the Catholic property at a time when all Chinese were expelled from the capital to what is today known as the Southern or Chinese city. The Jesuits were called back to their places in the Astronomical Bureau and, within a short time, they had almost completely recovered from the losses they had suffered from the change of dynasties.[1]

The discovery of the Nestorian tablet a score of years before[2] had answered the main objection of the scholars to the Christian religion by satisfactorily proving that Christianity had been preached in the empire under the T'ang dynasty, nearly one thousand years earlier. The added prestige which the Faith received from the discovery of this monument was soon reflected, the missionaries claim, in the great increase in conversions throughout the empire. The fortunes of Christianity were bright. It is estimated that in the fifteen years preceding the death of Schall the Church gained each year about seven thousand converts.

With the accession of Shun Chih began the important part of Schall's life. The emperor conferred on him the title of Most Profound Doctor (*tung kwan hsiao*) in an imperial rescript in which he praised the Jesuit's religion; and in 1650 he gave the missionaries permission to build a church, himself presenting them with a piece of ground

[1] For notes to chap. vi, see pp. 312–314.

near the southern gate. This was the first Christian church in the capital since the days of John of Montecorvino.³ In addition to the site the
emperor contributed a laudatory inscription, which in 1652 was carved
in letters of gold on a handsome white marble commemorative arch
(*p'ai lou*) erected in front of the building. In 1655 Schall acted as interpreter for the Dutch mission of De Goyer and De Keyzer and was
instrumental in defeating their plan to open permanent commercial
relations with the Chinese.⁴ "Looking back over the years 1651 to 1660,"
says Schall's biographer, "one might almost affirm that T'ang Jo-wang
was China's real ruler."⁵ Extreme as this statement certainly is, the
writer brings to the support of his assertion many interesting and significant facts, especially concerning the friendly attitude of the emperor. The young Manchu who succeeded to the throne in 1644 was
an impressionable youth on whom the cares of statecraft sat rather
lightly. Kind, sympathetic, and sincere, although at times rash, impetuous, and violent, he must have endeared himself thoroughly to
the Jesuit missionary. He had a passion for hunting and he would
often neglect his duties to follow the chase. With a virility bred on
the Manchurian plains he entered into everything that he did with
zest, though without persistence. At times, owing to his waywardness,
he must have been a trial to his foreign mentor, but he received the
rebukes which Schall did not hesitate to bestow on him with humility
and good grace. So plastic was the character of the young prince that
Schall probably had reason to hope that it could be molded along
Christian lines. The young emperor was sympathetic to the Bible
story and he received with emotion the account of the crucified Christ.
He showed always a capacity for moral reform which must have been
encouraging even in the face of his own continual lapses from grace.

Much of his submissiveness to Schall's teachings came undoubtedly
from a personal affection for the Jesuit. He very early bestowed on
his mentor the name *Ma Fa* or "Venerable Father," a term implying
an intimacy which was certainly unusual as between emperor and
subject. This intimacy was fostered by visits which he would make

to the house of Schall. Here ceremony was thrown aside and the young man talked to the old priest as friend to friend. Nowhere in the history of China can a European be found who played such an important role at court as did Schall. The young emperor, according to the Jesuit chroniclers, seemed to enjoy giving pleasure to the foreign scholar, and many were the honors bestowed on him. For some time Schall had had the privilege of presenting petitions direct to the emperor instead of through one of the boards. He was consulted on important affairs of state. When Koxinga in 1661 rebelled and threatened the empire, Schall bolstered the emperor's failing courage, made suggestions for a renewed resistance, and, the campaign succeeding, he was hailed as savior of the empire. He interceded for officials who had been victims of harsh punishment. Many titles were given him. He became rapidly Vice President of the Office of the Imperial Sacrifice, Superintendent of the Imperial Stud, Exploring Teacher of the Mysteries of Heaven, High Senator, High Honorable Bearer of the Imperial Banquet. (The last honor made him a mandarin of the first class.) High-sounding and empty titles these may seem, but they all showed that this priest was a man whom the emperor delighted to honor. To make these honors adequate, according to Chinese custom, Schall's ancestors were ennobled so that they would share with their descendant the favor of the emperor.

In the light of this treatment the ultimate fate of the young emperor must have been a bitter disappointment to the aged priest. Schall had always lamented the addiction of Shun Chih to the sins of the flesh. He had preached often of the evils of fornication. But the young emperor was an Oriental ruler, raised in the sensual atmosphere of an Eastern court, and when he conceived a passion for the wife of a Manchu official of his entourage, all the teachings of Christianity were of no avail. Inevitably the story of David and Uriah's wife was repeated. The Manchu official "died" suddenly and the beautiful widow became a member of the emperor's harem. Schall had preached that "the wages of sin is death," and this proved tragically true for the emperor. A child was born in 1660 who was to have taken Shun Chih's place on the throne, but he died after a few weeks, his death being followed by that of his mother. The emperor was inconsolable in his grief. The young imperial concubine was buried in great state. Two palaces which housed the remains served as a funeral pyre and thirty maidens of the court were forced to "mount the dragon" with their imperial mistress so that she might be adequately served in the future life. The whole empire was ordered into mourning, and Shun Chih, succumbing in his grief to the force of environment, turned to the Buddhist priests for comfort. Ma Fa and his Christian teachings were thrust into the background, the rule of the bonzes taking their place. The young monarch, however, never completely recovered from the shock. His lovesickness was followed by fever and, in February, 1661, by death.[*]

By his decease the mission lost a good friend. At the same time a way was opened to its enemies to obtain revenge. The Buddhist priests, who had gained much influence at court in the last days of Shun Chih, were dismissed on his death and for a time there were signs that the Jesuits were to be retained in favor. Schall was honored by being appointed a tutor to the new emperor K'ang Hsi, and the foreign scholars at court were permitted to continue their work at the observatory as usual. Soon, however, their fortunes began to change. The four regents who had charge of the empire for the young emperor showed themselves indifferent if not hostile.

There had already been a number of clashes between the Mohammedan clique and Schall. Verbiest graphically describes one of these encounters. In the calendar of the last year of Shun Chih, Schall had predicted that on the eighth month Mercury, the evening star, would not be visible, but Yu Ming-yuan, a specialist in the old Arab tables and a friend of Yang, had declared loudly that this was an error. The Board of Rites, appealed to, decided to let the matter prove itself. Schall was asked how this could be done conclusively, and he suggested that three officials learn the stars in that quarter of the heavens so that, with their naked eyes, they could verify the absence of Mercury. The three mandarins chosen entered into the affair with zest. The rumor of the test spread abroad so that on the eventful evening the observatory was filled to overflowing. Darkness came, and one by one the stars. As they appeared, they were named by the mandarins to the interested crowd of onlookers. Finally, with all the stars named, it was clear that Mercury was not to be seen. The Mohammedan astronomer was obviously at fault. The foreign scholar had triumphed. The punishment for such a grievous error was death, but Schall pleaded for Yu and he was forgiven, though this act of Christian charity did not lessen the Mohammedan's hatred of his opponent.[7]

The incident just described constituted a prelude to one of the bitterest fights in the history of the mission. Behind the scenes was the sinister figure of Yang Kuang-hsien, whom Schall had displaced in the Bureau of Astronomy, "a cunning, low old man, full of hatred."[8] With Oriental patience he was awaiting the chance for revenge. In 1659 he led the assault with a pamphlet attacking the truths of the Christian faith and passionately denouncing it as a menace to the state. A vigorous reply came from Buglio and Magalhaens who boldly announced that "the wisdom of China is only a dim light compared with the splendour of the Christian doctrine."[9] This brought forth a second diatribe entitled *Pu te i* ("I cannot be silent") to which Buglio replied with a pamphlet: *Pu te i pien* ("I refute because I cannot keep silent").

These were the opening skirmishes of the campaign. Yang was massing his heavy artillery. Funds came readily from the mission's chief enemies: the eunuchs, the Mohammedan astronomers, and the Buddhist bonzes. In September, 1664, Yang presented to the ministry an official indictment, and the battle had begun. In the center of the fight was the heroic figure of the paralyzed Schall, unable to bear arms but ready to share the brunt of the battle.[10] Behind him were ranged the newcomer Verbiest, Buglio, Magalhaens, and a group of faithful Christian converts. The indictment was read to the accused by the combined officials of the ministries of home affairs and of public education. The Christians were questioned and, through Verbiest, made a formal reply. The case was then referred to a judicial committee of the ministry of education when the first of three charges was presented, that of high treason. A hundred questions were addressed to the accused, to which satisfactory answers were forthcoming. It became evident that the charge of treason could not be sustained, and the second charge, the preaching of a false religion, was pressed. For twelve days the examination went on; in the end it seemed as if the missionaries' cause was to be victorious. Then followed a pause of three weeks, during which Yang once again burst into activity. Golden "arguments" passed between him and those in power. It is estimated that the sum of these "arguments" amounted to four hundred thousand taels. As a result, the atmosphere began to change. Hostility was felt on every side. Soon the old Chinese official was to be seen riding triumphantly through the city scattering lampoons of the foreign faith and its champions.

Then, on November twelfth, the accused were summoned to the palace, where they learned that henceforth they were prisoners. As a high official Schall escaped indignity for the moment, but the other three Jesuits and their Chinese allies were loaded with chains: three around the neck, three on the hands, and three on the feet. Cast into prison, they were bound to wooden pegs in such a way that they could neither stand nor sit, and there they remained for almost two months. Each day they were taken out, haled before their judges, and questioned. Finally, on December 27, the board of inquiry made its report. Schall was found guilty of numerous crimes and he and his fellows were turned over to the department of justice for punishment.[11]

The decision required the ratification of the regents, which was given after eight days' study of the question, and on January 4, 1665, it was read to the prisoners. The priests were then thrust into a filthy prison, only to be taken thence for further questioning. Ten days later came the announcement of sentence. Schall, as the chief offender, was to be strangled; the other three were to be beaten and banished from the empire. Their Chinese colleagues were to suffer a similar fate. The course of justice moved slowly, however, and there was further respite as the sentence was sent to the court of appeals for confirmation.

Then followed the first dramatic interlude in a case which had now become a veritable *cause célèbre*. The government decided to test the third charge against the foreign priests: that of spreading false astronomical teachings. It happened that an eclipse of the sun was due. It was decided that the three astronomical groups, the Chinese, the Mohammedan, and the Christian should each foretell the exact time of the phenomenon. In this way the Heavens should be the judge.

The affair was carried out in solemn state. At the Bureau of Astronomy were gathered the privy council, the ministers of state, the officials of the observatory, and a host of other mandarins. According to Verbiest, the struggle between the "Dragon" and the Sun should begin about three o'clock, the Mohammedan officials set it at a half-hour earlier, the Chinese three-quarters of an hour earlier. It was a tense moment in the hall where the crowd were gathered to see the discomfiture of the foreigners. Slowly the minutes went by; then from the mandarin in charge came the announcement "The hour of the forecast of Yu!" Nothing happened. Another fifteen minutes elapsed, then the announcement: "The hour of the forecast of Yang." But the sun was shining undimmed in the Heavens. Another half-hour went slowly by as the crowd waited in suspense. Would the foreign scholars fail like the others? Then, at precisely the hour named by Verbiest, a film began to protrude itself across the face of the sun. The sky gradually became darkened as the eclipse progressed. Once more the foreign priests had vindicated their learning.

But it did not save them. The court, which in China, as in the Europe of that day, presumed that the accused were guilty, proceeded with the conviction. In the beginning of February the prisoners were haled before the court of appeals and learned that the sentence of the ministry of justice was sustained. But one step more remained, the approval of the board of regents. This board, feeling the onus of responsibility involved in sending to death men who had been specifically favored by the late emperor, refused to ratify the judgment and ordered a renewed examination. So the trial began anew. Once more the prisoners were thrust into a cold and filthy dungeon, where they were chained like wild animals. Once more they were dragged from tribunal to tribunal and pestered with trivial and childish questions. From March to May the grand council met in the great hall of the palace. On raised seats covered with rugs sat the twenty princes, the fourteen *ko lao,* the twelve ministers of state, the eight officers of the staff and seventy-two other high officials, the elite of Chinese and Manchu officialdom. Before them, kneeling, were the aged missionary and his confreres, European and Chinese. To the left, the arch-accuser Yang reveled with silent malice in the situation. The issue was the truth or falsity of foreign astronomical science. The incident recalls that scene some three decades earlier in Florence when Galileo appeared before the judge of the Inquisition and was forced to retract. But here there was no retraction of the truths of astronomy, and the muttered *Eppur si muove* of the Florentine astronomer became an eloquent and bold assertion of the undeniable facts of science, as Verbiest with the aid of instruments and charts valiantly strove to uphold the truth. Through the spring days, the trial dragged on. The issue was never in doubt, for the foreign scholars were already judged. Finally, the decision came; European astronomy was condemned. Immediately the regents, able now to hide behind the authority of the grand council, ratified the sentence.

Then further charges hurled themselves on the unfortunate prisoners like an avalanche: Schall and his colleagues were guilty of the death of the second empress, of a successor to the throne, even of the emperor, Shun Chih himself. It was clear they had sought the destruction of the former Ming dynasty. So, in the middle of April, came a new verdict. Under the impulsion of these graver charges the sentence of the aged Schall was changed to the more severe one of beheading, that his ghost should be sent to wander mutilated through the Chinese Hades. His seven Chinese colleagues suffered the same fate. Persecution, however, had not reached its limits. The regents, encouraged by the turning of the tide against the prisoners and the clamor for their blood, again changed the sentence to the horrible *ling ch'ih,* the dismemberment by the slicing of the living body, the most severe penalty of the judicial code. A touch of irony here intrudes. To save the "faces" of the government, the cause of punishment was set down, not as a failure in astronomical knowledge (which would have cast doubt on the omniscience of officialdom, Schall being a mandarin) but as high treason. On Verbiest and his colleagues the sentence of beating and banishment was sustained.

Then came the second dramatic interlude, more startling and more terrible than the first. As the victims of this judicial murder were awaiting their fate, Nature struck swiftly and with terrible force. Suddenly an earthquake shook the palace and the capital. The great city wall was broken in a hundred places. A thousand houses collapsed and three hundred thousand people perished.[12] A dust storm darkened the sun. The Cross on the East Church was hurled to the ground. To make matters worse, a fire broke out in the palace where, for three days, quake followed quake, and the imperial entourage was reduced to a state of panic. In the face of this omen, the regents again hesitated. In their dilemma they appealed to the empress-mother, but she, it is related, refused indignantly to have anything to do with the death of a man who had been the friend of her imperial son. For a time judicial inquiry dragged on, but Yang overplayed his hand by demanding Schall's banishment to Tartary, and the regents began to tire of the whole affair.

The drama was played out. Frightened and at a loss what to do, the regents, on May 18, finally released the aged prisoner. Verbiest and the other two had already been freed.

The old man, broken in health and suffering from the effects of his stroke, was taken back to the mission house, where the priests had been living in seclusion for some time. He did not long outlive his freedom. The sufferings of the previous months had taken their toll of his frail body and in August, 1666, his noble and busy life came to an end.

Schall had experienced both the joy of victory and the bitterness of defeat. His successes had been astonishing. He was for many years the main support of Christianity in the empire. "We all, your brothers, rest secure under your shadow," writes Hurtado in 1647,[13] while three years later Manuel Diaz writes from Macao: "Would that we had one hundred Adams for, in spite of the distance, he affords us such an effective help that we need only to say we are companions and brothers and no one dare whisper a word against us." Verbiest tells us that the people called Christianity "the religion of the great Schall."

Lacking, perhaps, the tact of Matteo Ricci, Schall, nevertheless, stands next to him as the greatest of the Jesuit missionaries in China. Certainly, he is the most colorful. Nieuhoff, who saw him in 1656, describes him as "a very comely old man with a long beard, living in great honor and repute." In his later years, at any rate, he must have had the imposing personality of one of the Hebrew prophets. To the average person he is interesting on account of the contradictions in his character. Schall was not one of those meek, saintly, ethereal personalities who seem to dwell constantly on the verge of immortality. He was a red-blooded man with virile passions. Of a quick and lively temper, given to outbursts of verbal violence, ready always to level the sharp rapier of irony on his less intelligent brethren, impatient of ignorance and stupidity, he was at times an exasperating colleague. His fellow priests often found coöperation difficult on account of his independence and his refusal to give reasons for his actions. Scorn seems often to have taken the place of friendly explanation. Several must at times have disliked him thoroughly. Buglio and Magalhaens, for example, brought to the capital as prisoners from Szechuan under circumstances already described, found him unsympathetic and difficult, although he brought to their aid the prestige of his exalted post

Adam Schall von Bell

(From Kircher's *China . . . Illustrata*)

in the government and undoubtedly was instrumental in releasing them from a humiliating and even dangerous position. The coolness of their relations with Schall caused these two Jesuits to lead the opposition to his acceptance of the post of director at the Bureau of Astronomy. What is more reprehensible, however, it tempted them to lend their ear too readily to tales concerning their leader which reflected on his personal morality. In this way, they were instrumental in encouraging a campaign of calumny against the old priest.[14]

On the other hand, Schall was generous, tender to the poor and the weak, kind to children, strangely naïve in his imagination and fervent in his faith. His affection for the weak, wayward Shun Chih was more than an interest in a prospective convert. He must have stood much in the position of a real father to the boy, whose exalted position gave him many servants but few friends. The pictures which the Jesuit writers give us of the intimacy of their association prove that these relations were impelled by tenderness and affection on the one hand and, on the other, by real reverence for the priest's learning and character.

Undoubtedly, Schall had real talents as an administrator. At the beginning of the Manchu regime he rose rapidly to a position of great importance in the empire. For a time he seems to have been referred to on most matters of state. When the difficult question of a successor to Shun Chih arose, he was consulted by the empress-mother together with other great officials of the empire. The fact that he championed the cause of K'ang Hsi as heir to the throne shows the wisdom of his judgments, for a better choice could not have been made.

Schall's intellectual gifts, also, were outstanding. He seems to have had a mind that was eager and capable of grasping a wide variety of subjects. He possessed a good library of European books and, although constantly occupied with many and arduous duties, he spent much of his time reading. His remarkable memory, concerning which we have the enthusiastic testimony of his colleagues, helped him to retain well what he read so that it is no wonder that his culture delighted the emperor and scholar-officials at court.

In the uniqueness of his position and the strength of his personality one instinctively compares him with that great missionary of the Middle Ages, John of Montecorvino, but whereas the latter at the age of fifty was a worn-out old man, the Jesuit, up to the time of his stroke in 1664 at the age of seventy-three, was remarkably healthy and active, a man of great vitality and physical power. It is not surprising, then, that the mission prospered under his administration and that even the cloud which fell upon it with the Yang persecution was only a temporary eclipse.[15]

Schall's mantle fell on the shoulders of the Belgian Ferdinand Verbiest.[16] Arriving at the capital in 1660, he had been foremost in the defense of the missionaries during the Yang persecution and, when the priests had been banished to Macao, he and three others were permitted to remain in Peking on account of their scientific activities. For four years these men were virtually prisoners in the mission property at Peking, while their exiled brothers were discussing methods of evangelization at Macao and quarreling over the difficult question of the Chinese Rites.

This period of sequestration came to an end in 1671, when the young K'ang Hsi took over the cares of government himself and immediately began to show an interest in the foreign scholars. During the years of Yang's regime at the observatory errors had crept into the calendar. When the emperor took over the government, he saw the necessity of reform but did not think it wise to effect a change of regime at the observatory without sufficient reason. He therefore called a council of the empire at which the two rival groups were allowed to present their cases.[17] The Jesuit priests reviewed the work of the Mohammedan astronomers, showed that an intercalary month had been inserted in the year 1669 when there should have been none, and advised that it be eliminated. Yang replied with the *argumentum ad hominem,* reviling the missionaries and all their works. K'ang Hsi cut short the controversy by ordering an experiment which should test the ability of the two men. He called for a gnomon and commanded that each should calculate where the shadow would be at noon on the next day. Yang was helpless, being apparently ignorant of mathematics, while Verbiest clinched the argument by correctly making the calculation.

Yang had been supported by the president of the six boards. The latter, however, having lost face by Yang's defeat, now turned against him, with the result that the pseudo astronomer was disgraced and banished to the wilds of Tartary.[18]

Verbiest, having established himself again in authority, boldly suggested that the mistakes in the calendar be corrected forthwith. Aghast that this important public document should be altered, thus bringing into ridicule the fair name of the emperor under whose authority it was sent broadcast through the empire, the officials begged Verbiest to withdraw the suggestion, but the latter sternly replied, "It is not within my power to make the heavens agree with your calendar. The extra month must be taken out." And it was. Verbiest had won an astonishing victory.

It is strange that the Jesuit, whose order has always been famous for its skill in diplomacy, should have insisted on a course which must have involved a tremendous loss of face for a large number of officials. It may be surmised that, in making this display of his authority, he must also have gained not a few enemies. He may have believed of course, that the scientific aspect of his work in the bureau (which, in view of criticism at home, always had to be emphasized) demanded that he make no compromise with a condition brought about by ignorance. Whatever the reason, there is no doubt that, in the history of the Jesuits in China, it would be difficult to find a more striking example of triumph for their power and influence. It is easy to see how the fame of a man who could change the imperial calendar spread rapidly through the empire and how, for a time, a persecuted Christian (as the missionaries tell us) had only to mention the name of the Jesuit leader to obtain a fair hearing.

Installed as director of the Bureau of Astronomy, Verbiest soon found that his task was no sinecure. Among his duties was that of

giving a course of lectures on mathematics and astronomy to the students at the observatory. To these lectures flocked many of the officials,
who were curious to learn something of the science of the West. In
order to meet the demand for information, Verbiest set to work to
write primers on scientific subjects, and one may judge of the severity
of his labors in this field by the fact that, with the aid of Chinese
assistants, he composed thirty-three volumes on astronomy alone.[19]

On the reinstatement of the Jesuits at the bureau in 1671, K'ang
Hsi issued an edict putting an end to the persecution of Christianity
throughout the empire. The document is an excellent example of the
vagueness of terms in which Chinese official documents were often
purposely couched. In the face of strong opposition at court, which
had its center probably in the powerful Board of Rites, the emperor
undoubtedly felt it unwise to make a complete reversal of policy in
the matter of the foreigners. The edict allowed the missionaries to
return to their stations to preach their religion which "teaches nothing
contrary to the welfare of the State or the duties of subjects." It did
not, however, allow complete religious liberty. On the contrary, it forbade the emperor's subjects to embrace the foreign creed! The edict
left to the local official the task of interpreting its meaning.

The Jesuits had apparently a real friend in K'ang Hsi. That his interest in intellectual things was sincere there is no doubt. From his
earliest years he seems to have seen the possibilities of good in all kinds
of knowledge, and the inborn provincialism and chauvinism of the
Chinese scholar-official did not cloud his mental horizons. It was his
eagerness for knowledge that brought him more closely in touch with
the Jesuit scholars. Verbiest taught him geometry, translating into
Manchu the first six books of Euclid. He instructed him also in philosophy and music. In doing this he took advantage of every opportunity to introduce the subject of religion. As Abbé Huc says:

Verbiest, while cultivating the intelligence of the monarch, thought still more
of forming his mind to virtue and of inspiring in him a knowledge of salvation. He began by disabusing his mind entirely of the pagan fables and

superstitions and little by little taking advantage of favorable moments and the monarch's avidity to learn everything, he instructed him in the truths which are the objectives of the Christian faith. He explained to him its sublimest mysteries and showed him its holiness.[20]

Verbiest was made a mandarin of the sixth order. He had, in addition, a number of other titles, the most curious of which was President of the Supreme Court of the Imperial Sacrifices, a purely honorary title.

It is evident that the emperor, although he felt the value of the foreign scholars, did not treat them at first on the same intimate terms as had his father. Verbiest tells us that K'ang Hsi was at first haughty and suspicious in his attitude. He could not understand why the foreign scholars sometimes refused the mandarinate, imputing to them some hidden motive for doing so. Influenced by his interest in their learning, however, he became gradually trusting and even familiar. As the curiosity of the monarch in the wonders of Western science continued to grow, so also grew the influence of Verbiest at court, but it was not until after 1676 that he really began to exert a power at all similar to that which Schall had exerted under Shun Chih. In that year K'ang Hsi made Verbiest *Tung Chin Fu Ssu* and issued a decree ennobling his ancestors. During his later years, Verbiest held a position at the court which must have been the envy of all officials. Whereas most of the mandarins seldom came into the presence of the emperor—or even saw his face—Verbiest, at least in the years preceding the Wu San-kwei rebellion, came daily to the palace, arriving at early morning and returning home in the late afternoon. He was kept busy as a tutor of the emperor. At noon he would be served a delicate repast in one of the interior courts, often receiving on golden dishes meats from the emperor's own table. Moreover, his position at court must have been strengthened by his contacts with officials at the observatory, since among his pupils were more than a hundred who held official rank.[21] In his capacity as interpreter, too, Verbiest was able to exert influence on the foreign policy of the emperor.

But it was astronomy, mechanics, and hydraulics which provided the bond of union between the monarch and the foreign scholar. Verbiest spared no pains to stimulate and keep alive this interest. In a letter to his friend, Father de Rougement, written from Peking in 1670, he tells of two curious timepieces, built on the principles of optical illusion, which he presented to the emperor. He mentions also a number of hydraulic instruments, especially a pump for a well. Among his chief writings is a sixteen-volume work on the *Theory, Use and Construction of Astronomical and Mechanical Instruments.* We read also of a motor impelled by steam to furnish air for organ tubes—which imitated the nightingale's song—and to agitate little bells which played musical airs. In the making of these instruments he was greatly aided by Father Magalhaens, who seems to have been somewhat of a genius in mechanics.

Under Verbiest there was a period of increased activity at the observatory. In 1670, the missionary reported that the ancient astronomical instruments, made in 1279 by Kou Shou-ching for Kublai Khan on older models of the Sung dynasty, were cumbersome, overlaid with ornament, and difficult to handle. The emperor accordingly commissioned him to have five or six new ones made. The new instruments were of the same general character as their Mongol predecessors but more accurate in their construction and more easily adjustable. They included an azimuth horizon, a sextant, a celestial sphere, a quadrant, and an equatorial sphere. Together with a large armillary sphere in bronze, presented to the emperor by Louis XIV, these beautiful examples of Chinese craft, with their cunningly wrought decorations and exquisite workmanship, still stand on the great wall of the Tartar city of Peking. As scientific tools they have long been displaced by more modern apparatus, but they form a lasting and beautiful souvenir of the Jesuit regime at the observatory.[22]

Chapter VII

THE GROWING POWER OF THE JESUITS

WHILE THE JESUITS at court were trying to read in the heavens the course of the stars, the former Ming leader, Wu San-kwei, was endeavoring to change the course of history on the battlefield. In distant Yunnan he lived in almost imperial state; gradually it came to be realized that his power was a menace to the throne which must be removed. Taking advantage of a favorable moment, K'ang Hsi summoned Wu to Peking, there to put aside his official splendor and retire into private life. Thereupon, stung by the insult and by the ingratitude of the race whom he had assisted to power, Wu broke into open revolt. He murdered the Manchu governor of Yunnan, overran this and adjacent provinces and was soon threatening the safety of the reigning dynasty. Peking became alarmed, and the city's fear was increased by another severe earthquake in 1672, which destroyed much life and property. As if, in itself, this was not a sufficient disaster, it was looked upon as an omen of evil to come. Peking was said to be honeycombed with spies. Plots were discovered and wholesale arrests and executions followed. Undismayed, K'ang Hsi started preparations for a long and strenuous campaign.

The cannon made by Schall were either too heavy for field purposes or had fallen into disrepair, and Verbiest was called upon to repair them and to make new ones. The talented priest went about the task with diffidence; it was not until the whisper went around that the missionary was not unsympathetic to the rebels that he entered into the work with zest. He first made a piece throwing a shell of four pounds. This stood the test successfully, and the emperor then ordered twenty more, to be sent to the army fighting Wu in Shensi. Further demands for armament came in from the provinces, and soon three hundred cannon had been asked for—to make which would have taken a whole year. The task was, in many ways, a difficult one. It was made more arduous by the jealousy of officials at court and by the rapacity of the mandarins, who did not hesitate to steal the metal needed in the foundry, when occasion offered. Finally, however, the guns were finished and Verbiest, with a keen insight into the opportunities offered by the occasion, determined to consecrate them in public. On each gun he engraved the name of a Christian saint, according to the fashion of the time in Europe. Preparing an altar and clothing himself in surplice and stole, he sprinkled the cannon with holy water and offered prayers for the success of the imperial arms, while the dignitaries of the empire looked on.[1] The tests of the cannon were successful. The grateful emperor thereupon took off his own robe and gave it to the priest, an unusual mark of imperial favor.

The role of the Jesuits as cannon makers again drew on the order bitter criticism from their enemies in Europe, but Pope Innocent XI, in a brief addressed to Verbiest in 1681, praised him highly for having "used the profane sciences for the safety of the people and the advancement of the Faith."[2]

And so the routine of life in the imperial entourage continued. In 1687, Verbiest reached the height of his popularity, but it was no easy existence. K'ang Hsi, a man of splendid and tireless energy, demanded the same ardor from his servants. This was a severe strain on Verbiest, for the emperor, liking to keep the Jesuit near him, required his constant attendance.

The foreign scholars were called upon to do a remarkable variety of things. On one occasion, huge blocks of granite had to be transported across the Marco Polo bridge, the only solid bridge leading out of the capital, and the officials were afraid the structure would collapse under the unusual load. It was obviously a problem of practical physics, so in their dilemma they appealed to the foreign scholars. After careful study, the latter came to the conclusion that it could be done. Rejecting the suggestion that the stones be dragged across the river bed, as well as the jerky method of transportation by native

---

[1] For notes to chap. vii, see pp. 314–315.

cart, the fathers rigged up a system of pulleys and tackle by the aid of which the stones were slowly and evenly propelled over the bridge without harm to the structure. Once again the occasion was made a veritable triumph. To quote Verbiest's own words: "When all was ready, the signal was given to start and under the patronage of Saint Gregory the Thaumaturge, of Saint Symphonorosie the Martyr, and of the seven sons torn apart by pulleys (*moufles*) the stone was set in motion. Then with bands playing and flags waving the crossing was made."[8] At once Verbiest and other officials dashed off to tell the emperor the good news. K'ang Hsi was just returning from a hunt at which he had killed two stags. In gratification he presented one to Verbiest and the other to the officials in charge. Once more the Jesuits had used their technical ability to enhance their reputation and that of their faith.

On several occasions Verbiest accompanied the monarch on his periodic trips into the North, to the old camping grounds of his ancestors. These expeditions were organized, partly for the purpose of giving his people in Tartary an opportunity to see his power and to fear it, partly, probably, to keep his own officers and court in good condition. In his wisdom, K'ang Hsi saw that the greatest enemy of a dynasty was the slothful, enervating life of the palace, which sapped the virility of monarch and courtier. Ostensibly hunting expeditions, these trips were in reality military maneuvers. They were carried out with almost Spartan severity. With the exception of the journey of 1682 (when he took three of his queens to visit the family tombs), K'ang Hsi seems, on these occasions, to have indulged in marital abstinence. His followers were obliged to follow the example of the monarch. The excursions lasted two or three months and were carried out on a grand scale. Sometimes he would take cannon with him, which he would fire off in the defiles, making a great noise to impress his subjects in the vicinity.

In hunting he used the methods which had been characteristic of the Mongols since the time of Genghis Khan. He would take about three thousand men and, deploying them to left and right, he would swing them into a huge circle. The hunters would then advance, narrowing the circle until it was very small. Then all the animals within it would be killed. In this way tigers, bears, boar, and other wild beasts would fall into the emperor's bag. The sport must have been arduous as well as exciting, for the Jesuit writers tell us that the emperor would often tire out eight or ten horses in a single day. Both Verbiest and Gerbillon have left accounts of these trips. The former describes the consideration shown him by the emperor. In the intervals between the hunts the emperor would call the priests to him in order to talk with them on matters of philosophy and science.[4]

At this time K'ang Hsi was about thirty years of age. Already he was showing those qualities of leadership which made his reign a glorious period in the annals of his race. Verbiest speaks in glowing terms of his sense of justice, which caused him to treat rich and poor alike; of his distrust of eunuchs, court sycophants, and ignorant officials, and of his interest and participation in the details of government.

However, the difficulties of the journey, the long marches, the exposure to extremes of temperature—all a physical delight to the virile young monarch—must have been a strain on a man of sixty; finally the strenuous life of the court wore him out. In January, 1688, he was taken ill and after a short sickness passed away, to the genuine grief of his imperial master.

The funeral, the last "official" Jesuit funeral in Peking, was unique even for that city of interesting obsequies. Father Lecomte, just arrived from France, has left a description of the funeral procession:

In front was a banner-picture twenty-five feet high and four feet wide, ornamented with festoons of silk. At the bottom was a piece of red taffeta, inscribed with the name of the Missionary (Nan Huei-jen), and his dignities, in gold characters. Before and behind were bands of musicians and standard-bearers. Then came the Cross, in a large niche, ornamented with columns and various silk ornaments. Several Christians followed, some with flags and others with wax tapers in their hands. Then came the image of the Virgin Mary and the child Jesus holding a globe in his hand. A picture of the

Le Père Matthieu Ricci.   Le Père Adam Schaal.   Le Père Ferdinand Verbiest.

The three Jesuit leaders in China: Ricci, Schall, Verbiest
(From Du Halde's *Description . . . de la Chine*)

guardian angel followed, with more flags and tapers and then a portrait of
Father Verbiest, habited as an official, with all the honor conferred on him
by the emperor. We [his Jesuit confreres] followed immediately after in white
mourning, according to the custom of the country, and at intervals we expressed our grief by loud weeping, according to the manner of the people.
The body came next, accompanied by officers appointed by the emperor to
do honor to the remains of the famous missionary. They were on horseback.
Among them were the emperor's son-in-law and the captain of the guards.
The procession was closed by a party of fifty horsemen.[5]

The missionary was laid to rest by the side of Schall and Ricci in
the cemetery outside the western gate, and posthumous honors were
accorded him by the grateful emperor. His place at the head of the
mission was taken by Father Grimaldi.

Verbiest was the last of the great triumvirate who successively led
the Jesuit cause at the capital. All were men in whom the gifts of
leadership and diplomacy had been splendidly combined with the
wisdom of the scholar. Among those who followed them there may
have been some, like Gerbillon, who were as gifted in diplomacy;
there may have been others, like Gaubil, who were their superiors as
Sinologues. But in that combination of learning and worldly wisdom
so essential to the success of their cause they were without equal, and
certainly none of those who followed them came so near to the imperial sovereign or so successfully upheld the prestige of their faith
at court. With the passing of Verbiest the influence of the Jesuits
at court reached and passed its climax. Henceforth, the cause of Christianity was steadily to lose ground in the capital until its final disappearance with the missionaries who upheld it.

During the reign of the last Ming emperor there had been few
attacks on the Christian religion. The foreign scholars had been in
favor at court and their work had been carried on quietly but effectively in the provinces. A logical reason for this is to be found in
the condition of the country. During these years Chinese civilization was at a low ebb. Arts and letters were in a state of decadence.
Political conditions were in turmoil. There was not that feeling of

racial unity, that certainty of cultural excellence, which is so often present when a strong ruler is at the head of the state—that national consciousness to be found under Elizabeth of England and under Louis XIV in France. At such moments the nation is satisfied with its own culture and, as a result, is often contemptuous of that of its fellow nations. On the contrary, when a nation becomes weak, it is open to the invasion of ideas from without. Its nationalism begins to develop cosmopolitan tendencies, as happened so strikingly in France of the eighteenth century. The conscious solidarity of national culture, which had almost disappeared in the last years of the Ming dynasty, was to be regained under the "foreign" Ching dynasty, in the reigns of their great K'ang Hsi and Ch'ien Lung. Under them, Chinese civilization again began to assert its brilliant power. This return to a cultural nationalism is probably one of the reasons which made it increasingly hard, in the years which followed the death of Verbiest, for the Jesuits to hold what they had gained.

The event which helped the cause most in these early years was the discovery, already mentioned, of the so-called Nestorian tablet. The finding of this monument provided incontrovertible proof of the ancient character of the Christian religion and removed one of the chief objections of that class of literati who believed in nothing that was not hoary with age. The importance of the discovery is attested by the great increase in the number of conversions in the empire.[6]

The persecution directed against Schall stopped the growth of the Church for a score of years. Under the administration of Verbiest, however, the mission slowly recuperated, and it needed only the favor of the emperor to make it once more actively progressive. That this favor was bestowed in a gradually decreasing degree and that it was finally withheld altogether form the outstanding facts in the subsequent history of the Jesuits in China.

The *jus patronatus,* established definitively by the papal bull of November 3, 1514, enabled the Portuguese to exclude the missionaries of other nations, especially the Spanish who were their commercial rivals, and in this way it worked to the detriment of the Faith. Furthermore, whatever may have been the pious wishes of John III and of the government at Lisbon, there is no doubt that close coöperation between colonizer and missionary quickly disappeared. Except when it suited their purpose to use the priests, the Portuguese administrators and traders soon gave evidence of the lack of harmony in the aims and ideals of the two groups. Traders and officials objected to priestly criticism of their morality and looked upon them in general as busybodies. The *jus patronatus*, then, instead of being a useful weapon in the spread of the gospel came to be such a hindrance that finally efforts were made to break the monopoly.

The creation of the Sacred Congregation of the Propaganda[7] by Clement VIII in 1597 struck the first blow. With the same purpose of weakening Portuguese hegemony, Alexandre de Rhodes, a veteran French missionary in Tongking, had paid a visit to Rome in 1668. Finally, the Holy See named three French bishops, François Pallu, Pierre de la Mothe-Lambert and Ignatius Cotolendi, the first two being named vicars apostolic of Tongking and Cochin China respectively, with authority also in China proper. The difficulty was to get them to China and then to support them there. The Portuguese at first promised to take them, then refused; neither the English nor the Dutch wished to do anything which might lead to new commercial rivals in their Eastern trade. In this predicament, Bishop Pallu, who may be looked upon as the father of the French Jesuit mission, suggested that the Society follow the example of the English and Dutch and start a trading company. To supply priests for the new mission a training school was needed, and thus there were founded, about the same time, the Compagnie de la Chine and the Congrégation des Missions Etrangères.[8]

In the meantime, Verbiest had been making appeals to the king of France to send out French Jesuits to help him. Colbert favored the idea, but it was left to his successor Louvois to carry it out. In 1685, the latter appealed to the superior of the Jesuit Order in Paris for six priests of scholarly attainments to be sent to China. As a result, Fathers Tachard, Bouvet, Gerbillon, de Visdelou, de Fontaney, and Lecomte were chosen. They embarked early in 1685 on the "Oiseau," the ship which was taking the first French ambassador to the court of Siam. Their trip to that country was comparatively uneventful. The king of Siam[9] was much impressed with the foreign scholars and retained Tachard. The rest set sail for Ningpo in June, 1687, and, after an exciting and dangerous voyage during which they encountered the worst perils of the treacherous China seas, they reached the port. Here their presence seems to have caused a good deal of embarrassment to the local viceroy. Accordingly, they moved on to Hangchow, where there was a flourishing mission under the Italian Jesuit, Intorcetta. They were received enthusiastically, and before long word came from Verbiest that the emperor had summoned them to the capital. Arriving at Peking, they were given a satisfactory audience by the emperor, who treated them much more kindly (says Lecomte, who has left an illuminating account of the early days of the mission)[10] than he treated the Portuguese ambassador, who arrived about the same time. K'ang Hsi spoke to them concerning the dangers of the voyage and asked them questions about the greatness of France and conditions in Europe. Pereyra, the Portuguese head of the Jesuit mission at that time, desired to send the newcomers into the provinces, but the emperor wished to keep them near him. Finally it was decided that Gerbillon and Bouvet should remain in the capital while the others went to other places in the empire: De Visdelou and Lecomte to Shansi, and De Fontaney to Shanghai.

Such was the beginning of the French mission to China, which was destined to produce a number of brilliant scholars and Sinologues. Bouvet interested himself especially in the development of the mission and took an active part in the founding of the Compagnie de la Chine. This company bought a frigate of the French navy, the "Amphitrite," which made several memorable trips to the Far East.[11] On its first voyage in 1698, the frigate brought out additions to the mission in the persons of Fathers Dolzé, Parnon, de Broissia, de Prémare, Régis, Parennin, Geneix, d'Entrecolles, and Foucquet, and Brother de Belleville, besides the Italian painter, Gio Gherardini, and Fathers Dominigo and Barborier, who joined the boat at the Cape.[12] Gherardini and Prémare have left a graphic account of the voyage. On a subsequent trip others were brought, and soon the French mission had a personnel which was strong alike in numbers and talent.

Father Gerbillon, in particular, was gifted with those qualities of courtesy and suavity which had so largely contributed to the success of Ricci's labors. He set to work immediately to learn the language and in twelve months had so mastered Chinese and the equally difficult Manchu official language that he was able to act as court interpreter. In this capacity he rendered signal service to the empire, and incidentally to his order, by helping to negotiate the important Sino-Russian treaty of Nertchinsk.

War between Russia and China had long been imminent. For some fifty years the Muscovites had been pushing farther and farther eastward across Siberia until they threatened the whole vast country north of the Great Wall. In 1636 they had built the fort of Yakutsk, from which expeditions of semibarbarous Cossacks were sent east to explore the riches of the country north of the Amur River. In 1643 Poyarkof descended this river to the sea and took back with him valuable information concerning the fertile plains which stretched to the south. Seven years later Pavlof Khabaroff, with a band of adventurers, built a fort and trading station at Albazin (Yacsa) on the most northerly point of the Amur.[13] The Chinese claimed that the Russians were behaving with great cruelty and they appealed to Peking either to send them assistance or to allow them to become the subjects of the tsar. Khabaroff sent back to Russia glowing accounts of the country. "There are," he said, "inexhaustible riches, a superfluity of gold and silver, beautiful sables, cattle and agriculture and fruits."[14]

A mission, under Feodor Baïkof, was sent to Peking in 1656 to establish negotiations but, owing to the fact that the envoy refused to conform to Chinese diplomatic usage (involving the performance of the *k'o tou*), the mission returned without success.

In the next quarter of a century, several Chinese armies were sent against the invaders but no definite results were achieved. Albazin was taken, retaken, and destroyed, but so great was the lure of the immense riches of the Mongolian and Manchurian lands that the Russians returned again and again. Another envoy, Nikolai Spathary, was sent in 1676 but, although he presented his credentials and was received in audience, the only result of his mission was an increased knowledge on the part of Russia of the countries north of Peking. Spasmodic fighting continued for several years.

Finally news came that the tsar was sending another envoy to make a serious attempt to stabilize the situation, and hostilities ceased. After some delay, owing to the great distances which made communications difficult and to the fact that K'ang Hsi was at that time busy fighting the Eleuths and Kalkas, a meeting was arranged. The place chosen was the Russian city of Nertchinsk or Nipchou, which had been built in 1658. To this town came the Chinese emissaries: Prince Su Ko Tu (the "Sosan" of the Jesuit records), captain of the imperial guard and minister of state; Tong Kwei-k'ang, an uncle of K'ang Hsi; Tu Tung, chief of the Tartar troops; and other plenipotentiaries, with a following of five hundred officials, a large army consisting of one thousand infantry, fifteen hundred cavalry, and a train of three thousand camels.[15] With the mission went Thomas Pereyra and Gerbillon, who had been given the rank of mandarin of the third class so that they might act as interpreters. The envoy of the tsar was Prince Feodor Alexievitch Golovin, who had with him a "retinue" of fifteen hundred men. The negotiations began on August 12, 1689.

Du Halde has published Gerbillon's account of the meeting.[16] Both parties began with exorbitant demands, after the fashion of Oriental bargaining—each side, by diplomatic cleverness, seeking to take advantage of the other. In this way days passed and little was accomplished. "The Muscovites were proud," says the Jesuit writer, "and the

Chinese on their side believed themselves stronger because they had come with a good army."[17] The Chinese wanted to destroy Albazin and to thrust the Russians north of the Amur basin. Finally, when the Jesuits saw that the two sides had reached an impasse, they offered themselves as intermediaries.[18] Gerbillon was allowed to attempt the task of reconciling the contending lines of interest and soon he was traveling from camp to camp, smoothing ruffled susceptibilities, suggesting compromises, and using, as far as possible, his powers of personal persuasion.

The Chinese began to move their troops to what seemed a better strategic position. At the same time, the Russians found themselves deserted by Mongol allies on whose help they had counted. Fearing an attack, therefore, the Muscovites saw the necessity of quickly settling the affair. Finally, terms were agreed upon. The Russians gave up their claim to the Amur Valley and retreated beyond the Stanavoi Mountains, the rivers Argun and Gorbitza being chosen as boundaries. The fort of Albazin was to be destroyed, but the Russians were given the privilege of sending caravans periodically to Peking for the purposes of trade.[19]

The treaty was signed on September 7, 1689. Four copies of it were prepared, two in Latin, one in Manchu, and one in Russian,[20] and these were sworn to by the envoys of the two nations in the name of the "Sovereign Lord of All."

The success of the negotiations was, to a great degree, a personal triumph for Gerbillon for it was his tact and skill as intermediary which helped turn the conference from failure to success. Prince Sosan, the leader of the Manchu-Chinese envoys, was greatly pleased and showered praises and promises of friendship on the foreign priest. Gerbillon and Pereyra met his expressions of gratitude with a reminder of the chief purpose of the Jesuits' presence in China and a hint of their greatest need, religious tolerance. Subsequent events showed that the priests had indeed won a warm friend, who did not fail to keep his promises of assistance at court.

Chapter VIII

THE GOLDEN DAYS OF THE MISSION

As a result of a persecution which started in Hangchow, the missionaries in Peking, in 1692, through their friend Prince Sosan, boldly petitioned the emperor to put an end to persecution of the Christian religion in the empire. As a result the Board of Rites was persuaded—on March 22, 1692—to present the following decree for imperial approbation:

I, your humble servant Ku Pu t'ai, first President of the Imperial Board of Rites (*Li Pu*) and head of several other tribunals, present with respect this declaration to your Majesty, in most humble submission to his orders. We, I and my assessors, have deliberated upon the affair that has been submitted to us and we have found that these Europeans have crossed the wide ocean, and have come from the ends of the earth, so attracted by your high wisdom and by that incomparable virtue which charms all the nations and holds them in obedience. At the present time they are in charge of astronomy and the Tribunal of Mathematics. They have applied themselves assiduously to the founding of cannon and the making of war armaments, which were used in the recent internal disturbances. When they were sent to Nipchou [Nertchinsk] with our ambassadors to arrange a treaty of peace with the Muscovites, they succeeded in bringing these negotiations to a successful conclusion. They have, therefore, rendered great service to the empire. The Europeans in the provinces have never been accused of any misdemeanor or of having caused any disorder. The doctrines that they teach are not evil nor are they capable of leading the people astray or of causing disturbances.

Everyone is permitted to go into the temples of the Lamas, of the Ho-Shang and of Tao tze to worship but the people are forbidden to serve God in the European churches although the Europeans are guiltless of any crime, which does not seem reasonable.

We must then, leave all the churches of the empire in the condition in which they existed formerly and we must permit everyone to go there to worship God, without fear of molestation.

We await the order of your Majesty to promulgate and enforce this law throughout the empire.

Published the third day of the second moon of the thirty-first year of the Reign of K'ang Hsi.[1]

[1] For notes to chap. viii, see pp. 315-317.

The terms of the decree are given here in detail since it was the only edict issued during the whole period of the Jesuit regime in China which was unreservedly in favor of the tolerance of their religion. It is, therefore, an important document and one which greatly delighted the missionaries. Jesuit writers have pointed to it as evidence of the warm interest of K'ang Hsi in the Christian religion. It appears much more likely, however, that it is a proof of the open-mindedness of the great monarch, who recognized, on the one hand, the services that his foreign scholars were rendering to the empire, and, on the other, the absurdity of the charges made against their religion.

Whatever the reason behind the edict, there is no doubt of its importance to the history of Christianity in the empire. It definitely took Christianity out of the category of "false sects" and made it as respectable as the three official cults. By affixing his official seal to the document the emperor gave the foreign religion a definite status in the empire and by doing so he performed an act which marked the climax of the Church's prosperity. As the discovery of the Nestorian tablet had proved the antiquity of the Christian faith, so the edict of 1692 established its legality. Converts were now no longer afraid to admit openly that they were Christians. In the year following the publication of the edict the Jesuits alone record more than twenty thousand converts, a striking testimony to the importance of imperial favor.

The persecution of their religion having been stopped, its propagation having been permitted through the empire, and its approval by the Son of Heaven having been officially announced, the Jesuit scholars were now placed in an extremely favorable position at court. This position was to be further secured by another honor from the throne. The emperor was attacked one day by a fever which caused consternation among the courtiers. Court physicians failing to provide a remedy, a chance to cure the Son of Heaven was given to any random practitioner who was hardy enough to risk the consequence of failure. Medical practice had always been a private affair in China as in other Oriental countries. It is possible that many a potent remedy has remained hidden in the prescription books of a single family, to be handed down from father to son but not to be given to the world at large. To cure the emperor, however, was always a desperate gamble, for failure meant the death of the unsuccessful doctor and, for his mandarin sponsor at court, loss of rank and exile. Nevertheless, this did not prevent charlatans from appearing who, by uttering incantations over vials of water, hoped to produce the same results as the modern doctor who offers bread pills to hypochondriacs. Now, however, the emperor turned to the foreign scholars for relief. It so happened that a short time previously the French priests had received from a brother in Pondicherry an ounce of a new drug, quinine. News passed to the emperor of this powerful remedy and he wished to try it. At first the drug was administered to officials by Brother Rhodes, a skilled pharmacist attached to the mission, with negative results. Its efficacy was not tested but it was proved not to be poisonous, and finally the emperor was allowed to try it. After several doses the Son of Heaven, who was probably suffering from malaria, declared himself to be much better. He termed the medicine *chin yao* ("the golden remedy"), and, after a few more doses, his fever left him.[2]

The quinine incident is important only in its consequences. As a mark of gratitude, the Jesuit writers tell us, the emperor determined to give his foreign savants a permanent lodging within the imperial palace. In 1693, the missionaries were summoned to the court, where, kneeling reverently before the empty throne, they listened to the reading of the rescript awarding them a piece of land within the *huang ch'eng* ("the Imperial City"). On the following day they were permitted to make their obeisance to the emperor and to express their gratitude.

The priests took possession on July 2, 1693, of their new quarters, a handsome group of buildings near the palace. Their first thought was to build a temple within the imperial domain which should be worthy of their surroundings and at the same time an adequate material symbol of the Faith. Gerbillon, De Fontaney, and De Visdelou petitioned the throne to grant them an additional piece of ground for this purpose, pointing out that it was incompatible with their religion to live in handsome quarters when there was no fitting house of worship for the Lord of Heaven. K'ang Hsi replied by allotting half the ground asked for, permitting the building of the church, and providing some of the materials. In addition, he gave to each of the foreign scholars a sum of money to be donated as their contribution to the church.

The granting of their request is eloquent testimony to the friendliness of the emperor. That the temple of a foreign religion should be allowed within the sacred *huang ch'eng,* where, according to the Confucianist state cult, the emperor alone represents the religious destinies of the empire, was a remarkable and significant concession. The missionaries commenced the task of building with joy. "We have spared nothing," writes De Fontaney in January, 1704, "which might pique the Chinese curiosity and attract the mandarins and great persons of the Empire, that we might have an opportunity of speaking to them of God and of the mysteries of our holy religion." It was, in other words, to be a great center of attraction, a splendid example of Western ecclesiastical architecture, built for a people who were very curious concerning anything foreign.[3] The skillful Italian lay brother Gherardini, was the architect, and the great Sun King of France sent a complete set of silver and other ornaments for its adornment. Local Christians, too, showed their zeal for the Faith by adding to its beauty, "bringing their diamonds and other jewels as in ancient times did the women of the Old Law."[4] The building took four years to complete. The consecration ceremonies, which were held on December 9, 1703, were elaborate and impressive. They were made the occasion of a great gathering, to which came missionaries from all parts of China and from other lands. Princes, officials, and scholars attended, probably moved as much by the spirit of curiosity as by a desire to honor the Christian religion, and they bowed themselves as the priests, in full canonicals, knelt before the richly decorated altar.[5]

In the meantime more priests were arriving from France. K'ang Hsi demanded that five of these be left at court, the rest being allowed to go into the provinces. After a course of training in the new seminary at Nanking, at Macao, or elsewhere, they were sent to open new stations, particularly in the provinces of Kiangsi, Hukuang, and Chekiang where the field was unusually promising. They were allowed to go about freely, preaching the gospel without fear of molestation.[8]

In the capital, the foreign scholars were called upon to do many and sundry tasks. Grimaldi was occupied with the arduous duties of director of the Board of Mathematics; Pereyra, who had considerable technical ability, was working on certain mechanical devices which had attracted the attention of the inquisitive monarch; Gerbillon and Bouvet were performing the role of imperial tutors, instructing the Son of Heaven in philosophy and geometry, and Gherardini was conducting a school of oil painting. In the year 1704, the Yellow River, justly termed "China's Sorrow," overflowed its banks, causing profound misery throughout the province of Shantung. The victims, homeless and starving, turned their faces to the capital, where the Son of Heaven, theoretically the father of the people, was the last resort in such an emergency. Bound down by official corruption and court intrigue which kept him ignorant of the rapacity of the mandarins, K'ang Hsi lacked the machinery for carrying out a largely conceived plan of relief. In the exigency of the moment, he turned to the Catholic fathers for assistance. Giving them two thousand ounces of silver, he asked them to take charge of the situation in the capital. They built huge mat sheds outside the gates of the city and started rice kitchens. When the time of distribution came each day, a flag was hoisted, and the famished refugees gathered at the spot to receive their bowl of rice; the distribution, carried out with the assistance of Chinese converts, was so well managed that court officials, eager always for a new sensation, came to view the sight. For four months that winter the priests fed over a thousand a day, thus affording an interesting precedent for such modern efforts as those of the Red Cross in China.

Tientsin also had been suffering from floods, caused by the over-flow of the two small streams which reach the sea near that port. In 1705, therefore, the emperor commanded Fathers Thomas, Bouvet, Régis, and Parennin to survey the region with a view to starting a conservancy project and he ordered that the necessary material and assistance should be provided. The results were very satisfactory. The map prepared by the Jesuits for the project, besides containing some "seventeen hundred towns, villages and hamlets," gave a bird's-eye view of the capital with the enclosures of the imperial city and the palaces and parks in the vicinity. The emperor was pleased with the success of their efforts, and it may have been this piece of cartography which created the idea of having the whole empire mapped by the foreign scholars.

Then, in 1722, the emperor, aged sixty-eight years, caught a violent cold in the course of one of his periodical hunting trips in the north. He was forced to return to his palace, the Ch'ang Chun Yuan, on the outskirts of Peking where, in spite of the labors of the best physicians, he grew worse and passed away on December 20.[7] He was succeeded by Yin Chen, one of his thirty-five sons, who took the reign-title of Yung Cheng.

History has definitely inscribed the name of K'ang Hsi among its great ones, and the testimony received from Jesuit writings supports this decision. The political structure of a country like that of China imposes many limitations on the monarch. Although the ruler is theoretically omnipotent, practically he is at the mercy of court in-trigue, which leaves him to a very great degree ignorant of the politi-cal currents eddying around him. In spite of these limitations, K'ang Hsi seems to have been an extraordinarily efficient monarch. It was indeed fortunate for the Jesuits of this period that they had such a wise and discerning emperor on the Dragon Throne.

The first decade of the eighteenth century constituted the high-water mark of prosperity for Catholic missions in China. The em-peror, as has been indicated, appreciated his foreign scholars and adopted a tolerant attitude toward their religion, the moral precepts of which he undoubtedly admired. The sun of imperial favor was shining brightly when, comparatively late in his reign, the Rites controversy appeared like a small cloud on the horizon. This cloud, as it advanced, grew in size and in threatening aspect until it hid the sunshine of royal approbation and finally drowned the Church in a deluge of destruction. Gradually, during the last twenty years of K'ang Hsi's reign, the missions began to lose ground. K'ang Hsi became weary of the bickering and dissensions among the missionaries and, although he never took his support and favor from his foreign scholars in Peking, he ceased, after a time, to approve of their colleagues in the provinces. The remembrance of former imperial favor saved the missionaries during K'ang Hsi's lifetime but at his death the way was opened for a new persecution of the Faith.

In 1711, as a result of an abortive attempt at persecution in Shantung, the emperor had warned the priests that they must desist from indiscreet actions and words. About the same time letters patent (*p'iao*) were given those missionaries who accepted the Jesuit position on the question of the Rites. The names of such priests (the list included a number of Franciscans) were published and sent throughout the empire. This was done at the request of the Jesuits, but even this did not free them entirely from annoyances for unfriendly officials would endeavor to interpret the patents according to their malevolent whims.

In spite of limitations and obstacles, however, the records of the Jesuits show that the mission flourished during this period. One must be careful, however, not to trust too implicitly in the implications of the Jesuit statistics if one wishes to get an accurate idea of the true growth of the Christian religion among the people. The Jesuit methods were built upon enthusiasm, upon an appeal to the worker to achieve results of a kind which would supply striking evidence of Church growth. One sees a tendency in the Jesuit records to adopt much the same method as that of certain modern American newspapers, the managers of which certify to the excellence of their publications by issuing striking figures concerning their circulation. To gauge accurately the spiritual penetration of a religion among any people is at best a difficult task. This task is made the more difficult when stress is put upon numerical results. An interesting example of the inadequacy of statistics as a measurement of success is found in the Jesuit system of baptizing abandoned children.

A great deal has been written about the exposure of children—or infanticide, to use a more expressive term—in China. The consensus of opinion seems to be that it has existed in different localities at different times to a deplorable extent. Marco Polo claimed that ten thousand infants were exposed each year in Khanbaliq alone. That the practice existed in China during the seventeenth and eighteenth centuries there is ample proof from the records of the missionaries. The Jesuit Father d'Entrecolles, writing in 1720, reports that "there is not a year when our churches in Peking alone do not purify four or five thousand of these children by the waters of baptism."[8] Even with allowance for possible exaggeration in such a statement, it is safe to conclude, from this and other testimony, that the number of unwanted girl babies exposed to die in the capital each year must have exceeded three thousand. Other priests tell revolting stories of rescuing newborn children from the mouths of scavenging hogs and other animals. In Peking, five carts went around the city in the early light of day to gather together the small scraps of humanity, the dead to be thrown into a ditch in the outskirts of the city and burned with quick lime and the living to be taken to a foundling institution (*yu ying t'ang*), where the majority of them died through the carelessness of ignorant wet-nurses.

It was the practice of the Jesuits to send into those parts of the city where it was customary to leave foundlings native lay brothers to baptize those who were dying—a practice which still exists in Catholic missions in China. The living children would be taken sometimes to Catholic institutions founded by money supplied by pious French women. If they survived, a place would eventually be found for them

in Christian families. Prémare, in 1700, tells of plans to found homes
of this kind in five or six cities. That the missionaries made the baptism of moribund children an important part of their work is evident
from their frequent mention of the practice.[9] It would be completely
unjust and unhistorical to suggest that they did not consider the salvation of the souls of these little ones as vitally important. According
to the tenets of the Roman Catholic church, the spiritual salvation of
all baptized infants is as certain as is that of mature men and women.
One is justified, nevertheless, in believing that the practical test of
the success of the Jesuit efforts in China lies, not in the number of
baptisms recorded, but in the lives of their converts. A discussion
of the penetration of the effects of Christianity in China in this period
on the basis of statistics is relatively futile.

But whether their statistics are accepted or not, it is evident that in
the course of K'ang Hsi's reign the Jesuits had succeeded in establishing themselves firmly in the empire and in extending their work into
most of the provinces. The ranks of the missionaries had been increased by able, earnest men, chiefly from France, and the favor of the
emperor had allowed them to preach the gospel with little hindrance
from unsympathetic officials. Toward the end of the reign, however,
there were indications that these favorable conditions were not to
last. Bitter quarrels within the missionary bodies themselves, together
with tactless action on the part of a hierarchy in Rome unqualified to
judge of matters pertaining to the culture of China, nullified the advantages which the Jesuits had acquired and led the Church in China
to disaster.

Chapter IX

THE RITES CONTROVERSY: THE PRINCIPLES

THE QUARRELS over the Rites, which disturbed the Church in China for nearly two hundred years, were complicated by the abstruse nature of the religious questions which were at the base of the controversy. The doctrines of Catholicism had been the result of a development of seventeen hundred years. During this time the Church had been open to other philosophical systems, notably Greek thought, it is true. The main body of Christian dogma, however, had been the result, not of outside influence, but of the accumulation of the commentaries of great churchmen of the past, Saint Augustine, Saint Jerome, Saint Ambrose, Saint Thomas of Aquinas, and others. By the seventeenth century this accumulated religious wisdom of the Church Fathers had given to Catholic dogma a relatively static quality, which resulted in a general opposition to innovation and a tendency to charge with heresy those who advocated change in religious thought or interpretation of dogma.

Scholasticism, the intellectual outgrowth of this tendency, killed the spirit of eclecticism and resulted in comparative stagnation in Catholic religious thought. It frowned upon new explorations in the realm of religious experience and looked upon reform as a type of revolt. The quarrel between Bossuet and Fénelon, the two great leaders of the Church in France at the end of the seventeenth century, is an interesting example of this tyranny of the past in the Church. Because Fénelon showed a tendency to explore the vast field of religious psychology more than the doctrines of the Church seemed to warrant, he was practically outlawed by the man who was *par excellence* the representative of French Catholicism of the time. Influential bishop though Fénelon was, he came near to being accused of the taint of heresy by some of his ecclesiastical colleagues.

This intolerance in matters of dogma, this static element in Catholicism is almost completely foreign to the Eastern mind. Oriental religion in general has been peculiarly receptive to new spiritual influences.[1] To such an extent is this true that one might say that the most important element in the religion of the Orient is the spirit of eclecticism. It is particularly true in China, where there has grown around the nucleus of the *san ch'iao* ("three teachings") of Confucianism, Taoism, and Buddhism a vast corps of doctrines and dogmas and where a whole pantheon of deities has been developed to meet every human and spiritual need. In this system it is difficult to divide religion from ethics or from social morality. It was this inchoate character of the Chinese religious system which made it difficult to come to any definite agreement concerning the Rites, making the quarrel so rich in pointless debate and specious argument.

Even Confucianism, which seventeenth- and eighteenth-century Europe tended to look upon as a static code of religious and moral laws, had these impermanent qualities. It was a result of a slow development, in the course of which the intellectual tendencies of different periods left their mark. Chief among the influences which had modified Confucianist thought was the work of the Sung dynasty commentators, particularly Chu Hsi. The Sung school of thought had enjoyed a period of long popularity when Ricci appeared. When the Ch'ing monarchs came into power, Confucianism was still intimately connected with the state cult, but it was passing through a period of materialistic agnosticism. The scholars of this epoch were turning their backs on the transcendental mysticism of Buddhism and were preaching a frank agnosticism respecting the soul and the future life—a philosophical system which laid itself open to the charge of atheism.

It was difficult for the Jesuits to deny the existence of these agnostic tendencies. The mass of evidence was too great. The question which faced them was: How can we bring into the circle of accepted Chris-

[1] For notes to chap. ix, see pp. 317–318.

tian practice enough of the substance of Confucianism to make the cult appear not to oppose essentially the precepts of Christianity? They met the problem by an appeal to history. They attacked Chu Hsi, Wang Yang-ming and the later Confucian exegetists of the past, and, for their authority, appealed to the Confucian canon, pure and undefiled. As the foreign scholars studied the magnificent moral and religious tradition in the Confucian classics and became thoroughly absorbed in it, they tended to look upon Confucianism as being nothing more than the wisdom of these classics and they developed their ideas of the cult by a dependence on this material—precisely as a Western student of theology might reject Saint Thomas and Saint Augustine and go straight to the Scriptures, and to the Scriptures alone, for his conception of Christianity. They overlooked the fact that, exactly as Christian dogma had obtained a great deal of its vitality from the Church Fathers, so the Confucian canon had been shaped, colored, and often almost submerged by a mass of learned commentary which at times completely obscured its original meaning and precepts. The Jesuits, in general, tried to ignore this mass of exegetical material and to discover the Confucian doctrines *tout pur*. They went even further and tried to penetrate that past of which Confucius was looked upon as the great and final interpreter. What they discovered was a slowly developed mass of religious and ethical tradition reaching back into the mists of legend and fantasy. Long before Confucius were Yao and Shun. Before them were Shen Nung, the legendary creator of agriculture; Huang Ti, the first emperor; Fu Hsi, the great beginner and source of all civilized society and Pan Ku, the creator. The question had already vexed Chinese scholars. How many of these and similar figures were legendary and how many historical? At what time did the gods leave Olympus to become men? It was generally conceded that Chinese history certainly did not begin earlier than the time of the emperors Yao and Shun.

The Jesuit scholars studied the Chinese classics diligently to find a solution for this problem of chronology. As a result they found—or thought they found—in these ancient traditions several indications that in the earliest days the Chinese were under the influence of a monotheism which had not a few points of similarity with ancient Judaism. Whether the wish was father to the thought and their hopes influenced their scholarship is an open question. Many of the Jesuits stopped here, with the theory of an early Chinese conception of a Jehovah, but a small group of the priests went further and sought a more vital contact between early Chinese religion and Christianity. This they thought they had found in the so-called Noachide theory.[2]

According to this theory, at the time of the dispersion of the peoples, when the sons of Noah spread over the earth, the descendants of Japheth, the eldest son of Noah, traveled to, and occupied, northeastern Asia, taking with them the Ancient Law. In the course of centuries this Ancient Law became corrupted and lost its identity, but traces of it can still be found in ancient Chinese tradition, even the legend of the coming Messiah who should be born of a Virgin. This theory was believed, in varying degrees, by a number of members of the Society.

The group who held the most extreme views in the matter were called Figurists (a name given them by the French scholar Fréret). The chief of the Figurist group were Fathers Prémare, Bouvet, and Foucquet.[3] They associated their theories with the Y Ching, or "Book of Changes," that strangely enigmatical work, the obscurities of which no scholar, Chinese or foreign, has yet successfully fathomed. According to their ideas, Fu Hsi (the creator of the mystic symbols contained in the pa kua) probably was not a Chinese but was the original Lawgiver who appears in the tradition of every ancient civilization, the Hermes Trigesmetus of the Greeks, the Zoroaster of the Persians, and, finally, the Hennoch or Enoch of the Hebrews. This legendary figure was the creator of all learning and wisdom. The Law which he created was debased and almost destroyed in the corruption of the world which resulted in the Flood. This Ancient Law, however, survived in the form of symbols, and through a long series of

arguments the Figurists tried to prove that the mystic symbols of the
Y Ching (the *pa kua*) formed a geometrical representation of the
Ancient Law which, though it had lost its meaning, was still preserved in China. Then they set to work to examine the Chinese classics thoroughly. With their predetermined theory in mind they found
numerous references to the Law which Christendom knows in the
form of the Hebrew tradition. These theories, which appeared fantastic to the majority of their fellow Jesuits, nevertheless had sufficient
argumentative force to interest and almost to persuade the great
Leibnitz in Europe, while in China the emperor K'ang Hsi himself
studied them with curiosity.

It is interesting to note that, whereas Bouvet and Prémare used
their theories ultimately to support the thesis that Chinese were not
atheists and that their ceremonies should be permitted, Foucquet
became a black sheep—and was finally driven from the Society—by
insisting that the logical conclusion was that the modern Chinese
had completely fallen from grace; that they had, in fact, become idolaters, and that their ceremonies had become idol worship, the Golden
Calf of Moses' people.

Though most of the Jesuits refused to accept the fantastic theories
of the Figurist group, they agreed that in the beginning Chinese religion had been monotheistic, not to say orthodox, but had become
corrupted through the centuries. This corruption had taken place
long before Confucius, and the "good old times" to which Confucius
refers were those when the power of the Ancient Law still held sway.
According to the Jesuit theory, the forces of corruption in Confucius'
time found their expression in the doctrines of Taoism, or rather in
the historical development of the doctrines of Laotze. The Ancient
Law was further, and hopelessly, corrupted by the introduction of
Buddhism at the beginning of the Christian era, when the nihilistic
theories of *karma* introduced agnosticism which led to atheism. So it
was that the Jesuits gradually came to interpret the Chinese religious
system as a kind of dualism, with Confucianism (representing the

remains of the true Ancient Law) on the one hand, and the false sects of Taoism and Buddhism on the other. This dualism was implied rather than stated, but it lay at the root of the Jesuit apologia for Chinese religion and morals. Confucius was "canonized." His system was subjected to extravagant praise whereas other cults were decried. Ricci laid the foundations of this system of thought and action, and the Society, as a whole, accepted this point of view. A dualistic conception of the Chinese system was convenient since it held the same implications as the Christian system of a definite division into two classes, the "saved" and the "unsaved," or, more correctly, those capable of salvation, on the one hand, and those impossible of salvation on the other. In order to make this comparison appear likely the Jesuits, of course, had to prove their contention, that there was nothing in the ceremonies of the Confucianist to prevent him from being infused with that supernatural grace without which spiritual salvation is impossible. It was for this reason that Jesuit apologists, in the face of so much testimony apparently showing that the modern Confucianist scholar was an agnostic, expended so much energy to demonstrate the ancient purity of the Chinese cult. To show that Confucianism had a respectable origin was the first important step in proving that the modern Confucianist did not necessarily believe in doctrines opposed to the teachings of the Catholic faith.

The other orders of the Church, with rare exceptions, strove to uphold the traditional viewpoint: that ignorance of Revelation and of Redemption made a man a heathen regardless of his virtues. This was a narrow creed built on the supposedly irrefutable dogmas of the Faith. Its weakness lay in the fact that it was completely unsuited to the East where empiricism in religious matters had always made dogma a practical and mobile thing. It supported the necessity of accepting the Christian dogma *in toto,* to the exclusion of all other beliefs, cults, or ceremonies, particularly of those which had the slightest taint of idolatry. It refused to accept the theory that many Confucian practices were harmless.

In the system of the Jesuits' opponents the fundamental doctrine of the Crucifixion was so stressed as to cause one Franciscan missionary to remark that on his arrival in China he saw nothing but crosses and crucifixes. The orders other than the Jesuits, therefore, ignored the dangers which might come from their method. From the sole standpoint of the survival of Christian doctrines there were vital arguments on the side of the anti-Jesuit forces. The history of Nestorianism in the East, little as we know of it, seems to be the history of a cult which compromised its doctrines and liberalized the lines of its theology to such a degree that it finally gave up its identity, lost in the inchoate and changing mass of Asiatic religious practices. At the same time it must not be overlooked—again from the standpoint of the survival of Christian dogma—that Jesuit liberalism was a step along that road which the English Deists had explored and which their French disciples had taken to the verge of anti-Christian propaganda. In considering the history of the Chinese Rites, then, one must approach the subject in a spirit of tolerance, accepting the position that there were potent arguments on each side.

In a controversy in which the evidence was so obscure and so shifting there were many appeals to partial and questionable authorities and much specious argument. The Jesuits had three main sources of appeal: first, they summoned the authority of the ancient Chinese teachers, chiefly that of the Confucian canon; second, they cited the opinions of "favorable" Chinese scholars; third, they used quotations taken from the works and writings of their opponents, statements made by the latter when under the influence of the spirit of compromise, to prove that they were sympathetic to the Jesuit position. These misquotations were particularly galling to the persons involved and gave rise to minor controversies, which served only to add to the bitterness of the main quarrel. The Jesuit tactics were copied by their opponents, Ricci and others being cited to prove that their ideas on the subject were, at the best, not as definite as their confreres and followers wished people to believe.

And so, in the endless maze of specious argument, the controversy wound its sad course, fire answering fire and anger adding to the flame until all the traditional arguments against the Society bore their part in the quarrel and Catholic was arrayed against Catholic in a bitterness as bad as any which ever separated Catholic and Protestant.

The roots of this bitterness are to be found chiefly in institutional rivalries. Most important of these was the spirit of nationalism which made the Christian missionary the servant of a European king rather than a representative of the King of Kings. The gradual and forced surrender of the *jus patronatus* by the Portuguese was not brought about without a considerable amount of national jealousy. Even among the Peking Jesuits themselves this internecine strife created confusion. The Portuguese house, the father house, looked with extreme disfavor on the new establishment of the French Jesuit missionaries, and hostility grew stronger as the latter strove to preserve their national identity. A supreme example of narrow nationalism, at a time when unity of the Church was so necessary for its success, is Thomas Pereyra. This figure stands out on the canvas of the time clothed in the gloomy colors of intrigue. Not only did he fight an extra-Jesuit opposition, like that of Cardinal de Tournon, with all the forces of his cunning character but he incurred the distrust and lost the sympathy of the French Jesuits as well.⁴ In all the history of the order in China Pereyra best symbolizes the crafty, scheming minister of darkness which, however wrong, was the popular conception of the Jesuit in Protestant England.

But differences within the order were comparatively trivial. They were controlled and subdued by the elements of unity and obedience which were at the heart of the Jesuit administrative system. The nationalistic rivalry was reinforced when it was supported by a difference in ecclesiastical authority. It was shown, for example, in the struggle between Spain and Portugal, the former represented by the Philippines mission, chiefly Dominican, and the latter by the Goa-Macao organization, which was preëminently Portuguese. Rivalry be-

tween Portuguese and Spaniards was paralleled by that between the
Portuguese Jesuits and the French Missions Etrangères. The latter,
as has been shown, was a French institution and, although at first it
seems to have been sympathetic to the Jesuit policies regarding the
Rites, it was soon forced by the exigencies of political rivalry at home
to take a definitely hostile position. When the Pope appointed three
members of the Missions Etrangères as vicars apostolic to the Far
East, the hostility was greatly intensified. This spirit of restiveness
showed itself in the relations of the order with the titular bishops of
Macao, Nanking, and Peking. In July, 1692, the Congregation of the
Propaganda—the official institution in Rome of missionary endeavor—tried to settle these nationalistic and administrative rivalries by
dividing authority in China. Six provinces were given to the Portuguese, thirty-six to the French, two to the Spanish, and four to the
Italians and other nations. Furthermore, all of these were made independent of the three titular bishops named above. The latter often
found their lot a hard one. The Society was constantly criticized for
treating this important office of the Church with scant respect, and
the events connected with the De Tournon tragedy appear to show
that the criticism was merited.

Differences, national and internal, were so many chinks in the
armor of evangelical Christianity in China. They produced quarrels
and controversies which contributed to the final disaster. The De
Lionne affair is an excellent example of the many disastrous incidents
evoked by the quarrel. Monseigneur de Lionne, established at Nien
Chou, found himself in a position where he had to defend the title
of the mission property he had acquired. The local official was appealed to. In his report to Peking he said he thought the bishop's claim
could be sustained if De Lionne's identity could be established by
one of the foreign scholars at court. The Li Pu handed the query to
Pereyra, giving De Lionne's Chinese name, as was customary. Pereyra
replied that he did not know the man in question, and the missionary
therefore lost his suit. Grimaldi had had correspondence with De

Lionne and there is therefore basis for the charge that the Jesuit president of the Bureau of Mathematics must have known De Lionne's Chinese name. A Jesuit priest in Chekiang, consulted by the governor, seems also to have professed ignorance of the bishop's identity. The incident caused much discussion. De Fontaney, in Europe, tried to explain the mistake, when the affair threatened to assume the proportions of a minor scandal. Finally the French Jesuits, to close an incident in which they certainly appear to have been wrong, took up the question with the imperial court and got it settled satisfactorily.[5] This trivial affair is recounted to show to what a pass the inter-order jealousies and bitterness had come and to show the atmosphere in which the grave question of the Rites was discussed. Let us now look at the details of the questions involved.

The quarrel over the Chinese ceremonies had two chief aspects: (1) the question of the term for God and (2) the permission to converts to perform the rites to Confucius and to the ancestors.

The first question involved the interpretation of the words for the Supreme Deity, *T'ien* and *Shang Ti,* which were vague even to the Chinese themselves. This vagueness made it possible to marshal on either side a quantity of evidence gathered from reputable writers on the subject.

The Jesuits claimed that both terms could be used. They tried to prove that *Shang Ti* referred to a Supreme Ruler and could be used as a synonym for the term Jehovah. They claimed that in Chinese thought the term involved the conception of a personal entity who ruled over all things. They argued that the term *T'ien,* although it was sometimes used to mean the material heaven, "that inverted bowl we call the sky," was also used figuratively to refer to the dweller in the heavens, just as in English we use the word Heaven when we mean God in Heaven.

The position of most of the Dominicans and their allies was as follows: The Chinese are atheists. Confucius claims ignorance of a future life and of a Supreme Being. They have no conception of the spiritual apart from the material. Their idea of heaven is that of a material thing. The Chinese idea of a primal cause is purely material in its conception and makes no allowance for the spiritual. For them the primal cause is one immense substance, universal and infinite, from which emanates the *t'ai chi,* which comprehends in itself the same universal substance and takes upon itself various qualities and attributes, thus becoming the immediate cause of all things. This primordial matter is divided into two parts, the *Yin* and the *Yang,* the one referring to material, corporeal matter, and the other to less material things, like the air. The *Li* or *Tao* is best translated "infinite chaos." It is the physical as well as the moral final cause. The spirits (according to the *Li Chi*) are the agents of this final cause and are to be worshipped by man. Among the four classes of spirits is the *Shang Ti.* It cannot therefore be said that *Shang Ti* is equivalent to our term God (a living, omniscient, omnipotent Being without beginning and without end, the Creator of all things and the Ruler of all) since, according to Chinese authorities, *Shang Ti* is posterior and inferior to *t'ai chi.*

No attempt need be made here to interpret or to comment on the Dominican arguments on these matters. It may be stated, however, that their arguments concerning the term *Shang Ti* carry great weight. They go on to discuss the question of immortality: the human spirit, according to the Chinese belief, becomes merged into the *Tao* at death. There can be no question, therefore, of the immortality of the soul. The Chinese themselves (and many authorities are quoted in support of this) do not believe either in a future life or in future rewards or punishments. The Chinese are atheists, because they scoff at the term used by the Christian mission (*T'ien Chu,* "Lord of Heaven"), saying that *T'ien Chu* is merely the virtue that governs Heaven, which is in all of us.

The evidence of such prominent Jesuit converts as Michael Yang, Paul Hsü and Léon Li was produced in support of the assertion that the Christian God could not be *Shang Ti,* and that all modern scholars were atheists. If the Chinese really believe in one God, say the champions of the Dominican position, it is inconceivable that they should not have a system of worship or a ritual, and no one from the earliest times has ever worshipped *tao* or *t'ai chi*.

These, in brief, were the arguments of the Christian disputants. The Term question, then, resolved itself into a controversy whether the Chinese conception of God and of the immortality of the soul was of such a character as to justify a comparison with the Christian conception. It was chiefly a dispute on concepts of philosophy, theology, and eschatology which touched merely the scholars.

The Rites question, on the other hand, dealt with something much more vital to the life of the people. It struck at the very heart of the religious and social observances of the nation. "If I were called upon to name the most serious impediment to the conversion of the Chinese," said one of the wisest of the Protestant missionaries at the end of the nineteenth century, "I should without hesitation point to the worship of ancestors. Gathering to itself all that is deemed most sacred in family or state, it rises before us like a mountain barrier, heavy with age and buttressed on the bedrock of the Empire."[8] It is, perhaps, the oldest of the many ancient beliefs of China. According to the Book of History, the emperor Shun performed the filial rites at the ancestral temple of his adopted father, the great emperor Yao, and from that day to the end of the empire each ruler performed similar rites. And not the emperors only. The custom extended to the humblest in the land, who deemed it an impiety to omit the worship before the ancestral tablets at certain prescribed days during the year. Throughout the whole of Chinese history and for all classes of people within the empire the worship of the ancestors stands out as the greatest religious act of the people. The importance to Christian propaganda of any decision concerning these rites can therefore be readily seen.

In a more restricted way the rites to Confucius were equally important. They occurred twice a year at the temple of the sage, one of which is found in every town of any size in the empire. This was a cult not of the people in general but of the scholar-official class. The object to which the devotions were addressed was either a figure of the sage or a tablet, similar to the ancestral tablets, on which is written "Throne (or seat) of the Most Excellent and Most Saintly Great Master Confucius." At Peking, as long as the empire lasted, the ceremonies were attended by the emperor himself. In the provinces it was the duty of the highest magistrate or official to perform the rites. Ceremonies were observed somewhat similar to those used in the ancestral rites: fasting in preparation, testing of the victim, burial of the hair and blood, pouring of wine over the effigy, prostrations, offering of final supplications claiming benefits for the worship offered, offering of wine and flesh before the altar, and the prayers and chants. The Jesuits claimed that these acts had a social and political, and not a religious, significance. Their opponents asserted that they were idolatrous practices.

Chapter X

THE RITES CONTROVERSY: THE DEVELOPMENT OF THE QUARREL

THE HISTORY of the quarrel may be divided into five periods: first, from the death of Ricci (1610) to the appointment of Maigrot as vicar apostolic (1682); second, from the arrival of Maigrot (1683) to 1697, when the receipt of Maigrot's report in Rome caused the Holy See to order a reëxamination of the question; third, from 1697 to 1702, when the Missions Etrangères condemned Lecomte's work in France; fourth, from 1702 to 1710, the years of De Tournon's legation; and fifth, from 1710 to 1742, the period between the decrees of *Ex illa die* and *Ex quo singulari*.

Ricci died in Peking in 1610 after firmly establishing the order in China. Owing to his unusual talents and to the extraordinary success which had followed his efforts the Jesuits accepted his point of view in the matter of the Rites. At least during his lifetime there was no open revolt against his interpretation of the ceremonies. This unity within the order, however, was only superficial. Grave doubts arose very soon in the minds of some of Ricci's compeers. Chief among the dissenters was Father Nicholas Longobardi, who wrote a treatise the main argument of which was that the ancient Chinese had not had, any more than the modern, a knowledge of the true God. This treatise was condemned by the vice-provincial Hurtado. It survived in a copy, however, and was later published by Navarrete in his *Tratados*.[1] Apart from this written statement of his views Longobardi kept silence until the death of Ricci.

In the meantime Dominicans and Franciscans had made attempts to enter the mission field in southern China. It is claimed that they met opposition from the members of the Society, but after three

---

[1] For notes to chap. x, see pp. 318–320.

attempts Angelo Coqui, in 1631, managed to establish a mission in the South, and others followed him. In justice to the Jesuits it must be admitted that they had reasons to fear the rivalry of priests who felt that fervor and faith were adequate substitutes for wise planning in the missionary field. The Dominican and Franciscan methods of evangelization were entirely different from those of the Jesuits. They preached Christ crucified in a way that permitted no compromise with the religious practices of the country, which they branded off-hand as idolatrous. They preached publicly in the streets, using their own language and relying on interpreters of doubtful ability. They were dogmatic, unyielding, and either oblivious to, or careless of, the fact that they were constantly wounding the susceptibilities of the Chinese. These tactics had, it is true, been used with apparently great success by Francis Xavier himself in other Oriental countries but they were, nonetheless, unsuitable to the Chinese situation. From the start such methods had given the Jesuits a great deal of trouble, and it is not to be wondered at that the persistence of the members of other orders caused many misgivings among the Jesuits.

It was obvious from the first that the two systems would not mix. Soon reports began to arrive in Macao and Goa from missionaries in Japan that Ricci's methods were embarrassing them in their work. Longobardi, who succeeded Ricci in 1610 as titular head of the order, felt the time had come to seek a solution of the problem. Consulting Fathers Pasio and Ruiz, who shared his views, he called for an opinion from the missionaries on three points, namely: Whether the Chinese had a true conception of (1) God (as implied in the term *Shang Ti*), (2) spirits (*Tien shen*) and (3) souls (*ling huan*). Ruiz and De Ursis prepared treatises from the one point of view while Pantoja and Vagnoni presented the other. But this attempt to find a solution was unsuccessful. A conference was then called by the Jesuit visitor Father Rodriguez at Kiating in 1628. After a full month of discussion, however, the eleven members of the Society who met under the leadership of Father Emmanuel Diaz found it impossible to come to a categorical decision. Father Andrew Palmeiro, who had just arrived in China to replace Father Rodriguez as visitor, testifies to the harmony which prevailed at the conference: "In truth," he says, "I have not found the shadow of discord as far as their wills are concerned, nor any bitterness in their hearts."[2]

Then formal opposition began in the other orders, chiefly through Jean-Baptiste Morales, head of the Dominican Order in China and Father Sainte-Marie of the Franciscan brotherhood. The former was a man of considerable erudition and indefatigable zeal. During a long stay in the Philippines he had studied Chinese language and literature and had begun to have serious doubts of the rectitude and wisdom of the Jesuit position. For the purpose of settling the question he addressed a series of questions to Father Hurtado, vice-provincial of the Jesuits, and to Emmanuel Diaz, the Jesuit visitor in China. He appears also to have suggested a conference to discuss them. The two Jesuit officials wisely refused to accept the responsibility of attempting to solve such a grave problem without consultation with other members of the order. Receiving no definite reply, Morales determined to refer the matter to a higher court. Accordingly he prepared a list of fifteen "doubts" which he sent to his bishop in the Philippines.[3] The latter, while condemning the Rites, expressed his inability to legislate and ordered that the matter be referred to Rome. Morales, therefore, took it to the Holy See. The Dominican and his colleagues insisted—in defense of their action—that they used every effort to come to a peaceful solution by friendly discussion and argument before they made their appeal to the central authority outside China. There seems no reason to doubt this assertion since the Jesuits were slow in bringing the matter before a general council of the order—which, indeed, because of physical conditions was a very difficult thing to do. The members of the Society, in view of the gravity of the problem, evidently wished to consider carefully all the issues involved before making any formal pronouncement, whereas the Dominicans were impatient to get the matter settled.

It was not until 1642 that the members of the Society were able to meet again to discuss the question of the Rites. In April of this year at Hangchow they drew up a series of resolutions condemning: prayers to "idols"; appeals to the dead for assistance; the belief that the souls of the deceased dwell in the ancestral tablets; belief that the dead feed upon the food offered for that purpose; and the belief that paper money burned before the grave brings material aid to the deceased. The pronouncement expressed willingness to tolerate the salutations of respect before the tablets and the burning of incense and candles but suggested that the Christian convert place a crucifix or pious image on the table where those rites were performed.⁴ These decisions seem to have been arrived at in an admirable spirit of compromise.

By appealing to Rome Morales had lighted fires of controversy which were soon to blaze not only in the Orient but also throughout Europe. When Morales arrived in Rome, he found he had been preceded by Alvarez Semedo, a veteran missionary, as well as by Michel Boym, whose relations with the Ming pretender have already been described. Morales presented to the Holy See seventeen *quaesita*,⁵ and Pope Urban VIII ordered the Congregation of the Propaganda to examine the facts of the controversy. On September 12, 1645, a decision was rendered by Innocent X, Pope Urban's successor, which was hostile to the Jesuit position.⁶ The Papal pronunciamento was rendered *parte inaudita*. It contained a clause stating that the proclamation would stand until it had been decided otherwise.

The decree arrived in China in 1649. In a letter dated the next year Father John Garcia, a Dominican, attests that the Jesuits were paying no attention to the decision of the Pope. Bitterness had already begun to show itself, and the same priest repeats the assertion that Martini and other Jesuits were fomenting persecution of the rival orders.⁷

The Society, in 1655, decided to send to Rome one of the most experienced of its number, Father Martin Martini (the compiler of the first atlas of China). Once more the Holy See was treated to an expo-

sition of the problems of the controversy and once more a decision
was rendered favorable to the petitioner. Pope Alexander VII, on
March 29, 1656, issued a decree allowing the ceremonies under certain
conditions. This was the only decree in the whole controversy which
was outspokenly pro-Jesuit. The papal court evidently realized that
it was handling a delicate situation, since it added to each article of
the decree the words: *Juxta ea quae superius proposita sunt* ("According as the matter has been presented here"). The document is remarkable for its extreme tolerance.[8]

In presenting his facts, Martini had taken for granted that the
Rites in question were civil and political and in no way religious.
The source of the whole subsequent controversy is to be found in
this interpretation and in the fact that the Jesuits' opponents refused
to look upon the Rites as nonreligious ceremonies.

Much of the force of the Jesuits' victory was nullified by a decision
of the papal see (made in 1669 in answer to the head of the Dominicans in Rome, Jean de Polanco), that the second edict did not revoke
the first but merely supplemented it.[9] The attitude of the Congregation of the Propaganda at this time was dominated both by ignorance
of the facts and by caution with reference to the grave implications
of the problem. The hesitation of Rome served, however, only to fan
the flames of controversy. When the head of the Church was vague
or obscure in his findings and pronouncements, opportunity was
given for honest adherence to differences of opinion.[10]

In China confusion continued to prevail. In 1667, when the missionaries were exiled to Macao by the Yang persecution, already
described, they had the opportunity to discuss problems of evangelization. At the conference the Jesuits were in the majority. There
were nineteen members of the Society, three Dominicans and one
Franciscan. The Dominicans and Franciscans, according to their apologists, showed a spirit of compromise, but the Jesuits insisted on their
position that the Rites were originally pure and that superstitious
practices were later accretions. The conference lasted for almost five

years. As a result, forty-two articles were drawn up. The forty-first, dealing with the Rites, was as follows:

> As to the ceremonies by which the Chinese honor Confucius and their dead the replies of the Sacred Congregation of the Inquisition approved by our Holy Father Alexander VII in 1656 must be followed absolutely because they are based on a very probable opinion to which it is impossible to offset any evidence to the contrary and, this probability assumed, the door of salvation must not be closed to the innumerable Chinese who would stray from the Christian religion if they were forbidden to do what they may do licitly and in good faith and which they cannot forego without serious injury.[11]

This was undoubtedly a victory for the Jesuits, but their opponents, anxious to show a united front against Chinese opposition to the Faith, accepted it. Navarrete did at first refuse to sign the agreement, but he also saw the wisdom of compromise and temporarily withdrew his opposition.

Domingo Fernandez Navarrete now took the place of Morales as the chief opponent of the Jesuit position in the subsequent history of the controversy. After spending nine years in the Philippines, where the Dominicans had a large and flourishing mission, he had been one of the twenty-eight members of his order to cross to China with Morales. He had worked in Fukien and Chekiang until, in 1664, he was made head of his order in the Middle Kingdom. The decision reached in Macao was extremely displeasing to him, and he immediately set about gathering documentary and other materials to reopen the case. As a result of his labors he produced the most important of the anti-Jesuit works on the Rites, the widely read *Tratados historicos, politicos, ethicos y religiosos de la Monarchia de China.*[12] In this work he developed, in the formal scholastic manner with numberless quotations from the Classics and the Church Fathers, all the chief arguments against the Jesuit point of view, reinforcing them with many documents, one of the most important of which was Longobardi's protest against Ricci's interpretation of the question.

With this material Navarrete left for Rome, arriving in 1673. His formidable battery of over a hundred questions relating to doctrine and morals, which constituted the differences between the orders, was presented to the Congregation of the Propaganda in the following year.

The success of Navarrete's book was counterbalanced by a treatise written at this time by the Dominican Gregory Lopez, vicar apostolic of Nanking and the first Chinese to hold a high post in the Church, which seemed to favor the Jesuit position. Accordingly the first phase of the controversy ended with the issues hopelessly involved, with Rome in a state of bewilderment, and with a feeling of bitterness rapidly growing. It was not, however, until later that this bitterness became general. In the early stages of the controversy there seems to have been a sincere desire on the part of the moderate elements of all orders to approach the important problems involved in a dispassionate spirit. Had this spirit subsequently prevailed, much harm to the China missions would have been avoided.

Up to this point the affair was chiefly a question involving Rome and China. In the years following, the controversy spread so that the whole of Europe became involved. Until now the Holy See had made no serious and intelligent effort to solve the problem but had been willing merely to temporize, to listen to the different arguments as they were presented by each side, and to render decisions which, by the very nature of the circumstances under which they were given, could not be final. The Pope was urged to send someone to the field to obtain accurate and unprejudiced information and to suggest a solution. Though this decision was reached rather late, it might still have been possible to rescue the Christian cause in China from the fires of controversy, had the authorities in Rome chosen priests who were first-class diplomats as well as theologians. The task demanded men of unusual ability and attainments who should be able to enter the empire without bias; men who would attempt to understand the Oriental mind and to see the relative unimportance of lesser dogma in view of the great need of Christian unity. Unfortunately, the envoys chosen were either of mediocre talents or, by their peculiar temperaments, were unfitted to cope with the difficulties of the problem.

Meanwhile, to improve the situation in the missions of the Far East, the Holy See had instituted a system of sending out vicars apostolic with much the same administrative duties as those pertaining to bishops.[18] On March 26, 1693, this rank was conferred on Charles Maigrot (afterwards Bishop of Conon) who had started missionary work in China twelve years earlier. Since Maigrot had been sent out at the suggestion of the Missions Etrangères, which had become by this time the open enemy of the Society of Jesus, the taint of prejudice was with him from the start and his efforts were foredoomed to failure. It was also doubtful whether, at the beginning of his ministry in Fukien, he legally possessed the title and power of vicar apostolic, since these powers had been conferred, not by the Holy See, but by his predecessor, Bishop Pallu. On March 26, 1693, Maigrot issued a mandate to the Christians within his jurisdiction by which he hoped to put an end to the controversy. The injunction commanded the use of *T'ien Chu* (instead of *T'ien* or *Shang Ti*) for God. It condemned the *Ching T'ien* tablets and, in effect, forbade the participation of the neophytes in the Confucian and ancestral ceremonies, except under circumstances which would completely clear them from the charge of participating in "idolatrous practices." Furthermore, it discouraged any system whereby the ancient Chinese religion was made to show affinities to the Ancient Law of the Hebrews and to the doctrines of the Redeemer.[24]

The publication of the injunction was met with indignation throughout the mission field of China. It was looked upon as a declaration of war and annoyed even that group of non-Jesuits who had assumed a liberal attitude to the question,—a group including many Augustinians and Franciscans and a few Dominicans. The Jesuits raised their voices in indignant protest, and it was not long before unfortunate incidents produced a state of open revolt.

In Fuchow the Jesuit Gozani, perhaps rightly, refused to recognize the authority of the vicar apostolic when, in 1693, Maigrot strove to enforce his commands.[15] Maigrot replied by depriving Father Gozani of his priestly functions. The latter was therefore forced to announce to his neophytes that the power of hearing confession and of granting absolution had been taken from him. The neophytes of the Society were known as "Jesuit converts" rather than as Christians, a sad commentary on the lack of unity within the Church. A convert died at this moment, unconfessed and unabsolved. As a result, a mob rushed into the church where Maigrot happened to be performing Mass, and the vicar apostolic, together with a Dominican priest who strove to defend him, were kicked and cuffed for a period of three hours. It is hard to absolve Gozani from blame in the matter; the best that can be said is that the forces of hatred and bitterness roused by his action got beyond his control. In his defense it must be asserted that he forced Maigrot's assailants to express to the vicar apostolic contrition for their violent acts.

Maigrot, seeing the serious pass to which the situation had come, tried to compromise and, for the good of the cause, gave up for the moment his presumed ecclesiastical jurisdiction over the order.

Here, as elsewhere, the Jesuit argument for disobedience was that the vicar apostolic lacked jurisdiction. There were at the time only two episcopal sees in China, those of Nanking and Peking. (The number was increased to twelve in 1696, at which time Fukien became a separate vicariate). These two bishoprics had been placed under the jurisdiction of Portugal, and the Portuguese claimed that the province of Fukien belonged to the diocese of Nanking. As a matter of fact, the Portuguese archbishop of Goa had, in 1693, named the Jesuit father, Joseph Monteiro, vicar general of Fukien, but, owing to the refusal of Maigrot to surrender his claims, Monteiro apparently never took over the duties of his office. Under this ruling Maigrot would have had no ecclesiastical authority over the Society. The argument concerning lack of jurisdiction, therefore, must have had a high degree of validity for the priests on the spot at the moment, even though, to a non-Catholic observer of today, it might seem a very inadequate reason for stimulating what developed into something very like a schism in the Church in China.

In the meantime the quarrel had spread to Europe. No longer was it a question of a difference of procedure in a faraway mission field. It had become involved in the great struggle between centers of authority and between different interpretations of Christian doctrines which rocked the Christian church throughout the seventeenth and eighteenth centuries. Father le Tellier, the Jesuit confessor of Louis XIV, whom the opponents of the Society make out to have been a sinister power behind the throne during Louis' last days, entered into the fray with enthusiasm. In a work entitled *Défense des nouveaux Chrétiens,* he summed up the chief Jesuit arguments and launched a strong attack on their enemies. It was at the time when the Jansenist polemist, Antoine Arnauld, was writing his violent *Morale Pratique des Jésuites,* a seven-volume work which reviewed the whole question of weaknesses in Jesuit methods—a pale but equally violent copy of Pascal's famous *Letters.* In answer to Le Tellier's book the Dominicans fired a broadside when they published their *Apologie des Dominicains.* So the quarrel over the Chinese Rites became mixed up in the theological controversy over the *grâce suffisante* and the *grâce efficace,* the theories of probablism, and the politics of casuistry.

The quarrel reached its climax in the Lecomte incident of 1700. Louis Lecomte had been one of the first group of French Jesuits sent to China in 1685. He had returned to Europe to gain recruits and in 1696 had published a two-volume work entitled *Nouveaux Mémoires sur la Chine.* At first the work had passed with little notice. It appeared at the moment when the new translations of Confucius were being received by scholars in France and Germany. Leibnitz had just written his *Novissima Sinica.* Undoubtedly a number of the clergy were a little disturbed at some of Lecomte's assertions, but their criticisms must have been ignored, since the work passed into a second edition in 1699. A year earlier another Jesuit, Father le Gobien, had published his *Histoire de l'Edit de l'Empereur de la Chine*. It was here that the members of the Missions Etrangères definitely entered the fight. The head of the establishment in Paris, Father Brisacier, had (probably unthinkingly) given his approbation to Father le Tellier's *Défense*, when it had been written in 1696. He now retracted this approval and decided the moment had come to open an attack on what he felt to be a menace to the Church.

The Missions Etrangères, therefore, addressed to the Pope a letter, which was published in April, 1700.[16] It was the first important statement issued by the Paris organization on the subject of the Chinese Rites. It accused the Jesuits of insincerity, lack of uniformity in their beliefs, quibbling, and a doctrine tainted with the evils of probablism. It asserted that the members of the Society wanted to convert the world without hurting anyone's feelings or ideas. The letter of the Missions Etrangères is a frank and outspoken attack on Jesuit methods in China. Although adding little that had not already appeared in the Dominicans' *Apologie*, it clinches and emphasizes the arguments developed in that work. The letter also accuses the Society of Jesus of wishing to postpone the papal decision and it appeals to the Pope to take action immediately to put an end to an intolerable situation. The Missions Etrangères offered to sign with the Jesuits a promise to cease from propaganda until a final papal decision should appear. The Jesuits in a *Réponse* retorted that they had kept silence for years after the Maigrot injunction, in face of a flood of pamphlets against them, but now they answered point by point the accusations of their opponents. The *Réponse* is an interesting example of the specious arguments into which the controversy had deteriorated.

The letter of the Missions Etrangères resulted in a series of pamphlets in French, Spanish, and Italian, as ardent priests on both sides flung themselves into the controversy. Le Gobien, the procureur of the Society in Paris, replied to the letter, accusing members of the Missions Etrangères of ingratitude, of being troublemakers, and of a bigotry which delighted the enemies of the Church.[17] The letter was condemned as a "tissu artificiel de duretés, de faussetés, d'équivoques, de traits de satire, de réflexions odieuses," showing a spirit in striking contrast to the evident desire of the Jesuits to understand the heart and mind of the peoples they were striving to convert.

It was under these circumstances that the Lecomte affair occurred, to add to the bitterness of the controversy. In July, 1700, the Missions Etrangères turned against Lecomte's book, bringing it to the attention of the Holy See and at the same time denouncing it before the faculty of theology of the university. On the pretext that the matter had already been referred to Rome, the Jesuits and their friends tried to avoid discussion, but their opponents were successful in causing the matter to be brought before the faculty. The latter appointed a commission of eight members to examine the Lecomte volumes as well as Le Gobien's work. Apparently the commission was prejudiced from the start. Its chairman, the Abbé Boileau, launched a violent attack on the members of the Society, "this faction feared by our ancestors who always dreaded to fall into their hands or even to have dealings with them; this faction that we have seen (according to the words of the prophet Hosea) suckle princes and kings with the malice of their lying."[113]

The commission sat until October in an atmosphere torrid with passion and prejudice. Neither Lecomte nor his representative was allowed to present a defense, but the opinion was taken of one hundred and sixty doctors of theology. The question was an extremely important one; grave theological dogmas were involved. Although there were other propositions discussed, the crux of the debate centered around the doctrine involved in the statement, "the people of China have preserved for about two thousand years the knowledge of the True God and have honored Him in such a manner as to serve as an example and model even for Christians." All the old problems involved in the doctrine of the Chosen People and the salvation of the virtuous pagan, which had embarrassed the Church for centuries, are latent in this phrase. The theology of the question was argued by many learned doctors of the faculty, but the issue was never in doubt, in spite of the warmth of the arguments and the bitterness of the debate. The judgment appeared in the form of stinging censure in which the offending proposition was condemned as *falsa, temeraria, scandalosa, erronea, sanctae Religioni Christianae injuriosa.* The other propositions, less harmful though they certainly were to Christian theology, were condemned in equally strong language.[19]

The Jesuits could not remain silent under such a rebuke. Le Gobien published a *Protestation* which inspired a *Remarques de M... sur la Protestation ...* which, in turn produced a *Réfutation d'une Réponse ...* ; and so the ludicrously solemn game of the religious pamphleteer went on, as pious priests and learned theologians argued, in anger and in bitterness, the "facts" concerning eternal mysteries. Rumors and accusations were sown broadcast. It was even suggested, by the enemies of the Society, that Lecomte had never been to China. The author of the *Mémoires* withdrew a little from his first position by affirming that the Chinese, in any event, could not be saved without a knowledge of the Saviour. Although still asserting that they had had at one time a knowledge of the true faith, Lecomte admitted the "difficulty of knowing how long this religion which came from Noah through Shem lasted." He insisted, however, that idolatry did not enter China until after the birth of the Redeemer.

The satirists in the meantime were not idle, and the Jesuit adoption of Confucius was laid open to ridicule for a Parisian public which set more value on a *bon mot* or a witty epigram than on a dozen volumes of theological arguments.

The history of the quarrel over Lecomte's work has been described at length because of its effect on the spread of Sinophilism in Europe. There is ample testimony to show that the circle of those who were fascinated by the story of Chinese civilization was becoming larger and larger. Galland, the French translator of the *Arabian Nights* and an eminent cosmopolite, receives news from Paris that the quarrel is creating as much disturbance as the Jansenist controversy. Silhouette, the author of an important book on China, testifies that the discussions "have given rise in the minds of everyone to a desire to know China." Deplorable as the quarrels were for the welfare of the Church, they served the purpose of making the name of China a household word in France and elsewhere.

While these events were taking place in France, Father Charmot arrived in Europe with a copy of Maigrot's injunction. He presented the document to the Pope together with a number of communications from representatives of the orders in the Far East, condemning the Rites. The Jesuits claim that Charmot's evidence was partial and that he suppressed documents which supported their viewpoint. Whether this was so or not, his arrival caused a fresh outbreak of controversy. Conditions became so bad that the Pope was once more forced to intervene.

The members of the Society in Peking now took a significant step. They appealed to K'ang Hsi, as titular head of the religious system in China, for an expression of opinion concerning the Rites. The petition to the throne was couched in the following terms:

We, your faithful subjects, although natives of distant lands, respectfully beg your Majesty to give us positive information on the following points.

The scholars of Europe have learned that in China ceremonies are performed in honor of Confucius; that sacrifices are offered to Heaven and that special rites are performed to the Ancestors. Persuaded that these ceremonies, these sacrifices and these rites are based on reason, European scholars, who are ignorant of the true meaning of these matters, are urgently begging us to enlighten them concerning them.

We have always judged that Confucius is honored in China as a legislator; that it is to this end and solely with this in view that the ceremonies established in his honor are performed. We believe that the Rites which are performed to the Ancestors are established only with a view to communicating the love in which the latter are held and to consecrate the memory of the good which they accomplished during their lifetime.

As for the sacrifices to Heaven (T'ien) we believe that they are addressed not to the visible Heavens that we see above us, but to the Supreme Ruler, Author and Preserver of Heaven and Earth and of all that they contain.

Such is the meaning which we have always given to the Chinese ceremonies. But as foreigners cannot be expected to be capable of pronouncing upon this important matter with the certitude of the Chinese themselves, we take the liberty to beg Your Majesty not to refuse the enlightenment which we need. We await your elucidation with respect and submission.[20]

The emperor replied briefly as follows:

What is written here is without fault. It conforms to our holy doctrine. To honor Heaven; to serve the prince and parents; to honor one's master and one's superiors is the universal doctrine of the Empire. In all this [petition] there is not a word which needs changing. Respect this.[21]

It will be seen that in this document of the Jesuits there was an attempt to represent the matter not as a question of controversy by the missionaries in China but as a series of doubts entertained by the scholars of Europe. In a single phrase the petition may be summed up in the query: Are not the rites in question civil and political ceremonies? The emperor's reply appears emphatically affirmative.

Much has been written in support, as well as in condemnation, of this appeal of the Society to the emperor. The act, of course, brought on the Jesuits the bitter criticism of their opponents. The champions of the Jesuit position claim that the appeal was made merely in order that Rome might have, from the highest authority in China, an unequivocal interpretation of the nature of the ceremonies involved, in order to furnish a basis for judgment in Rome. Nevertheless it would seem to an impartial observer that by appealing to the head of a "heathen" nation for interpretation of a matter which was still *sub judice* at Rome the Jesuits had committed an act of indiscretion which was not likely to allay bitterness or to bring nearer the solution of the problem. Had the Jesuit missionaries taken this step after they had asked permission of the Holy See to do so, they would certainly have freed themselves of the charge of appealing to a "heathen" authority over the head of the leader of their religion.[22] It can be clearly seen why their opponents in China and Europe looked upon the act as a clever move to cut the ground from under the opposition by enlisting the support of an authority which was infallible and without question in China.

The period from 1700 to 1702 is the high-water mark of the controversy in Europe. Printing presses were kept busy with a flood of pamphlets on both sides. The Missions Etrangères and others were pressing for an immediate and unmistakable pronouncement from the Holy See. The Jesuits appeared to be willing to let the matter slide, for they vehemently asserted their intention of obedience to the papal decisions. Meanwhile, Louis XIV's Jesuit confessor, Father la Chaise, was trying to rally the bishops of France to the side of the Society. In a letter addressed to several of the most influential prelates he pointed out that the Church would become the laughingstock of the heretics if it was proved in Rome that for more than one hundred years the Holy See had acquiesced in practices which were later condemned as idolatrous, and he invited their opinions. The reply of the great Fénelon is a masterpiece of wisdom and tolerance but it did not, any more than the other replies, give the Jesuit the satisfaction he was seeking.[23]

Chapter XI

THE RITES CONTROVERSY: THE
DE TOURNON LEGATION

THE CONTROVERSY had reached a critical stage when Pope Clement XI decided on a step which might well have been taken earlier. He appointed a *Legatus a latere* to go to the Indies and China for the purpose of investigating causes of disharmony in various mission fields, particularly that of the Rites controversy. The ecclesiastic chosen for the purpose was Charles Thomas Maillard de Tournon, Patriarch of Antioch, a man but thirty-six years of age, who nevertheless, by his fervor and piety, had attracted the attention of the Holy See. Jenkins, who has written an account of the legation, speaks highly of his naturally religious temperament: "His beautiful and saintly character," he says, "might well have fitted him for all the higher dignities with which he was crowned in the last years of his truly evangelical life."[1] Mere saintliness, glorious as it is in the character of a Christian priest, was not, however, sufficient for the successful accomplishment of such an enormous task as had been thrust on the young Savoyard.[2] To offset his saintliness and charm of personality he was burdened with three great weaknesses: a total ignorance of the languages and customs of the countries he was to visit; a persistent malady which kept him a semi-invalid during his stay in the Middle Kingdom; and a sensitive temperament which showed itself in occasional fits of temper and in a haughty attitude toward his opponents. It can readily be seen how easy it was for him, with these drawbacks, to fall a prey to men, skilled in the ways of diplomacy, who were masters of the facts with which they had to deal.

From the beginning De Tournon's mission was weighted down with troubles. Secrecy, an element which is often a sad necessity in diplomacy, was used to keep from the ecclesiastical world the fact

---

[1] For notes to chap. xi, see pp. 320–321.

[148]

that the young legate was carrying with him an injunction from the Holy See which, in effect, prejudged the cause he was supposed to arbitrate. In a secret meeting of the Propaganda at Rome resolutions had been passed which included: (1) a condemnation of the terms *T'ien* and *Shang Ti* in favor of the term *T'ien Chu,* (2) a forbidding of the use of the inscription *Ching T'ien,* (3) a condemnation of all oblations and ceremonies to Confucius and to the ancestors, and (4) a prohibition of the use of ancestral tablets by converts. If the news of this act on the part of the Propaganda leaked out and preceded the legate to China, that fact affords a logical explanation of the hostility which awaited him and of the attitude of the Society toward him. At any rate, it is probable that De Tournon left Rome with his mind made up about the Rites.

The legate's stay in China lasted five bitter years. When he landed in Canton, he had already taken action to straighten out differences in other mission fields. At Pondicherry he had examined the question of the Malabar Rites and had issued a decree regulating the practices of the Jesuit Order. At Manila he had deposed a *procureur* of the Society accused of usury, and had confiscated his ill-gotten wealth. These decisions seem to have given the Jesuits in China the impression that the legate was prejudiced against them even before he arrived in the empire.

De Tournon arrived in Canton on April 7, 1705, to face a clergy which was, on the whole, hostile. He was, perhaps, able to gain a little comfort from the statements of De Visdelou, the Jesuit "rebel," who told him that the Jesuits were wrong and the vicars apostolic were right in their attitude. The legate spent a year in Canton accumulating facts concerning the controversy and preparing for his visit to the Chinese capital. Even while he was in Canton, the inevitable failure of the legate was foreshadowed in a number of minor incidents which showed how difficult his task was to be, owing to the unsympathetic attitude of the Jesuits at Peking. While in the southern city, he was attacked with the same malady which had caused him trouble at

Pondicherry. Recovering, he ordered the missionaries at court to obtain permission for him to travel north. K'ang Hsi replied that arrangements should be made for De Tournon's journey but stipulated that the latter should come merely as an unofficial observer and not as an envoy—which, it must be remembered, the legate did not claim to be.

The imperial edict declared:

Since To Lo (De Tournon) is a virtuous man and since he has come to gather information concerning our Law, and since he is sent by no prince of Europe to bring tribute, let him clothe himself after our manner. Write to the highest officials and to the viceroy that he be treated honorably.[3]

The legate was met in Tientsin by representatives of the emperor and was conducted to the Jesuit mission in the Forbidden City. Father Thomas, who has left the best account of the mission from the Jesuit point of view, emphasizes the almost unprecedented honors accorded De Tournon: the monarch's solicitude concerning his health; the food sent to him from the imperial table; New Year's gifts and other tokens of imperial benevolence. It is evident that, although his visit was not considered an official one, the emperor wished to honor him as a representative of the head of the Christian church.

K'ang Hsi received the legate with kindness and accepted with evident pleasure the gifts sent him by the Pope. These presents provided, nevertheless, the occasion of one of the many unpleasant incidents with which the legation was tainted. The emperor wished to send gifts in return, and Father Mariani of the Propaganda was chosen to accompany them. The Jesuits were surprised and displeased that one of their number was not named for this honorable mission. Ever on the watch lest their favored position at court be threatened, they suggested to the throne that one of their number be appointed to accompany Mariani. In compliance with this suggestion Bouvet was chosen. Then followed a struggle between the two priests for precedence—with the result that neither was sent. Later the emperor replaced them by the Portuguese Jesuit Barros and the French Father Beauvoilliers. These two priests started on their long journey but, overtaken by a storm at sea, were drowned. For a number of reasons news of this tragedy did not reach the emperor until fifteen years later.

A stern battle started between the young legate and the members of the Society. The former was armed with the authority of the Church but sadly lacked the methods and means of approach to the throne; the latter had long experience in the methods of Oriental diplomacy and enjoyed the protection of powerful friends at court. K'ang Hsi himself, although he did not approve of certain actions of the Jesuits, seems to have supported them out of a sense of gratitude. He showed, for example, a tolerance for the violent, quarrelsome nature of Pereyra, saying that a master does not tolerate seeing an old dog murdered who has served him faithfully in his youth.[4] The Jesuits had a valuable ally in the person of Ch'ao Chang, the mandarin who had charge of foreign relations. They were also able to gain the favor of one of K'ang Hsi's sons who had great influence with the monarch. Through avenues of approach which their position as scholars near the emperor had opened for them they were often able to exert influence which the legate did not possess, and they seem to have used this advantage again and again, with much success.

The first struggle came when the death of the legate's surgeon, Sigotti, occurred. De Tournon asked the Jesuits to obtain for him a piece of ground for a burial place. They refused at first to do this, perhaps because they thought the legate wished to use the ground for the establishment of a permanent residence for a representative of the Holy See in Peking. They yielded only when the legate formally demanded obedience.[5] It is evident that De Tournon had in mind the establishment of an official home for the direct representative of the Roman see in Peking, which would, of course, have taken precedence over all other Catholic establishments in the capital. When he sought the support of Pereyra and Grimaldi, and of Gerbillon of the French Mission, the legate—according to De Tournon's supporters—was received with silent hostility. It is evident that any request to establish headquarters of a foreign power, political or religious, in the capital would be met—as, in fact, it always had been met—with the strongest imperial opposition. The charge that the Jesuits stimulated this opposition is beside the point. Any favorable action on the part of the Society would have been ineffectual in face of the tremendously strong Manchu sentiment against such an establishment. Under these circumstances the members of the Society may well have felt that such a request was highly indiscreet, and this may have been the chief motive for this refusal.

The problem was settled with true Oriental wisdom. The emperor approved the legate's request but stipulated that the superior general whom De Tournon wished to appoint should have resided in the capital for ten years. This would, of course, have excluded nearly all but the Jesuits. De Tournon was astonished at the decision and naturally sensed the intrigues of the Society behind the emperor's reply.[6]

According to Jesuit apologists, the legate, on learning of the imperial decision, lost his temper in the monarch's presence and actually accused him of trickery, persisting in his accusation even though his fellow priests strove to get him to modify his demeanor. If this is true, it is striking evidence of the unfitness of the papal representative for his task.

It is obvious that De Tournon, weakened by illness and exasperated by the cabal which he felt had been formed against him, undoubtedly found it difficult on several occasions to refrain from giving expression to his anger. Seldom are intense religious fervor and suavity of manner combined in the same person—although it might be argued that the Jesuit was often a remarkable exception to this rule. Had the legate possessed more suavity, his mission might have had a greater chance of success. It is not strange, then, to find the members of the Society accusing the legate of lack of tact, of insolence in the presence of the emperor, and of an obstinate pride which would admit of no compromise.

Hostility to the legate was at times but thinly veiled. When he wished to visit the Portuguese house in the Western city (*Hsi T'ang*), his representative, the Bishop of Peking, whom he sent to prepare for the visit, was met at the gate by the superior of the mission, Father Barros, who refused admission on the ground that the Jesuits admitted only the authority of the Pope and recognized no episcopal jurisdiction—convincing evidence of the state of affairs in the capital.

The same hostility became apparent in the dealings of the Jesuits with those who supported or helped De Tournon. The subordinates of the legate became the victims of an open opposition, which the members of the Society did not quite dare to show to the Pope's direct representative. The chief sufferers were Fathers Pedrini, Appiani of the Missions Etrangères, and Ripa. Appiani had been brought from Canton by the legate to be his interpreter, since he naturally wished to have someone speaking for him who would be sympathetic to his views. In this capacity Appiani was often the mouthpiece of De Tournon and, therefore, an important figure in the controversy. According to the legate's supporters, the Jesuits forced Appiani into a position of disfavor with the emperor and caused to be revived against him an old accusation of sedition and disturbing the peace in Szechuan, for which, they said, he had been driven from the province. According to the Dominican Saint-Pierre, the emperor sent a eunuch to examine Appiani, in the presence of Pereyra and other priests. The eunuch, after the usual procedure of Chinese officialdom which took for granted a prisoner's guilt before he was proved innocent, treated him with unnecessary harshness. Instead of protesting against this violence, Pereyra adjured the accused to confess his misdeeds while Appiani continued to protest his innocence. Even when the prejudices of the narrator of the story are taken into account, the picture of a Christian priest aiding and abetting an ignorant and cruel minor official in the persecution of a fellow priest is not a pleasant one to consider, but it shows to what extent human passions had by this time taken the center of the stage.[7]

In the meantime a much more serious charge against the Jesuits had been brought to the legate's notice. The son of a prominent official had borrowed money from the missionaries and, not being able to pay the principal when it was due, had had moral pressure of an objectionable nature brought to bear on him by the priests, despite the fact that he had always paid the interest promptly. Acting under advice of his friends, the debtor took the case to the legate, opening up the whole question of the business affairs of the Jesuits. Complaints had come from other native Christians, and the insistence of these rumors forced the legate to take action. He made a formal inquiry into their methods and, on May 17, 1706, rendered judgment against them of lending money at an usurious rate of interest and of being harsh in the enforcement of their contracts. Considering the fact that all lending at interest was forbidden to churchmen, the business dealings of the Society provided material for grave charges against them.

There is no doubt that the financial condition of the mission at this time was very good. The editor of the *Memorie storiche* gives the following facts:

The Jesuits have three houses in Peking. Every house has virtually a trade of interest to the value of fifty to sixty thousand taels. The interest given in China is ordinarily thirty for a hundred. The Jesuits pretend that they take only twenty-four, or 2 per cent per month. It is easy to calculate the profit. The capital of sixty thousand taels for every house makes, for all taken together, the sum of seven hundred thousand livres and the income about one hundred eighty thousand livres, for the support of twelve poor clergy.[8]

After an examination of the facts, the legate by formal decree suppressed and annulled all usurious contracts and, on the 18th of May, 1706, he took from Pereyra and Grimaldi their rank of apostolic missionaries. This act inevitably brought added bitterness to his relations with the foreign scholars at court. It was looked upon as an open declaration of war. The opponents of the Jesuits accuse them of threatening De Tournon not only with the ruin of his legation but also with personal molestation if he did not revoke his censure and send to Rome a favorable report concerning them. The charge of personal threats may well be looked upon as an imaginative product of the violent atmosphere of the quarrel, but it is significant of the animosity and hatred which had been injected into the controversy by these purely mundane affairs.

It was at this moment, May, 1706, that Maigrot took the center of the stage and assumed the unpleasant role of scapegoat at court. The Bishop of Conon had been a resident in China for a decade. Since 1693 he had been occupying the position of vice-provincial of the province of Fukien where, as we have seen, he had come into open hostility with the local Jesuits on account of his injunction against the Rites. Apparently he had studied the Chinese language with little success, since subsequently he showed a startling ignorance of Chinese characters. This was an unpardonable weakness in one who had assumed the role of legislator in a matter demanding an accurate and profound knowledge of the facts involved, and his Jesuit opponents exploited this weakness to the fullest extent. They turned to ridicule Maigrot's lack of knowledge and through him they brought contempt on the party he represented. So successful were they in this that, when Mezzabarba visited China fifteen years later, Maigrot's name still stood at court for everything which the emperor condemned in the Catholic quarrel.

Probably at the suggestion of the legate, who badly needed expert advice, Maigrot was summoned to Peking to give evidence. He arrived on June 29, 1706, and immediately found himself in trouble. The emperor commanded him to expound in writing all the passages in the classics which he found to be opposed to the Christian faith. Maigrot saw the trap but, knowing no way to avoid it, he prepared, under protest, a list of fifty citations from the works of scholars, with explanatory comments. At the same time he declared that he did not recognize the right of the emperor to legislate in a purely religious matter. Father Beauvoilliers was chosen by the Jesuits to answer Maigrot's suggestions and objections and to prove that the passages cited were not opposed to Christian teachings. Several times in the history of the Christian religion in the Far East public debates had been held before the emperor in which a representative of the Christian faith upheld the doctrines of his religion, but this was, probably, the first occasion when Catholic fought with Catholic "for the glory of the Lord."

The storm center had now fairly shifted to the Bishop of Conon. Together with the Jesuits Parennin, Gerbillon, and Antoine Thomas, on the one hand, and Appiani, Angelita, and Guetti on the other, Maigrot was summoned to Jehol, where the emperor was staying at the moment, and on the fourth of August K'ang Hsi gave an audience in which the unfortunate bishop was forced to defend himself.

The scene, as Maigrot faced his enemies, was not lacking in drama. For the first time the two parties were placed face to face before an umpire who, though not unprejudiced, was in the eyes of the non-Catholic world at least authoritative. On the one side were the defendant and his sympathizers, all hostile to the Rites and waging a courageous fight for the integrity of their religion, as they saw it; on the other, the Jesuits, secure in their position as the allies of the national cult and convinced that their point of view was the only one which could save the mission from ruin. The interview turned on the competence of Maigrot to be a judge of matters of Chinese thought and practice. K'ang Hsi commanded the Bishop of Conon to repeat a passage from one of the classics, which he was unable to do. Thereupon the emperor exposed the missionary's extreme ignorance by himself repeating several pages of the work in question. The unfortunate bishop was then asked to interpret four characters on a scroll which hung behind the throne. He was able to name only one of them. In the conversation which followed he seems, according to the Jesuit accounts, to have shown not only a lack of knowledge of Chinese but also an ignorance of the history of the Jesuit mission. He failed to recognize the Chinese name of Ricci when it was mentioned, and he admitted he had not read the Italian Jesuit's famous apology for Christianity (*T'ien Chu shih I*) which many an official at court must have read.[8]

The Bishop of Conon had been introduced by the legate as a man well versed in the language of the country; thus, by the end of the interview, the legate himself had suffered, according to Oriental ideas, the greatest possible humiliation, a complete loss of "face." How much of this humiliation was due to the maliciousness of the members of the Society it is neither necessary nor possible to determine, but the fact of Maigrot's ignorance is important since it illustrates, in an illuminating way, the strength and weakness of the opposing forces.

Matters went from bad to worse for the unfortunate champion of the legate. In a rash moment Maigrot had publicly called the emperor an atheist and, not content with this, had asserted that China was a land of atheists! When faced with this remark, he refused to retract. His condemnation, therefore, was a foregone conclusion. After several days of official censure and abuse he was dismissed from the capital, together with Father Mezzafalci and Guetti, a mechanic attached to the mission—a liar and a troublemaker who seems to have played an ignoble part in the quarrel. The three men were banished.

K'ang Hsi's opinion of Maigrot appears in a document sent by the emperor to an official in August, 1706. He says:

I have ordered Yen Tang (Maigrot) to come hither to examine him. He knows a little Chinese but cannot speak so as to be understood, whence he is obliged to have an interpreter. Not only does he not understand the meaning of the Books [the Confucian Canon] but he is even ignorant of the characters. A man in this empire who should show such ignorance would move the hearers to laughter. Not understanding the sense of the Books he cannot say what they contain, as he affirms.[10]

It is no wonder, then, that the emperor's attitude toward him swung between scorn for his ignorance and anger at his obstinacy. It was a serious mistake on the part of the anti-Jesuit party to have chosen Maigrot for their champion and a lack of wisdom on the part of the legate to have accepted him in that role.

The Bishop of Conon arrived in Europe in May, 1708, and hastened to Paris to lay bare his griefs before the Missions Etrangères.

Here this important actor in the Chinese drama leaves the scene. His role had been a courageous one, and it is to be regretted that he had to perform it with the meager resources of ignorance and indiscretion.

The story swings back to the legate. In the capital the controversy seems by now to have become a *cause célèbre* in Chinese official circles. Charges and countercharges were hurled from one party to the other. Personal violence was threatened and feared. The illness of De Tournon brought rumors of poison, a charge never long absent from the plottings of an Eastern court. In this fetid atmosphere the young legate, sick, indignant, beaten down by the forces of intrigue ranged against him, presents a spectacle worthy of pity. The situation became more and more difficult. De Tournon's petition to visit the provinces was flatly refused. It was now clear, even to the legate, that nothing good was to come of his labors. Finally, he was made to understand that his mission was ended and that he was at liberty to retire from the capital.

Hard as his experiences in Peking had proved to be, however, he was destined to suffer even worse. He started for Canton but stopped en route at Nanking. Here he published an apostolic letter to the missionaries, giving his decisions concerning the points in dispute. This letter ordered the use of the term *T'ien Chu;* forbade the use of *T'ien* and *Shang Ti* for God; and refused to allow the *Ching T'ien* tablets in the churches. It also forbade the granting to neophytes of the right to participate in the ceremonies to Confucius and to the ancestors and refused consent for them even to appear, on the grounds that the cult was steeped in superstition. It withheld permission, also, from a Christian official to participate in the Confucian ceremonies. It forbade offerings in the ancestral halls of oblations to the dead or association in any way in the rites before the tablets which claimed to be the dwelling place of the souls of the departed.[21]

De Tournon's injunction, the clearest and most condemnatory which had yet been issued on the subject, was received with a storm of indignation. The Bishop of Macao refused to accept it, giving as his reason that it infringed on the prerogatives of the king of Portugal.[12] He claimed the document had not been registered before publication at the chancellery at Lisbon, as should have been done according to the rights of Portugal implied in the *jus patronatus,* and supported this rebellious position by accusing the legate of being an avowed enemy of Portugal.

Not less angry was the emperor who saw in the legate's act an open defiance to the will of the throne. K'ang Hsi immediately gave orders for De Tournon's arrest. He was taken to Canton and handed over to the Portuguese, who, subjecting him to the hardest treatment, transferred him to Macao. The legate now had three forces ranged against him: the emperor, whose dignity he had insulted; the Portuguese, whose supposed rights he had infringed; and the members of the Society, whose policies he had outspokenly condemned. The subsequent history of this unfortunate man is a dark one, lightened only by the calm heroism with which he met his fate.

On August 31, 1707, he writes to the vicar apostolic of Tongking: "I have received from the bishop and the governor of this city [Macao], acting at the instigation of the Jesuits, such a barbarous treatment as I have never met with among the Gentiles."[13] Jenkins, who has carefully investigated the evidence, exonerates the Jesuits from blame for what happened at Macao and places the responsibility on the representatives of the king of Portugal. Their leader, Diego de Pinho Texeira, the captain general, was De Tournon's most bitter persecutor. He was abetted by Juan de Cazal, the Bishop of Macao, who was himself instructed in the matter by his superior, the Archbishop of Goa. These representatives of the Catholic church aided the civil authorities in making life miserable for the imprisoned legate. De Tournon seems to have felt that François Pinto, the provincial of the Jesuits, was also among the tormentors, though there seems to be little evidence to support this accusation. The latter refused to recognize the legate's jurisdiction in spite of three monitions commanding him to do so, monitions which, according to De Tournon, he received with such scorn that the legate was finally forced to put him under the ban of excommunication.

The legate was at first given miserable quarters but, as he protested, they were changed for better. Guards were placed around his house; free access to him was denied. One of his retinue, a French priest named Hervé, was thrown into prison for a slight indiscretion, and the efforts of the legate to release him failed. Augustinian missionaries who visited him were rebuked by the Bishop of Macao and enjoined to do so no more. As the legate attempted to exert his ecclesiastical powers, persecution became more bitter. The auditor of the city visited him and, failing to persuade him to surrender his apostolic jurisdiction, made a formal arrest of his person. In spite of the most solemn protestations of his retinue, his guards were doubled and everything but the merest necessities of life was denied him. Father Pedrini seems to have considered a dramatic attempt to rescue him with the aid of a piratical junk hired for the purpose, but at the last moment the prisoner refused to accept this way out of the situation.[14]

On July 6, 1707, the provincial of the Society showed the legate an order from the viceroy of the Indies forbidding the recognition of his jurisdiction. Two weeks later the bishop took from De Tournon the support of the priests of his diocese and the Three Estates of the city, convened by the captain general, signed a document supporting the latter's attitude in the matter. To these acts the legate replied with the ban of excommunication.

A gleam of hope came to him from the Philippines when messengers from the governor of that place brought to the prisoner the insignia of a cardinal which had been bestowed on the legate by the Holy See in August, 1701. De Tournon summoned to his presence the clergy of Macao and, in solemn ceremony, in the chapel of his prison lodgings, he was invested with the crimson biretta. This sign of papal favor, however, did not lessen the opposition to him. At times even water was withheld from him, according to the account of his secretary and last companion, Father Angelita.[15]

Under these conditions it is not surprising that his health grew worse. Finally, on June 8, 1710, he suffered an attack of apoplexy and succumbed, dying at the age of forty-one. His supporters do not hesitate to bring forward once more the accusation of poisoning, and anti-Jesuit historians have repeated the charge.[16] When one bears in mind the ravages of dysentery in Oriental lands, however, one must reject entirely such accusations and attribute his death to natural causes.[17]

The complaints of the legate and his supporters against the Society have been answered at length by Jesuit apologists,[18] but if these charges are only half true, it is clear that De Tournon had great cause to complain. The legate accuses his enemies of a lack of respect for his person and of communicating this disrespect to the officials, beginning with the viceroy of Canton, who (he claimed) should have paid a visit of courtesy to him when he first arrived.[19] He asserts that the Jesuits omitted the ceremonies of reverence due one of his exalted rank; that they withheld their advice from him when they were in a position to guide him; that they opposed his plan of founding a permanent House for the Propaganda in Peking, and that they defeated his efforts to place near the throne a physician of his suite. (The Jesuits claimed that the man in question, Signor Borghese, was incompetent, ignorant of the literature of his subject, and nothing more than a menial in the retinue of the legate.) Finally, the cardinal accuses the Jesuits of preventing him from visiting their mission as visitor and of arousing rebellion against him in the minds of their converts.

The Jesuits answer these charges by declaring that the legate was given a reception more honorable and splendid than had ever before been given a foreign envoy; that from the beginning to the end of his visit he was the recipient of distinguished honors from the emperor and that the Jesuits themselves were careful to demand for the legate all the honors that the throne seemed disposed to grant. They assert that they did all in their power to cover up his ignorance of Chinese etiquette, court procedure, and national or racial psychology and that, time and again, they stood between the tactlessness of the envoy and the anger of the monarch. That his mission failed, they claim, was owing to his own lack of tact and to his unwillingness to accept a situation which, by the very nature of things, was from the first inevitable.

Whether these assertions represent the whole truth or not, it is obvious that the forces arrayed against the legate were too strong, and that he himself was too lacking in the qualities which alone could have brought his task to a successful conclusion. De Tournon, like many another Christian martyr, was imbued with the majesty of the great Church he represented, particularly in its aspect as controller of the destinies of men. He was jealous of its prerogatives and sensitive to any slights put upon it. It is clear that much of the persecution of the last days, at least, came from his violent opposition to the Portuguese hegemony in the Far East. Perhaps this was his most serious tactical blunder. At Macao he might have escaped many of the indignities heaped upon him, had he been willing to waive the question of his ecclesiastical authority. To a man of his temperament this seemed a cowardly surrender, which he rejected with scorn. Endowed with the delicate nervous balance of a mystically religious temperament, he demonstrated his pride in the Church and his responsibility to the role he had been given by anger against his and the Church's opponents.

The spirit of self-sacrifice may have made of De Tournon a figure of noble proportions and raised him by his death to the glory of martyrdom, but it did not assist in any way in the accomplishment of the task which he had left Europe to perform. The situation demanded not a Savonarola but a Benedict XIV, a man willing to meet other men in the council chamber in that spirit of comradeship which is an indication of open-mindedness. This, apparently, De Tournon refused to do. He adopted throughout the attitude of a high ecclesiastical official who had come to legislate for the infallible head of the Church. In this attitude is to be found the chief cause of his failure.

But what of his opponents, of the men who have, perhaps right-fully, been accused of acts contrary to the spirit of the Christian priest-hood; the men who alone had real access to the emperor and whose attitude had much to do with determining the moral tone of the controversy? There is much to be said on the Jesuit side. Jenkins' words, in exoneration of the acts of Pereyra and Grimaldi, might be applied to the Society as a whole. Jenkins says:

They had been the founders and the architects of the greatest missionary work which the world till then had seen. By the most consummate prudence and skilful diplomacy they had opened to the Western world an empire which had hitherto been closed to every explorer. The method they had adopted had succeeded beyond their most sanguine expectations and now their life work was to be suddenly broken down and destroyed by Dominican and Franciscan rivals who were absolutely unable to estimate or even to com-prehend the plan upon which the building was laid out.[20]

The fundamental soundness of the Jesuits' position in the matter of the Rites is, however, scarcely justification for their continual oppo-sition to the legate. The power of interpreting and defining the dogma of the Roman Church rests alone with the head of that church and with his advisers, even though his counselors be weak, his envoys the least enlightened, and his information inaccurate and insufficient. The liberal verdict of the world would probably support the Jesuits' position, but their insistence on this in face of formal papal con-demnation is difficult to condone.

De Tournon left the situation of the Church in the Middle King-dom much worse than he had found it. The bishops in China had ap-pealed from his edicts to Rome. The Archbishop of Goa had ordered his suffragan bishops to regard the acts of the legate as null and void, and the theologians of the king of Portugal had confirmed this order. The bitterest animosities had been engendered. The emperor's sym-pathy had been utterly alienated, and Christianity in the Far East had received a serious blow. In answer to the legate's decree, K'ang Hsi announced that only those who would promise to accept the Rites and to stay in China all their lives would be allowed to remain and would be given the imperial *p'iao* ("license") and that all those who did not possess the *p'iao* would be driven from the empire. The majority of the missionaries, including the Franciscan Bishop of Peking and the Augustinian Vicar Apostolic of Kuangsi, decided, for the good of the mission, to postpone obedience to the legate until they could hear from Rome.

Chapter XII

THE RITES CONTROVERSY: THE
END OF THE QUARREL

IN THE MEANTIME in France the bitter struggle between the Jesuits and the Missions Etrangères had flared up again. In February, 1710, the Missions Etrangères petitioned the Pope to force the Jesuits to submit to the orders of the papal see. In October the Holy See forbade further controversy and, five years later, in March, 1715, issued the Constitution *Ex illa die*. After summing up the previous actions of the Holy See regarding the Rites the decree expressly forbade: (1) the use of the terms *T'ien* and *Shang Ti* for God, (2) the use of the *Ching T'ien* tablets, (3) sacrifices to Confucius, (4) other ceremonies in the Confucian temples, (5) sacrifices to ancestors, (6) oblations offered before the ancestral tablets, before the body of a deceased person, or at the graveside, (7) the possession of tablets bearing the legend, "Seat of the Soul of X...." It tolerated, however, the use of these tablets if they contained only the name of the deceased, and it permitted all ceremonies which were unquestionably only of a civil or political nature.

The document went on to ratify the decree of Cardinal de Tournon, to condemn pretexts for eluding obedience to the papal orders and to demand unequivocal obedience on the part of all ecclesiastical functionaries to the terms of the decree.[1] Mosheim says:

> There is not one among all the decrees of the Holy See so accurately and cautiously worded or so minutely guarded against possible exception and evasion. The lawyers who prepared it exhausted their whole stock of such words as might be effectual to disarm those who study to transgress under cover of the law.[2]

The terms of the *Ex illa die* Constitution being so clear, it would seem that the decree would have put an end to the controversy, but

---

[1] For notes to chap. xii, see pp. 321–323.

this was not so. For thirty-two years the question continued to be debated while efforts were made to induce the Holy See to revoke its decision. The Constitution arrived in Canton in August, 1716. The situation was a tremendously difficult one. The problem which faced the Jesuits and the other orders was: How could the mandate be promulgated without causing immediate ruin to the mission? The success or failure of more than a hundred years' hard toil hung upon the decision. Mgr. della Chiesa, Bishop of Peking, would not accept the grave responsibility and fell back on a promise of Rome that a legate would be sent to guide the Church in China. He therefore refrained from making a definite pronouncement. The Jesuit visitor, Father Stumpf, issued an encyclical letter to the members of the Society ordering them to obey the commands of Rome, but the Jesuits in the Chinese capital, lacking the leadership of the bishop, waited for future events to bring light to the situation.

In November, Father Castorano, vicar of the Bishop of Peking, arrived in the capital and was given the task of promulgating the papal edict. The Jesuits were dismayed, but they appear to have offered the use of their churches for the act of promulgation. In the meantime news reached the court of the purpose of Father Castorano's visit and the priest was summarily arrested, imprisoned, and finally banished to Canton. It is probable that the intercession of the Jesuit priests at court saved him from harsher treatment.

K'ang Hsi issued a statement that he was awaiting the return of Father Provana from Rome and, until that time, he expected the missionaries to take no action. The papal document was, therefore, sent back to Father Geron, Procureur of the Propaganda at Canton, who referred it to Rome with the emperor's comments and a detailed report on the situation.

The Holy See was nonplussed. It had already issued a command that controversy cease under threat of excommunication. In September, 1711, Louis XIV issued similar commands. Portugal sided with the Jesuits, and a request from the Most Catholic King to the Pope that the decree be suspended until further investigation was ignored. Thus ended what might be called the fourth phase of the quarrel.

In the meantime the Jesuits were apparently trying to consolidate their position by attacking their opponents in China. Among these were Father Pedrini of the Lazarist Mission and Father Matthew Ripa, an independent missionary of the Propaganda. Father Ripa has left an interesting account of life in Peking, where he lived for twelve years (1711–1723); an account which, in many respects, is the antithesis of the panegyric of the Jesuits. Judged by his own words, Ripa was a narrow and bigoted, although fervent and well-meaning, character—the kind of priest whose role in an ecclesiastical quarrel is to add fuel to the fires of controversy. In the capital his vocation was that of a painter, in which he succeeded fairly well; his avocation was the establishment of a school for the training of native clergy, a plan which ran headlong into Jesuit opposition. The little English version of his experiences[3] is steeped in bitterness and the disillusionment which comes with failure, the failure of a sincere but narrow soul who is constricted by the limitations of his bigotry.

Pedrini, the first missionary of the Propaganda to get to Peking, is much more interesting and a much more worthy opponent of the Jesuit strategists. Designated to bring the biretta to De Tournon, he made a thrilling journey to China by way of South America, Mexico, and the Philippines. After several attempts to reach Canton he finally disguised himself as the captain of a frigate and at length arrived in Macao on January 1, 1710. Later at court he gained the favor of the emperor on account of his skill in making and mending musical instruments. In spite of persecution he seems never to have lost entirely the protection of the emperor.[4]

Pedrini refused to obey the decree of the emperor concerning the Constitution, *Ex illa die,* and, occupying a position at court which gave him a certain amount of favor, was able to show K'ang Hsi that the members of the Society had withheld from him, the emperor, evidence showing the attitude of the Pope, notably the papal decrees of 1704 and 1710. In spite of the opposition of the Jesuits, Pedrini succeeded in getting into the emperor's hands a memoir concerning the Rites which contained information harmful to the Jesuit cause. This act brought about his ruin. His enemies poisoned the mind of the emperór against him. He was accused of writing to Rome a letter hostile to the imperial decree concerning the Rites. The emperor angrily referred to him on one occasion as "a seditious, tumultuous man, a rough fellow, ignorant of Chinese letters." Then began a series of humiliations and insults which stopped just short of death. He was forced to retract what he had written. On February 8, 1720, he was arrested, ostensibly for having failed to pay the formal New Year's visit to the court, and was thrown into prison.

During the visit of Mezzabarba, Pedrini was called upon to sign a report of the audience of the legate and, not knowing what was in the document, refused to do so. For this he was beaten in the presence of the emperor, again thrown into prison, and later handed over to the Society to be incarcerated in their mission.[5] His enemies did not hesitate to accuse him of being the originator of the *Ex illa die* decree and his name was coupled with that of the other bête noir of K'ang Hsi, Maigrot. Although Pedrini may have been lacking in tact, one cannot fail to admire the courage of the Italian priest who, with almost no support from his colleagues, pitted his strength against the combined forces of the emperor and the Society.

So the quarrel over the Rites dragged on until, ten years after De Tournon's death, the Holy See made a new attempt to settle it. In 1719 it was decided to send another legate to China. The man now chosen for the mission was George Ambrose de Mezzabarba, Patriarch of Alexandria. Leaving Rome in 1719, he arrived in Macao in June of the following year. On the way he had taken the precaution to stop at Lisbon to obtain the official recognition of the Portuguese monarch.

The history of the De Tournon legation was, in its main outlines, repeated. Landing at Canton, Mezzabarba was met by Laureati, the

Jesuit visitor, who subsequently, in the presence of the emperor, tried to persuade him to repudiate De Tournon—which, of course, the new legate refused to do. He was asked by local officials why news had not been received from Fathers Barros and Beauvoilliers or from Father Provana, who had gone to Rome as the emperor's envoys. Mezzabarba's replies were vague but, inasmuch as he was allowed to travel north, were evidently satisfactory to the local officials. He had been receiving most discouraging news from Peking. Father Jean-François Foucquet, whose views on the Figurist theories had brought him into disfavor with his Jesuit confreres, had written the legate that he would have grave obstacles to surmount.° At a short distance from the capital the legate was met by officials of the court and again questioned on his purposes. His replies suggest·that the Holy See had profited by the De Tournon fiasco and had chosen a man who had at least some gifts of diplomacy. Undoubtedly Mezzabarba came to Peking with a sincere and honest intention to carry out the wishes of Rome. When he arrived at the capital, however, he was overwhelmed by the complexities of the situation.

At Peking the Jesuits informed the legate that "without a Brief which permits the modification of the Constitution everything will be hopelessly ruined." The first struggle came over interpreters. The emperor refused to accept either Ripa or Pedrini (who, he said, were creatures of Maigrot), or Appiani. K'ang Hsi was apparently obsessed with a violent prejudice against the Bishop of Conon. Time after time he referred to Maigrot with harsh invective. He threatened to send the new legate back to Canton in chains if he should try to follow the tactics of this earlier representative of Rome.

Mezzabarba's audience with the emperor was not unsatisfactory. K'ang Hsi expressed his bewilderment in the face of the bitter quarrel between the orders, for, although he made use of Jesuits and for that reason supported them in their controversy, he seems to have had no illusions as to the reasons for the Society's efforts. The emperor promised to read Mezzabarba's brief and subsequently did so, calling the legate again to an audience. At this meeting Ripa and Pedrini were allowed to be among the interpreters, together with the Jesuits Bouvet, Parennin, and De Mailla. At this audience the legate explained that the mission had a fourfold purpose: to inquire concerning the health of the emperor; to thank His Majesty for past favors to the missionaries and to the Christian faith; to beg the emperor to allow the Christians to follow the practices of their religion as defined in the Constitution which the legate carried and to concede to the Pope spiritual authority over the converts.

The emperor replied that only the missionaries at court, and not the Chinese converts, would be allowed to recognize the Constitution.[7] Finding himself running into hopeless imperial opposition, the legate then sought a compromise. He begged the emperor to read the papal letter which set forth the arguments regarding the *Ex illa die* decree, and he presented eight "Permissions" which he had drawn up as a substitute for the latter. The "Permissions" marked a sincere attempt on the part of the legate to compromise in an almost impossible situation. Without denying the force and validity of the papal edicts they attempted to find a tactful way of carrying out these edicts. That they served to nullify the papal pronouncements is evidence of the extreme difficulty of the problem. There is no doubt that the "Permissions" had the effect of putting the controversy back to the time prior to the promulgation of the *Ex illa die* decree.

Then followed a long diplomatic struggle, during which the legate had several audiences with the emperor. In the end K'ang Hsi showed himself ill disposed to withdraw from his position. He reiterated the view that there was no difference between the Chinese and the Christian conceptions of God and that those who condemned the Rites were ignorant and foolish men.

On seeing this decree [said the Manchu emperor], one wonders how the ignorant and contemptible Europeans dare to speak of the Great Doctrine of the Chinese, these men who know nothing about either its rules or its practices and cannot perhaps even understand the characters in which they are written.[8]

Finally the Constitution was translated and read to the emperor. In reply the latter angrily declared that the Europeans would not be allowed to preach their religion in China. The legate, alarmed, petitioned the throne that the priests be allowed to remain and promised that all dissensions should cease. According to the historian of the legation, the missionaries of the Propaganda subscribed to this promise while the Jesuits replied by taking the attitude that the Constitution was not a papal bull but merely a *Praeceptum ecclesiasticum* and that they were not therefore bound to obey it. The legate was alarmed and shocked at the attitude of the Jesuits but, in a tactful though persistent manner, he continued his struggle with the throne. K'ang Hsi seemed now to be tiring of the whole matter. He became in turn ironical, angry, insulting. Although he subsequently granted several audiences to Mezzabarba he does not appear to have taken these conferences seriously. In the meantime the Jesuits did their utmost to persuade the legate to suspend the Constitution.

The emperor, though conceding nothing, continued to treat the legate with distinction, bestowing on him the honors generally bestowed on an envoy. He made him handsome gifts, had feasts prepared for him, and sent him food from his own table. He asked of the legate a Christian relic, assuring the priests that it would never be deposited in a "heathen" temple. These friendly actions, however, were merely expressions of formal imperial condescension and must not be taken as indicative of the emperor's true attitude.

Mezzabarba's chronicler shows how pitifully mean the quarrel had become and how fiercely burned the fires of dissension in the minds of men who were in the empire to represent the cause of Christ. It is not to be wondered at that the emperor insisted that the legate stop the discord. But Mezzabarba, with all his powers of tact and diplomacy, was able to do nothing to clear the atmosphere of intrigue and jealousy. Finally the emperor became tired of the legate's persistence and inability to put an end to the quarrel and intimated that, the purpose of his mission having been accomplished, he was at liberty to leave. In his last audience K'ang Hsi received the Roman envoy graciously, sent handsome presents to the Pope, and asked in return that the legate send him news from Europe and the latest books on mathematics.

Mezzabarba left Peking on March 3, 1721, and arrived at Macao in May. Here he addressed a pastoral letter to the missionaries containing the text of the eight "Permissions." In Peking he had left the impression that he himself had misgivings concerning the *Ex illa die* decree and was returning to enlighten the Pope. This must have been a diplomatic subterfuge, for, once outside the jurisdiction of the emperor, he reaffirmed the legality of the Constitution and insisted on its enforcement, with the reservation which he had expounded in the "Permissions." The words of the instructions, issued November 4, 1721, are as follows:

The decree of our Holy Father, Pope Clement XI, having already been published and having acquired the force of law to be enforced on each and every one, we judge that it is not necessary to issue a new injunction for the purpose of publishing it. So, without giving new orders, we believe we ought to leave matters in the condition we found them, that is to say, we in no way suspend the Bull *Ex illa die* and we do not in any sense permit what it forbids. Nevertheless we judge it fitting to accord a certain facility in carrying it out, by means of eight "Permissions."

Under penalty of excommunication we forbid the translation of this text into either Chinese or Tartar [Manchu] and we prohibit the divulging of its contents to any others than missionaries.[9]

It is a serious question whether the methods of diplomatic secrecy which had already been used with disastrous results in the controversy were the wisest tactics on the part of the legate. Judging from the circumstances, from the standpoint of the present, it seems puerile on Mezzabarba's part to have believed that such a document, issued under such conditions, could have been kept secret.

The mission of Mezzabarba failed, but this failure was not, apparently, due to lack of wisdom or tact on the part of the legate. Nor can it have been due entirely to the opposition of the Jesuits, who appear to have wished for its success even while disagreeing with some of the legate's tactics. Rather was it caused by the fact that at this stage of the controversy no compromise was humanly possible.

The Bishop of Peking, Mgr. François de la Purification, issued two letters in 1753 ordering the clergy of his diocese to base their acts on the "Permissions," but two years later the Pope annulled these orders as well as the "Permissions" themselves. In Europe the "Permissions" displeased the Jesuits' opponents.

The injunction of M. Mezzabarba [says one writer] does not permit all that the Bull [*Ex illa die*] condemns but it leaves the serpent an opening to insert his head and he will have no scruples about inserting the rest of the body.[10]

In February, 1721, K'ang Hsi sent another envoy to Rome in the person of the Jesuit Gianpriamo. Traveling by way of Russia, he arrived in Italy in October, 1722, but his mission had little success. He was silenced by the heads of the Church, who would neither listen to his pleas themselves nor allow anyone else to do so. Then, on September 1, 1723, Innocent XIII, basing his decision on the report of the legate, issued a pronouncement in which he not only condemned the practices of the Jesuits, but accused them of disobedience to the Holy See. The general of the Jesuit Order, Tamborini, addressed a memoir in reply.[11] Again a flood of literature on the subject was let loose. In a seven-volume work entitled *Anecdotes sur la Chine* the case against the Society was only too amply and virulently set forth. This work represents the high-water mark of vituperation in the quarrel and is a shameful document in the literature of ecclesiastical controversy.

On receipt of the news of the outbreak of persecution in China in 1724, Benedict XIII sent two Carmelites, Fathers Gothard and Ildefonse, to Yung Cheng, ostensibly to congratulate the emperor on his succession. They were received formally. In his letter of thanks Yung Cheng included the following statement:

As regards the Europeans who have been in my country for some time, I, the emperor, have taken pains to instruct them and to teach them the submission due to superiors, the moderation and the conduct which they owe to their elders and the repose which will permit them to avoid the defects of a troublesome temper.

If indeed they resolve to observe the laws of the empire and to do nothing reprehensible, I shall shower favors on them. I shall favor them in everything, and I shall honor them with much affection.[12]

Obviously this document was both a promise and a threat. The embassy of Gothard and Ildefonse had no ultimate effect on the fortunes of the mission, and finally the quarrel threatened to assume such alarming proportions in Rome that Pope Benedict XIV, to settle the matter for all time, issued (July, 1742) the bull *Ex quo singulari*.

The bull began with a recital of the history of the controversy including a summary of the mandate of De Tournon and the text of the *Ex illa die* Constitution. It condemned the eight "Permissions" of Mezzabarba (which had never, indeed, been accepted by the Holy See). Finally, by supporting the *Ex illa die* it gave the final and irrevocable decision of the Church of Rome concerning the Rites. It enjoined obedience in the following stern phrases:

Furthermore, concerning the regular missionaries of any Order, Congregation, or Institute whatsoever, even those of the Society of Jesus, if any of them (which God forbid!) refuse an exact, entire, absolute, inviolable and strict obedience to the things which are legislated upon and ordered by Us through the tenor of the present Constitution, we expressly enjoin ... that these bold and refractory men be dismissed without delay from the Missions and sent immediately to Europe and that we be informed so that we may punish them according to the gravity of their crime. That if the provincial Superiors or Generals are not sufficiently obedient to this order which we give them, or carry it out negligently, we shall not fear to proceed against them and among other penalties we shall deprive them for ever of the privilege or the faculty of sending members of the Order to the Missions of these countries.[13]

The Constitution ended by prescribing the following oath to be taken by all missionaries in the China field:

I, N ... Missionary sent to China (or destined for China) or the kingdom N ..., or the province N ... by the Holy See (or by my Superiors, according to the powers which the Holy See has accorded to them), will obey fully

and faithfully the apostolic precept and command regarding the Rites and
Ceremonies of China, contained in the Constitution which our Holy Father
the Pope Clement XI has given in this matter, where the form of oath is prescribed and is perfectly known to me through the reading which I have made
of the entire Constitution, and I will observe strictly, inviolably and absolutely and I will accomplish it without any tergiversation, and I will make
every effort that this same obedience be rendered by all Chinese Christians
of whom I shall have the spiritual direction, of whatever manner it be. And,
furthermore, as much as it shall be possible to me, I will never allow the Rites
and Ceremonies of China, permitted by the pastoral letters of the Patriarch
of Alexandria issued at Macao, November 14, 1721 and condemned by our
Holy Father Benedict XIV, to be put into practice by these same Christians.
That, if in any possible way (which God forbid!) I disobey this, and every
time that that happens, I recognize and declare myself subject to the penalties
imposed by the same Constitution. I promise, avow and swear this, on the
Holy Scriptures. So may God help me and his Holy Apostles.

I, N ... with my own hand....[14]

This oath was obligatory and remained unchanged until recently,
when the Holy See judged it superfluous. Under a decree of the
Propaganda, dated December 8, 1938, the oath was abolished. This
recent decree further permits the presence of Catholics at ceremonies
in honor of Confucius; the use of the picture of Confucius, or of a
tablet dedicated to him, in schoolrooms; and the performance of gestures of respect to the sage and to the ancestors when done unequivo-
cally as acts of resｊect and not of worship.[15]

The Roman decree of 1742 was promulgated in Peking by the
Portuguese Jesuit, Bishop Mgr. Polycarpe de Souza, and was regret-
fully accepted by the native Christians.

By the bull *Ex quo singulari* the Rites controversy was definitely
brought to a close. There were complaints that the Jesuits did not
obey the spirit of the bull,[16] but with the decline of the mission these
accusations ceased, and today the question of the Chinese Rites is no
longer a live issue in the Catholic Church.

Chapter XIII

THE DECLINE OF THE MISSION

BY THE END of K'ang Hsi's reign (1722) the Jesuits had passed the summit of their success. Under the Ming emperors they had created for themselves a strong position at court, chiefly through the influence of powerful converts and through the novelty of their Western science. Under the Manchu dynasty their position had been confirmed, chiefly through the greatness of an emperor who recognized their intellectual worth. The mission grew in power and numbers as long as it retained the sympathy of the emperor. This sympathy, however, as has been indicated, was gradually and almost completely alienated by the quarrels involved in the Rites controversy so that, by the end of K'ang Hsi's reign, the foreign priests had lost, or almost lost, the only effective guarantee of their continued stay in the empire.

K'ang Hsi's place on the Dragon Throne was filled physically, if not intellectually, by his fourth son, who became emperor in 1723 with the reign-title of Yung Cheng. The early years of his reign were marked by domestic quarrels. Since he had many brothers, the opposition to his accession was keen, and there were soon attempts to displace him.[1] His greatest enemy was the eighth prince, Yun Ssu, the ablest of K'ang Hsi's children. This man conspired with his brothers to get rid of the emperor.[2] Some of the princes were known to be friendly with the Jesuit missionaries and, when the conspiracy was sternly suppressed by Yung Cheng, missionaries and Christian converts also suffered from the imperial anger. The chief victim among the Jesuits was Father Juan Morao, superior of the Nan T'ang mission, who had had many friends at court during the last days of K'ang Hsi. Morao was arrested and sent into exile while the emperor decided what his fate should be. When news was received that a Portuguese

---

[1] For notes to chap. xiii, see pp. 323–325.

envoy was being sent to intercede for the foreign priest, however, the emperor forestalled such action by commanding that the Jesuit be executed. Accordingly he met his death by strangulation or poisoning in Turkestan on August 18, 1726. It is noteworthy that Father Morao was the only important member of the Jesuit mission at Peking to meet a violent death at the hands of the government in the entire history of the mission of the seventeenth and eighteenth centuries. Among the native Christians who were punished at the same time were the noble family of Sounou or Sourniama, whose sufferings have been graphically described by Father Parennin in the *Lettres édifiantes*.[3]

Family quarrels undoubtedly influenced the mind and actions of the monarch. He has been accused of querulousness and vindictiveness in his acts.[4] Undoubtedly he felt keenly the disturbances caused by his own family. He saw in these rivalries a menace to the tranquillity of the state and tried to do away with them by every means in his power. If his methods were at times open to criticism, his object—the security of the throne, with resultant peace and prosperity for the empire—was, at least, a laudable one. It was perhaps this sense of political instability which caused Yung Cheng to look with suspicion on anything not conforming to the well-established order of things Chinese. Although he was by no means a blind bigot, he was ultraconservative, and he classed all new systems of thought with the "false sects."

As a youth the emperor must have heard much about Christianity from his tutor, Father Pedrini, and he appears to have admired many of its tenets. His admiration for the doctrines of Christianity was weakened, however, by his belief that the religion as a whole was revolutionary and subversive of Chinese institutions. While he was striving for stability and the continuation of the *status quo,* he saw the foreign priests disturbing the capital with quarrels concerning the fundamental institutions which he, in common with all his Chinese subjects, so firmly supported. Yung Cheng explained his views one day to several of the missionaries.

You say that your law is not a false law. I believe it. If I thought it were false what would prevent me from destroying your churches and driving you from them? What would you say if I sent a troop of Bonzes and Lamas into your country to preach their doctrines? You want all Chinese to become Christians. Your Law demands it, I know. But in that case what will become of us? Shall we become subjects of your king? The converts you make recognize only you in time of trouble. They will listen to no other voice but yours. I know that at the present time there is nothing to fear, but when your ships come by the thousands then there will probably be great disorder . . . The emperor, my father, lost a great deal of his reputation among scholars by the condescension with which he let you establish yourselves here. The laws of our ancient sages will permit no change and I will not allow my reign to be laid open to such a charge.[5]

In his famous commentary on his father's still more famous edict he approves of Christianity being classed with the "uncanonical doctrines," or false sects. This document, which is known as the Sacred Edict, was revered by all the subjects of the emperor, and the condemnatory mention in it of the doctrines of Christianity must have had considerable influence on the attitude of scholars and officials toward the religion which the Jesuits preached.[6]

Yung Cheng attacked many of the important doctrines of the Faith. He condemned the Incarnation as a trick to fool the simple, and he criticized the idea of the special interposition of God as being unworthy of the Deity. His chief attack upon Christianity, however, was as an enemy of filial piety, that great cornerstone of Confucian tradition. The Jesuits tried to show him that the filial piety of the West, although it differed slightly in its social implications, was essentially the same as that of China and that it was an integral part of their Holy Law. The acid of distrust, however, had eaten too deeply into the mind of the emperor for him to be persuaded by their arguments. He continued to look upon Christianity as a menace to the state.

It was not long before this change in the attitude of the monarch began to react on the situation in the provinces. Persecutions sprang up in different parts of the empire and the life of the mission in China was endangered.

Portrait of Ch'ien Lung by the Jesuit artist Brother Panzi
(From the *Mémoires concernant l'histoire ... des Chinois*)

It was probably a desire to put an end to this state of affairs that influenced the king of Portugal to send an embassy to Peking. Several years previously (1721), Father Antoine de Magalhaens had been sent by the China mission to the Pope and to John V of Portugal, but for various reasons his return had been delayed. When he came back to China three years later, he was accompanied by Don Alexandro Metello de Sousa y Menezes, an envoy from the Portuguese monarch. The ostensible purpose of the embassy was to bring to Yung Cheng the congratulations of the Portuguese monarch on the occasion of the emperor's accession. Soon, however, the rumor spread that Don Metello had in reality come to intercede on behalf of Christian missions. This angered the Son of Heaven, who immediately made known to the Jesuits that, if such a plan were contemplated, he would be unable to grant an audience to the envoy. With their keen sense of the undercurrents of court feeling the priests realized that Metello, under the circumstances, could do them more service by creating a favorable impression at court than by carrying out his previous plan, thereby incurring the anger of the emperor.[7] Accordingly, they advised him to make no mention of Christian missions, and they let the emperor know that he would not do so.

The question concerning the nature of the embassy having been settled, Yung Cheng decided to receive the ambassador. On May 14, 1727, Don Metello and his brilliant entourage entered the capital, where they made a profound impression on the people as they rode magnificently through the streets, scattering largess—a custom unknown in China. The emperor and his court were also impressed by the richness of the robes of the Europeans; by the splendor of their equipage; by their grave, but courteous and polished, demeanor and by their rich gifts, enclosed in beautiful cases. There was a hitch in the proceedings because the ambassador refused to place his credentials anywhere but in the hands of the monarch (which Chinese custom forbade), but, since a precedent had already been established by the Russian embassy of Ismaïlov in 1720, Metello finally gained his point. Yung Cheng received him cordially. He was feted and dined. At the Yuan Ming Yuan, the Summer Palace, the ambassador was shown the splendors of that magnificent place, feasts and theatrical entertainments being arranged for his pleasure. When he left in July, he carried with him thirty-five cases of presents for the king of Portugal, as well as many for himself and his suite, the good will of the emperor (who had found him a courtly and pleasant man), and happy memories of imperial entertainment. As far as practical results were concerned, however, he had accomplished little, and his plan to influence the monarch to grant treatment more favorable to the Christian religion had utterly failed.

To make matters worse for the Jesuits, support in Europe was beginning to fail them. Their enemies were attacking them in Spain and France. In the latter country the spiritual domination of Louis XIV by his Jesuit advisers was causing great alarm among the hostile elements. Elsewhere their brilliant scientific studies were causing their Catholic colleagues to fear that they would seek to change the very fabric of Christian dogma by their extreme liberalism. To such an extent had opposition to the Society grown that after the accession of Clement XII the new Pope issued a decree (September 26, 1735) forbidding the Jesuits to continue their work in China. The decree, however, was not enforced.[8]

Yung Cheng died in 1735, leaving the throne to his fourth son, known to history as Ch'ien Lung. When the former had "mounted the Dragon," there were no Christian priests legally residing in the empire except the scholars at Peking, and even the existence of these was threatened.[9]

Ch'ien Lung was destined to rank with Wu Ti of the Han, with T'ai Tsung of the T'ang dynasty, and with his own imperial grandfather, K'ang Hsi, as one of the most illustrious emperors of China. During his long reign (1736–1796) he made constant use of the Jesuit scholars at court. "Since the establishment of the missionaries in China," writes Father Amiot, "no emperor profited so much by their services as Ch'ien Lung, nevertheless no monarch ill-treated them more harshly or published more deadly edicts against Christianity."[10] One of his first acts was the ratification of an edict forbidding members of the Manchu banners to remain or to become Christians.

It was at this critical period that the mission lost its most influential and brilliant member by the death of Dominique Parennin.[11] Arriving in China in 1698, this able man had, for nearly half a century, represented Christianity in the capital in such a way as to earn for himself universal esteem. Unequal, perhaps, in profundity of scholarship to Gaubil and Prémare, he made up for this by the unusual breadth of his knowledge, by his personal charm, and by the tirelessness and fervor of his work. For twenty years he followed K'ang Hsi in hunting and military expeditions into the North. It was during one of these expeditions that he drew the attention of the emperor to the need for accurate maps of the empire. Thus he became the inspirer of the Jesuit work in cartography. Parennin's letters cover a wide range of subjects; from the origins of the Chinese to the qualities of certain medicinal roots or to the making of artificial flowers. His knowedge of Spanish and Italian, in addition to his versatility in the Chinese and the Manchu languages, fitted him well for the post of interpreter, a duty which he undertook time and again with such skill and tact as to earn the gratitude of many. He helped the Portuguese envoys on several occasions. His services to the ruler of Russia were so important and so much appreciated, that he was showered with praises and presents to such an extent that he aroused the suspicion of the emperor.

Parennin succeeded Gerbillon as corresponding member of the Académie des Sciences of Paris, to which he sent many interesting and enlightening brochures.

The Jesuit named Parennin [wrote Voltaire], a man celebrated for his learning and the wisdom of his character, spoke Chinese and Tartar very well. He made himself necessary not only as interpreter but also as mathematician. It is he who is principally known among us for his wise and instructive answers to certain intellectual doubts of one of our best philosophers [Dortous de Mairan] concerning the sciences of China.[12]

Voltaire's frequent mention of the Jesuit proves that the great leader of European liberalism was a fervent admirer of the missionary's wisdom. His correspondence with Dortous de Mairan, the secretary of the Academy, has been published, thereby affording an excellent opportunity of judging his erudition.

Parennin's knowledge of China was profound. While possessing a deep admiration for the Chinese, he was not blind to their shortcomings, which he explained with a justness and a discrimination that serve to add weight to his panegyric of the people. His linguistic skill helped him in his relations with K'ang Hsi, who often required him to translate into Manchu some example of Occidental erudition in geometry, natural history, astronomy, medicine, or other branches of science of which he possessed a knowledge.

If [says Huc], all the works he translated to satisfy the savants of China, of France and of Russia were collected, we would be astonished that a missionary with so many other occupations should be able to write in so many languages and to make himself useful in so many phases of learning.[13]

On the death of K'ang Hsi Parennin was relieved of many of his duties at court, whereupon he turned his attention to Sinological research, correspondence with Europe, and pastoral duties. In these he engaged until the time of his sickness, a long and painful malady which ended in his death on September 29, 1741. At the command of Ch'ien Lung he was given an elaborate funeral.

Parennin was the last of the second generation of Jesuits who were the close and trusted servants of the Manchu emperor. From the time of the accession of Yung Cheng the foreign scholars ceased to occupy the position of eminence and importance in the state which Gerbillon and Parennin, as well as their predecessors, had held. From this time on the foreign priests were merely skilled servants of the emperor, their voices no longer being heard in the councils of the empire.

Deprived of their status of councilors of state, robbed of much of their prestige at court, the missionaries were forced to be content with minor duties, with a multitude of unimportant matters, which, though trivial in themselves, were sufficient, nevertheless, to keep them in touch with the emperor and with national affairs.

Among the numerous things which provided points of contact between emperor and priest was Western painting. From the beginnings of the mission efforts had been made to interest the Chinese in the art of the West, for the purpose of using the great religious masterpieces as instruments of propaganda.

The story is told, for example, of a painting presented to Shun Chih, which was a realistic picture of the fate of Sodom and Gomorrha. The young Ch'ing monarch prized the work highly but—to the great chagrin of the priests who were at that time hoping for the emperor's conversion—the moral of the picture entirely escaped him.

In the early days Ricci had brought a Jesuit-trained artist from Japan, and, until the death of Ch'ien Lung (1799), there were always Jesuit painters at court.[14] The best known of the foreign artists were Gherardini, Castiglione, Attiret, Panzi, and Sichelpart. Gherardini was a specialist in murals, whose decoration of the chapel at the Hsi T'ang was greatly admired. The result of his efforts at foreshortening on this occasion were a source of wonder to the Chinese, who knew little of western perspective. The picture which he painted behind the altar, where the landscape seemed to recede into the far distance, was so realistic—the Jesuit writers relate—that native visitors hit their heads against the wall trying to walk into it.

Brother Attiret was one of the most industrious and most admired of the Jesuit painters. For thirty years he worked in the palace, the halls of which were decorated with much of his work. All these paintings appear to have been lost, though copies have survived of the series that he drew, in collaboration with Sichelpart, Castiglione, and Jean-Damascene, to celebrate Ch'ien Lung's victories over the Eleuths.[15] Modest and devout, Brother Attiret is a shining example of the type of Jesuit who, under most trying limitations of health and environment, used his talents for the glory of the Faith.

Father Ignatius Sichelpart, a German Jesuit and pupil of Cas-

tiglione, was also a great favorite with the emperor. Following a precedent set in the honors paid the Italian painter, Ch'ien Lung, on the
occasion of Sichelpart's seventieth birthday, sent him valuable presents: six scrolls of silk, a mandarin robe, and other things, the most
important of which was a laudatory scroll bearing characters written
by the Son of Heaven himself. The gifts brought in stately procession
to the Nan T'ang mission from the Yuan Ming Yuan palace, preceded by twenty-four imperial musicians and accompanied by four
officials on horseback, attested to the prestige of the foreign artists
at court. "Any of the ten thousand scholars in the capital," says a
Jesuit writer, "would have given his right hand to have been similarly
treated."[16] Sichelpart died in 1780 after having served at the court for
nearly thirty years.

Brother Joseph Panzi was the last of the noted Jesuit painters. It
was his portrait of Ch'ien Lung which was best known to eighteenth-
century Europe. Like Attiret, he was a man of mild and gentle disposition whose evangelical labors were limited almost entirely to the
use of his art as a means of service. He painted many pictures of religious subjects, notably a "Vision of the Prophet Daniel," done for
the emperor, and, in 1776, a large canvas of the Immaculate Conception for the new church at the Nan T'ang mission.[17]

But the most famous of the Jesuit artists was Brother Joseph Castiglione, a Milanese of outstanding artistic ability. Court painter from
1715 to 1766, he served under three Manchu emperors. His wisdom,
coupled with his years of service, gained him a reputation which he
frequently used to the advantage of the mission. In times of persecution it was he who appealed personally to Ch'ien Lung when such
a measure was felt necessary. Castiglione attracted the notice of the
emperor by his clever decoration of the foreign building at the Yuan
Ming Yuan, the plans of which he helped to design. He painted the
monarch's picture several times as well as the portraits of many court
officials. Probably more of his paintings have survived than those of
any of his colleagues. He was particularly famous for his painting of

horses. The most famous of these, the "Hundred Horses," a series of twelve panels, was painted in 1728.[18]

Another great loss overtook the mission in 1759 through the death of Antoine Gaubil. For a quarter of a century this talented priest had played an important part in the history of the mission. In 1741 he had succeeded Parennin as head of the French establishment. In the troublous times under Ch'ien Lung it was he who had to smooth out the obstacles at court to the progress of the Faith in the provinces. For several years he was official interpreter for the foreigners, a position which gave him much prestige. He had charge, also, of the Imperial College, where noble Manchu youths were trained for the diplomatic service—at that time confined almost entirely to relations with Russia.[19] As an interpreter Gaubil gained many friends. He developed cordial relations with the Russians and was elected a member of the Imperial Academy at Saint Petersburg, which had on its rolls the names of some of the most brilliant men in Europe. The language used in the Russian diplomatic correspondence was Latin and it fell to Gaubil to translate into the official Manchu the documents arriving from Russia, and into Latin those emanating from the Manchu court. The work of interpreter demanded an exact knowledge of places and peoples, particularly of those areas and races occupying the vast territories bordering on China and Russia. Such knowledge Gaubil possessed to a remarkable degree.

In addition to his membership in the Russian Imperial Academy, Gaubil was a member of the Royal Society of London and of the Académie des Inscriptions of Paris. He was also official correspondent in China of the Académie des Sciences of the French capital. Through these scholarly affiliations he became acquainted with many of the outstanding savants of Europe.

Not only was he well versed in European culture, in classical and modern history, in physics, astronomy, and theology, but he had in addition a profound knowledge of Chinese literature, history, and culture. In his scholarship he was both thorough and precise. He composed many works dealing with the institutions and civilization of China, the erudition of which mark him as undoubtedly the greatest of the Jesuit Sinologists.[20]

Besides his erudition he possessed, as had Ricci and Aleni before him, that mildness of character, that courtesy and tact which had endeared the two earlier missionaries to the hearts of those with whom they came in close contact. He was a man, therefore, who possessed at the same time the resiliency of demeanor of the courtier and the rigid and careful standards of the scholar. It is not to be wondered at that his colleagues referred to him as a man who knew everything and seemed fitted for everything.

Another of the Jesuits whose services were greatly used by Ch'ien Lung was Father Benoit. Trained in mathematics and physics by such masters as Lemonnier and De la Caille, this priest went to China well equipped to meet imperial needs and demands. Of the missionaries in the capital none worked harder and none was called upon to perform such a variety of tasks. He was simultaneously mechanic, engineer, and architect. In conjunction with Castiglione he was responsible for the Western-style buildings at the Yuan Ming Yuan Summer Palace, which until 1860 constituted the chief material record of the Jesuit labors in China.

It was K'ang Hsi who ordered the building of the magnificent Yuan Ming Yuan palace in the Western Hills near Peking but it was his son, the emperor Yung Cheng, who first occupied it, and it was Yung Cheng's son, Ch'ien Lung, who enlarged and beautified its pavilions and gardens. One day Ch'ien Lung was looking through a book of foreign pictures when his eye fell upon an engraving depicting a large fountain in the gardens of a French château. He asked Castiglione about it and, when the latter explained its nature and use, the emperor determined to have one like it. The next question was: Who should construct the fountain? None of the Jesuit missionaries had ever had any experience in the making of fountains. Finally the choice fell on Father Benoit who set to work to make plans and

Portrait of the Jesuit painter Brother Castiglione, done by himself;
an interesting example of the blending of Chinese
and foreign elements

(Reproduced by permission of the owner, Mr. Chen Chao-Ming)

models. These delighted the emperor, as had his other mechanical toys. Then someone suggested that the *shui fa,* as the Chinese called the fountains, should be put in a suitable setting. This decided Ch'ien Lung to build a foreign palace, a Versailles in miniature, within the vast enclosure of the Yuan Ming Yuan. In consequence a piece of ground in the eastern part of the palace, called the Ch'ang Ch'un Yuan, was allotted and Father Castiglione was appointed architect.

In addition to the difficulties inherent in their task the Jesuit builders had to struggle against native prejudice. The people's most widely spread religion was animism. Numbers of them believe to this day in the *feng shui*—that mysterious action of wind and water which has such potent influence on human destiny before and after death. They found, therefore, something to dread in water which gushed many feet out of the ground and in buildings which raised themselves several stories high without respect to direction. However, the priests, with the backing of the emperor, undertook the work. From their lodging in the neighboring town of Hai T'ien they went every morning to the palace. Rules of court etiquette were laid aside that they might enter the gates, and through the oppressive Peking summer they worked steadily at their tasks. When the first fountain—and the hydraulic machine which controlled it—was installed, Ch'ien Lung ordered others to be made. The foreign palace took a number of years to complete, but when finished, it formed as handsome and imposing an architectural group—a "pleasure dome" for the Manchu emperor—as any ever decreed by his Mongol predecessor, Kublai Khan. There were seven or more buildings, mostly of white marble, constructed in the ornate style of the period of Louis XV, with exterior horseshoe staircases and rococo ornament combined with Doric columns and classic Greek peristyles.[21]

The largest of the foreign-style buildings contained the hydraulic machine and the tank from which flowed the water for the fountains. On the west side of this building was the famous "clock of the hours," consisting of twelve marble animals which marked the time by spouting, in succession, a stream of water from their mouths at two-hour intervals. The water fell to the level of this clock by a series of cascades in a marble aqueduct. To the east and to the west of this building were the largest of Benoit's fountains.

In 1860 the Yuan Ming Yuan was looted and destroyed by British and French troops as an act of reprisal for the Sir Harry Parkes incident, and the foreign buildings suffered the common fate. Nothing was left but picturesque marble ruins, with here and there a beautiful Greek column, a handsome window frame or a piece of rococo ornament to tell of the former magnificence of the palace. Moreover, recent acts of vandalism have caused almost all of these ruins to disappear.

Among Benoit's avocations was that of cartography. On the occasion of Emperor Ch'ien Lung's sixtieth birthday he presented to the monarch a map of the world in hemispheres, each five feet in diameter. This map superseded the famous Ricci map, of which mention has been made. Ch'ien Lung ordered it to be sent to the Bureau of Maps where Benoit further embellished it. Later he was given the task of engraving on copper the maps for the atlas of China which had been drawn earlier by his Jesuit colleagues. The emperor had for long admired the fineness of European engraving, which was much superior to the native woodcuts. Finally he determined that the atlas should be engraved according to European methods. The resulting work contained one hundred and four maps, each about one foot by two in measurement. About one hundred copies were made of the volume.

Most of the artists at court had, at one time or another, been commanded to paint studies of Ch'ien Lung's military victories. Late in his reign the emperor decided that engravings should be made of the best of these. He chose sixteen pictures, from the brushes of Castiglione, Attiret, Sichelpart, and Jean Damascene. The missionaries, fearing they could not succeed in engraving these delicate subjects, suggested that they be sent to Europe to be done by the best artisans there. At first it was decided that they should be sent to England, but the French priests in Canton pointed out the preëminence of France in the arts—and so to Paris they went instead. The first four were shipped in 1765, the rest later. They were received with interest, not so much on account of the excellence of their painting as on account of their imperial origin, and the work of engraving was begun under the direction of the celebrated Cochin.[22]

In February, 1775, the beautiful Church of the Immaculate Conception in Peking (*Nan T'ang*) was destroyed by fire. This edifice had been a source of great pride to the Jesuits. Decorated by Gherardini, it was looked upon as one of the finest in the Orient. On its completion K'ang Hsi had presented to the establishment ten thousand taels and a congratulatory scroll. When it burned, the missionaries hastened to court in self-condemnatory contrition for the loss of an imperial writing. Ch'ien Lung received them in a kindly manner and, after causing the records to be searched to see what his father had done in the matter, he donated a similar sum toward a new building. More important still, he gave the priests a scroll, written with his own hand, to replace the lost one.

Considering it an unfilial act to reign longer than his grandfather, Ch'ien Lung abdicated in 1796. Thus the Jesuits were robbed of a patron who, though far from being a champion of their religion, was not blind to the merits of the Faith and, particularly, of the European scholars whose presence in the empire was caused by a desire to spread that Faith. Twenty-three years before the abdication, Pope Clement XIV, in the bull *Dominus ac Redemptor,* had acceded to the demands of the enemies of the order in Spain, Portugal, and France and had suppressed the Society of Jesus.

The last days of the Jesuit mission were clouded with sadness and with quarrels. The news of the suppression of the Society did not officially reach Nanking until June, 1775, but long before that date rumors of catastrophe had reached the Chinese capital. Two problems immediately arose: the jurisdiction of the Jesuit mission and the individual claims of the missionaries in the settlement of the Jesuit "estate." Into the latter problem was injected a bitterness which accorded ill with the profession of priests who had taken the vow of poverty. Fathers Ventavon and Grammont appear to have insisted on an immediate division of property. They were opposed by Father Bourgeois, the superior of the mission, and by the other French Jesuits. The bickerings which ensued and the extraordinary virulence of language may be passed over in silence as the products of disillusionment and despair. The other phase of the quarrel, however, the question of jurisdiction, is more important inasmuch as it introduces questions of national rights and conflicting national interests.

On receipt of the news of suppression, the establishment of the Propaganda in Peking wished to take over the Jesuit property.[28] The members of the Society resented this and appealed to France to name a French successor. Amiot was the leader in this nationalistic movement. "Nous ne sommes plus jésuites," he writes to a friend in November, 1774, "mais nous sommes encore français," and he boldly asserts that the mission is a French, and not a Jesuit, establishment. In answer to Amiot's pleas Bertin, contrôleur général des finances, appointed Bourgeois administrator of the mission and persuaded Louis XVI to write forbidding the French Jesuits to recognize any authority but his own.

The question of jurisdiction was complicated by the fact that the See of Peking was at that time vacant. The nearest bishop, Geoffrey-Xavier de Laimbeckhoven of Nanking, an Austrian Jesuit, asserted his authority. His action was contested by the Bishop of Macao, who had newly arrived bearing the *Dominus ac Redemptor* decree. Each sent his representative to Peking. Most of the French Jesuits accepted the authority of Nanking whereas the Portuguese accepted that of Macao. The Holy See and, as a result, Lisbon, supported the claims of Laimbeckhoven. After much unseemly discord a new bishop, the Augustinian Jean-Damascene Sallusti, arrived to take charge of the vacant see—unfortunately, however, without the documents of his appointment. Thereupon the French Jesuits, led by Amiot, refused to recognize his appointment, basing their action on a ruling of Boniface VIII that a bishop may not assume authority without a copy of the bull appointing him. In spite of opposition, nevertheless, Sallusti was consecrated by the local representatives of the Propaganda and, the opposition persisting in their refusal, the "Bonifacians," as they were called, were excommunicated.

Sallusti then took a significant step. Like the Jesuits in the Rites quarrel, he made the appeal to Caesar, asking the emperor to judge in the matter of the disputed property. A Chinese named Fu was appointed as imperial commissioner to examine the matter and to report. In his report to the emperor, Fu stated: "We have reason to conclude that Bourgeois has not administered the property in a seemly manner and that Ventavon is not exempt from the charge of cupidity."[24] The judgment commanded that the Jesuit priests should administer the property in turn, drawing lots for the post. Grammont drew the first and proceeded to divide the mission property funds, keeping, according to the Jesuit historian,[25] the lion's share for himself!

Meanwhile, under the stress of bitterness and hostility engendered by the quarrels, three of the French priests, Cibot, D'Ollières, and Collas, now old men, succumbed, leaving Amiot and Bourgeois to champion the interests of France. Bishop Sallusti, too, died, after only one year of office. The Franciscan Alexander de Gouvea, who was appointed to succeed him, finally brought peace and amity to the mission.

Amiot had suggested to Paris that the Missions Etrangères should succeed the Society. The Paris mission organization, however, declined the responsibility. Finally it was offered to the Congregation of the Priests of the Mission, known as the Lazarists, who accepted it and took control in May, 1784. Father Raux, who was appointed to take charge of the work, was, apparently, an excellent choice, making himself respected and liked by all parties.

So the members of the great missionary order slowly left the scene of their activities. Ventavon died in 1787; Bourgeois in 1792. Amiot, the greatest of this last group of Jesuits, lingered on for three years more. His last days were saddened by news of the Revolution in France. As if the passing of his order and the ruin of his lifework were not sufficient, he was forced to contemplate across the distance which separated them, the passing of the glory of his beloved France. A stout champion and an ardent lover of his native land, the aged priest grieved at seeing her overrun by "men who were without law, without restraint, without religion, without morals."[26] He died on November 9, 1795.[27]

The life of the mission did not long survive that of its founders. The French Revolution stopped the flow of funds, and, under the new emperors, Chia Ch'ing and Tao Kuang, persecution made the position of the priests in the capital untenable. Christianity in China entered once more a period of eclipse.

Chapter XIV

PERSECUTION AND PROGRESS

THE HISTORY of the Jesuit achievements as Christian missionaries has its periods of growth and decline, which are directly related to the measure of success that the Western scholars were enjoying in the capital. Before Ricci succeeded in reaching Peking, there was constant opposition to the foreign cult, expressed in spasmodic persecution in the provinces of the South. This opposition was offset by acts of friendliness on the part of local officials who had become interested in the scholarly visitors and their strange learning.

While Ricci was in the capital, his constantly increasing reputation protected the mission, but, following his death, official hostility soon began to show itself. The first important attack came in 1616 when Shen Chueh, a member of the Board of Rites, angered at Father Vagnoni, denounced the missionaries as members of a seditious sect—comparing them to the notorious White Lotus Society whose activities were always a matter of concern to the government. In Shansi Fathers Vagnoni and Semedo were seized and put in an iron cage for thirty days while they were being transported south to Kwangtung. This attack resulted in an edict ordering all the missionaries to Canton for deportation. Not all the priests obeyed the order. Many of them hid themselves and continued their work secretly. Several lay brothers lost their lives at this time, as well as a number of Christian converts. The same malevolent official reopened the attack in 1622, with similar charges against the foreign priests. Once more the missionaries were forced to flee. The persecution, however, appears to have died out with the death of its originator.[1]

The last days of the Ming dynasty were comparatively free from organized persecution. The next period of danger for the mission came from Yang Kuang-hsien who launched the attack on Schall,

[1] For notes to chap. xiv, see pp. 325–327.

described in a previous chapter. There seems to have been no wide-spread persecution at this time, although Christianity was again officially denounced and several foreign priests lost their lives as a result of the hardships they had to undergo. Following this short period of opposition to the Faith (1664–1671) came years of undoubted prosperity during which the mission grew rapidly. Then, in 1692, the viceroy Chang at Hangchow turned against Father Intorcetta, who for years had been laboring in that city. This official, who had been a friend of the Jesuits' arch-enemy Yang Kuang-hsien, issued an edict which he caused to be posted in the public places of seventy towns of the province of Chekiang. The document was a fair example of official vituperation. It set forth the adequacy of the three official cults (*san ch'iao*) to fill the spiritual needs of the people and forbade the adoption of Christianity "with many blasphemies against the Faith." Chang then ordered the arrest of Father Intorcetta on the charge of printing religious books with painted images of God, for distribution among the people. The Jesuit priest, who was then over sixty, was seized and dragged before the magistrate of Hangchow. When the latter showed signs of being just to the foreign priest, his report to his superior was rejected, and other officials were sent to harass the missionary. Chang was, perhaps, kept from more violent measures by the knowledge that Father Intorcetta had been treated with singular honor when the emperor had passed through the city three years earlier. The Jesuit priest, fearing a general persecution, wrote urgently to his superiors in Peking, whereupon Father Gerbillon appealed to his friend, Prince Sosan, for assistance.

In the meantime the persecution spread through the province. The servants of God were "tracked like wild beasts and were obliged to flee to the mountains after hiding their images and books, to save them from profanation at the hands of idolaters."[2] Prince Sosan's efforts to obtain the release of Intorcetta by direct negotiation with Chang proved fruitless, and Fathers Pereyra, Thomas, Gerbillon, and Bouvet determined to appeal directly to K'ang Hsi. On December 1,

1691, they appeared at court and were received by the high imperial official Ch'ao. Throwing themselves on their knees they laid their case before him, begging the Son of Heaven to revoke all edicts inimical to the Faith and to allow the messengers of God to preach freely throughout the empire. As a result they were allowed to present a formal petition. In this document, couched in the servile terms with which it was customary to address an Oriental monarch, they dwelt on the purity of the Faith and its teaching of the highest virtues and the strictest morality. They denied that there was anything in it subversive of public morals or of the laws and traditions of the empire.

The Board of Rites, to whom all petitions of this character were referred, sent in a hostile report to the emperor. The latter returned it, thus intimating that a more favorable reply was expected. A second report, still unfavorable, was prepared. The Jesuits, hearing of this, appealed once more to their friend, Prince Sosan, who personally took the case before K'ang Hsi himself. He was so successful that he was able to appear before the Board of Rites with the approbation of the emperor and to speak forcefully and eloquently in favor of the missionaries' cause. As a result the *Li Pu* drew up the famous edict of 1692 in favor of the Christian religion, which has already been discussed. This edict effectively put an end to persecution for a number of years.

It was a quarter of a century before the mission ran into serious difficulties again. In 1717 Chang Mao, a high official of Canton and a hater of the Christians, memorialized the throne advocating the prosecution as rebels of all those who professed the Faith; the demolition of their chapels and the punishments of lax officials. The result was an edict forbidding those who did not possess the imperial patent (*p'iao*) from residing in the empire. This edict led the way for others of a harsher nature.

The Board of Rites, meanwhile, had decreed that Canton should be closed to foreigners and that the Christian religion should be banned, but, in answer to long and continued protests from the mis-

sionaries, the emperor refused to endorse the decree. He ordered the
port to be reopened and the decision of the board suppressed, giving
as his reason that he was not willing to retract his edict of 1692.[3]

The next trouble started in Fukien. In 1723 the viceroy of that
province suddenly turned against the Christians. According to De
Mailla, the immediate cause of the persecution was the indiscretion
of two Spanish Dominicans who had violated Chinese notions of
propriety by holding services common to men and women. The
Jesuits had long since learned that among the customs of the country
which could not lightly be ignored were those dealing with the
mingling of the sexes and also with the native prejudice against the
practice of monasticism by either men or women.

The prefect of the *hsien* of Fu An, in Fukien, had notified the
viceroy of Christian activities in his district. The viceroy, Mu An-pao
by name, thereupon issued a proclamation publicly condemning the
foreign cult. At the same time he memorialized the throne, citing
cases in which the "sect" had violated Chinese traditions. He advised
that it be suppressed and that the Europeans (with the exception of
those at court) be banished to Macao. Before action was officially
taken by the Board of Rites in Peking, Mu An-pao issued another
edict, calling on the missionaries to surrender their imperial *p'iao*
and retire to Macao. The edict also ordered that their temples be
confiscated.

In the proclamation which announced the imperial edict the viceroy Mu An-pao gives his reasons for opposing the Christian religion.
He says:

I have examined this religion carefully and I have found this: Those who
profess it regard our Sages and ancestors as demons, do not bear them any
respect and do not perform the usual ceremonies. At the death of their
parents they do not grieve. After the death of a wife the husband does not
marry again. They look favorably upon young men and women who do not
marry. Men and women speak in a low voice to the master in a retired place
[referring to the confessional]. These customs are contrary to the five relationships [of the Chinese classics] and they ruin the doctrines of our Sages. I consider this sect the most pernicious of all the false sects.[4]

The edict of the viceroy was one of the strongest and most violent which had been launched against the Christian mission. Since Mu An-pao was of the highest rank and enjoyed a great reputation throughout the empire, his attack on Christianity was seriously received in the capital. His memorial was finally acted upon by the Board of Rites in accordance with his suggestions and ratified by Yung Cheng on January 11, 1724. However, the emperor added a note commanding all local officials to give the foreign missionaries proper escort to Macao so that they would be protected from indignities.

The Jesuits soon saw that this edict, if strictly carried out, meant the ruin of Christian missions all over China. The priests at court, therefore, used every effort to obtain a reconsideration of the question. Day and night they lingered in the antechambers of influential princes. They kowtowed in the imperial courtyards to men who had the ear of the Son of Heaven and on bended knees they implored the assistance of their official friends, begging that those missionaries at least who had received the imperial *p'iao* might be allowed to remain. They desisted from their efforts to obtain reconsideration of the edict only when they were told that further importunity would endanger their own position at court and even bring about their expulsion from the empire. The only concession they obtained was that the priests in the interior should be sent to Canton instead of to Macao.[5]

In the meantime, even before the edict had been published, rumor had carried to the provinces the news that a change in court favor was imminent. Immediately persecutions arose. Churches were destroyed in Chihli, Shansi, Honan, Kwangsi, Fukien and elsewhere. In some places mission stations were turned into hospitals, granaries, schools, and other public buildings. Priests were insulted on the streets, and native converts suffered severely.

The edict of 1724 had been published throughout the empire with the result that all missionaries were forced to leave their stations to retire to Canton, where they were allowed to remain. Before long, however, they were secretly stealing back to their flocks, who were faring ill without their guidance. More than forty of them succeeded in reaching their stations, but the task was an arduous one.

Owing to its proscription everywhere, Christianity had now reached a stage where the European servants of the faith, by their very presence in the country, marked themselves as transgressors of the law of the empire. From this time on there was constant need of secrecy. To meet this need the priests evolved a system of quiet preparation and penetration for both old and new missionaries.[6] The new priests were met at the port by a Chinese convert in whom the mission had implicit confidence. It was the duty of this man to pilot the new-comer through all the dangers and perils of the road; to do this he relied chiefly on the Catholic communities in the country through which he and the newcomer passed. The priest would be dressed in Chinese clothes but, knowing little or nothing of the language, was entirely at the mercy of his guide, on whose ingenuity depended his life. Often the new missionary would be forced to feign sickness to avoid awkward questions; now and again he would simulate dumb-ness to relieve himself of the necessity of answering questions. Arriv-ing at his station, he would shut himself off from all but a few converts, for whom he would perform such offices of the Church as his vocabu-lary permitted, and for a period he would do nothing but study the language. Then, having become sufficiently proficient in it, he would take over the work of the mission.

The life was difficult and dangerous. Father Couteux relates how, in 1727, he returned from Canton into Hupeh and Honan, traveling as much as possible by boat, in constant danger of being discovered and dragged before a magistrate. Attacked by illness, he suffered greatly from the heat and the inconveniences of the voyage.[7] About the same time Father Barborier made the journey from Canton to Chekiang in a coffin, coming out only at night for fear of detection by customs officials.[8] Father Loppe, penetrating to the central prov-inces, was betrayed by a renegade Christian and obtained his liberty only by a bribe of two thousand taels to the local magistrate.[9]

It soon became known in Peking that the missionaries were returning secretly to their stations, and Parennin, whose natural astuteness
and close connection with the court kept him constantly in touch
with the trend of events, began to fear a storm of unprecedented violence. He therefore urged the priests to refrain from such a procedure
for the time being; moreover, he advised the missionaries in the country, wherever possible, to retire again to Canton. At this port they
remained, preaching in a quiet way and going about the ordinary
business of their calling until, in August, 1732, they were summarily
ordered to Macao. Even their church in Canton was threatened. The
local officials offered to pay a nominal sum for it, but the priests refused to surrender the title deeds. Some of them, being altogether discouraged by the situation, wished to embark for Europe on a vessel
which happened to be in the harbor at the time. Even this they
were not allowed to do, however, because the officials suspected them
of wishing to land again on another part of the coast. They were
forced, then, to Macao. As soon as they had left Canton, the local
mandarins began to imprison and torture their converts.

The situation in the provinces was an extremely gloomy one. In
the meantime, the fortunes of Christianity in the capital were going
from bad to worse. After agreeing to allow a few missionaries to remain in Canton to act as agents for those at the court in Peking,
Yung Cheng suddenly took a different course. Influenced, doubtless,
by the vitriolic attacks of the Canton officials, he called Pedrini and
others to court, immediately after the New Year of 1733, and told
them that he had decided to expel them all from the empire. He gave
as his reason their supposed lack of reverence for their ancestors. The
missionaries replied that filial piety was a Christian as well as a Chinese doctrine, and they presented a copy of their religious books to
prove the truth of their assertions.[10] The emperor consented to recon-
sider the matter, and the affair dragged on from month to month
without anything being done. The attitude at court continued to be
distinctly hostile to the priests, and they were forced to be careful

in order not to make an enemy who might start active propaganda against them. They were often close to disaster, as is shown by the fact that in 1734 they were reduced to bribery in order to persuade the scribes to omit from an edict a clause ordering a search for missionaries in the provinces.

When Ch'ien Lung ascended the throne in 1736, it soon became obvious that conditions would be little better for the Faith. The first important persecution began in the capital itself. In 1737 a native catechist named Liu Erh was caught by an official in one of the houses for newborn foundlings supported by the government in Peking, in the act of baptizing moribund infants. He was taken before the local court and tortured in order to make him confess that Christian converts were acquired by bribery. After considerable ill-treatment he was burdened with a *cangue*—a huge wooden collar used to humiliate criminals—on which was written the inscription "criminal for being of the Christian religion." Then hostile officials, taking advantage of a temporary absence of the Jesuits' official representative at court, placarded the city with virulent attacks on the Christian religion. In reply the missionaries, in a long memorial, appealed to the emperor, referring to past services and former imperial favors. The affair was referred to the Board of Punishments which protested against the assumption, by the Jesuits, of judicial authority over their converts. The missionaries were told that they themselves were allowed to carry on the functions of their religion but that the Chinese and Manchus were forbidden to take part in them. The answer of Parennin is an eloquent argument: "We have not come ten thousand leagues," says the aged priest, "to ask permission to become Christians; to pray to God in secret."¹ Castiglione, long a favorite with the emperor on account of his skill in painting, took the bold step of appealing directly to the monarch. Finally, a compromise was made. Official announcement was made that Liu Erh was punished for disobeying the laws and not for being a Christian, and the hostile placards were suppressed.

Soon, however, it came to the ears of the missionaries that the written attacks had been scattered through the provinces without their being followed by the more favorable government announcement. The results were disastrous. Once more the Jesuits were forced to use their powers of diplomacy until they succeeded in getting the favorable statement included in the official gazette. In order to obviate the ill effects of the omission, they caused thousands of copies of this pronunciamento to be printed and scattered throughout the empire. The evil, however, had been done. Minor persecutions arose everywhere. News of trouble came from Shansi, Shantung, and other provinces. It may be presumed that opposition to the missionaries at this time was general; the friendly viceroy of Chihli told them that he alone had suppressed seventeen denunciatory documents, addressed to him by scholars and officials. Government hostility having once raised its head, all who, for one reason or another, had a grudge against the foreign religion and its foreign or native exponents took the opportunity to pay off old scores.

Again the attack slowly died down. Then, in 1746, there broke out the most violent persecution in the history of the mission. At this time there seems to have been a general disquietude throughout the empire regarding so-called false sects. The Mahayana Buddhists were being bitterly attacked in western China. In the west and southwest the White Lotus Sect (*Pai Lien Kuo*) was giving the government a great deal of trouble. In 1749, the *Lo Hwei* society was so severely persecuted in Fukien that it broke into open revolt, resulting in an active campaign for its extermination. Evidently there was great uneasiness in the minds of the officials. They were suspicious of anything which produced crowds or gatherings or which involved strange rites of any kind. What more natural, then, than that the Christian church, now classified among the "false sects," should be suspected and that persecution should follow?

The attack on Christianity which began in Fukien at this time is peculiarly interesting on account of the number and variety of accusations brought against the missionaries. An official named Fan was sent by the viceroy to investigate certain charges against Christians in the city of Fu An, the scene of the 1723 persecution. He quickly made himself notorious by the harshness of his methods. Rushing soldiers into the territory under suspicion, he invaded houses, made wholesale arrests, even of people who were in no way connected with the religion, and haled the miserable natives before the local magistrate. The accusations against the mission, formulated in his report to his superior, sum up clearly the anti-Christian attitude of officialdom. They were as follows:

1. That the priests are preaching in China contrary to the laws of the empire.
2. That they obtain converts in return for a payment of two taels and through the hope of paradise and the fear of hell.
3. That they choose the most fervent and make them catechists, placing them at the head of fifty Christians.
4. That the Christians do not honor their ancestors but pay extravagant honors to a man named Jesus.
5. That the missionaries have a rule requiring all converts to come twice a year to confess their sins.
6. That Christian girls and women wear neither silks nor ornaments nor jewels and among them there are some who have renounced marriage.
7. That in some Chinese houses there are secret chambers where the priests administer bread and wine and anoint with oil.[12]

This persecution arose in a district where Spanish Dominicans were working. The importance attached to the cult of virginity in Catholic conventual life resulted in the bringing forward again of the old charges of moral laxity. Fan seized a number of nuns and tried unsuccessfully to induce them, by means of torture, to confess having had immoral relations with the priests. During the following year five Dominicans, including the aged Peter Sanz, Bishop of Mauicastre, and Fathers Royo, Alcobar, Serrano, and Diaz were seized and accused of impudicity and magic, of the killing of little children, and of the drawing from their heads of a philter to be used as an aphrodisiac. They were also accused of the use of European drugs for purposes of abortion. Candles found in their possession were supposed to be made from the fat of little children, merely because they were whiter than the native product. The remains of a dead brother awaiting transportation to Europe were seized and said to be the bones of murdered children. Although the officials were probably not so ignorant as to believe any of these silly rumors, such reports served—as the officials intended—to stir up the people against the Christians. The priests were dragged from tribunal to tribunal, cruelly tortured, and finally sentenced to death. The viceroy himself went to Peking to obtain the necessary permission from the Board of Punishments for the carrying out of the sentence. On May 26, 1749, the bishop was publicly beheaded—the other four Dominicans being later strangled in prison.[13]

Shortly afterwards an order was sent to all officials ordering them to make an investigation concerning Christianity and to punish all minor officials who had been lax in their duty. This order, like many others, was interpreted according to the feelings of the local official. Churches and mission property were seized in several of the provinces. Converts were imprisoned and tortured; stories of apostasy were mingled with tales of heroism under cruel treatment. Many, like Father Beuth, fell into the hands of virulently hostile officials. This priest, while on his way to Macao, was seized by a petty magistrate of Canton named Hsiang. He was beaten and so badly abused that he died shortly afterwards.[14] The same official was responsible for the harsh treatment meted out to Father Abormio. Arrested in Shansi and dragged from prison to prison for eleven months, this priest had suffered several kinds of torture before he fell into the hands of Hsiang, who had him placed in a dungeon where an attempt was made to stifle him with fumes from damp paper. This having failed, through the sympathetic actions of a fellow prisoner on his behalf, Father Abormio was locked in a narrow cell and chained in such a way that he could neither stand nor sit. Another priest, Father Lefevre, was treated in the same manner and left in this position for months.

Meanwhile persecution spread to other parts. "On all sides," writes

Father Benoit, "one hears nothing but the groanings of the Christians who are enchained, put to torture and treated in every harsh way imaginable that they may be forced to renounce Jesus Christ."[15] In Hukuang, where there were flourishing Christian communities, persecution and torture accompanied devastation and general ruin of the mission. In Kiangnan two Jesuits, Tristram de Artemis, an Italian, and Antonio Joseph Henriques, a Portuguese, were arrested by the viceroy, a friend of Hsiang, the anti-Christian bigot of Canton, and were strangled on September 12, 1748. In many places converts were seized and tortured, and nuns were beaten on the feet to make them apostatize.

The persecution was felt in Peking, in the very shadow of the throne. Father da Rocha was arrested by the governor of that city for giving reliquaries and images to native converts. Ch'ien Lung, being appealed to, met the prayers of Castiglione with a stern rebuke, although Da Rocha was finally released. At the same time the Portuguese authorities at Macao were forced to sign a document forbidding the teaching of Christianity to Chinese.[16]

It is probable that other disasters to foreign priests were prevented by the general amnesty proclaimed by the emperor on the occasion of his victories in central Asia.[17] Nevertheless, for a number of years the edicts against Christianity continued to be rigidly enforced. The constantly lengthening duration of these periodic attacks on the work of the missionaries shows that opposition to the Faith was slowly increasing. Gradually the persecution of 1747 subsided, however, and the priests attempted to return secretly to their labors. They were forced, generally, to live in the country, at the house of a convert, since they dared not risk living in the cities. For places of worship, native dwellings replaced the churches now in ruins. Conditions were sadly changed from the time when they had been secure in the protection of the emperor and had preached openly throughout a large part of the empire. Father Roy, a French Jesuit, declares that it was the rich convert who suffered most from persecution, which, he says, "was pushed to an excess against all the customs of the country." The same priest, in a gloomy letter written in 1795, says:

Without fire or shelter, almost always wandering and vagabond, like outlaws who dare not settle in any one spot and whose best friends dare not shelter them, we have for several years, in different places and at different times, seen the storm fall on our Orders. The monks of St. Dominic and of our Order have been put to death for the Faith and others have been imprisoned and tormented with the most frightful tortures.[18]

In 1769 a violent attack on the Christian religion occurred in Hukuang, in the course of which natives were imprisoned and tortured. About the same time persecution arose in Peking, where members of a seditious sect were discovered with rosaries in their possession, said to have been given them by a Chinese Christian. On investigation this Chinese could not be found, and the persecution would have died out, had it not been for a memorial addressed to the throne by the Manchu president of the Board of Mathematics. This document was referred to the Board of Punishments. This board ordered all Christians to report to the local official but, as this action involved the danger of being forced to deny their Faith, the converts neglected to do so. The memorial mentioned a score of Christian officials at court, who were brought before the board for examination. Some apostatized, others were whipped and tortured. Finally, the persecution died out.

Among the mandarins was Joseph Ma, an important official in the capital, where he was in control of the police. Brought before the court of the grand officials of the empire he refused to give up his Faith and was therefore turned over to the Board of Punishments. Taking advantage probably of one of the periodic absences of the emperor from the capital, his judges condemned him to be beaten and sent into slavery. Loaded with chains he passed through the streets, amid the tears of the populace, the Jesuit writer tells us.[19] This incident was followed by a thorough examination of the bannermen, some of whom were discovered to have embraced Christianity and were accordingly treated with the utmost cruelty.

In more or less constant difficulties in the provinces, the Jesuits nevertheless continued to retain friendly relations with the emperor at Peking. It is a curious commentary on the inconsistencies of the situation that Ventavon is found writing, in the year of the Joseph Ma incident, praising the clemency of the emperor while Cibot, in 1771, reëchoes his praises. In an edict which appeared the same year, Christianity was condemned as being contrary to the laws of the empire but having nothing in it which was false or bad.[20] It is doubtful whether Ch'ien Lung himself was personally very hostile to the Faith. In a system of theoretically absolute monarchy such as that of China, the monarch was forced to rely on the judgments of his closest officials. When persecution occurred, Ch'ien Lung seems to have acted always at the wish of some mandarin who was impelled by jealousy or ignorance.

The practice of secret penetration into the empire still went on. A letter from the hostile president of the Board of Mathematics to the viceroy of Kwangtung in 1765 resulted in such a strict inspection of the avenues of ingress that for a time missionaries, unable to penetrate into the provinces, were forced to return to Macao. In 1767 two German Franciscans were seized in Canton, and the viceroy threatened the Portuguese authorities at Macao with dire punishment if the practice were not stopped. Two other priests caught in the neighborhood of the port, obtained their release only after giving a bribe of twenty thousand taels.[21] In Shensi a revolt of the White Lotus sect was suppressed, and the Christians once more suffered as a result of the rebellion. In 1769 trouble arose in Szechuan where Father Gleyo of the Missions Etrangères was seized, cruelly beaten, and imprisoned for eight years.[22] This incident brought on an investigation and subsequent persecution. Once again Christians were classed with rebellious sects or tribes, this time with the semisavage Miao-tze! "It is very strange," writes Bourgeois at this time, "that two hundred years of experience has not taught the Chinese that Christians are faithful subjects of the empire." The answer to such an enigma must lie in the fact that even after this lapse of time the Christian religion was still misunderstood by a large number of people and its strange doctrines, even when the officials deigned to study them, were associated with attempts to break down the social and political order.

In 1774 the rebellion of Wang Lun in Chihli was put down with great severity; here again the Christians were confused with the dreaded White Lotus sect. Another attempt was made to place Christianity on the list of all false sects, but the Board of Crimes, possibly acting in accordance with the wishes of the emperor, refused to do this. Ch'ien Lung with his military victories behind him and the country unified, was disposed to be more moderate toward the religion of his foreign scholars. The last ten years of the Jesuit mission appear to have been relatively calm.

But against this story of intermittent persecution stands a solid record of accomplishment. The statistics available are for the most part fragmentary and to a great degree unreliable but they serve to give some idea of the Jesuit success in opening missions and in converting the natives.

The period of early struggle, which came to an end in 1610 with the death of Ricci, shows the mission expanding slowly. Trigault reports that, whereas in 1607 there were only seven hundred Christians in the empire, in 1613 there were five thousand. In 1611 a church was built at Nanking, where Fathers Semedo and Vagnoni were working. The most prosperous of the early missions, that of Hangchow, was established in the following year by Father Cattaneo. At this time there were four chief centers of propaganda: Ch'ao Chou in Kwangtung, Nanchang in Kiangu, Nanking in Kiangsu, and Peking in the North. Gradually these areas were enlarged until there were missionaries in every province of the empire. The decade 1620–1627 showed encouraging development. By 1624 the Peking mission had three Jesuit fathers and a brother and reported several conversions at court. Nineteen new priests arrived at this time to take care of the six mission centers in the provinces. It was toward the end of this period, too, that the mission at Sianfu, Shensi, one of the most successful of the Jesuit establishments, was started.

The first quarter of the seventeenth century was the period when Jesuit achievements included the conversion of a number of eminent scholars. Under the influence of Ricci, Paul Hsü and Léon Li had been baptized and had proved themselves valiant fighters for the Faith in the capital. At Hangchow the latter had been responsible for the conversion of one of his relatives, Yang Ting-yun, an ardent Buddhist, who was baptized with the name of Michael.[23] These three form the great triumvirate of Chinese Christian officialdom. They were able to interest many other scholars in the foreign religion, and it is not surprising to find Father Semedo writing at this time: "The wintry season of tempests and persecutions is past, and spring is bringing into being flowers worthy of the paradise of God."[24]

The thirteen thousand converts reported in 1627 had by the close of the following decade been increased to forty thousand.[25] By the end of the Ming dynasty there were missions in all the provinces but Szechuan, Yunnan and Kweichow.[26] In 1657 fourteen Jesuit recruits arrived and two years later the mission was augmented with an additional twelve priests. When the attack of Yang Kuang-hsien occurred, the mission had arrived at a degree of prosperity which attests itself in striking figures. Father Martini asserts that in 1650 there were 150,000 Christians in the empire; according to Father Intorcetta, 104,980 converts were added in the period 1650–1667.[27] Untrustworthy as some of these figures may be, they indicate, at any rate, a rapid expansion of Christianity in the empire at this time.[28]

In the meantime the other Church orders had not been idle: the Franciscans, the Dominicans, the Augustinians, and later the Missions Etrangères and the Lazarists, all sent their representatives to join in this harvest of souls. The early attempts of the Franciscans and Dominicans in Ricci's time were generally unsuccessful, but both the orders later expanded their mission work with success. Spanish Franciscans started work in Fukien as early as 1635. Five Italian Franciscans, who arrived in 1684, labored chiefly in the northern and central provinces. Joining those who had arrived in 1672, they had, by 1687, established missions also in Kiangsi and Kiangnan. By the end of the century there were twenty members of the order in the empire.

The Dominicans, working from their base in the Philippines, which had been established at the end of the sixteenth century, made repeated attempts to enter the empire in the early days.[29] Angelo Coqui, who arrived in 1630, appears to have been successful for a short time. When he died in 1633, he was succeeded by Juan Baptista de Morales, mention of whom has been made in connection with the Rites controversy. In 1637 the records show that five Dominicans— and three Franciscans—entered Fukien and were forced into hiding.[30] In 1655 the Dominicans built a church at Foochow in the same year that the Franciscans, with the assistance of Schall, started their mission at Tsinanfu in Shantung. The Dominicans shared with the Jesuits the prosperity which preceded the Yang persecution. In 1665 they had eleven residences, about twenty churches and some ten thousand neophytes in Chekiang, Fukien, and Kwangtung alone. Between 1673 and 1674 eight new priests arrived to work, chiefly in the province of Fukien. Chief among the Dominican converts was Gregory Lopez, who had the distinction of being the first native bishop. He was made vicar apostolic of Nanking with the title of Bishop of Basileus in 1674.[31]

The Augustinian missionaries arrived a little later. By 1722 eleven priests of the order had entered China. As early as 1687, however, they reported twelve hundred converts.[32]

The eighteenth century opened with the Jesuit mission in a flourishing condition. The arrival of the French Jesuits in 1688 had started a new and important chapter in the history of Christianity in China. By 1700 the members of the Society had established themselves in Chihli, Shantung, Shansi, Shensi, Honan, Hupeh, Kwangtung, Chekiang, Kiangnan, and Kiangsi. In the last-mentioned province alone, there were one hundred churches. New priests were continuing to arrive: fifteen in 1698, sixteen in 1701.[33]

By the end of the seventeenth century the French arrivals were beginning to take over part of the work heretofore carried on by the Portuguese.[34] Father Noël, in 1703, writes optimistically of the situation. He speaks of the new Portuguese missions at Tsinanfu and at Tientsin, of the French establishments at Jaochow, Kiaking, and Wuchow, and of others in the provinces of Hukuang[35] and Chekiang. He admits, however, that the majority of the converts were from the poorer classes. Persecution had by this time begun to alienate the sympathies of the scholar-official class and the Rites controversy was bringing suspicion of the Faith to the minds of those who had been brought up to look upon the Confucian canon as the supreme law, the cornerstone of the state.

At this time there were very few missions in the border provinces of the West. There were only four or five in Honan and Shensi and as yet there were none in Szechuan, Yunnan, or Kweichow. In the other provinces, however, the additions to the Church in the last decade of the seventeenth century were great in number. The Jesuit records claim that in this period (1685–1705) thirty thousand were baptized in the capital alone. The period marks the climax of the Jesuit success. It is possible that the number of Christians throughout the empire may now have reached the sum of three hundred thousand.[36]

Then persecutions began to take their toll. Henceforth the figures in the records are smaller and more indefinite. It became progressively more difficult to work in the provinces, and much of the work had to be carried on in secret. The work did go on, however. In 1728 records show that more than four thousand converts received communion in Peking. In the same year there were ten priests in Shansi, Shensi, Hukuang, and Szechuan, nine priests in Kiangsu province,[37] and twenty-four or twenty-six in Kwangtung. The success of the foreign cult was, of course, greatest in the capital, where the emperor was always a potential check on the malevolence of officials. When Ch'ien Lung succeeded to the throne, the three churches in Peking were still openly served by twenty-two European Jesuits—though seven of these devoted most of their energies to the court—and six Chinese. The French Jesuits annually baptized between five hundred and six hundred natives and the Portuguese an equal number. In 1740 it was reported that there were thirty to thirty-five thousand converts in the region north of the Chinese Wall alone. Three years later the Peking mission announced the baptism of twelve hundred converts.[38] In 1745 the mission in Honan appears to have been flourishing; fourteen years later it was reported that there were two to three thousand Christian converts in the neighboring province of Hupeh, served by six foreign and three Chinese Jesuits.

There are few statistics for the last twenty years of the Jesuit regime, although in 1773 the Nanchang mission in Kiangsi reported the baptism of one hundred Chinese. The historian of the Macartney embassy, which visited China in 1793, learned from the Jesuits that there were at most one hundred and sixty thousand Christians in the empire at that time.[39]

The Lazarists arrived in 1784 to take the place of the Jesuits.[40] From that date until 1830 apparently only eighteen members of the Congregation worked in China and fourteen in Macao.[41] This small number is eloquent testimony of the decline of the mission.

Chapter XV

PRIESTS AND COURTIERS

JESUIT DIPLOMACY, which had been put to such rude tests in Europe and which had so brilliantly met them, had no field more difficult, no task more arduous, than the spiritual conquest of the Middle Kingdom. For the missionary in China it did not suffice to show the courage and spirit of martyrdom of a Lallement or a Brébeuf. Not by the supreme sacrifice of an exemplary death could the European missionary hope to achieve his ends but by the arduous act of living on a high intellectual and moral plane; by the constant exercise of his mental powers, by his tact, and by his prudence. It was as a scholar, primarily, that he was to be weighed in the balances of Chinese favor. The difficulties of his task were inherent in the solidity and relative impermeability of the civilization of the country he was invading.

Nowhere were intellectual arrogance and narrow provincialism supported by such a solid structure of racial accomplishment and national culture. Across the centuries the Chinese saying, reported by the medieval traveler, Haytoun the Armenian, rang persistently: "The Chinese have two eyes, the Franks one—the rest of the world is blind."[1] The Confucian official class—whose inspiration came from a system equally as persuasive as the scholasticism of medieval Europe; whose regime was guided by the unquestioned wisdom of the classics; whose authority was established by the highly centralized power of the throne and reaffirmed and strengthened by the force of local tradition based on the family—this class formed a wall of conservatism hard to demolish.

That the gravity of the task was never underestimated by the Jesuits was demonstrated from the beginning. Francis Xavier himself, although realizing that the qualities of a true missionary were pa-

---

[1] For notes to chap. xv, see pp. 327–330.

tience, prudence, purity of habits, and mildness of speech and demeanor, soon discovered that for China something more was necessary.
By his first contacts with the Far East he was persuaded that a civilization so deeply rooted in cultural ideals of a high character could be
reached only by an appeal to the intellectual qualities which produced
those ideals. Of the Japanese Xavier had already written:

> Only because they believed we were scholars were they disposed to listen to
> us on the subject of their religion. ... Men of letters and of virtue are those
> whom we receive most readily because they are the ones who will be most
> useful in converting the people.

These words are significant as forecasting the strategy of the order in
China.

This policy of winning the country from the top down was adopted
enthusiastically by the first great missionary, Matteo Ricci. There
were several things in China which augured well for the success of
the mission. In the first place there was the nature of the government,
which was in form that of an absolute monarchy with the emperor
as the representative of Heaven on earth. In a sense the government
was semi-theocratic. A contemporary writer points out that this was
a form of political organization peculiarly suited to the Jesuit methods:

> Not being able to conquer the globe by the force of arms, they resolved to
> subdue it in the name of the Eternal God. This is why they never ceased to
> exalt the theocracies. Under this emblem they strove to disguise their sacred
> despotism. This was the picture of the government which they desired ar-
> dently to establish in all countries.[2]

In the second place the appeal to the rational in man was an outstanding element of Jesuit strategy. Mysticism the members of the
Society certainly possessed, and a willingness to sacrifice themselves,
as the records of their missions clearly show; but at bottom their system rested on a humanistic basis, derived from a recognition of the
spiritual limitations of man. The Confucian system, the chief source
of government and morals in the China of their day, seems to have
been specially created to meet their needs. It was a system which had

as its center the moral aspirations of man, his excellencies, and his weaknesses. Under it the scholar and the official were of one class; learning and statecraft were bound in close alliance. Nothing is more natural, then, than that Ricci and the early Jesuits should have made their primary aim the winning of this class.

They had to deal with a group which for centuries had been hidebound in its knowledge and motivated by the conviction that outside the borders of the empire there was nothing but ignorance and barbarism. "The more knowledge there is in the head of a scholar," says one of the missionaries, "the more conceit there is also. That is to say, the more obstinacy concerning his learning and the more esteem for the Chinese doctrines, the greater prejudices against foreign nations"; and he adds, "What a long way a Chinese scholar must go before he begins to realize that a European can teach him anything."[3] Jesuit policy was, of course, dependent on two things: first, on impressing the scholar-officials with the wealth and power of foreign scholarship and, second, on so hiding or disguising these new ideas and new riches that they would not offend the susceptibilities of the ultra-conservative native scholar. It was a narrow path to tread between an undignified excess of humility on the one hand and an assumption of superiority on the other. Ricci and his colleagues could never have succeeded, had they not been willing to lose, to a great degree, their identities as men from the West. They endeavored, therefore, to eliminate from their appearance and personalities all foreign character and, meticulously and carefully, to cultivate Chinese psychology.

The first lesson they learned was in externals. Very soon they discovered that in adopting the garb of the Buddhist bonze they had made a serious mistake, since Buddhism at the moment was in a state of eclipse and the priests of that faith were heartily despised by the intellectuals. They therefore discarded Buddhist robes for the dress of the scholar-official; the grave deportment, the slowness of movement, the cult of the *li* of Chinese behavior, all were studiously copied.

At the same time they let their beards grow to give themselves the venerable appearance befitting a scholar.[4]

In their conversations with native scholars the Jesuits quickly learned that certain topics were dangerous. At first they had to refrain from any reference to religion, thus bringing on themselves the bitter criticism of their opponents in the other orders of the Church. Parennin, writing as late as 1735, has well expressed their position:

Experience has taught our older missionaries, that when it is a question of preaching to the nobles and literati of this nation, one does not generally succeed by starting with the mysteries of our holy religion. Some of these appear obscure to them and others incredible. The arguments they put forward are that foreigners have no conception of religion which is comparable to their great doctrine. If they listen for a moment, therefore, they quickly turn the conversation to another subject.[5]

It was this concession to the prejudices of their scholar hosts which created the impression in Europe that the missionaries were refraining from teaching some of the important mysteries of the Christian faith. Pascal leads the attack in his widely read *Lettres provinciales,* in which he violently condemns the Jesuits for their reluctance to preach Christ crucified, a charge repeated again and again in the course of the next hundred years. It is true that Ricci in his famous work *T'ien Chu shih I* passes lightly over this cornerstone of Christian doctrine. The same missionary, in the early days, took down from his walls a picture of the Virgin Mary because he found that the portrait of a woman in such a place offended Chinese ideas of propriety. But there is no proof that Ricci or his colleagues ever willfully suppressed the traditional figure of the Mother of God any more than there is evidence that they eliminated the teaching of the Passion because on certain occasions they thought it unwise to display the figure of the crucified Christ. Jesuit apologists point out that even Saint Paul himself, in the presence of the great culture of Greece, used the same eclectic methods. It seems clear, that, although they may at times have acted with excessive prudence, they cannot justly be accused of sacrificing any of the tenets of their religion.

Their policy at the beginning, then, was to find a middle ground on which they could meet the native scholar, gradually gain his confidence and admiration, and, that obtained, expound and develop their religious views. To make use of this strategy both unlimited tact and profound knowledge were necessary. With tact, Ricci and his colleagues seem to have been well supplied. It was one of the chief glories of their mission that they were equally well supplied with knowledge. Ricci himself was a pupil of the famous Clavius, and most of his colleagues were trained in at least one branch of science. It was their role to focus their knowledge on the goal they had in mind.

When, later, it was realized that some of them were to become courtiers, it was necessary that they be trained in the *savoir faire* of that intricate and bewildering life which surrounded the foot of the throne. The missionary had to learn to forget his own personality or to merge it in that of a sycophant, a hanger-on at the court, a humble seeker of imperial favor. This proved often the most difficult of their many tasks. "A layman," says De Fontaney, "is naturally quick, ardent, impetuous, and curious. When one comes to China he must absolutely change these characteristics and resolve to be all his life mild, complacent, patient, and serious." If we add to these qualities servility, sagacity, and watchfulness, we shall get some idea of the mental and moral equipment necessary for the courtier which the foreign priest tried to be.

Several of the Jesuits, notably Schall and Parennin, became astute politicians, masters of the Oriental art of specious argument. The first lesson they learned was a formal humility. Parennin says:

I began, according to the custom of the country, by admitting that he, the emperor, was right. This method pleases Oriental princes; they enjoy it and it disposes them to receive the reasons by which you prove imperceptibly that they are wrong.

It was of course this constant practice of self-abnegation which caused the hostile Father Ripa to call the Jesuit priests "honorable galley slaves." But amid the sinuosities of an Oriental court, with its intricate rivalries and its constant shifting of forces, its reliance on the whim of the monarch and on the subtlety and address of the courtier—where the emperor, powerful as he was, remained always more or less the victim of the vicious circle revolving around him—it was easy to make enemies and extremely difficult to make friends to whom to appeal in time of need. The Jesuits realized this and were willing to fit themselves into this new environment with a power of adaptability which cannot fail to arouse our admiration, even though we may at times condemn their methods.

That they were highly successful, particularly in the early days, there is no doubt. The official records of the time bear witness to the popularity of the foreign scholars. The annals of the Ming dynasty describe them thus:

Those who come to the East are, generally speaking, all clever men, scholars specially sent for the purpose of propagating their teaching without seeking rewards or wealth. The majority of the books which they have written are what the Chinese have not yet treated of. And so all those who are fond of curiosities continually honor them and scholars and officials like Hsü Kuang-ch'i and Li Chih-tsao and P'ei Shou approved of their words and added polish to their style of writing so that their teaching prospered rapidly.[8]

Coming from a Chinese official document this is eloquent testimony of the early success of the Jesuits in establishing for themselves a reputation at court.

It was as a result of this first wave of popularity that the Jesuits obtained a footing in one of the most powerful departments of the government. This position influenced the whole of their subsequent history in the empire, gave them immense opportunities for prestige, and provided a kind of brake on the downward movement of fortune, when that prestige was rapidly vanishing. With such a start how is it possible that the Society allowed itself to lose what it had won?

The answer to this question is to be found chiefly in the nature of the officials with whom they had to deal and in their attitude to the foreign scholars. The chief motive of the rapprochement between

Christian priests and Manchu-Chinese mandarins was the curiosity of the latter. These "foreigners of undoubted learning," coming from a distant land, reported strange customs, expounded strange theories, and, better still (because more concrete), displayed strange machinery and curious books of learning. To minds always fascinated by the unique these things appealed even when their intellectual significance was ill understood. So Ricci and his colleagues were able to entertain for hours crowds of curious admirers who filled their courtyards and naïvely commented on the foreign objects, which they handled with childlike wonder. The Jesuits made full use of this means of contact. Every occasion was used to stimulate and vivify this curiosity. On one occasion, Parennin was traveling with the emperor's suite in Tartary and, in the course of one of his conversations with the officials, he averred that he could freeze water over a brazier of coals. The officials were incredulous and demanded a demonstration so urgently that there was nothing to do but to take up the challenge. Slipping a little nitre into the water at the right moment, Parennin successfully performed the experiment to the great astonishment of the onlookers—a trick more worthy, perhaps, of a charlatan than of a priest but nonetheless capable of enhancing the reputation of the foreign scholars and the cause they represented.[7]

The same Jesuit has explained his theories on the subject. He says: "Curiosity must first be stimulated by natural phenomena that they are eager to understand, such as the explanation of hail, thunder, etc." And he continues:

One must add a great deal of patience in listening to and in solving the difficulties they present, whether good or bad, making it appear that one is impressed by their intelligence and their personal merit. For it is by these wise tactics that one insinuates himself into their minds and unconsciously instils in them the truths of religion.[8]

To stimulate curiosity, then, was the first step. To reinforce it with concrete evidence was also necessary, and so the priests equipped themselves with globes, maps, crystals, clocks, charts, books, engrav-

ings, and other objects. From the displaying of these things to the
giving of them was another step. Soon the Jesuits were fairly launched
upon the practice of distributing clocks, compasses, books, and maps
in order to gain favor or to ward off disaster. For example, Semedo
tells us that Father Pantoja, when he wished to obtain a burial place
for Ricci, distributed to influential officials a number of ivory sundials.
This method of persuasion was later frequently resorted to. Often
a Western map or painting, a book or a mathematical instrument
smoothed the path of the foreign priests. Even in the last days of the
mission we find a priest writing home for these things with the
comment:

A watch given at the right moment, a picture, a miniature, some little article
in coral, enamel or crystal which in Europe is little more than a vain and useless ornament, presented in China to a Governor or a Viceroy will serve as
a support for our Religion, will create protectors for us and will sometimes be
the occasion of changing the situation in an entire province.[9]

A volume might be written concerning the influence of the clock on
the infiltration of Western ideas in China, so great was the importance
of this popular form of gift.

By their conversation and their gifts the foreign scholars gained a
reputation for themselves which must often have been embarrassing.
They were credited at times with a mild form of omniscience, which
they felt they had to sustain at all costs. A remark of Verbiest consti-
tutes an interesting proof of the fact. Writing to his friend Father de
Rougemont, he tells of a comet which appeared in 1666 and of his being asked for an explanation. "I might," he says, "if I had been talking
with a Tycho Brahe or a Ptolemy have expressed ignorance, but to
these fat-bellied mandarins one must immediately give a reason without blinking an eye, if one does not want to lose his reputation."[10]

By the exercise of such strategy the Jesuits found themselves officials of the empire and were called frequently to Peking. It is difficult
to overestimate the importance which a summons to the imperial
court gave to the recipient of the honor. Verbiest writes that, when

he was called from Sianfu to Peking in 1660, his cortege was almost
a mile long. On his litter was a banner bearing the legend: "The most
wise scholar Ferdinand summoned by the emperor." At each town
he passed through, its chief official sent messengers out to greet him.
He arrived at the city gate to the sound of trumpets, the clashing of
cymbals, and the beating of drums. Salutes were fired in his honor at
his arrival and at his departure.[11] No occasion was missed by the astute
priests to surround themselves with a display of power and the marks
of favoritism. The Dominican Father Garcia—like many members of
his order disgusted at this ostentation—describes for us a meeting with
Father Martin Martini on the highway.

> He came with great pomp, purely secular, being a mandarin of the first rank
> (superior even to that of a viceroy). He was garbed in robes which had a
> dragon embroidered on the chest and he was accompanied by lancers, cross-
> bowmen [*arquebusiers*], banners and other marks of his rank.[12]

The Manchu code rigidly prescribed the ceremonial dress of the official with its richly embroidered garments, plumed hat surmounted
by a button of material distinctive of the rank of the wearer, its neck-
lace of 108 beads, its girdle with pendent ends, its fans, and its boots,
its jacket with *pu tzu* or medallion on breast, and back embroidered
with figures of birds for civil officials and of beasts for military officers.[13] Jesuit officials were forced to conform to the rules of dress and
of demeanor. They soon learned that the question of ceremony in
China was bound up with the important question of "face," the *sine
qua non* of existence—to ignore which would have rendered useless
all their efforts.

These tactics were necessary even when the Jesuits had obtained
a secure footing in the empire; for the fear of opposition constantly
haunted them. With the officials in their administrative capacity their
relations were always precarious. The government of the country was
based on the theory of direct personal responsibility. The emperor
was the father of his people and, as such, was directly responsible to
Heaven for their welfare. In theory, any evil that attacked the country

was the result of his own misdeeds or misgovernment. The viceroy and other officials were in turn directly responsible to the emperor for everything that went on in their districts. Sometimes the official was punished for a disaster over which he could not possibly have had any control. This threw on him a great burden and forced him often to act in an arbitrary manner. In the absence of a code of plainly written laws he was often left to interpret for himself the edicts which came from the throne, and these were frequently couched in purposely obscure or ambiguous language. His position gave to the imperial official almost unlimited power—even though the decision of life or death rested theoretically with the emperor. When he was tolerant, Christianity was often ignored, in spite of hostile edicts; when he was ignorant, bigoted, or vindictive, the Christians in his district suffered. A hostile official, like Mu An-pao, viceroy of Canton, was able, as has been shown, to stir up great trouble for the foreigners.[14]

At court matters were more stable, but even here the missionaries existed only through the pleasure of the Son of Heaven. It was the close contact between the Jesuits and the person of the emperor which made possible the development of missions throughout the empire. During his ten years at court (1600–1610) Ricci did the work of a pioneer and did not personally come in contact with the emperor. Schall, however, saw much of the reigning monarch, especially during the missionary's later years when his venerable appearance and reputation for wisdom brought that respect which all Chinese show to old age. He had unusually intimate relations with Shun Chih, and this friendship was reflected in cordial relations with the officials.

Under the later Manchu monarch, relations between priest and emperor were more formal. K'ang Hsi accepted Schall as a wise old man whose learning and reputation had been well established— a tradition in a land of traditions. As the emperor came to know the Jesuit missionary better, he developed an admiration of the priest's character. The same thing happened with Verbiest, whose intellectual talents and moral rectitude K'ang Hsi came greatly to value.

The young emperor's teachers report him assiduous in his studies. He often required them to rise for the imperial audiences at four in the morning, a duty which, since they had sometimes spent a large part of the night in preparing the lessons for the imperial pupil, must have been somewhat difficult. It may be, as Ripa asserts, that K'ang Hsi was merely a dilettante in the realm of Western knowledge,[15] but the evidence seems to show that he had a real interest in these subjects. In this respect K'ang Hsi takes his place by the side of Louis XIV, Catherine II, Peter the Great, Frederick of Prussia, and other royal patrons of learning in Europe.

K'ang Hsi's failure was his inability to adopt and apply in his realm the Western science which interested him so greatly. He had in his palace modern instruments, such as the telescope and the microscope, but half a mile away across the city the astronomers of the observatory were still using the inaccurate instruments in use for centuries. The force of conservatism in the empire was so strong that it limited the emperor's belief in up-to-date foreign methods to a mere academic curiosity.

This emperor's interest in foreign science must not, therefore, lead us to believe that he was converted to Western ideas. His attitude toward strange sects was that of the typical officials of his time, who were trained in the Confucian tradition. In a famous decree, revered by succeeding generations as the Sacred Edict, K'ang Hsi exhorts his subjects to degrade strange religions in order to exalt "orthodox" doctrines, a term defined in Yung Cheng's commentary on the edict as the doctrines of the sect of the learned (Confucianism), of the sect of Fo (Buddhism), and of the sect of Tao (Taoism), these being the *san ch'iao* or "three teachings," which were the basis of Chinese moral and religious philosophy.[16]

There were political reasons for K'ang Hsi's distrust of all things foreign. He had studied the history of the Ming dynasty and he felt that what had happened in China before might happen again; that it was not impossible that another revolution might sweep away his dynasty as it had swept away the Mings. More and more, as his reign advanced, did his political sagacity lead him to dwell upon the possibility of foreign invasion. His friendship for the Jesuit scholars, from whom he gained an insight into the power of foreign nations, contributed to accentuate this fear. He was keenly alive to the necessity of preserving the cultural and social solidarity of the nation. In his last edict, which may be looked upon as a political testament, he advocates constant vigilance on the part of the government, and then adds the warning: "If the government becomes feeble, the foreigners will do with China what they wish."

Whatever K'ang Hsi's attitude may have been toward the missionaries, however, it is evident, from the testimony of the Jesuits, that they regarded him as a wise and capable ruler. Lecomte, seeing the emperor for the first time in 1689, gives us the following picture:

The emperor appeared to me to be above medium height and stouter than men in Europe who pride themselves on their good figures . . . He has a full face marked by smallpox, a wide forehead, a small nose and eyes after the Chinese fashion, a fine mouth and the lower part of his face very attractive. In addition to this he has a good deportment and one can see in his appearance and in all his gestures something that savors of royalty.[17]

Of the emperor's character we must of course expect to hear little but praise from his Jesuit courtiers. Parennin, writing in 1723 to Fontenelle, the great secretary of the Académie des Sciences, says: "This prince was one of the most extraordinary of men, such as one finds only once in several centuries."[18] De Mailla writes:

During the fifty-six years that he has been on the throne he has rendered each day memorable by some good action; his glory increases daily. By the wisdom of his government he equals and even surpasses not only the kings, his predecessors, but even those ancient emperors of the three most illustrious families.

Du Halde, with the letters of the missionaries before him, joins in the chorus of praise:

True it is that this prince possesses to the highest degree the art of reigning and that he gathers in himself all the qualities which make the *honnête*

homme and the monarch. His bearing, his figure, the features of his countenance, a certain air of majesty, tempered with mildness and kindness in-
spire at first sight love and respect for his person and announce from the very
first the master of one of the greatest empires of the universe.[19]

The Jesuits praise his sense of justice, his personal abstemiousness,
the economy of his government, its freedom from corruption, his
simple mode of life, and his tirelessness in matters of state. It is not
to be wondered at that they liked to compare him to Louis XIV, *roi
soleil* of France.[20] Indeed, when we remember those scathing pages
in the memoirs of Saint Simon which describe the weaknesses of the
French monarch, it is the Chinese emperor who gains by the comparison. The missionaries had every reason to admire the splendid
character of the monarch.

But when the Jesuits dwell upon K'ang Hsi's intellectual endow-
ments, they lay themselves open to the charge of excessive flattery.
Thus De Mailla: "His mind is so keen that he understands without
difficulty all that is in the books. He knows perfectly astronomy, arithmetic and philosophy."[21] As an antidote to this fulsome praise the
comment of the stern, disgruntled Father Ripa might be recalled.
Although admitting that the Chinese monarch was a man of wide
understanding, Ripa adds that K'ang Hsi had little real knowledge
of foreign subjects and that, like most Oriental potentates, he was
inordinately vain and given to fits of cruelty.[22]

There is good reason for the Jesuits' praise, however. The Chinese
monarch appears to have taken a deep and friendly interest in the
learning of the foreign scholars. At court he would sometimes lay
aside the burdens of empire and converse with the Jesuits, "chatting
with them," says Father Gerbillon, "like a father with his children."
It was in conversations such as these that the emperor not only learned
the rudiments of Western sciences but also acquired a knowledge
of the customs of the different courts of Europe, the ancient and modern history of countries far distant from China, and the social habits
of the rest of the world. Knowing the skill of the Jesuit courtier, one

is not surprised to learn that from these talks with the French scholars the Chinese monarch acquired a high regard for the French people and a particular esteem for Louis XIV.[23]

The emperor's interest in Western knowledge put him sometimes on almost intimate terms with his foreign scholars. Verbiest relates a significant incident which occurred during one of the emperor's trips in the North. With considerable difficulty the imperial party had crossed a flooded stream in the vicinity of Kirin. K'ang Hsi had taken the Jesuit with him in the royal barge. "When they had crossed," relates the priest:

> the emperor sat on the bank of the river and made me sit by his side with the two sons of the Governor of the West and the first *ko lao* of Tartary. The night was fine and the sky clear. He told me to name in Chinese and in the European language the constellations which appeared in the heavens, first naming the ones he already knew. Then, unfolding a little chart which I had presented to him a few years earlier, he began to calculate what was the hour by the northern star.[24]

The picture of the Son of Heaven seated on the river bank under the starlit northern sky with the foreign priest, studying the beauty and significance of the stars, is more eloquent than many pages of Jesuit panegyric in disclosing to us the relation of emperor and foreign priest. It is probably in accounts of such moments as these, and not in the study of the cunning diplomacy of the priests, that we can find the key to their influence in the empire under K'ang Hsi.

Yung Cheng's relations with the Jesuit scholars, in spite of the fact that he was a pupil of a foreign priest, were on the whole governed by suspicion—if not by hostility. When he began his reign, the quarrels of the Christian missionaries had already served to deprive them of many of the privileges possessed by Ricci and Schall. Henceforth the priests were to wear themselves out as servants of the emperor— but they were never to regain that solid footing in the court which they had enjoyed in the earlier days of the mission. True, they remained in office at the observatory, but at court they became artisans, mechanics, artists, paid servants of the emperor, hardworking menials of the royal entourage. Nevertheless, they had a good word to say for their imperial master. Father Contancin, in 1725, writes:

One cannot refrain from praising the qualities which render him [Yung Cheng] worthy of the Empire ... This prince is indefatigable in his work. He is thinking day and night of the establishment of a wise government and of procuring the happiness of his people. There is no better way of currying his favor than to propose some plan which has to do with public welfare or with relieving the distress of the people. ... [25]

Under the last of the Mings the Jesuits had been advisers; under K'ang Hsi they were honored scholar-guests; under Ch'ien Lung they were merely servants of the crown. The grandson of K'ang Hsi was destined to occupy a place in history equal, if not superior, to that of his brilliant grandfather. The latter had been interested chiefly in philosophy and the mathematical sciences. Ch'ien Lung was of a more practical turn of mind. He was interested in the concrete rather than the abstract. He enjoyed things that moved: the stroke of the brush on canvas, the play of moving water, the coördinated movement of machinery in motion. Even the eddying life of the streets fascinated him. Within his great palace outside Peking he caused a small city in miniature to be built and here, at certain times of the year, he would send some of his servants to play the part of the populace, while he would sit intently watching the artificially busy thoroughfares and listening to the clamor of the vociferous buyers and sellers, the actors sometimes becoming so absorbed in their roles that they forgot they were merely playing for the benefit of their imperial master. Near by he had caused a whole street to be built according to Western architecture, which in his imagination he must have peopled with such crowds as daily passed the Porte Saint-Martin or crossed the Pont Neuf in that capital of France about which he had heard so much from his Jesuit servants.

Foreign portraits of the monarch are not lacking. Attiret, Panzi, and Castiglione all painted him, as well as Alexander of the Macartney mission. Verbal portraits pay tribute above all to his energy. "I do not know," says Ventavon, "how he can attend to so many details."[26]

He is a prince who superintends everything for himself [says Father Cibot]. He is full of fairness and equity. He will not suffer the least injustice. Mild and accessible, he listens with pleasure to the innocent who is attempting to justify himself; but prompt and severe, he humiliates and punishes the oppressor. It would seem that flattery has little effect on his mind.[27]

The Jesuits praise the almost Spartan simplicity of Ch'ien Lung's private life, which was in strong contrast with the gorgeous pomp of his public affairs. Cibot comments on the stoical passivity of his posture as he sits at audience or at meals, and he adds interesting details concerning the emperor's daily routine. After a heavy morning's work the latter would go by chair or boat through his palace grounds, visiting the various buildings and especially examining the multitude of curious things he had gathered there or inspecting the alterations or repairs he had ordered. At the Yuan Ming Yuan one could, at any rate until recently, see the remains of the marble throne, placed against a background of panels sculptured with foreign armorial bearings, where the emperor would sit watching the play of the foreign fountains or admiring the rococo ornaments of the building opposite, with its horseshoe staircase and beautifully carved doors and columns.

The energy of such an exacting monarch called for a corresponding energy on the part of his courtiers, and the Jesuits were kept busy satisfying his whims. Whatever he desired—a butterfly painted on glass, a delicate engraving, a hydraulic machine, a fountain, or a palace—had to be provided immediately. There could be no excuse on the ground of ignorance or lack of time. Indefatigability and a kind of omniscience were a necessary part of the Jesuit equipment. Often the fathers would be forced to spend most of the night preparing plans or sketches to be presented to the Son of Heaven the next morning. Ch'ien Lung rose often at four or five o'clock in the morning to begin the life of the day. At dawn the missionaries left their lodgings at the near-by town of Hai Tien in order to arrive at the

palace gates when they were opened, ready to obey the imperial summons. Often they were forced to spend hours in the antechambers
awaiting the monarch, who would then give them some task to be
executed in an absurdly short time. Sickness itself was no excuse for
delay. Then would follow hours of feverish activity, often with little
or no break for food, until the task was accomplished, the picture
painted, or the machine perfected. A word of approbation from the
imperial taskmaster, coupled with the realization that what they had
done had been done for the Faith, was adequate reward.

And how trivial were some of these tasks! The best efforts of the
Jesuit scholars were often devoted to satisfying Ch'ien Lung's desire
for mechanical objects. Many hours of strenuous labor were given
to the making of clockwork toys, one of the most ingenious of the
toymakers being Father Chalier. In spite of his successes, we find this
clever priest bemoaning the fact that he had not received better training in his youth. He says, in a letter to a friend, "We are called upon
to invent everything, for, although there are four thousand clocks and
watches in the palace, products of the best masters of Europe, the
emperor is constantly demanding more."[28] When this happened, the
missionary artisans set to work to make another more ingenious than
the last. As soon as it was finished and presented, the emperor would
call his courtiers to see it and, repeating the priest's explanation of its
movement, would imply that the clock in question was his own
invention. Thereupon the courtiers would overwhelm the monarch
with servile praise and, Father Chalier adds, "the best part of the affair
is that I myself would have to join in this adulation."[29]

Each member of the Society in Peking made himself a master of
some form of mechanical construction. Brother Brossard accomplished
wonders in spun glass, and the delicate results of his skill were to be
found in the throne room of the palace, side by side with a host of
objets d'art from Louis XV's court. In 1754 Brother Thibault made
an automatic lion, while Father Sigismund of the Propaganda outdid
him in making a clockwork man. Father Amiot writes humorously

that they looked forward with dread to the day when the emperor would demand a "robot" who should be able to talk. Considering the ingenuity with which the Jesuits met every other emergency of this nature, one can judge that such a situation would have been adequately met if it had arisen.

On the occasion of the empress mother's sixtieth birthday in 1752 the priests put their heads together to make something worthy of the occasion. It took the form of a semicircular stage three feet high, on which was a large statue holding a congratulatory scroll and other statues with cymbals. When the hour struck, the figure came forward displaying the scroll while the attendants played a tune on their cymbals. In the foreground, a goose marked the time with his beak on a dial carved around the bank of a pool.[30] The ingenious toy was received with enthusiasm and greatly added to the reputation of the priestly inventors. One can gauge the amount of time required by these labors from the statement of Father Ventavon that he had been giving his leisure hours for more than eighteen months to the making of two toy men carrying a pot of flowers.

It would, perhaps, be too much to say that the fate of Christianity rested in China on the success of a mechanical toy. But it is obvious that the making of these toys was a powerful aid to the keeping of the emperor's good will, without which Christianity in the empire would have been doomed. The Jesuits, realizing this, were willing to submit to the most trivial duties.

That these menial tasks were often harrowing to the soul of the priest who had come to the empire for other reasons we can quite understand. Father Amiot has left us a graphic account of the arduous labors as court painter of Brother Attiret,[31] a gentle soul who joined the Society late in life. The latter was summoned one day to accompany Ch'ien Lung to Tartary, when the latter was receiving the submission of the Eleuth chiefs whom he had subdued. At the end of an exceedingly strenuous journey, which was made more difficult by the artist's ill health, Attiret was forced in the short space of forty days to paint

twenty portraits in oil, as well as four large pictures of court ceremonies. Often painting against time, constantly harassed by curious,
boorish Tartar chiefs who got in his way and showered him with foolish questions, exhausted and sick, he "carried on" in the best tradition
of his order.

Similar complaints were made by the other artists at court. It was
not easy for them to forget the principles of their art, or to put
aside the technique in which they had been trained, to satisfy a
whim of emperor or official which appeared to them naïve and
childish. The letters of the missionaries abound in stories concerning
imperial eccentricities. The artists, for example, in accordance with
Chinese custom, were forced to paint the emperor's face with the
light falling equally on each side. The first portrait done with the
shadow falling on one side of the imperial countenance had angered
the monarch, who did not like the idea of being painted as a black
man. Accordingly, his portrait henceforth appeared devoid of shadow.

Native prejudices, too, determined their use of materials. They
began to paint in oils, as they had been accustomed to do in Europe,
and for a while Ch'ien Lung was amused at this new technique. He
soon tired of it, however, and the foreign artists were then forced to
limit themselves to the use of water colors. Often they would be commanded to collaborate with native painters, the Jesuit doing the figures and the Chinese filling in the background. On rare occasions the
emperor himself began a painting, to have it finished by one of the
missionaries. All these limitations to their work were exasperating
and often made their lives a real martyrdom.

At the same time the Jesuits were slaves to the intricate ceremonies
of the court. They were forced to stand for hours in respectful silence
in some vast hall or courtyard in the imperial palace.[32] They learned to
perform the *k'o tou* before the empty throne. More galling still, they
became accustomed to abasing themselves before some high official
without whose aid their request could not reach the ears of the emperor. Rarely did they find it possible or expedient to speak directly

to the Son of Heaven regarding affairs of interest to the mission. Only
when matters had reached a desperate pass, did they resort to direct
appeal to the monarch, which happened only once or twice in the
Ch'ien Lung period.

Sometimes their astuteness and learning failed them. Ripa tells of
a lay brother, called in to treat the twentieth son of K'ang Hsi for
some illness. Not being able to diagnose the case accurately, he
declared the royal patient was in no danger. This was unfortunate,
for the youth died, and the lay brother, as was not uncommon, was
"kicked, cuffed, and beaten so severely that he became seriously ill."
Although not all their tasks were as hazardous as that of medical
adviser, it is clear that the margin between imperial favor and displeasure was slight, and the priests, like all other courtiers, had constantly to be on their guard against disaster.

One of the most important functions of the Jesuits at court was
that of interpreter for European diplomatic missions. In those days few
Westerners spoke Chinese or Manchu, and no Manchus or Chinese
at court spoke a European tongue. The Jesuits, then, often found
themselves the arbiters of the fortunes of Europe in China, with the
power to make or break a foreign embassy.

It has been shown how the Jesuits used their position at court
to oppose the De Tournon mission. National enemies were treated
in the same way as ecclesiastical opponents. Their great common
enemy was the Dutch, who, in the middle of the seventeenth century
were making violent efforts to establish trade connections with China
and who, for some time, had had a factory at Amoy.[38] In 1655 a Dutch
mission headed by Pierre de Goyer and Jacques de Keyzer arrived
in Peking. They were received with polite ceremony, and it fell to
Schall and his colleagues to act as interpreters. The Jesuits met them
with politeness, but they had already received secret word from
Macao to bring about the failure of the embassy. Appended to the
English translation of Nieuhoff's account of the mission is a letter
from a Jesuit which is enlightening as showing the tactics of the mem-

bers of the Society in their role as go-between.[34] Failing by other means
to prevent the Hollanders' arrival in Peking, they resorted to bribery
in order to cause the final failure of the mission. For this purpose they
had been promised financial assistance from Macao. An important
official guaranteed for the sum of eight hundred taels to bring about
the ruin of the mission, but demanded cash in advance. The Jesuits,
having no ready funds, offered two beautifully embroidered vests at
an evaluation of one hundred and fifty taels, and the official was on
the point of accepting the offer when he suddenly discovered that the
garments in question were gifts of the emperor to the Jesuits. He
feared to accept them and therefore withdrew his offer. Failing in
their efforts at bribery, the Jesuits then tried the effect of propaganda.
"We spared not to acquaint them with the villainous and perfidious
disposition of the Hollanders," says the Jesuit writer, "with their apostasy from their ancient professed religion and their rebellion against
their lawful sovereign."[35] These charges, uttered by the grave and
eloquent Schall, had a striking effect on the Manchu officials, as one
can well imagine—an effect which was no doubt heightened by a
reminder concerning the Dutch attack on Macao in 1622.

As a last resort, the Jesuits made full use of the advantage of their
role as interpreters. The members of the embassy were summoned
to the palace to present their gifts. When the presents were uncovered
by the examining official, Schall "sighed deeply" and pointed out that
only a small part of them actually came from Holland. During these
proceedings the emperor sent for Schall and inquired privately concerning the nature of these foreigners. The Jesuit criticized the Dutch
in no uncertain terms, and it is impossible to believe that his judgments did not have a vital influence in bringing about the failure of
the mission. In fact, when the decision had been put into writing and
shown to Schall, it was the Jesuit who protested against the mildness
of the terms of refusal used, though he was unsuccessful in getting
the document changed.[36] The mission was courteously discharged
without a promise concerning the opening of trade posts, and one

must conclude that the Jesuits had scored another victory. They had effectively prevented the "heretics" from getting a commercial foothold in the empire. The Jesuits undoubtedly salved their consciences with the theory that the presence of the Dutch would have been inimical to the interests of their Faith in China.[37]

Verbiest was also successful in opposing the efforts of the Dutch to obtain a factory site. He gave as his excuse that he feared the Calvinism of the Hollanders. It is certainly true that the presence of the Dutch in Peking, or for that matter anywhere in the empire, would have added another and more powerful element of discord to an atmosphere soon to be troubled with the quarrel over the Rites.

But the Jesuits' hostility to the Dutch did not extend to the Russians. The first Muscovite embassy to China arrived during the reign of Shun Chih (1656). It was followed by several others during the Jesuit regime, most of which were aided by the foreign priests. Behind the Jesuit relations with Russia was the hope that an overland route to the Far East might be opened to them across northern Asia. As early as 1628 Schall, then in Sianfu, had apparently foreseen this possibility, since he established cordial relations with the Mohammedan mission passing through that city from the Near East. This mission came across Asia every five years to bring tribute to Peking. When he came to the capital, Schall continued his efforts to gather material on the possibilities of a trans-Asian route. In 1657 Goa had been blockaded for a year by the Dutch; accordingly, the need of an alternative for the sea route was keenly felt. Verbiest, like Schall, was friendly to the Russians. His correspondence shows that he had constantly in mind the possibility of a route across their country.[38]

For this reason, if for no others, the Jesuits rendered good service as interpreters to several Russian embassies. The first thus aided was that of Nikolai Gavrilovitch Spathary in 1676. Spathary was of Greek origin and had an excellent knowledge of Latin. When he arrived at the Chinese capital, he was pleasantly surprised to find someone who could speak that language fluently, as well as the native tongue. K'ang

Hsi, on his part, was astonished that the two foreigners could understand each other. Verbiest translated the tsar's letter from Latin into Manchu and was of the greatest assistance to the mission in the difficult and protracted controversy over the question of the ceremonies for the embassy's reception. The ambassador and the Jesuits were on excellent terms, and Father Grimaldi speaks with evident pleasure of Spathary and his suite.[39] When the envoy returned to Russia, he carried to the tsar a book on astronomy as a present from the Jesuits.

The role played by the Jesuits in the negotiations leading to the Treaty of Nertchinsk has already been described. The importance of this effort is enhanced by the fact that the treaty arranged with Gerbillon's assistance continued to be effective (with only small changes) for one hundred and sixty years.[40]

When the mission under Evart Isbrand Ides arrived in 1693, Gerbillon, together with the Portuguese Jesuits, again rendered valuable services, as did Parennin and Stumpf for the Ismaïloff mission in 1720. When, however, as a result of the last-mentioned mission Lawrence Lange was allowed to remain behind in Peking, with the obvious purpose of founding a Russian establishment in the Chinese capital, the friendliness of the Jesuits changed to a prudent aloofness. Indeed, they finally intrigued against the Russian agent to such a degree that he was unable to accomplish anything.[41]

The Jesuits felt that it was above all things necessary that they should retain their hegemony in international relations at the court of China. Only by the absence of European competition would the members of the Society appear to be indispensable to the emperor. Their role as interpreters for the representatives of European powers was, therefore, dominated by this fear of potential rivals.

Had the members of the Society been able indefinitely to retain the prestige at court which they had enjoyed during the early years of K'ang Hsi, they might have been powerful diplomatic agents for the European powers, particularly for France. Even with their limited prestige, they were able to exert their influence so that in the diplomatic as well as in the cultural sphere they stood as mediators between the Orient and the Occident.

In addition to the opposition which they found at court the Jesuits had to face the hostility of their fellow priests of the other orders, notably the Dominicans. As already indicated the *jus patronatus* caused the Portuguese to claim a spiritual hegemony in Asia. This right was challenged in turn by the Spaniards and the French. Shortly after the Portuguese had established themselves at Macao (1557), the Spaniards had come to the Philippines and founded the *Congré-gation de la Rosalie* at Manila, in charge of the Dominican order. Henceforth this order was to represent unofficially Spain's interests in the Far East precisely as the Jesuits represented the other Iberian power. When the Spaniards at Manila saw the probable success of the Jesuit organization centered at Macao, they contemplated the acquisition of a port in China for themselves. In the Philippines they had accumulated a huge amount of silver from their Mexican and South American colonies. This they wished to use to purchase Chinese commodities. They therefore sent Juan Bautista Roman and a Spanish Jesuit, Alfonso Sanchez, to the Jesuit mission at Macao in 1582 suggesting that the Society negotiate with the local officials for the sending of a Spanish embassy to Peking, the Jesuits to accompany it as spiritual advisers. The latter seem to have made progress in the affair when they were ordered by their superior to let the matter drop. The Portuguese evidently felt that the competition of such wealthy rivals would mean the death of their own commerce and so killed the enterprise before it was well begun.[42] It is probable, too, that the Jesuits in China found the ignorance which the Catholics in the Philippines—Jesuit and non-Jesuit alike—showed concerning the situation in China so embarrassing to this work as to offer a distinct menace to its success.

It may have been the failure of this scheme which made the Spanish colony anti-Jesuit. Gradually the Spanish Dominicans in the Philippines became more and more outspoken in their criticism of the actions and policies of the Society of Jesus in China, and the rivalry between the two orders, based on essential differences in tactics and methods, became a form of national rivalry. This fact must not be lost sight of when one examines the quarrels over the Rites. Much of the opposition to the Jesuits in this quarrel, at least in the early stages, had its source in Manila. It was an international as well as an inter-order quarrel.

When, toward the end of the seventeenth century, France decided to send her own Jesuits to China, a new element of opposition to Portugal was created. From the beginning the French mission was highly national in character. The purpose of its patrons in France was to get into commercial and cultural contact with China, and with the arrival of the French Jesuits the leadership in Sino-European cultural relationships passed definitely to the kingdom of Louis XIV. The French mission was subsidized by Paris. It came to China with definite instructions from its government. That it did not accomplish much in aiding French commerce in the Far East was probably more because of the fact that France at that time was not a strong commercial nation like Portugal—and the Netherlands and England later—rather than because of any absence of desire to join in the lucrative trade. Nevertheless the French mission at Peking under the leadership of Gerbillon and his confreres strongly maintained its national identity and at times aroused the angry opposition of Pereyra and his Portuguese colleagues.[43] By the time Cardinal de Tournon reached Peking in 1705 the quarrel between the two groups had become intense. According to Gonzales de Saint-Pierre, K'ang Hsi asked the legate whether the Pope was aware of these quarrels which "had been pushed so far the emperor had been obliged on several occasions to warn them seriously to give up their disputes."[44] International rivalry was subordinated to the general opposition of the Society to the legate during the latter's visit, but it flared up again after his departure, especially during the last days of the Jesuit mission.

These, then, were the chief methods and results of Jesuit diplomacy in China. They form a brilliant chapter in the achievements of the Society. Their very success, however, created for the Jesuits enemies among the other orders and aroused opposition which at times was difficult to combat. In overcoming this opposition the members of the order were often guilty of acts of indiscretion or even of duplicity, laying themselves open to serious criticism, some of which must have been justified. These criticisms were seized upon by enemies of the Society in Europe and used as potent weapons against it.

In spite of all the charges leveled against them, however, the impartial observer is forced to admire the perfection of the system they created. Faced with enormous difficulties, they met them with skill, perseverance, bravery, and a spirit of consecration and sacrifice unsurpassed in the annals of the Christian faith. That they did not achieve ultimate and final success can in no way dim the glory of their efforts.

ORIENT AND OCCIDENT

Chapter XVI

JESUIT SINOPHILE LITERATURE OF THE
SEVENTEENTH CENTURY

To the Roman world China meant chiefly silk. Geographically, the country was a vast entity on the dim eastern limits of the world. Its people were known to be pacific and good traders. Of the culture of silk itself knowledge was vague. Pliny wrote that it was grown on trees, and other writers for centuries repeated the error. It seems certain that any knowledge of the Far East which the Romans may have possessed came through the Persians and Scythians, intermediaries in the Oriental trade. In the European conception of the Chinese character were woven many of the traits of the peoples on the eastern rim of the Roman empire.

China itself was almost a closed book to the West until Genghis Khan arose and changed the face of the world. Henceforth the course of history was to bring together East and West in spite of powerful influences to prevent this meeting. Across the highway that Genghis made came the friars in their role of ambassadors to the Mongols. They returned to Europe to report what they had witnessed and heard. John of Plano Carpini, William of Rubruck, Haytoun the Armenian, and others took back to Europe fascinating stories of the Mongols and their customs. Other travelers added to this store of information: Shah Rukh, the Persian chief who was sent across Asia on a mission in 1304; Nicolò Conti, who visited the Far East toward the end of the fifteenth century; John of Marignolli, a Florentine monk, who was sent to Khanbaliq in 1338; Jean de Cora, Bishop of Soltania, who, though he himself did not visit China, gathered information which he published in a book dated 1330; Rashid-ud-din, who passed his life at the court of Abaga Khan toward the end of the thirteenth century and, much later, Fernand Mendez Pinto, whose fantastic, although not entirely mendacious, account of the Chinese empire of the Mings was widely read in the West. All these men added their small contribution to the sum of knowledge of the eastern rim of the world.

They speak chiefly, however, of the customs of the Mongols, of the court of the Great Khan, and of the vast stretches of mountain and plain to the north of the Great Wall. Their remarks on China proper are scanty and, for the most part, vague. Not until after Kublai Khan had shifted the center of Mongol power to his new capital of Khanbaliq, south of the Wall, was the first authentic information brought to Europe of the great eastern empire. The two documents which provide this knowledge are the works of Odoric and of Marco Polo. Of Odoric and his book mention has already been made. His account was, of course, eclipsed by that of the Venetian, but it has enjoyed a popularity second only to the latter's work and, in many ways, corroborates the evidence contained therein.

The book of Ser Marco Polo was a revelation to Europe which, up to the thirteenth century, had relied for information concerning China and its people mainly on the vague generalities of the classical writers, on the one hand, and on the fantastic uncertainties of Ptolemaic geography on the other. Marco Polo traveled the length and breadth of China and, as an official of the khan, was given the opportunity to acquaint himself with the customs of the people and with the details of administration. As a result, the Venetian was able to give to Far Eastern geography a degree of certainty which it had not until that time attained.

The Romans had not been interested in discovery of new lands far removed from the Mediterranean basin, and, when their empire fell, Europe forgot even what little knowledge the classical writers of Rome had been able to gather. With the coming of the great explorers, however, came also a new kind of world consciousness. The Renaissance brought a tremendously increased interest in cosmography. Dozens of works appeared describing the new countries and attempting to place them within the framework of universal geography. In this period almost the sole authority on the Far East was Marco Polo, and Renaissance cosmography, as far as this part of the world was concerned, was built almost entirely on material found in his book, although many writers still clung to the authority of Ptolemy and the legends of Biblical geography.

The material which Marco Polo presented, however, was fragmentary, ill arranged, and mingled with marvels and legends. The digestion of this material to form a coherent body of knowledge was beyond the power of the Renaissance geographers, who themselves were standing on the threshold of a new science.

In tradition China continued for three centuries to be bound to the chain of Genghis' and Kublai's conquests and to the medieval traditions of Prester John. Its geographical extent and limits were unknown. Its great cities were dimmed by the haze of a romantic exoticism. Certain curious facts and customs—such as the use of paper money, the prevalence of a new fuel (coal), and so forth—were repeated; a strong and stable government—often confused with the Mongol regime—was hinted at, it is true, but nothing was known of China's religions, the cult of Confucius, the philosophical systems of the empire, its great literary works, and its moral codes.

At the beginning of the seventeenth century, then, China was still a land of marvel and legend, a great but little-understood country on the still vague eastern limits of the earth. Then the Jesuits sailed eastward, and little by little they unfolded before the eyes of the western world the glory of this great empire in all its vastness, in all the richness of its traditions, in all the power and beauty of its ancient culture. Almost without rivals in their task, they poured into Europe, during a period of nearly two hundred years, quantities of letters, documents, and books, which in an increasing degree caught the imagination of Europe and made of the members of the Society the supreme contemporary interpreters of the Orient.

Strange to say, the first important work in this rich Sinological literature was not written by a Jesuit. It was a compilation by the

Augustinian Juan Gonzales de Mendoça entitled *The History of the Most Notable Rites and Customs of the Great Monarchy of China*[1]— written in Spanish and published in Rome in 1585. Mendoça himself had probably never been to China. His material was taken from the accounts of Augustinian and Franciscan priests who had visited the Middle Kingdom and from "other soldiers that went with them, that did see and have intelligence of that kingdom."

In geographical details Mendoça's account still clings to the old "Cathay" tradition of Marco Polo. It must not be forgotten, however, that whereas this tradition centered in the North, for the later books, based on the Portuguese conquests, the point of departure was the South. These two currents finally met and coalesced when Ricci arrived in Peking in 1600. Thenceforth, in the mind of Europe, northeastern Asia and southeastern Asia were placed in their proper relations to each other.

Concerning the beliefs, traditions, and philosophy of the country Mendoça's work is full of unassimilated facts. According to his informants, China was still a land of fantastic heathen beliefs and superstitions, which Mendoça made no attempt to evaluate or to harmonize. Confucius is not mentioned, but in the confused account of Taoist superstitions and Buddhist practices is included the statement, "there are found in this kingdom many moral things the which do touch very much our religion, which giveth us to understand that they are a people of great understanding, in especial in natural things."[2]

There is an interesting chapter exalting the paternalism of the government, culminating in the incredible assertion that poverty and beggars are nonexistent—upon which the editor of the English translation remarks: "I would the like were with us." In addition, there is a description of a score of interesting customs, of race *mores* and of curious facts. The work shows a knowledge of the country which is still extremely vague and uncritical, but it contains the beginning of a broader and more accurate conception of China. Mendoça's inform-

---

[1] For notes to chap. xvi, see pp. 330–332.

ants, in spite of the superficiality of their knowledge, had begun to get a true vision of the greatness, the richness, and the worth of the empire and its civilization. For this reason his compilation stands out as an important pioneer work in this field.

After Mendoça comes the first group of books by Jesuits, the works of Trigault, Semedo, and Kircher. The *History of the Christian Expedition to China*[3] by Nicolas Trigault, published in Amsterdam in 1615, is based upon information found in the papers of Matteo Ricci. It is, therefore, a document of the highest importance. Trigault was a missionary who had spent a number of years in the empire.[4] In a book of some six hundred pages he unrolled the splendid panorama of the land he and Ricci had attempted to convert. For the first time Europe was given a well-rounded account of the Chinese systems of moral and religious thought. For the first time, also, it heard of the great teacher Confucius and of the classical writings which are at the heart of the nation's culture. In the apology for his book, the author dwells upon the differences between the earlier travel books on China and the Jesuit works. He says:

We [the Jesuit missionaries] have seen their most noble provinces; we enter every day into conversation with the principal citizens, the magistrates and the men of letters; we speak the native language of the Chinese; we have learned by careful enquiry, their habits, customs, laws and ceremonial and, finally (what is of the greatest importance), day and night we have their books in our hands.[5]

The claims of authority and excellence implied in these words are justified. Reading the pages of the work, one is struck by the fact that they contain the first description of the Chinese empire which is serious and fairly adequate. The vague generalities of Mendoça are displaced by explanations and distinctions which, though lacking sometimes in illuminating details, present a satisfying summary of the importance and the complexity of the Chinese moral and religious code. The author emphasizes the dignity and worth of the scholar class and the high value placed upon learning in a land where the

Golden Rule—negatively expressed though it be—is the ideal of the law. For the first time Europe was given an exposition of the relation and differences between the *san ch'iao*—Confucianism, Buddhism, and Taoism—and the multitude of animistic practices which are accretions thereto. Apart from these matters, in which the Jesuit writer is naturally interested, there is a wealth of facts concerning the customs of the country. The tone of the writer is, on the whole, fairly dispassionate throughout, but he does not conceal his admiration for the country and its institutions. In spite of omissions, then, it may be claimed that Trigault's book was the first really significant contribution to Sinophile literature.

The volumes of Semedo[6] and Kircher are similarly important. In the work of the former, the author, a missionary who had spent over twenty years in the country, shows the same degree of sympathy and admiration for Chinese institutions as that expressed by Trigault. Although not so long as the latter's account, the summary of the religious system of China is clear and precise. The work forms a fitting complement to that which had preceded it.

The *China Illustrata*[7] of Athanasius Kircher, published in 1667, is noteworthy as being the first important work by a Jesuit scholar who had never visited the country. Kircher was a friend of the philosopher Gassendi, and one of the most learned men the Society had produced. His interest in hieroglyphics had led him to a superficial study of the Chinese language, despite the fact that his desire to go to the Far East had not been fulfilled. His book, although based only on information supplied by Fathers Boym, Grueber, and d'Orville, shows the influence of a keen and analytical mind. It suffers from its author's distance from the source of material, but it has the advantage of dealing chiefly with facts. Like Semedo, Kircher makes much of the Nestorian monument, which had been discovered about forty years before the publication of the work. The learned author includes Father Boym's translation of the inscription, accompanied by the romanized Chinese text and the Syriac characters. The *China Illus-*

trata, in addition, contains an account of early Christian missions in the Far East, as well as an erudite, though not always accurate, description of the language and some interesting comments on the flora and fauna of the empire. The most valuable part of Kircher's book, however, were the engravings. For the first time the reading public of Europe was shown pictures, not only of Ricci and Schall in their Chinese robes, but of the great emperor K'ang Hsi and of his subjects. The pictures appear curiously unreal to the modern eye but to the seventeenth-century reader they were fascinating in their novelty. They aroused great curiosity and helped to create a vogue for Chinese subjects among lovers of engravings. In this way they were the forerunners of numerous prints of the same kind, the inaccuracy of which did not in any way detract from their interest and popularity.

Within ten years of the date of publication of Kircher's work a number of lesser, but still important, volumes had enriched this field of literature. Among these were the *Tratados* of the Dominican Navarrete,[8] a controversial work, the second volume of which was suppressed by Rome on account of its frank discussion of Jesuit missionary methods in the Far East. The first volume is filled with a multitude of facts concerning the *mores* and habits of the Chinese but is marred by frequent inaccuracies. At this time there appeared also the highly important Intorcetta translations of the Confucian classics, of which mention will be made later.

These works came at a critical period in European thought. The great age of discovery of the sixteenth century had given place to an epoch when Europe was beginning to draw cultural dividends from the energy and hardiness of the explorers. The West was becoming vaguely conscious of its place in the universe. Old and respected traditions and doctrines were being questioned by men who had begun to read of strange countries and remarkable customs, of virtuous practices among unknown tribes, and of admirable rules of living prevalent among "heathen" peoples. America had found a place on the literary map with the eloquent pleas of Garcilaso de la Vega for the

Incas and their brilliant civilization. Gomara had written his important *History of the Indies,* while the monk Las Casas had added his
voice to the condemnation of Spanish cruelties. At the same time
the works of Bernier, Tavernier, Chardin, and others were interesting
Europe in the civilization of the Near East and of India.

This type of literature reached its climax toward the end of the
seventeenth century and gave rise to another literary form, the imaginary voyage.[9] Offspring of Utopia on the one hand and of the travel-
books on the other, the imaginary voyage was an attempt to foist upon
a legendary people customs and institutions which had their source
in the ideas and ideals of the writer. The source of these books is more
important than the works themselves, for at heart they were the
expression of dissatisfaction with European social and moral conditions and of a desire to find in foreign lands models for reformation
or amelioration of these conditions.

Reform was in the air, particularly in the realm of religious thought
and practice. Christian theology was being put on the defensive; its
authority in moral affairs was even being seriously attacked. The
medieval system which strove to limit man's historical and ethical
horizons to the Bible, the Church Fathers, Plato, and Aristotle found
itself in the presence of a new cosmopolitanism, which was beginning
to question Biblical cosmography and chronology and, at times, even
the basic dogmas of Christianity. The problem of the fate of the "virtuous heathen," for example, which had troubled the Church for
centuries, was assuming an added importance in the light of new
knowledge. In the middle of the seventeenth century the French
freethinker, La Mothe le Vayer, had, for the first time, coupled the
name of Confucius with those of Socrates, Aristotle, and other virtuous pagans for whom he claimed exemption from the law of eternal
damnation.[10] At the same time authors of books on the New World
were beginning to sing the praises of the American Indian and to
evolve that fantastic literary tradition of the "noble savage" which
was to persist in European literature for nearly two hundred years.

This accumulated evidence appeared to suggest to the thinkers of Europe that the Church could not have a monopoly on virtue and that it was a question whether religion ought not to be divorced from morality. In a world racked with ecclesiastical abuses and other evils this suggestion struck with startling force.

Then came the evidence of the Chinese classics. For the first time since the Middle Ages Europe began to hear of a great and ancient civilization which, for perhaps four thousand years, had had a noble conception of ethical distinctions and a firm and successful system of private and public morals. In the history of European thought only the cultures of Greece and Rome had presented to Christendom such a worthy rival to the Christian system of ethics and morals. It is not surprising, then, that China almost immediately took a definite and permanent place in European thought.

In this movement the literature of the Jesuits played a preponderant part. About the time when the great churchman Fénelon was describing for his royal pupil, the Duke of Burgundy, the little utopia of Betica, there appeared the *Nouveaux Mémoires sur la Chine*[11] by Father Louis Lecomte. The furor which this work created among the theologians of Paris has already been described. As a result of the controversy over the book the religious system of China came to be closely associated with the cult which at that time was making such headway in Europe as a substitute for Christian theology—the cult of Deism. In this way China became an important stimulus to the chief philosophical movement of the period.

Meanwhile, at the other end of the Eurasiatic continent, a small group of Jesuits, under the leadership of Father Intorcetta, had been laboring to put into the languages of the West the crystallized wisdom of the Confucian canon. Almost contemporaneously with Lecomte's book there appeared a small volume entitled *Confucius Sinarum Philosophus* (1687).[12] This had been preceded, five years earlier, by a work entitled *La Science des Chinois*[13] which expounded the teachings of the Chinese sage. In addition to these two interpreta-

tions of Chinese philosophical thought, there was a translation of the
Four Books, published in 1711 at Prague by Father Noël.[14]

To many of the intelligentsia of Europe the wisdom of Confucius
appeared almost as a revelation. The Jesuits had portrayed him not
so much as a philosopher as a great religious teacher. Here is a man,
they said, whose doctrines are so pure, so lofty that they seem to
breathe the very spirit of the true Faith. Here, they asserted, is a system which has stood the test of more than two thousand years and
still remains the spiritual guide of countless millions of people. In
this way a little of their reverence for the Chinese sage was communicated to Europe. In Germany, Leibnitz read the teachings of
Confucius with astonished admiration; in France, the freethinker
La Mothe le Vayer, felt himself constrained to exclaim "Sancte Con-
fuci, ora pro nobis!"; in England, the Deists found in these teachings
the epitome of their Natural Religion. The emphasis on the social
rather than on the mystical needs of man which characterized the
Confucian system appealed to thinkers who were beginning to use
their skepticism of the Biblical miracles as a point of departure for
a new creed.

The Jesuits, taking advantage of this enthusiasm to enhance the
reputation of their mission work in China and to obtain support for
their policy of compromise, proclaimed that a system which was such
a worthy competitor of Christianity must have had a common source
with the latter. Accordingly, they diligently studied the ancient Chinese canon for support of such a thesis. Their arguments, which found
the most extreme form in the theories of the Figurist group, were
ingenious, extravagant, and generally unacceptable to the Church as
a whole, but they deeply influenced such minds as those of Leibnitz
and others who were seeking for a universal system of philosophy
and ethics.[15]

Bound up with the Figurist theories was the question of chronology. Here again the Jesuit writers had a distinct influence on contemporary thought. The horizons of the people of Europe at this time

were being thrust back temporally as well as geographically. Anthropology had not yet come to the aid of man in his search for origins, but scholars were beginning to push further back into the past to discover the origins of life and society. The Biblical stories of Adam and of the Flood were being questioned more and more. In the history of China Christian theology found itself faced by another chronological system, well authenticated and based on records which forced themselves upon the attention of Western scholars. Curiosity was aroused, and soon the Jesuit missionaries found themselves the recipients of many eager inquiries.

The cornerstone of Biblical chronology rested on the Genesis account of the Flood. It had been discovered that other lands had a legend of a great deluge. The question arose: Did these traditions deal with the same Flood or merely with a local phenomenon? When this tradition came from a country which had no long, authenticated record, no problem arose, but when it came from China, a land with a continuous history reaching beyond the scriptural date of the Deluge, the problem of the correctness of Biblical chronology, as well as that of pre-Deluge history was involved.

The controversy placed the Jesuits on the horns of a dilemma. If they insisted on the validity of the Chinese records, they struck at the roots of authority in the scriptures. If, on the other hand, they remained true to Biblical tradition, they threw doubt on the authenticity of the ancient canon of the culture which they were praising so highly. They met the situation by putting aside the authority of the Vulgate in favor of the Septuagint version of the scriptures, the chronology of which seemed to harmonize with Chinese figures. Jesuit ideas greatly interested such scholars as Fréret and La Peyrère; in the ensuing discussion, Western knowledge of China was further broadened and deepened.

It was in Germany that the influence of the new knowledge was first seen. In the middle of the seventeenth century the scholar Isaac Vossius had composed a treatise in which the virtues of the Chinese were enthusiastically praised.[16] Vossius' work was the forerunner of a number of works on this subject by German scholars.

Leibnitz, who was the greatest exponent of a kind of spiritual cosmopolitanism relatively widespread in Europe at this time,[17] immediately saw the importance of this newly discovered system of social ethics and religious tolerance. As early as 1669 he began to express his admiration for the Chinese sage and his teachings. At the end of the century he published his work entitled *Novissima Sinica* which contains much of the material he had gathered from Jesuit sources. This study emphasized the value of Jesuit activities in China and the importance of the Confucian canon to European thought.

The distinguished German philosopher advocated the founding of Protestant missions in China and, in fact, inspired A. H. Francke to establish such a mission. Leibnitz had, however, a much broader purpose than the spread of Christianity in the Far East. He envisaged a real exchange of religious "ambassadors." "I almost think it necessary," he wrote, "that Chinese missionaries should be sent to us to teach us the aim and practice of natural theology as we send missionaries to them to instruct them in the revealed religion."[18] The plan was a noble one. Its proponent sought an exchange of scientific and philosophical knowledge. Europe should provide the East with Christian doctrines and theoretical science, and the Orient should give the West the benefit of its wisdom in practical philosophy and in what is called today the social sciences.[19]

Leibnitz sought in the Orient—and thought he had found there—arguments for his theory of universal harmony. His theory of binary arithmetic seemed to him a rediscovery of the principles involved in the symbols of the Chinese *pa kua,* and in 1703 he published in the memoirs of the French Academy of Sciences a discussion of this relationship. For some years he carried on a highly illuminating correspondence with Jesuit missionaries, notably Bouvet, Foucquet, and Gaubil. His letters show an intense desire to acquire all the knowledge they could give of Chinese thought and philosophy. In the

new spiritual world order of which he dreamed the German philosopher felt that China must play an important part. He it was who first
saw the supreme importance of the Jesuit role as cultural missionaries
and was anxious for their success in this role. He may, therefore, be
looked upon as the first great European Sinophile.

The enthusiastic admiration of Leibnitz for the culture of China
was echoed by his disciple, Christian Wolff. The latter took advantage of the opportunity afforded by his farewell oration as Prorector
of the University of Halle in 1721 to proclaim a fervent eulogy of
Chinese philosophy.[20] Asserting that the Chinese doctrines con-
formed to his own philosophy of life, Wolff expounded the theory
that the Confucian canon was, in reality, the teaching of the ethical
and political power of natural reason. Though he did not, as his
enemies later claimed, state that the Chinese were atheists, he emphasized the efficacy of a system which appeared to harmonize the happiness of the individual with the welfare of the state. There is much
in his views which implies—as did Voltaire thirty years later—that
this alone was a doctrine adequate to support the religious aspirations of a people. Wolff's oration created a furor in Halle. His enemies, notably Francke and Lange, accused him of atheism and they
succeeded in getting him dismissed from his professorship at the
university. Wolff went to Marburg, where he was enthusiastically
received, and there continued his teaching. Among his pupils was
Bülffinger, who published a work in 1724 to demonstrate how the
Chinese system preached the practices of virtue in both public and
private life. By the middle of the eighteenth century, then, Jesuit literature with its eulogy of Chinese thought had made a deep impression
on German minds.[21]

In England the first reaction to the philosophy of Confucius is to
be found in the writings of the Deists, who were leading the movement toward a more liberal interpretation of the scriptures and a wider
conception of religion. In general the Deists followed Leibnitz in his
admiration for Chinese thought. The most enthusiastic of them was,

perhaps, Matthew Tindal. Supporting his thesis that Christians had not arrived at any higher state of perfection than the rest of mankind, Tindal made frequent references to the Chinese. He interpreted the moral code of Confucius not as an enemy but as an ally of Christianity. "I am so far from thinking the maxims of Confucius and Jesus Christ to differ," he writes, "that I think the plain and simple maxims of the former will help to illustrate the more obscure ones of the latter, accommodated to their way of thinking."[22]

In England, as later in France, the humanistic basis of the Confucian canon was looked upon as a potential antidote for the obscurantism which the Deists declared they found in the Christian scriptures.

In France the fame of the Chinese sage developed more slowly. The country was under the intellectual tyranny of Louis XIV's regime, which was attempting to suppress the rising tide of free thought in religious matters. But Confucius was appreciated by the freethinkers, like La Mothe le Vayer, from the middle of the seventeenth century.

In 1708 the celebrated Oratorian philosopher Malebranche wrote the *Conversation between a Christian Philosopher and a Chinese Philosopher on the Existence of God.*[23] Father Gollet, one of the Figurist group of Jesuit missionaries, had made known to Malebranche the delight of the Chinese in his writings. Malebranche, therefore, was persuaded by the Jesuit opponent, Mgr. de Lionne, Bishop of Rosalie, to write a treatise on the Deity. In this treatise he attempted to refute the Chinese idea that matter is eternal and that *Li* or supreme wisdom, also eternal, is associated with it, being a purified form of matter expressing itself in the intelligence of man. The work of Malebranche has a curious similarity to Ricci's great treatise, *T'ien Chu shih I,* written in 1595, but since the latter work was not translated into French until the end of the seventeenth century, there was probably no direct borrowing from the Jesuit book. The *Conversation* of Malebranche may have been written as a reaction to Maigrot's account of his experiences in China. At any rate the Jesuit *Journal de Trévoux* attacked the work for its implication that the Chinese were atheists, to which Malebranche replied that the book was in no sense meant to be a reproach of the Jesuit missionary work in China. Malebranche seems to have had only an imperfect knowledge of Chinese philosophy but he was keenly interested in the subject, for he thought he saw in the Chinese system many points of similarity with the philosophy of Spinoza.

It is significant that in this period the three great representatives of Cartesian philosophy, Spinoza, Leibnitz, and Malebranche, were all associated with the new cult of Confucius. By the beginning of the eighteenth century, then, the knowledge and appreciation of Chinese culture was in the process of being built on the solid foundations of a study of the Confucian canon and, what is more important, on a comparison of these doctrines with European Christian thought.

In the meantime members of the Society of Jesus in the Middle Kingdom were continuing their work as purveyors of Chinese culture to Europe. At the end of the seventeenth century the controversy over Lecomte's *Mémoires* brought the debate over the Chinese Rites to a head in France. The quarrel died down after a few years, but to take the place of the books it inspired there appeared two monuments of Sinophile literature which were to exert a profound influence on the European reading public. The first of these was a series of volumes entitled *Lettres édifiantes et curieuses écrites des Missions Etrangères,* published periodically throughout the century.[24]

These letters are valuable, particularly, for the variety of information which they contain. Intended primarily as a source of propaganda for the foreign missions, they supplied the European reading public with a panoramic view of the rich and complex culture of China. They deal with a host of subjects, ranging from the making of artificial flowers to the history of the Jews in the Middle Kingdom; from the nature of the cochineal bug to the annals of Christian persecution. The tone of the letters is sometimes naïve, sometimes erudite, always informative. They give illuminating evidence of the role of the Jesuit missionaries as *entrepreneurs* between East and West.

The second of the literary monuments of Sinophile literature is the *Description de la Chine* of Father du Halde.[25] This priest, having been delegated the task of editing the *Lettres édifiantes,* had received a mass of material which was not suited to publication in that work. He decided, therefore, to publish this material separately, and it appeared in a four-quarto-volume edition in 1735, accompanied by an atlas of maps engraved by the celebrated French engraver, D'Anville. Du Halde's work was carefully edited to make it suitable to the needs of its public and at the same time to glorify the achievements of the members of the Society. Indeed in some instances Du Halde incurred the displeasure of the missionaries on account of the changes or emendations which he made in the material supplied to him—displeasure which was probably justified. In spite of frequent inaccuracies and misrepresentations, however, the work was an extremely valuable contribution to the literature of the subject. It deals with many phases of Chinese life and thought. In its pages are to be found a great amount of statistical material concerning the geography and history of the empire, a short description of the dynasties, brief translations from Chinese poetry and proverbs, and interesting glimpses into other branches of Chinese literature. It contains also accounts of the journeys of Gerbillon and Verbiest with K'ang Hsi into the Manchurian country and a translation, by Father Prémare, of a Yuan dynasty drama, the *Orphan of the House of Chao.* The last-named is noteworthy as providing inspiration for one of Voltaire's most successful plays, *L'Orphelin de la Chine*—a most significant literary byproduct of the Sinophile movement.

Du Halde's work was enthusiastically received by the scholars and literary public of Europe. It was quickly translated into English and German. Voltaire refers to it frequently in laudatory terms and in his *Age of Louis XIV* he places the author on the list of great men of his time. Montesquieu leaned heavily on the work for his knowledge of China when he discussed that country in his *Esprit des lois.* In general, Du Halde's work was a source book for most of the authors whose writings aided in the spread of cosmopolitanism in the eighteenth century. No single work on the Far East, before or since, has had such a profound influence on European thought.

Before we leave the subject of Jesuit literature on China, mention must be made of the most ambitious contribution to that literature, the *Mémoires concernant les Chinois par les missionaires de Pékin*,[26] a work in sixteen quarto volumes which appeared toward the end of the eighteenth century. In general it presents, in a more scholarly way, the material found in Du Halde. Because of its learned nature, however, and because of the variety and value of the Chinese classics of which it gives translations, the work still remains unrivaled in its field. It represented the efforts of scholars like Amiot, Gaubil, and Prémare, the last representatives of the French Jesuit mission in China before the dissolution of the Society. Whereas Du Halde's work may be said to be an attempt at popularization of the subject, the *Mémoires* had a definitely erudite purpose. Most of the material consists of translations from Chinese documents; relatively little space is given to the comments of the missionaries themselves. The work was the direct result of the curiosity expressed by scholars in France. Its aim was to meet ever-increasing demands for further and more accurate information about Chinese culture.

It was not alone in the seclusion of the study, however, or in the heated atmosphere of controversy that the new knowledge from, and concerning, China was being disseminated. Before the Middle Kingdom was known as the land of Confucius, it had gained a wide reputation as the source of the most delicate and artistic handicraft Europe had seen since the golden days of the Italian Renaissance. Even before the beginning of the seventeenth century a stream of Chinese *objets d'art* had begun to flow to the West. Articles in porcelain, bronze, jade, and ivory, lacquered screens and cabinets, painted panels and fans were imported and began to exert a profound influence on the modes and fashions of the time. Through Russians in the North, through Portuguese adventurers, through Dutch and English traders, through Jesuits, and through trading companies a delighted Europe received large quantities of the exquisite products of Chinese artists and artisans.

The Jesuits urged the French government to participate in this lucrative commerce. Partly as a result, the ship "Amphitrite," sent out in 1693, returned with a cargo rich enough to give the shareholders a dividend of 50 per cent on their investment. The vessel made a second trip, which was moderately successful. A third was not attempted, probably on account of the opposition of manufacturers in France who were producing imitations.[27]

It was not long before French and other artisans were striving to reproduce the perfection of Chinese *bibelots*. At Delft in Holland, at Sèvres in France, at the royal pottery of Worcester in England, Chinese porcelain—always considered, *par excellence*, the supreme gift of China to the West—was receiving new interpretations at the hands of European craftsmen.[28] Strange distortions of landscapes and figures, curious men and women in pseudo-exotic landscapes, of which the ever-popular willow-pattern plate is the most lasting and typical example, had their provenance in European factories.

In France, the Martin family, under the patronage of La Pompadour, perfected the manufacture of lacquered articles. At Lyons, French manufacturers began to lay the foundations of that city's reputation in the making of silk goods. By the end of the seventeenth century the cult of Chinese art motifs and objects had developed from the admiring and collecting of these objects to a period of imitation, the period of *chinoiserie,* during which Chinese designs were copied—more or less—and incorporated into new styles in decorations and furnishings.

As the eighteenth century passed, the craze for things Chinese became ubiquitous. It must not be thought that *chinoiserie* represented an attempt at a faithful, realistic picture of Chinese life and manners. Foreigners in China and Japan in the last twenty-five years have been often amused at the unlovely and often ludicrous products of Oriental attempts to imitate Western models. The same inexactness, the same *gaucherie,* the same lack of comprehension of exotic canons of taste were to be found in the *chinoiserie.* The cult came to satisfy the desires of a period when classicism, with its severe standards and cold logic, was losing its charm for the greater part of the upper classes and was becoming, artistically speaking, an empty shell. In France the Regency with its license brought only disillusionment; boredom became the prevailing disease of the *beau monde.* Society tried to find a way of escape in works of fantasy: in the cult of the romanesque typified by the charming comedies of Marivaux; in the delicate sensitiveness and fairy backgrounds of the landscapes of Watteau, Boucher, and others. Delicacy and grace combined to give artistic expression to the nostalgia of the time.

It was in this atmosphere that *chinoiserie* was fostered, and here it flourished. It was these qualities which dominated the interpretation of Chinese art and life in the artizanship of the period. *Chinoiserie* was the reproduction not of living models but of Oriental artistic creations—the imitation of an imitation. The figures on a Chinese fan or a porcelain vase served as inaccurate models. The copies were often grotesque and fantastic, even though charming, so that the Chinese motif ended by conjuring up a land of fantasy filled with exotic but graceful birds and flowers and queer people, that unreal land so characteristic of the landscape painters of the time.

In the meantime the upper classes of France, who were tiring of classical restrictions, were becoming weary also of the geometrical symmetry of the classical out-of-doors, of those stately but cold garden landscapes brought to their perfection by Lenôtre at Versailles and elsewhere. Consequently, Chinese influence overflowed from the salon into the outer air. If *chinoiserie* is preëminently a French cult, the effect of the application of Chinese ideas to gardens was chiefly felt across the Channel, where the natural landscape garden had always been a rival of the classical type.[29] At the beginning of the eighteenth century in England a need was felt for a more intimate form of garden architecture—something dominated by the spirit of play, which more closely met the demands of leisurely recreation. At the end of the seventeenth century Sir William Temple, an ardent Sinophile, advocated a new type of garden architecture,[30] and a few years later Addison and Pope were to seize upon his ideas, setting up the Chinese garden as a model worthy of emulation. Here again the Jesuit influence is noteworthy. Brother Attiret's letter of 1743, published in the *Lettres édifiantes*, gave an illuminating description of the gardens at the Yuan Ming Yuan palace outside Peking. Speaking of the palace grounds he says:

> It is truly a terrestrial paradise. The artificial streams (*canaux*) are not arranged symmetrically, as they are with us, but are laid out, bordered with stone in a rustic fashion, with pieces of rockery, some protruding, some set back, and placed with so much art that one would say it was the work of Nature. Sometimes the stream is wide, sometimes narrow; here it winds, there it makes a sharp bend as if the course were really regulated by hills and rocks. The banks are planted with flowers, springing from the rockery in such a way that they seem to have been placed there by Nature. . . .[31]

He then describes the summer arbors, bridges, and other buildings and decorations which add to the charm of the landscape. Brother Attiret's detailed and enthusiastic description is an important document, since it furnished the foundations for the European conception of a Chinese garden. Most subsequent treatises on the subject make reference to his letter.

But here as elsewhere insufficient evidence of a definite nature, such as pictures or plans, brought about a misunderstanding of Chinese garden architecture. It was at first thought that the Chinese aimed at imitating natural wildness and not, as Father Benoit says in a letter written from Peking in 1767, to "employ art to perfect nature." What the rebels against classicism were seeking was a kind of beauty without order, a *"beau désordre,"* an asymmetrical garden where the element of surprise, together with a feeling of intimacy, would displace the cold formalism and lineal rectitude of classicism.[32] The result was the Anglo-Chinese garden which, at least on the continent and up

Jesuit architect's drawing of one of the foreign buildings, the Hsieh Ch'i Ch'ü, at the Yuan Ming Yuan, the Imperial Summer Palace of Peking

to 1771, meant almost everything that was contrary to the spirit of the Lenôtre ideal of garden landscape. Like the products of *chinoiserie,* it was a hybrid creation, the sole unity of which was to be found in the satisfaction it gave to the demand for variety and recreation in gardens. The Anglo-Chinese garden kept its classical ornaments, its temples to Love, and its Greek and Gothic structures, but it added to them the "pagoda," the curved bridge, the lily pond with its "gondola," the Chinese *tingtze* or kiosk, and the *p'ei lou* or "Oriental arch." The most important of the innovations was the pagoda, which had its prototype in the famous porcelain tower of Nanking, a picture of which had been published in Kircher's work in 1672. With this as inspiration, imitations appeared in the gardens of many a European king and nobleman: in the grounds of the Trianon, at Frederick of Prussia's Sans Souci, at Chanteloup in France, at Kew Gardens in London, and at a score of lesser known places. Most of these were frail structures, disappearing in the early eighteen-twenties when the Romantic landscape with its Ossianic wildness and its ruins created a new vogue. Nevertheless, the pagoda and other exotic ornaments added to the European conception of Chinese garden topography and exerted a great influence on the time. So profound was this influence that it has been asserted that the idea of beauty without order, the *coup de grâce* of eighteenth-century neoclassicism, was Chinese in origin.[33]

In this movement the Jesuits had their part, although indirectly. They supplied the only authentic descriptions of Chinese gardens many years before Chambers wrote his well-known work on the subject. They sent to Europe Chinese prints as well as designs made by themselves or by their pupils expressly for the Occident. Moreover, they undoubtedly contributed their share to the trade in Chinese *objets d'art* and, consequently, to the development of *chinoiserie.*[34]

Chapter XVII

THE JESUITS AS INTERPRETERS OF THE CULTURES OF EAST AND WEST

T HE CONTRIBUTION of China to the intellectual life of the West was as important as its influence on European arts and crafts. It will be illuminating, therefore, to examine briefly the nature of this contribution in different fields of learning. With the exception of the Confucian studies mentioned, the most important field of learning covered by the Sinological labors of the Jesuits was that of history. Few writers on China have avoided the temptation of reflecting that admiration which the Chinese themselves have for the antiquity of their culture. The Jesuits found it a facile instrument with which to play upon the imagination of Europe. In general their works on Chinese history fall into three classes: first, those of the ancient period, consisting of translations or adaptations of old classics, often imperfectly done; second, those relating to contemporary history, the materials for which came from eyewitnesses and from official records; and third, works of a general nature. Martin Martini was the first to write on the ancient period.[1] He was followed, and surpassed, by the most brilliant of Jesuit Sinologues, Antoine Gaubil. This missionary was a historian of distinguished ability. More than any of the others he developed a broad and scholarly attitude toward his subject. He searched Chinese records for evidence which appeared to link the history of the empire to that of other lands and often made possible the solution of problems which had troubled Western learning. His *History of Genghis Khan*,[2] published in 1739, was the first version of the Mongol leader's life, based on Oriental sources, to reach Europe. It was a careful piece of scholarship and has won praise even from those Chinese scholars who are slow to see any merit in the Sinological labors of the Jesuits or other Western scholars.

[1] For notes to chap. xvii, see pp. 333-335.

De Visdelou had already explored the vast field of north-Asian history in so far as it was contained in Chinese sources. He was content to transfer the facts found in Chinese books without any process of selection. Gaubil, on the other hand, chose his material carefully, trying to put each fact in its place and to evaluate it correctly. He brought to his subject the force of a keen intellect, which showed itself in suggestive notes and brilliant commentaries. The greatest of his works is his translation of the Book of History (*Shu King*),[3] that classic which spreads before the reader part of the pageant of ancient Chinese civilization. To this masterly work Father Prémare, another Jesuit of marked erudition, added a summary of Chinese chronology.[4] Among the most important of Gaubil's scholarly works, a list of which fills several columns, must be placed his *History of the T'ang Dynasty*,[5] published in the *Mémoires*.

The greater part of the Jesuit historical studies had to do with contemporary history. Martini wrote an account of the wars which had ruined the Ming dynasty and allowed the Manchus to come to the throne. To the same subject Father d'Orléans contributed a *History of Two Manchu Conquerors*,[6] a historical essay which did not fail to interest eighteenth-century Europe. Bouvet's *Portrait of the Emperor of China*,[7] a valuable source for the life of K'ang Hsi, and Le Gobien's account of the publication of the edict of 1692,[8] both written as contributions to the Lecomte controversy, added many facts concerning the China of that day. There can be little doubt that, looking at the matter from the standpoint of its contribution to historical knowledge in general, the Jesuit works in this class were of the most importance. The relations between the Jesuits and the throne enabled them to give historical data which is not be found even in the Chinese books of the time.

Perhaps the most important of Jesuit historical works of this period—at least as regards the development of European Sinology—is the translation by Father de Mailla of the *T'ung Chien Kang Mu*, one of the classics of Chinese historiography.[9] The emperor had ordered his scholars to make a Manchu translation and De Mailla used this version. He revised and brought the work up to date, adding from the sources at his disposal the more recent history of the empire, particularly of the Jesuit mission in China. The work appeared in twelve quarto volumes in 1778. Severely criticized for its inaccuracies, it is not so scholarly as some of the other Jesuit writings, but it was extremely valuable to the savants of Europe since it was the first work of importance covering the whole sweep of Chinese civilization to be made available in a European language.

No discussion of the Jesuit contribution in the field of history would be complete without reference to the extracts from the annals of the empire, published by Du Halde. These had a wider and more popular appeal than the more erudite works of the priests in the field. They added a picturesque touch to Chinese history. Du Halde reproduced a large number of anecdotes relating to the moral excellence of Chinese emperors and officials and of virtuous women. These went to swell that literature of edification and amusement which, since the Middle Ages, had kept alive stories of such heroes as Alexander, Alfred the Saxon, and Henri Quatre. Du Halde's tales had also a distinct didactic effect, serving as they did, more than any other source, to create the eighteenth-century tradition of a benevolent despotism in China.

Many of the Jesuit historical works have been superseded by modern scholarship, but this in no way detracts from their importance as sources of Europe's knowledge of China in the eighteenth century and as contributions to the development of Sinology in the West. Here, as in so many channels of culture, the missionaries were pioneers. They blazed the trail of historical studies which later Sinologists made broader and smoother. By the end of the eighteenth century, thanks to their efforts, Europe had a fairly accurate account of the magnificent panorama of Chinese culture.

The Jesuit contribution to the knowledge of Far Eastern geography is equally striking. As has already been indicated, the only reliable source of information on this subject before the seventeenth century—with the exception of occasional facts gleaned from other medieval travelers—was the book of Ser Marco Polo. Such information, obscure and vague as it was, could not be effectively used. Until the middle of the fifteenth century, indeed, the geographers made scarcely an effort to reform their maps in the light of the new materials. The Catalan map (1375), the oldest extant document which makes use of the new knowledge, is a vast improvement on previous attempts at Far Eastern geography but it still leaves the picture of eastern Asia in a vague and incorrect condition. Not until the middle of the sixteenth century did Munster, Ortelius, Thevet, and others begin really to take advantage of Marco Polo's contribution to Far Eastern geography. In all these works, however, Cathay—essentially Mongol northeastern Asia—took the central place, and the distinction between it and China proper was ill defined. The age of scientific cartography had not yet arrived.

The enthusiasm of Henry the Navigator brought modern geography into existence.[10] However, it was not until much later, indeed, until well into the seventeenth century, that the proper coördination of geographical facts brought about the publication of accurate maps of the Far East. Ortelius, Mercator, and their contemporaries might have benefited from much information obtainable from Portuguese sources but they continued to identify China with the Manzi of Marco Polo. This was the situation when Ricci printed his map of the world in 1584.[11]

For centuries there had existed Chinese maps of the empire which, although abundant in information, lacked scientific detail. When Ricci and his confreres came to China, they soon became acquainted with these maps and noted their superiority over anything the Portuguese possessed.[12] They set to work to verify the material and to collate it with their own observations and studies. They determined the latitude and longitude of "key" places and were able to correct certain errors made by the Chinese. As a result, Ricci's map, although it still contained inexactitudes, was considerably better than anything which the West possessed at that time.

Ricci's cartographical labors were continued by Fathers Aleni and Boym and by the Jesuit missionary to Japan, Jean Rodriguez Tçuzzu. The great contribution to Europe's knowledge of Chinese geography came, however, in 1655 when Father Martini published his *Novus Atlas Sinensis*,[13] the first truly scientific atlas of the Middle Kingdom. Martini had personally traveled in seven of the fifteen provinces of China and, with the geographical facts he obtained from his fellow priests, he had an excellent knowledge of a great part of the empire. Martini, modest though he was, showed himself a great geographer. Making intelligent use of Chinese material at hand and adding to it his own knowledge, he described in detail each province and each prefecture, giving innumerable facts which had been unknown to Europe before the publication of his work. Until the nineteenth century Martini's atlas remained the most complete and the most illuminating in the West.

Great as was Martini's work, however, it contained serious errors, as, for example, the placing of the city of Samarkand near the border of Kansu. Little by little the Jesuits who followed him were able to correct these errors. Verbiest's travels with the emperor in Tartary helped to solve certain of the geographical problems of that region. Fathers Noël, Thomas, de Fontenoy, and others also helped by checking data with astronomical observations.

The geographical material presented by the early Jesuits was not immediately assimilated in Europe. For some years there remained the old confusion between *Sinarum regio, Serica regio,* Cathay and the China of Renaissance cartography. Not until the travels in central and northeastern Asia of Brother Bernard Goës and of Fathers Grueber and d'Orville—all Jesuits—had taken place was the confusion definitely ended.

Although Verbiest had first interested K'ang Hsi in the possibility of mapping the whole empire, it was probably Parennin who finally persuaded the emperor to order the undertaking of the work. When at last the Jesuits were placed in charge, all the resources of the government were at their disposal. In their surveys they used the most scientific methods of the time, triangulation and verification of long distances by the study of eclipses. Great care was taken to make the work accurate and definitive. The task took ten years to complete. Nine priests participated, in addition to a large number of Chinese assistants.

The work was started in July, 1708, when Bouvet, Régis, and Jartoux began a survey of the Great Wall and adjacent territory. Six months later the results of their labors were presented in a fifteen-foot map which greatly pleased the emperor. In the following year Régis, Jartoux, and Fridelli—the last-named a German Jesuit—crossed the Great Wall to map eastern Tartary (Manchuria), the ancestral home of the reigning dynasty. The priests went as far north as the fourth degree of latitude and as far south as the borders of Korea, covering for the most part a desert country with few landmarks of importance. K'ang Hsi was delighted with this first cartographical description of his great northern empire, in parts of which he had recently ordered constructed a number of forts. As a result, in accordance with imperial orders, the Jesuit scholars were split into several bands to map the land south of the Wall, in China proper.[14]

The results of the surveys were brought to the capital and collated by Fathers Jartoux and Régis in a general map, which was presented to the emperor in 1721. K'ang Hsi immediately had it engraved on thin sheets of white jade.

The cartographical labors of the Jesuits were not carried on entirely without difficulty. Under the orders of the emperor, local officials did indeed give assistance, but at times they appear to have acted under secret orders from Peking—which may or may not have emanated from the throne—not to trust the foreigners too far. Certain territories they were not allowed to penetrate. They were not, for example, permitted to go as far north as the Russian frontier or eastward thence to the sea.[15] The emperor turned a deaf ear to the pleas of Parennin for permission to map this *terra incognita*. Nor were the Europeans allowed to enter Korea or Tibet. The emperor sent only Chinese or Manchu officials into these regions to bring back measurements later collated by the foreign scholars.

The maps were first printed in Chinese, then recopied with Latin characters. Since the art of engraving in China was inferior to that of the West, the Jesuits persuaded K'ang Hsi to send the maps to Europe, where they were engraved under the direction of D'Anville in Paris. When they appeared as a supplement to Du Halde's work in 1735, they aroused much interest and contributed greatly to the popularity of that work.[16] The result of this concerted effort of the Jesuits to map the Chinese empire remains definitive. It has been the basis of all subsequent geographical study of and in China.

The great D'Anville atlas of the Jesuits was not, however, the last of their contributions to Far Eastern cartography. K'ang Hsi, Yung Cheng, and Ch'ien Lung were often concerned about their vast dominions in the north and were constantly seeking information about them. The Jesuits were permitted to get into touch with officials from the border countries, obtaining from them much valuable data. This information was incorporated into new maps, not only of China proper, but also of north-central Asia and northeastern Asia as far as the Arctic Ocean.

In another direction Ch'ien Lung's anxiety over the menace arising from nations on his borders helped the work of cartography. He apparently feared an alliance of the Mohammedan peoples against him and therefore demanded information concerning their countries. Gaubil, in consequence, was commanded to make a map of the frontier lands of Turkey, Persia, and India, and this was added to the map of Sungaria made a short time previously. In 1769 Father Benoit, ordered to make a new atlas of central Asia, produced a collection of 104 plates. The missionary knew nothing of the art of engraving and was forced not only to study the matter himself but also to train assistants in the difficult task. Here, as elsewhere, the result of his efforts has been of use to subsequent geographers of these regions.[17]

In geography, then, as in history the Jesuits were the first to supply the West with extensive and accurate information concerning the Chinese empire. They laid the foundations on which not only European but also Oriental scholars have since built their structure of knowledge.

Considering that the most spectacular part of the Jesuits' work at Peking was their labor at the Bureau of Astronomy, their contribution to European knowledge in that field, at first sight, appears disappointingly meager. It must be remembered, however, that Chinese knowledge of astronomy had been based chiefly on Arabic materials—the Chinese themselves having done little to develop the science. It is not surprising, therefore, to find that the only noteworthy work on the subject by a Jesuit missionary deals chiefly with the history of the Jesuit regime at the Bureau of Astronomy and of the success of members of the Society in introducing European methods into that bureau.[18]

If Chinese astronomy was a barren field, Chinese medicine was equally fruitless. For ages the practice of medicine in China had been carried on through a kind of closed corporation consisting of individuals who handed down their knowledge from father to son. There were a few treatises on different phases of the subject, which were in general unreliable. Father Boym prepared for publication a number of these, including Wang Shu-hua's work on the pulse and a study on the diagnosis of diseases. Boym's manuscript fell into the hands of the Dutch, and a scientist of that nation, André Cleyer, published it, together with other articles on Chinese medicine, in a volume entitled *Specimen medicinae Sinicae* in 1682.[19]

Another slight contribution to European knowledge was the description of Chinese methods of inoculation against smallpox, published by Father d'Entrecolles in the *Lettres édifiantes*.[20] This reached Europe about the time that the famous Doctor Tronchin of Geneva and others were trying to persuade the skeptical that inoculation was a scientific preventative and not the work of the Devil. In the end the Chinese method of inoculating through the nose was rejected in favor of the method now in use, but there exists an account of experiments made on the prisoners at Newgate Prison in 1721, which relates that the Chinese method was tried on one of the prisoners. The Jesuit contribution in this field of medicine, therefore, is interesting rather than important.

In botany the missionaries had a more encouraging field of research, but here also their contribution was not impressive. They made known to Europe a large number of Chinese plants but merely gave the native names without attempting to identify them. Father Boym published in 1656 a *Flora Sinensis,* describing a score of Chinese plants (as well as several animals); twenty-three engravings illustrated the work. The *Letters* and *Memoirs* also contain a few articles on the flora and fauna of the empire, but for a comparatively adequate treatment of the subject Europe had to wait until the nineteenth century.[21]

Scientific linguistics is a relatively modern science; therefore, in this period not much that is definitive can be expected in this field.[22] There were, of course, a number of treatises on the subject, but only one of them is of importance. This is Father Prémare's *Notitia Linguae Sinicae,* a combination grammar and rhetoric, which even in this day of efficient language study is not entirely unnoticed.

In the fields of literature and of belles-lettres little was done. The magnificent T'ang poetry, which was to fill nineteenth- and twentieth-century Europe and America with admiration, was almost completely overlooked, while the golden age of Chinese drama, the Yuan period, was represented by only one example: Prémare's translation of the *Orphan of the House of Chao,* published, as before noted, by Du Halde. The same Jesuit work contained a few examples of Chinese literature, notably the *Ku Wen,* a collection of prose readings compiled by order of K'ang Hsi, and eight odes taken from the *Shih King,* both translated by Hervieu.

In addition, Ch'ien Lung's poem on Mukden and his verse in praise of tea found their way into French through the medium of the *Mémoires* and aroused the interest of Voltaire. The aged philosopher-poet immediately penned some graceful verses to the monarch, hailing him as a fellow artist—a piece of presumption the Son of Heaven could scarcely be expected to appreciate. The verses, however, brought to Voltaire a gift of porcelain from his Oriental "confrere." This meeting, in the high realms of poetry, between the greatest monarch of his time and the famous leader of European thought, brought about through the medium of the missionaries, is an interesting, if trivial, incident in the history of the Jesuits as go-betweens in the relations of East and West.

Although not remarkable in detail—since the members of the order were rarely profound scholars—the quantity and variety of the literature and thought of China presented to Europe by the Jesuits was striking and significant. They gave the West an alluring insight into the breadth, depth, and richness of Chinese culture; they aroused a spirit of curiosity and suggested a starting point for a more scholarly and searching study of the subject. That the Sinophilism which this body of literature inspired was tainted with dilettantism may be true, but superficiality was a characteristic of eighteenth-century science, which in many fields served merely to clear the ground for more certain advances in the centuries which followed.

The role of the Jesuits as purveyors of culture is more important in their contributions to Europe than in their achievements as introducers of European culture to China, but the latter are neither uninteresting nor unimportant. Their greatest work was, of course, in astronomy. In the course of their stay in China there was a tremendous advance in astronomical science in the West. It was the period of Galileo, of Tycho Brahe, and of Kepler. In 1608 the telescope was invented. With this instrument scholars revolutionized the science and added enormously to human knowledge of the universe. At the college of the order in Rome Father Clavius, a friend of Kepler and

Galileo, was an enthusiastic exponent of the new discoveries. Ricci and De Ursis had been among his pupils. When Galileo went to Rome in 1611 to defend his theories at a formal meeting of the Roman college, it is probable that among his audience were Adam Schall and Jean Schreck. The latter, under the Latin name of Terrentius, was to distinguish himself in after years (1626–1630) through his scholarly activities in Peking.[23] In 1611 he was a member of the academy of Linceus, a group of scholars active in liberal thought in the Eternal City. The new discoveries in astronomy, with their disturbing repercussions on orthodox religious thought, were creating a stir in Rome. It was in this atmosphere that the training of those priests who were to have such an influence on Chinese astronomy took place. When Father Trigault arrived in Rome in the year 1614 with insistent demands for missionary astronomers, he was enthusiastically received, and many wished to return with him to the Far East. Those who were chosen took with them to the Orient their enthusiasm for the new knowledge. In Peking they kept up their interest in the progress of the science in Europe and awaited with eagerness news of further achievements. An account of Galileo's discoveries had arrived in China in 1612, and two years later Father Diaz was making use of the new theories in his *Explanation of the Celestial Sphere.*

The Church, however, although willing to accept Galileo's theories in themselves, was unwilling to accept their implications. Rome condemned his conclusions, particularly the theory of the rotation of the earth around the sun,[24] and in 1614 the general of the Jesuit order forbade the dissemination of the idea of the "liquidity of the heavens." Clavius, a champion of the new school of thought, had died in 1612, and other astronomers of the Society remained silent in face of the general's pronunciamento. In China the missionaries tried to keep in touch by correspondence with Galileo; failing this, they turned to Kepler for advice. The condemnation of Galileo must have embarrassed and hampered them a great deal in their work. They finally sought refuge in the system of Tycho Brahe who, though turning his back on the outmoded Ptolemaic system, had nevertheless retained the theory of the stationary position of the earth in relation to the sun. The Jesuits appear to have had a dual method of procedure: within the palace they taught the Copernican system, but in their work at the observatory they relied on the treatise of Manuel Diaz which was based on the old Ptolemaic theories.[25] Not until 1865 were the discoveries of Galileo and Kepler publicly made use of in the Catholic missions in China.

The Jesuits have been much criticized for their adherence to an obsolete system but here, as so often in the history of the Chinese mission, they were victims of a conflict between rational methods, necessitated by the logic of their situation at the Chinese court, on the one hand, and restrictions of ecclesiastical authority on the other. In this predicament they can scarcely be blamed if they subordinated the uncertain wishes of Rome to the exigencies of the immediate and local situation.

In mathematics they were not hampered by theological restrictions—and here their contribution was important. As early as 1607 Ricci, with the aid of Paul Hsü, translated the first six books of Euclid, and Trigault taught the Chinese the use of logarithms.[26] It was not an easy task to teach mathematics to Chinese in the Chinese language, since the priests had often to create a terminology to describe concepts which were nonexistent in the native science. Their efforts, respectfully received by many scholars, led to a curious renaissance of Chinese knowledge in the field. The savant Mei Ku-cheng noted the fact that the algebra expounded by the Jesuits was much the same in principle as the Chinese "celestial method," which had fallen into disuse. This discovery brought about a revival of the ancient science, and for a time new and old terminologies were used side by side.

In arithmetic the Jesuits added little to what the Chinese already possessed, but in geometry they introduced a new science. To the translation of Euclid was added a compendious work entitled *Su le tsing yun* containing the latest knowledge in mathematics and geometry obtained from Europe. A number of other treatises of lesser importance were also written on the subject.

As might be expected, the greatest part of Jesuit writings in Chinese and in Manchu dealt with philosophy and theology. In China as in Europe at this time books of theology and religion by Western scholars outnumbered works on all other subjects. When one examines the bibliography of Jesuit writings prepared by Father Pfister recently, it becomes clear that few of the missionaries failed to supplement their propaganda by the use of the printed page. In the early days of the mission, when it was considered inadvisable to stress too bluntly the dogmas of Christianity, this literature took the form of treatises on morality and ethics.[27] Pantoja wrote *Seven Victories*[28] and Ricci *Twenty-five Moral Maxims*[29] as well as a treatise on the *Art of Memorizing*[30] and an *Essay on Friendship*,[31] all of which were greatly admired. Ricci's *Ten Conversations with Chinese of High Rank*,[32] a brochure on morals, contains little concerning Christian doctrines, but it expounded a system of morality greatly admired by Chinese scholars.

The best-known of the early moral works is Ricci's *True Doctrine of the Lord of Heaven* (*T'ien Chu shih I*), written in 1595 and revised in 1601. Many Chinese have looked upon this book as a masterpiece of style. It was included in Ch'ien Lung's famous catalogue of classics because of its literary excellence, and it has remained popular to this day. Here again there is little exposition of Christian dogma, although there is a vigorous attack on the tenets of Buddhism.

As part of their policy of appealing to the Chinese intellect the Jesuits became prolific writers. By 1631 they had published no fewer than 340 treatises on non-Chinese subjects, and this high rate of publication continued throughout their regime. Most of their works, of course, deal with Christian apologetics, but others cover a wide range of material, from astronomy to hydraulics, from Aesop's Fables to Western music. In all this the Jesuits were assisted by native scholars who helped them in the difficult task of translation. The value of the treatises varied, of course, with the ability of the European writer to use the native language. The mistakes of the less competent were corrected by Chinese associates; the more talented, however, at times produced works which compelled the admiration of the Chinese and gained for the writer a very considerable reputation. For example, Father Aleni, on account of the excellence of his style, was known to his friends as the Confucius of the West—somewhat extravagant praise when we remember the veneration in which the name of the great sage was held![33]

A discussion of the Jesuits' contribution to Chinese knowledge would be incomplete without further reference to their work as court painters. Attention has already been directed to the peculiar nature of the difficulties involved in this task. Did the efforts of the Jesuits result in permanent contribution to the culture of the empire? This is a difficult question. The two chief innovations of the foreign artists were the introduction of European ideas of perspective and the use of chiaroscuro. In neither of these did they profoundly influence Chinese art. Native artists in the main looked upon the foreign notion of perspective as a clever trick—something to amuse but not to be copied. The use of light and shade in painting was more seriously regarded. There are extant several paintings by native artists in which Jesuit influence in this respect may be clearly seen. That there was a tendency on the part of a few artists to profit by the teachings of the Jesuits may be appreciated by a remark of Tsou I-Kwei, one of their pupils: "Students make use of a small percentage of the methods of the Westerners but they are entirely devoid of style. Although their painting shows skill and technique, it cannot be classified as true painting."[34] This presents the point of view of the conservative native artist. The Chinese of this age were too closely bound to the centuries-old technique of the brush to profit greatly by the new methods of the Westerners. Although the ideas of Lang Shih Ning (Castiglione) seem to have left a few slight traces upon the works of modern artists, the ultimate influence of the foreign painters was extremely slight.

In addition to interpreting China to the West, then, the Jesuits took much of Occidental learning to the Orient. This was the most delicate part of their task. Whereas they found in Europe a reading public which avidly seized upon any knowledge they were able or willing to transmit and accepted it with enthusiasm, in China they met with skepticism, based on a long-established contempt for everything foreign, or with a curiosity which envisaged most of this new knowledge as amusing but not fundamentally important or sound. Considering this opposition, it is not surprising that most of the Western science that the Jesuits took to China was not permanently incorporated in the native thought. A small part of it persisted, however, and remained until the empire, about the middle of the nineteenth century, was opened once more to Western intellectual influences.

Chapter XVIII

JESUIT SOURCES OF THE RÊVE CHINOIS
OF THE AGE OF ENLIGHTENMENT

D URING THE PERIOD in which the Jesuit missionaries in Peking
were engaged in building an intellectual bridge between East
and West the effects of their work were being felt more and
more strongly in Europe. Sinophilism in the seventeenth century was
characterized, as we have seen, in the material realm by the adoption
of Chinese art forms and in the realm of the intellect by the discovery of Confucianism. In art the movement had reached and passed its
climax; in the domain of thought the foundations only were being
laid as the century came to a close. It was in the following century—
the Age of Enlightenment—that the spirit of Chinese culture reigned
supreme. Gradually the civilization of the Far Eastern empire began
to impress the imagination of the West as something almost infinite
in its antiquity and its perfection. Europe had discovered a new world,
one which was socially and morally more perfect than anything it
knew. "Of all the kingdoms of the earth," says the English editor of
Lecomte's *Mémoires* (1698), "China is most celebrated for politeness
and civility, for grandeur and magnificence, for arts and inventions."
The movement grew as the century developed to such a degree that
by 1768 Voltaire was able to claim that "China is better known than
some of the provinces of Europe."[1] For many writers the Far Eastern
empire seemed to be the long-sought Utopia.

In England the spread of Sinophilism was contemporaneous with
the declining fortunes of classicism. At the close of the seventeenth
century Sir William Temple, in a significant chapter of his work *On
Heroic Virtue,* had sung the praises of the Chinese. Later Horace
Walpole, that great cosmopolite and lover of the Gothic, was converted to the art of China. Thomas Percy, the English antiquary, was

---
[1] For notes to chap. xviii, see pp. 335–336.

another of her admirers. He edited the first Chinese novel to appear
in a European language and was, in addition, the author of a number
of Chinese studies. Percy's friend, Oliver Goldsmith, also caught his
enthusiasm. The latter's *Mr. Tatler of Peking* was the application of
the Chinese motif to the "observer" type of literature made famous
fifty years previously by Montesquieu's widely read *Persian Letters,*[2]
a genre in which the exotic country is made to serve as the framework
of the author's views and ideas. Other writers added their minor contributions to the movement. Thus by the middle of the century Sinomania had become one of the chief cults of the time. In a poem *On
Taste* written in 1756, James Cawthorne gives amusing expression to
this craze for the exotic:

> Form'd on his plans our farms and seats begin
> To match the boasted villas of Peking.
> On every hill a spire-crowned temple swells,
> Hung round with serpents and a fringe of bells.
> In Tartar huts our cows and horses lie,
> Our hogs are fattened in an Indian stye;
> On every shelf a joss divinely stares,
> Nymphs laid on chintzes sprawl upon our chairs;
> While o'er our cabinets Confucius nods,
> Mid porcelain elephants and China gods.[3]

   This satirical protest against the dominance of Asiatic motifs in
art is accompanied, about the same time, by a skepticism concerning
certain phases of Chinese culture. Goldsmith pokes fun at the Sinophile excesses of his time. Daniel Defoe looks askance at the novelties
introduced from this strange land, while John Shebbeare, William
Nichols, and others add a healthy note of doubt to the chorus of panegyric. In spite of occasional protests, however, the movement continued to grow and in the third quarter of the century had become an
important element in determining English taste and thought.
   Sinophilism in England exerted its influence in two directions. In
the first place, it provided material for those who were beginning to
rebel against the cold classicism of the first part of the century; in

the second place, it provided a model and a philosophy for those who, in the latter half of the century, were preaching the doctrine of the English *honnête homme*. The rule of the Golden Mean of Confucius, with its condemnation of excess in thought and manners, supplied excellent arguments for that theory of deportment of which Lord Chesterfield was an outstanding exponent. The Confucian "superior man" was, then, the philosophical prototype of this class of English gentleman. The intellectual appeal of Sinophilism in England undoubtedly centered around the cult of moderation, and the similarities of the two doctrines—the Oriental and the Occidental—could not have failed to add to the influence of Chinese thought in this country.

The sources of the intellectual Sinophilism in England are to be found in Jesuit literature on China. All the important works on the subject were translated. Kircher's volume, with its pictures, was greatly appreciated. It is to this work that Mr. Pepys undoubtedly refers when he records in his diary on January 14, 1667, "To my bookseller Martin and there did receive my book I expected of China, a most excellent book with rare cuts." Du Halde's *Description* had as important an influence in England as it had across the Channel. Lecomte's two volumes were widely read. Moreover, a number of the *Lettres édifiantes* were done into English for those who could not read them in the original. The journals of the time, the *Spectator,* the *Tatler,* and others, contained laudatory reviews of these books, which stimulated their sale and increased their popularity.

To the studies just mentioned must be added the works of Voltaire, D'Argens, and their fellow philosophers treating of Chinese affairs, as well as the large novelistic literature with a Chinese motif, such as Gueulette's *Contes chinois,* which were also translated. There were, indeed, occasional books by English authors which touched on Chinese affairs, like the well-known *Voyage* of Admiral Anson.[4] On the whole, however, these were few and unsatisfactory, and the English reading public had to rely for its knowledge of China mainly on Jesuit material.

In France also Sinophilism was leaving an indelible mark on the Age of Progress. In the country of Louis XV it became the most important element in the larger movement of cosmopolitanism. The harsh absolutism of the seventeenth century with its worship of tradition and of the theory "un roi, une foi, une loi" was giving way to the doctrines of relativism and universalism. The inhabitants of the land of Boileau and Descartes had forsaken the cult of classical Reason and were worshipping the new goddess Progress. They were beginning to learn that the history of mankind is the history of a large number of epochs and a wide variety of cultures. The cult of *philosophie* was finding its high priest in Voltaire and its gospel in the great *Encyclopédie*. To the advanced thinkers of the time the Bible and the works of the Church Fathers, as sources of inspiration, were no longer potent. Even the classics of Greece and Rome had been dealt a serious blow in the course of the quarrel of the Ancients and Moderns. In place of these two traditional sources of wisdom the intellectual public was turning for enlightenment to the new literature of travel and research. The works of this nature suggested to the philosophers that the American redskin, the Japanese islander, even the despised Hottentot, could supply material to prove their thesis that Christendom did not possess a monopoly on virtue and truth. So the systems of other lands and other periods were searched for evidence. What more natural, then, than to believe that Chinese civilization, the oldest and obviously the most highly developed of foreign cultures, was worthy of study and emulation? And the more the Europeans studied Chinese civilization, the more they were impressed. China was a land, they were informed, where the ruler was a truly benevolent despot, the father of his people, the friend of philosophers, even a philosopher himself; a land where the scholar was more admired than the soldier; a land where industry produced craftsmen of unrivaled excellence; a land where intolerance had been displaced by a wise and salutary system of social ethics; a land where the great Confucius had proclaimed and established the ideal *honnête homme.* To this ideal land, therefore, intellectual Europe turned for inspiration and enlightenment.

Pierre Bayle, whose *Dictionary* was the great source book for eighteenth-century liberals in Europe, included a study of the Chinese people among his encyclopedic labors. He found them an eminently respectable race in spite of their atheism—for he believed them to be atheists in the face of the Jesuit testimony to the contrary. Bayle was thus provided with striking proof of his theory that, if one had to choose between an idolater and an atheist, one should take the latter as potentially the more valuable member of society, since he would be tolerant whereas the idolater would be fanatical.

Montesquieu, whose *Persian Letters* (1721) provided the first great monument of exotic literature in France, published his *Esprit des lois,* in 1748. Voltaire's famous remark that the work had restored to humanity its lost title deeds testifies to the importance of the book. The cosmopolitanism which was at the base of Montesquieu's discussion of the nature of laws centers around two poles, England and China. The French philosopher was greatly impressed by what he had read about the Far Eastern empire. Dogmatically he placed the Middle Kingdom on the list of absolute monarchies as he asserted: "China is governed by the rod," a declaration which aroused the ire of the Sinophile Voltaire. When, however, Montesquieu came to examine the evidence more closely, he found in the Chinese system not only fear (the foundation of despotism) but honor and virtue (the characteristics of the monarchy and the republic). This author's contribution to the Sinophilism of his time was to place China among those countries the study of the history and institutions of which might provide Europe with material for the objective examination of the principles of government.[8]

Not all the philosophers, however, were admirers of China. Diderot, the most typical mind of his age, adopted a dispassionate attitude. He was willing to admit the antiquity, the solidity, and the excellence of Chinese social and political institutions, but he could not forgive

the Chinese for the fact that their culture, raised to such a high standard many centuries earlier, had in more recent times been—as he had
been led to believe—static and unproductive. For the great compiler
of the *Encyclopédie* China was a sinner against one of the important
doctrines of his school, the law of progress.

Jean Jacques Rousseau, whose thought and personality dominated
the latter part of the eighteenth century, naturally had little that was
good to say of the empire of Ch'ien Lung. Confucian ethics formed
the antithesis of Rousseau's theories regarding nature and society,
and he was therefore prejudiced from the beginning. He would not
admit a comparative social perfection in China but could see only
its faults.

The enemies of the China cult were, however, comparatively few.
The philosophical movement, in this respect, is characterized by the
attitude of its leader, Voltaire. The sage of Ferney made the cause
of China peculiarly his own. He was never tired of singing the praises
of the land of Confucius. At the time of his most effective writing,
when he was composing articles for his *Philosophical Dictionary,* he
was frankly and violently Sinophile. His *Essai sur les mœurs,* that
brilliant attempt at a synthesis of the lessons of history, marks the
climax of the movement.[7] The *Essai* places China in the forefront of
civilization, since the author gives to the Far Eastern empire the place
of honor in the book. For Voltaire it represented par excellence the
land of tolerance. In a score of dialogues, articles, and treatises he
emphasizes this fact. Faced by the sad events of the Rites controversy,
Voltaire seems to rub his hands in unholy glee as he dwells on the
spectacle of two Christian orders fighting each other bitterly in the
tolerant land which they were trying to win to the Christian cause.
Time and again he repeats the pertinent question of the emperor
Yung Cheng addressed to the Jesuits: "What would you say if I were
to send missionaries to your country who would stir up trouble and
dissension among your people?" In Voltaire's polemic works China
emerges, more than does any other nation, as a foil to Christian intol-

erance. That remarkable historical work, the *Age of Louis XIV*,[8] ends
with a chapter devoted to the Rites quarrel, an apparently irrelevant,
but in fact highly significant, conclusion to the work, which the
author undoubtedly meant as a sermon on the eternal text, *Ecrasez
l'infâme*.

As Voltaire used history, so he used drama as a vehicle for his
Sinophilism. At the time he was writing his Chinese play, *L'Orphelin
de la Chine* (his "Confucius in five acts"), his correspondence shows
how infatuated he was with his subject and how ardently he wished
for the success of the piece. And a success it was! Eighteenth-century
audiences were enraptured by a terrible Genghis Khan subdued by
the charms of love. For the poet himself, however, the merit of the
play lay in its value as a sermon against intolerance.

Voltaire, following the Jesuit literature which he had thoroughly
studied, sees China as a utopian state, ruled by wise men.[9] Years before, in pursuance of his theory that the institution of monarchy was
great when the monarch was wise, he thought he had found his ideal
philosopher-king in Frederick of Prussia. The tragi-comic events of
his three years' stay in Berlin, however, brought disillusionment. He
discovered that his idol had feet of clay. Then he turned to distant
China to find in Ch'ien Lung the supreme example of the philosopher-king. A country ruled by such a monarch, and possessing so
ancient and unbroken a record of culture, could not fail to be great.
Furthermore, wisdom in monarch and people had produced a creed
which was devoid of religious bickerings and of the devastating effect
of dogma. It was with intense satisfaction that the arch-enemy of
organized religion thought he had discovered a successful cult—that
of Confucius—which was no more and no less than a system of pure
morality. In this way the Sinophilism of Voltaire was linked to the
Deism which was the dominant religious trend of the age.

It may be argued that Voltaire's China was a result of wishful
thinking—that there never was a nation which possessed the virtues
attributed by him to the land of Ch'ien Lung. Undoubtedly Voltaire

accepted, and used, the materials supplied by the Jesuits in an undis-
criminating manner. This does not, however, detract from the importance of his Sinomania. All the arguments of his contemporaries
concerning the worth and richness of Chinese culture were unified
and emphasized by him. He showed that the discovery of the culture
of China was an event in the intellectual world equal to the discoveries
of a Vasco da Gama or a Columbus in the physical world. With him
the *rêve chinois* reached its apotheosis.

While the sage of Ferney was evoking the example of China in
the face of ecclesiastical conservatism and bigotry, a group of econo-
mists was, in an equally definite way, turning to the land of Confucius for enlightenment. These men, the Physiocrats, constituted
the only definite school of economic thought in France in the eighteenth century. Their views, therefore, although not widely accepted,
are of importance. The theories of the Physiocrats centered in the idea
that the products of the soil are the real and only basis of national
wealth. They believed they had found the most striking support for
this idea in the Chinese empire.

Of all the pictures of China which fascinated the West in this
period one of the most copied was the description of the ceremony
of the *keng chi,* the spring plowing, when the emperor, or his representative, with his own hands turned the first furrow for the spring
cultivation. Du Halde described the ceremony at length. Voltaire,
Diderot, Raynal, and a score of other writers enthusiastically commented on it. Gradually it came to represent the acme of eighteenth-
century sentimentality applied to affairs of government. One of the
first to be influenced by this picture of imperial paternalism was
Etienne de Silhouette, a pupil of the Jesuits, who in 1729 published
a book on the government of China.[10] In this little work Silhouette
develops the theory that political society should model its structure on
that of the family, citing the example of China where the emperor
was father of the country and the local official the father of his district.
Silhouette became contrôleur général in 1759—but his admiration of

the Chinese system does not seem to have influenced his official acts as administrator of French finances.

In 1768 there appeared a small volume by Pierre Poivre[11] entitled *Voyage of a Philosopher.* This work contained a warm eulogy of agriculture in China and its relation to the government of the empire. "This great nation," declared the author, "unites under the shade of agriculture, founded on liberty and reason, all the advantages possessed by whatever nation, civilized or savage." Poivre's book immediately gave the Physiocrats the inspiration they were seeking. Madame de Pompadour's physician, François Quesnay, who, as the leader of the movement, came to be known as "the Confucius of Europe" published a brochure entitled *The Despotism of China,*[12] which contained, in essence, all the politico-economic theories of the group. Doctor Quesnay had already become fairly well versed in the philosophical thought of the Chinese, which he considered greater than that of the Greeks. His book is an interesting example of the Sinophile literature of the time. Making use of Du Halde, Lecomte, Magalhaens, Navarrete, and others, Quesnay developed a glowing picture of the organization of the Chinese system, as the Jesuits had described it. He saw China as a land of wise rulers, humane laws, and clean (!) prisons. All government, he asserted, must be based on natural laws. The knowledge of these laws can come only through education, through the application of reason, and through the intelligent study of a country's resources. All these he found in the land of Ch'ien Lung. So, from a study of agriculture, the theories of Quesnay and his colleagues broadened to a discussion of government in general. Opposing Montesquieu's idea of a despotism based on fear as its characteristic trait, they developed the theory of a benevolent despotism, a system of government and economics which had at its head a sort of Voltairian philosopher-king. This theory of Quesnay and his confreres was one of the most striking of those intellectual chimeras which gave color and variety to eighteenth-century French thought.

Among the thinkers of the group which followed Quesnay in his
admiration for Chinese institutions was Turgot, minister of finance
and the most brilliant economist of his time in France. Turgot had
had the opportunity of coming in contact with two young Chinese,
Ko and Yang, sent over by the Jesuits to prepare themselves in the
French capital for the task of aiding the missionaries. The studies of
the young Chinese had been supervised by members of the Acad-
emies and they had been given special training, not only in the
sciences, but in such practical subjects as printing and engraving, the
weaving of silk, and the making of cannon. After studying in Paris
for ten years they returned to China in 1766, but before their departure
Turgot met them and talked with them concerning Chinese institutions and the studies they were to make in their native land for the
French Academy of Sciences. In order that they might have definite
ideas of the scope and methods of their research Turgot prepared for
them a series of fifty-two questions, with commentaries and explanations. Since these formed an exposé of certain current economic problems, Turgot, at the request of his friends, published them with the
title *Reflections on the Formation and Distribution of Wealth*.[18] The
work attracted attention and was reprinted several times. It is today
still considered one of the most important documents of economic
theory of the eighteenth century. Although it contains no passages
directly traceable to the influence of Chinese thought, it is a significant example of intellectual rapprochement between France and
China in this period. It shows how the Jesuits, indirectly, were responsible for aiding in the development of the thought of one who,
with a little more luck, might have been instrumental in guiding his
country out of the financial morasses which led to the Revolution.

By 1750, then, and during the two decades which followed, China
was omnipresent in French thought. The culture of the empire left
its imprint upon religion, philosophy, economics, and theories of government. The Chinese social system was considered by its admirers
to contain the panacea of most of the social, financial, and economic

ills of France. Baron Grimm reports that the Sinophile minister Bertin, discussing one day with Louis XV the problems of his country's government, told the French monarch that the surest cure for these problems was for France to be inoculated with the Chinese spirit.[14] Thus in the French councils of state as well as in the salon, China, for a period, was widely discussed and was set up as a model to follow.

Bertin carried on a highly interesting correspondence with several of the missionaries concerning their Sinological labors. He provided the chief stimulation from French officialdom to the publication of the *Mémoires concernant les Chinois.* In 1777 he wrote to Father Amiot:

As regards the literary correspondence I beg you to urge your workmen to undertake the translation of Chinese works, whether treatises on morality, legislation, government, history or other subjects ... in general, the works of the Chinese from their own writings accompanied, if advisable, by notes from the pens of the missionaries. Indeed everything of which the original is from the Chinese documents themselves will succeed far better in Europe; will have more attraction for us and will be infinitely more useful for our customs, our government and our happiness than all that the missionaries can send of their own composition. It is the Chinese themselves that we want to see. It is their writers, their critics, their authors, orators, and artists.[15]

The words of this French official are illuminating. They show that European intellectuals were no longer satisfied by the narratives of travelers or by the propaganda of missionaries. They were now asking for scientific theories, for systems of thought to ponder over, and not for pictures to amuse or edify. Sinophilism in Europe was becoming the field of the scholar as much as the playground of the intellectual dilletante.

The direct result of this new spirit was the beginning of a scientific study of Oriental literatures and languages. Materials, in the form of Chinese books, were gradually accumulated. By 1720 the royal library in Paris could boast of over a thousand volumes. In England Thomas Hyde interested himself in acquiring for the Bodleian Library an adequate collection of Chinese works. Etienne Fourmont in

Paris set about the task of compiling a Chinese-Latin dictionary and inspired several of his students to become specialists in the field of Oriental culture. These early scholars studied Chinese as a dead language, often as an adjunct to Sanskrit or Egyptian. They had little direct contact with the Middle Kingdom, and their knowledge was often, therefore, theoretical and bookish rather than empirical. It was their role to bring the languages of the Far East within the field of research of scientific linguistics. In so doing they made an important contribution to Sinological science.

The scholar seized upon the study of China at the moment that it was beginning to lose its popularity as a popular cult. The eighteenth-century movement of Sinomania reached its zenith in the 'sixties. From this date calmer minds began a consideration of facts in a more objective way. The disparaging remarks concerning China in Lord Anson's *Voyage* and elsewhere caused people to stop to think. Panegyric gradually became tinged with a healthy amount of skepticism. Other enthusiasms, notably a growing admiration for Hindu culture, began to displace Sinomania as a popular fad. In 1773 the writer of Grimm's *Correspondance* compared China to an old man, cold, harsh, and dominated by the traits of prudence, mistrust, stubbornness, and weakness. In the last great expression in the eighteenth century of the philosophical mind, Condorcet's noble work on the development of the human intelligence,[16] composed during the throes of the Revolution, China is depicted as a land where progress has been retarded by the superstition of an ignorant priesthood. Slowly France of the prerevolutionary years awakened from its *rêve chinois*. Slowly the excesses of an unbalanced enthusiasm, based on partial knowledge, were eliminated, to leave a residuum of solid, if still far from complete, information concerning the great Far Eastern empire and its culture.

CONCLUSION

Chapter XIX

THE ACHIEVEMENTS OF THE JESUIT MISSION IN CHINA

T HE PROBLEM of rapprochement between East and West is chiefly a psychological or spiritual one. To achieve harmony the mind of the Occident must meet that of the Orient, and the two must arrive at a degree of fusion or compromise. The agents of the process must be men who appreciate and understand distinctions and differences in thought patterns as well as the repercussions of these differences on social and moral phenomena. In judging the success or failure of the Jesuits in the Far East, therefore, it is pertinent to ask whether the members of the Society possessed these gifts and, if so, whether they used them intelligently and effectively.

Few human institutions have been the recipients of such mixed praise and blame as has the Society of Jesus. By their enemies the members of the order have been looked upon as dark and Machiavellian plotters, arrogant dissemblers of the truth, sources of danger, indeed, to the cause of Christianity. To their admirers they have always been stalwart soldiers of the Cross of Christ, intrepid and devoted, the finest stuff of which martyrs are made.

What is it which makes possible such a widely different conception of the role and achievements of the Jesuits in history? The answer, if there is one, lies probably in the startling contrast between the nature and structure of the Society and its intellectual and moral strategy.

In its organization is was militaristic, unified, highly centralized. The priest obeyed his superior as the soldier obeyed his captain, without question. In the mission field some degree of liberty of action, made necessary by the exigencies of time and space, undoubtedly existed but, generally speaking, there was more unquestioned obedience to superior by inferior within the order than there was between the Jesuit and those in ecclesiastical authority in the Church. This discipline resulted in two outstanding characteristics: on the one hand it gave to the Society unity and steadfastness of purpose; on the other, it created a sense of solidarity which gave to the members remarkable effectiveness in their disputes with their fellow Catholics but which often resulted, unfortunately—as was conspicuously true in China—in an extreme aggressiveness. This aggressiveness on the part of many of its members developed, in the eighteenth century, more and more into a pride of power, which finally brought about the suppression of the Society in 1773.

But although the organization of the Jesuits was centralized and authoritative, its philosophy was broad, liberal, accommodating, conciliatory, humanistic. In contrast to the absolutism of its structure and tactics the moderation of its philosophy is startling. In the earliest years, at any rate, the aim of the order's diplomacy was to be "all things to all men." In furtherance of this aim the members of the Society showed themselves highly tolerant to new systems, new ideas, and new habits of thought. So frequently was this liberalism present in their acts and decisions that one is almost tempted to say that the Jesuits represented the resilience of philosophy as opposed to the intransigence of dogma. Within Europe, this resilience had its source in the recognition of the frailty of the human will; in the mission field of China, from the sixteenth to the eighteenth century, it was derived from the contemplation of hitherto unknown moral systems, manners, and customs.

Casuistry, that moral blemish so virulently condemned by Pascal and a hundred other non-Jesuit defenders of the Faith, was essentially based upon a realization of the inability of the average human being to cross in one bound the great gulf between the temporal and the eternal—to grasp the immensity of the Infinite. Realizing the impossibility of making a saint of the average man, the Jesuit tended to bring religion to man's level rather than to attempt to raise mankind in one effort to the skies. In this humanizing process the system may have sacrificed much that others thought essential to salvation. It may sometimes have treated certain phases of Christian dogma with scant consideration. It may even have used the study of "cases" to permit ignoble compromises. Nevertheless, at its best, it had at its center the desire and needs of man, and it strove, in the most effective way, to meet those needs. It was the liberal answer to the many impasses of dogma. As an attempt to make man the starting point in the interpretation of theology, it was essentially a system of humanism.

One of the chief aspects of this humanism during the period under consideration was the Society's emphasis on the works of the intellect. It encouraged education; it appealed to the mind of man and used his intelligence to win him to higher things. As a result, the Jesuits became the teachers of Europe and were praised even by such enemies of the Faith as Voltaire. They helped to uphold the beauty and worth of the classics of both East and West to a degree not practiced or appreciated by Westerners even to this day. They joined their great enemy Pascal in admiration of the power of the human mind.

The fundamental humanism of the order, with its glorification of the intellect, made possible the role of its members as purveyors of culture. Here the Jesuits in the foreign field excelled their confreres in Europe. In spite of the admirable record of the order in the realm of education it is the achievements of the Jesuits as missionaries which constitute the greatest glory of the Society. Amidst the lights and shadows of Jesuit history nothing stands forth more clearly than their work as propagandists of the Faith in foreign lands. In this work they were pioneers—and great pioneers—in the dissemination of culture. Whether in the pathless forests of America, the windswept plains of North China, or the steaming tropics of India and Siam, the Jesuit blazed the trail for universal truths, both Christian and secular.

The members of the Society helped also to build into a science the geographical knowledge of a great part of the earth's surface. To vitalize this new knowledge, they forwarded to Europe accounts and interpretations of laws, customs, and institutions new to the West.

Theoretical and practical knowledge of the variety and richness of human institutions caused the Jesuits to develop a sympathy for social and religious phenomena which they thought might be useful in the struggle between Christian light and heathen darkness. Although they continued to hold the doctrine that no non-Christian people could have an adequate conception of truth, they felt, nevertheless, that such human beings might possess elements capable of providing a nucleus around which truth might grow and develop. The vision of this possibility brought to the Jesuit missionary understanding, sympathy, and tolerance for non-European systems of life and thought. Writing of the American Indian, Father Lafitau pointed out many customs of theirs similar to those among nations of antiquity which Christian Europe had long since accepted as respectable; in India, Father Nobili, immersing himself in the lore of the Brahmins, was won to a conviction of its merits; in China, Father Ricci found Confucianism a sane and admirable philosophy.

It is this attitude toward "strange" peoples which made of the Jesuit missionary a true cosmopolite, despite restrictions of ties which bound him to Rome and to his order. This cosmopolitanism, however, had dangerous implications for a religious organization. It tended to encourage a spirit of relativism. The Jesuit panegyric of non-Christian moral codes was used by the enemies of the Church as evidence that all morals are relative and that religion itself is not a gift of the Eternal, divinely revealed to a favored people, but the residuum of the aspirations and longings of man, uniform in their essence the world over—universal, as mankind is universal. So the Jesuits, unconsciously and unwillingly, seemed to become the champions of eighteenth-century Natural Religion or Deism. The outstanding ironic fact of early Jesuit history is that, perhaps more than any other organization, the members of the Society put into the hands of anti-Christian forces one of their most effective weapons against the Church. Fortuituousness of circumstances made the missionary field a stronghold of liberalism within the order, while from it went forth many ideas and theories which greatly embarrassed the Church in Europe.

The problems of the order in China, its achievements, and the causes of its failure were, broadly speaking, much the same as those in other parts of the world. But China was the Society's most promising field of endeavor. No other country was as suited to Jesuit methods and strategy as was the Middle Kingdom. The eclecticism of Oriental thought, the scholarly basis of Confucianism, the essential relationship between this cult and the state, these conditions seem almost to have been made especially for Jesuit purposes and tactics. Here, if anywhere, were to be found moral and ethical doctrines suitable as a basis for building a Christian structure. The Society of Jesus was not slow to realize this advantage, and its members began immediately to develop a strategy fitting to time and place. This, of course, meant compromise. The greatest concession to circumstance was, perhaps, the suppression of intellectual aggressiveness in the face of the insularity and mental arrogance of their potential allies. In their relations with the native officials the Jesuits appeared to adopt an intellectual humility which at times was in striking contrast to the lack of spiritual humility present in the dealings of some of them with their fellow priests in the other orders. However, after the manner of Asiatic officialdom, they managed to squeeze the last drop of authority out of any situation which gave them temporary prestige or power.

The other fundamental compromise made by the members of the Society was with local religious or quasi-religious ceremonies, chiefly the Rites to Confucius and the ancestors. From the previous discussion of the quarrel it can be seen that the controversy at bottom involved a definition of what is really meant by the term "religion" as well as the question whether the practices—if religious—were consonant with Christianity. The Jesuit attitude toward the problem springs from a profound conception of the ideas involved.

Chinese ancestor worship is based upon a theory of life as an unending stream not limited to the short space between the cradle and the grave but reaching, in both directions, into infinity. The most intelligent of the Jesuits—and intelligence, as has been shown, was an

outstanding characteristic of the members of the mission—grasped
the spiritual significance of this conception. They appreciated the social value of ancestor worship, which gave strength, continuity, and
dignity to Chinese society. They were willing to thrust into the background narrow interpretations of these native customs, and even certain dogmatic interpretations of Christianity, and to look upon the
ceremonies of the cults as nothing more than imperfect attempts to
give concrete expression to eternal mysteries. Hence their insistence
that the Rites had social and not religious significance.

By this interpretation, of course, they removed the Rites from the
category of dogma and reduced the controversy to a quarrel over facts.
The assertion of the Jesuits' opponents that the ceremonies were of
a religious nature, however, although of course denied by the members of the Society, seemed to put the latter in the position of ignoring
one of the fundamental doctrines of the Church. The enemies of the
order argued that compromise in such a matter would be deadly to
the Faith. Here, in the light of history, they would appear to have
been on solid ground. It is probable that, had the Jesuit position been
whole-heartedly accepted, the Catholic church in China might sooner
or later have lost its identity and become merged in the relatively
formless chaos of native philosophical thought. As has been shown
earlier this was the fate that had overtaken Nestorianism in China—
in which country the high mysticism of ancient Taoism had also de-
generated into a system of magic and charlatanry.

This is the focal point of Jesuit history in China during this period.
Around it revolved the bitter opposition of critics to Jesuit methods
and the aggressive and angry defense of those methods by the members of the Society. It is true, as has been shown, that the bitterness
injected into the controversy was stimulated by animosities which had
grown up elsewhere between the order and the rest of the Church,
but in China the struggle was protracted and opportunities for compromise were ignored, because both parties felt that the issues involved
were a matter of life and death to the Faith in the empire.

Furthermore, the quarrel was aggravated by temporal and geographical limitations. In the twentieth century, when an airplane can circle the earth in a few days, it becomes increasingly difficult to understand the importance of the fact that in the seventeenth century it took a ship several months to reach the Far East. Often action was taken by Rome to meet a situation which had arisen in the China mission and the action became ineffective because, by the time the envoy bearing the news arrived in China, the situation had completely changed. At times authorities in the mission took action or accepted an interpretation of facts, only to have their position reversed by Rome, even though it had been put into effect for months or even years. This naturally led to confusion among the priests and their converts.

Another source of aggravation was the problem of authority, which showed itself in the claims of bishop, vicar apostolic or superior general to control over priests and policies. It has been shown that much of this difficulty was caused by national rivalries. To a non-Catholic, however, who may have less respect for hierarchy, in its institutional phases, than has a member of the Roman Church, it is clear that the complexity of that organization contributed greatly—and, considering the two centuries' course of the controversy, unnecessarily—to the misunderstandings involved in the Rites dispute. It is not expected that the central authority of the Church should have radically surrendered its responsibilities in matters of doctrinal jurisdiction, but it is clear that a greater degree of local autonomy would certainly have hastened the end of the quarrel. It would appear not unreasonable to believe that an autocracy as venerable and as experienced as that of Rome might have collected data and acted definitively upon it in less than two hundred years. Indeed, after examination of the facts, one is tempted to draw the conclusion that it was not so much the issues involved that caused the catastrophe as the length of time taken to solve the problem.

The most tragic element in the controversy is, of course, the fact that the two opposing factions ignored the greatest danger of all: that of disunity, of presenting to the enemy a front disrupted by dissension. This was a danger far greater than that of doctrinal differences. Ignoring this great threat to their work, the Jesuits and their opponents—as well as those in control in Rome—brought about the temporary ruin of the Faith in China. After two hundred years of splendid, and often successful, effort the outcome of their evangelical labors was practically nil.

If the attempt of the Jesuits at spiritual conquest of the empire was unsuccessful, what can be said of the great byproduct of their missionary work, their attempt to convince the intelligentsia of China of the excellence and worth of Western culture? At first glance it would seem as if they made little permanent contribution to Chinese thought. They established no new system of philosophy or ethics. They did not greatly or permanently influence the social and political institutions of the empire. With the exception, probably, of awakening a renewed interest in mathematics they apparently contributed no new methods or technique in science. Were their efforts, therefore, entirely in vain?

It is a difficult task to trace the influence of one cultural system upon another.[1] The works of the human mind are evanescent, imperfect in their entirety, and impossible of acceptance definitively. In the process of transference they become so changed and modified by the intellectual milieu of the country they strive to penetrate that they almost inevitably lose their identity as a coherent system or group of ideas. Much of the science of the Arabs was absorbed almost unconsciously in European medieval culture just as, earlier, a part of the wisdom of Greek philosophy was adopted by early Christianity, losing not a little of its identity in the meantime. This is what may have happened to the Jesuit attempt to introduce Western science and learning to the Middle Kingdom.

In the realm of morals and philosophy the Jesuits had a much easier task than in the artistic and scientific fields. Their religious efforts had

---

[1] For notes to chap. xix, see p. 336.

a strong native system of ethics on which to build, but their scientific efforts found few such antecedents. These met a kind of intellectual void, sank into it, and were lost. Perhaps not entirely so. Though the European scholars established no new systems, founded no new philosophy, created no new industry, here and there they may have planted an idea or started a new habit of thinking or action which, dropped into the amorphous mass of Chinese thought, may have provided a leaven, which went on working unobtrusively and unconsciously, to add to the richness of native culture. In the multitude of scientific and artistic facts which they communicated some undoubtedly did survive.² This is all that can be said of the efforts of the Jesuits as purveyors of Western culture—but this is by no means a negligible achievement.

In the other cultural movement in which the members of the Society participated, namely, the introduction into Europe of Oriental thought, the importance of their contribution stands unquestioned and unrivaled. They brought to Europe the picture of a world, the vision of a society, which, ancient in themselves, were new to the West. The intellect of Europe was ripe for new ideas. The Renaissance, which had liberated men's thinking, had been temporarily blocked by ecclesiastical and political reaction, but the dam was weakening, and in the eighteenth century it broke, flooding Europe with the New Enlightenment. In the creation of the new spirit of cosmopolitanism which followed, China, thanks to the Jesuit panegyric, had an important share. When one compares the literature on China from non-Jesuit sources with that supplied by the members of the Society, one fully appreciates the role of the order as a disseminator of Oriental culture. Through the Jesuits the glories of Greece and Rome came to be rivaled, and even surpassed, by the splendors of the Chinese empire, ancient and contemporary. For the astonished intellectual and social elite of the Occident they continued to present fact after fact, new aspects of the development of the human mind, new-old social phenomena and moral precepts, until they finally created in the minds of these same intellectuals beliefs in the existence of a utopia which never really existed, in China or in any other Oriental realm.

At first these facts were slowly and imperfectly assimilated. Liberal aspirations tended to confuse ideals with reality. Much was exaggerated, inviting reaction, which did not fail to come. But in spite of such drawbacks Europe obtained through the medium of the Society a new conception of a great Asiatic culture. Scholars—and a few statesmen—striving desperately for tolerance grasped the value of the sane and mild philosophy of Confucius. A world restive under governmental oppression envisaged the ideal—chimerical and distorted though it was—of a benevolent despotism in which the rights of the people were explicit and the duties of the monarch as clear as his privileges. Leaders of a society in which the man of letters, the "philosopher," was gaining an increasing influence saw in China an example of the value of the scholar to the state and of the softening and beneficent effect of what the times called "philosophy."

The new ideals involved in this vision helped to shape the course of future events. It is true they did not produce immediate benefits. On the contrary they worked for disruption and disaster—but it was the disruption of tyranny and disaster to social and judicial despotism. It cannot, of course, be said that the great movement of liberation which took place in France and elsewhere had its source preponderantly in the Sinophilism of the time, but it may certainly be affirmed that in the creation and fostering of this movement the example, real or imagined, of China was of tremendous importance.

Chateaubriand, in his remarkable panoramic view of the cultural and aesthetic beauties of the Christian contribution to civilization, wrote of "the immeasurable services which the Jesuits have rendered to human Society." Undoubtedly he was thinking chiefly of their contribution to science and learning, of their achievements in astronomy, physics, geography, and other sciences. Few will disagree with this assertion. Even the enemies of the Society are forced to admit the value of its work as a channel of human culture. Nowhere is the contribution of its members so brilliant, nowhere is their influence on the period which prepared the modern world more striking than in their share in creating that cosmopolitanism which is at the heart of modern civilization.

"Within the four seas all men are brothers," says an oft-quoted Chinese proverb. The realization of this age-old ideal as a fact is yet tragically far from completion, but it is to the everlasting glory of the Society of Jesus that, by helping to bridge the gulf between Orient and Occident, it made an outstanding contribution to this ideal of universal brotherhood.

NOTES

NOTES TO CHAPTER I

CHRISTENDOM AND THE MONGOLS

[1] Budge, *The Monks of Kublai Khan*, p. 15.

[2] Yule, *Cathay and the Way Thither*, Vol. I, Introduction, p. lxxxix.

[3] Arnobius, *Adversus Gentes Libri Octo* (Rome, 1542), fol. 18.

[4] Mosheim in *Historia Tartarorum Ecclesiastica* (English translation by Murdoch [London, 1750], II, 422), rejects the theory, but the Protestant missionary Edkins (*These from the Land of Sinim* [Philadelphia, 1845], p. 35) says, "There can be little doubt that the country of the Seres includes the province of Shensi in China and the mention of them by Arnobius (who died in 1326) shows that before his time the Gospel had been carried there." For a discussion of the subject see A. C. Moule, *Christians in China before the Year 1550*, pp. 10–24, and Chabrié, *Michel Boym*, pp. 223–224.

[5] Budge, *op. cit.*, p. 32.

[6] E. O. Windstedt, *The Christian Topography of Cosmas Indicopleustes* (1909).

[7] Mingana, "The Early Spread of Christianity," *Bull. John Rylands Library*, IX, 299.

[8] Stewart, *Nestorian Missionary Enterprise*, p. 77.

[9] Mingana, *op. cit.*, p. 325.

[10] A Latin translation of the tablet was made, probably by Trigault (Pelliot thinks it is the work not of Trigault but of Jacques Rho), and Semedo made a version in Italian. A more nearly complete Latin version by Michel Boym was published by Athanasius Kircher in his *Prodromus Coptus sive Aegypticus* (1636). The best translations are to be found in A. C. Moule, *op. cit.*, Havret, *La Stèle chrétienne de Si-ngan-fou*, Saeki, *The Nestorian Monument in China*, and translation by A. Wylie in Carus, *The Nestorian Monument*. See also Gaillard, *Croix et swastika en Chine* (2d ed.; Shanghai, 1904), and Heller, *Das Nestorianische Denkmal in Singanfu*. Pauthier also translated the inscription into French, and Neumann into German.

[11] Saeki, *op. cit.*, p. 157. Chinese records make no reference to Nestorians as occupying important places in the court life of the time.

[12] Many of the statements made on the Nestorian tablet are corroborated in a little manuscript found in 1908 by Professor Pelliot at Tun Huang. This document, dating from 800 A.D., contains a *Gloria in Excelsis* in Syriac, a list of saints and holy books, and a short historical note. See A. C. Moule, *op. cit.*, pp. 52–57.

[13] Latourette (*A History of Christian Missions in China*, p. 58) suggests the following reasons for the disappearance of Nestorianism: (1) In China it was always a foreign religion, supported by non-Chinese people; (2) it arrived in China at a moment when the country had no special need of a new faith; (3) it was separated by enormous distances from its source of inspiration. For a full discussion of the subject see Latourette.

[14] Bar Hebraeus (*Chronicon Ecclesiasticum* [Paris, 1872], §2, p. 451) calls them "Yagûrâyê" (Montgomery, *The History of Yaballaha III*, p. 18, note).

Pelliot ("Chrétiens d'Asie Centrale et d'Extrême-Orient," *T'oung Pao* 1914, pp. 630–636) thinks that Markos at least may have been an Ongut.

[15] The Syriac manuscript came into the possession of Father Paul Bedjan of the Chaldean church in 1888. The best modern versions of the work are: Chabot, *Histoire de Mar Jabalaha III* (Paris, 1893); Montgomery, *The History of Yaballaha III* (New York, 1927); Budge, *op. cit.;* A. C. Moule, *op. cit.,* chap. iv.

[16] Koshang or Kâwshang, about fifteen days' journey from Peking (Budge, p. 130). Chabot thinks this is the Cacianfu of Marco Polo, but others have identified it with the modern Ho Chien fu, 120 miles south of Peking (see Montgomery, p. 30, note).

[17] The manuscript says: "He was minded to go and subjugate the lands of Palestine and Syria . . . So he desired the Catholicus that he should send him a wise man, one useful and fit for the embassy, to send to those Kings" (Montgomery, p. 51).

[18] The Paizâh (Chinese *pai-tse*) or Mongol warrant of authority (see Budge, p. 61).

[19] The knight chosen was Gobert de Helleville. The business records of the Templars under the date of February 2, 1288, allot to him twelve hundred livres "pro expensis in via ad regem tartarorum."

[20] Montgomery, *op. cit.,* p. 73.

[21] A good account of the Prester John story is to be found in Sir Denison Ross, *Travels and Travellers of the Middle Ages.*

[22] Howorth, *History of the Mongols,* I, 534.

[23] Beazley, *The Texts and Versions of John de Plano Carpini and William de Rubruquis,* p. 213.

[24] William of Rubruck mentions also a brother whose name was Ung or Unc. He was first an ally, then an enemy, of Genghis Khan and through him several Nestorian women entered the Mongol harem, one of whom became mother of Kublai Khan.

[25] Yule, *The Book of Ser Marco Polo* (rev. ed.; London, 1921), pp. lxv-lxvii. On the globe of Martin Behaim (1491) Central Asia is marked as the habitat of Prester John. In Sebastian Cabot's atlas of 1544 mention is made of a mighty king of Central Africa "whom some call Prester John, but this is not Prester John because Prester John had his empire in Eastern and Southern India until Genghis Khan defeated him in a very cruel battle in which he died" (Beazley, *John and Sebastian Cabot,* p. 233). The reference is evidently to Ung Khan.

[26] Yule, *Cathay and the Way Thither,* I, 154.

[27] According to Harold Lamb (*March of the Barbarians,* p. 376) Paul Pelliot believes that Genghis Khan was born in 1667

[28] In January, 1249, Louis IX sent one of the Preaching Friars, Andrew of Longjumeau, to the Mongol court of Karakorum, with two companions. When they arrived, they found that Kuyuk had just died and the empress Ogoul Gaimiz was acting regent. Apparently the sending of this embassy was looked upon as an act of homage.

NOTES TO CHAPTER II

THE MISSIONARIES OF THE MEDIEVAL PERIOD

[1] Beazley, *The Texts and Versions of John de Plano Carpini*, chap. xxviii, p. 138.

[2] John was told that there were more than four thousand ambassadors, but this can hardly be anything more than an empty boast. The list of tribute includes: "a sun canopie, a small tent set full of precious stones, a company of camels covered with Baldakan [cloth], in addition to five hundred carts, full of silver, gold and silken garments" (*ibid.*, p. 139).

[3] Beazley, *Prince Henry the Navigator*, p. 92.

[4] Beazley, *Carpini*, chaps. iv and v.

[5] *Ibid.*, chaps. xvii and xviii.

[6] *Ibid.*, chap. xxxiv.

[7] Yule, *Cathay and the Way Thither*, III, 137–171.

[8] Beazley, *Carpini*, p. 219.

[9] *Ibid.*, chap. li.

[10] A short time after William's departure, another Christian visitor arrived at Karakorum. This was Haytoun the Armenian, a vassal of the Mongols, who probably came to obtain an abatement of the amount of tribute he was forced to pay annually. Apparently he returned after a stay of a few weeks.

[11] In reality it was Mandeville who borrowed from Odoric's narrative. The latter's work, like that of Marco Polo, was dictated to a companion (the monk William of Solanga), in 1330, and put into writing as Odoric reported the facts.

[12] H. Cordier, *Les Voyages en Asie au XIVe siècle du bienheureux frère Odoric de Pordenone*.

[13] Yule, *Cathay*, I, 160.

[14] A. C. Moule, *Christians in China*, chap. vi.

[15] Nestorianism continued to flourish in other parts of Asia. Nicolò Conti, in the fifteenth century, found Nestorians scattered in all parts of India, with ten thousand at Meliapur. Ludovico of Varthema, in 1506, met Nestorian merchants from the kingdom of Siam and went with them to Pegu, where the king had ten thousand of them in his service. The Indian church, however, has been the only one to preserve its identity to the present time. When the Portuguese arrived in India in 1542, they found it flourishing, although cut off from the patriarchate. Roman Catholics led by Xavier, proceeded to persecute this church. On account of the bitter hostilities which resulted, the Jesuits were replaced there by the Carmelites in 1657 (Yohannon, *The Death of a Nation*).

[16] Yule, *Cathay*, III, 46.

[17] A. C. Moule, "Minor Friars," *Jour. Royal Asiatic Soc.*, 1914, p. 580.

[18] George died in 1294 leaving a baptized son, but on the father's death the Nestorian influence succeeded in undoing this work of conversion (A. C. Moule, *Christians in China*, p. 174).

[19] A. C. Moule, "Minor Friars," p. 584.

[20] Marco Polo, Odoric, and the other medieval travelers who visited Zaitun speak of the city in terms of profound admiration. The evidence of many medieval travel records proves it to have been at least as large as the greatest ports of Europe at that time. Today it has almost entirely disappeared, and modern scholars have difficulty in identifying it with the town of Ch'uan chou in Fukien, near Amoy.

[21] A. C. Moule, "Minor Friars," p. 593.

[22] *Ibid.*, pp. 593–595. The letters of John of Montecorvino are in the Bibliothèque Nationale. They were found by Luke Wadding and printed in his *Annales Minorum* (Vol. III) in 1635. They were reprinted by Mosheim in his *Historia Tartarorum Ecclesiastica* (1741), pp. 114–123. A. C. Moule, "Minor Friars," gives the Latin text and translation.

[23] On the site of Zaitun several small stone crosses have been found attesting to the presence there of Nestorianism in the fourteenth century. In the north of China, the Rev. P. M. Scott of the Anglican mission found, several years ago, in the neighborhood of the Yellow River, a number of small bronze ornaments bearing the cross, probably relics of King George's Ongut Christians (A. C. Moule, *Christians in China,* chap. III).

NOTES TO CHAPTER III

Francis Xavier, Apostle to the Indies

[1] Ignorance of Far Eastern history at that time is shown by the fact that comments in Columbus' copy of Marco Polo's book (now in the Columbian library at Seville) imply that the explorer thought that the Great Khan was still reigning at Khanbaliq, though the Mongol dynasty disappeared from China more than a century earlier.

[2] A. P. Newton, *et al., The Great Age of Discovery,* p. 86.

[3] *Ibid.,* p. 46.

[4] *Regimini militantis Ecclesiae,* September 27, 1540. A French translation of the bull is given in Crétineau-Joly's *Histoire de la Compagnie de Jésus,* I, 36 *et seq.* The Constitutions and Declarations of the order were written in Spanish by Loyola and translated into Latin by his secretary, Father Polanco. They were published in 1558 (*ibid.,* p. 45).

[5] René Guettée, *Histoire des Jésuites,* I, 64.

[6] Crétineau-Joly, I, 153.

[7] *Ibid.,* p. 154.

[8] *Ibid.,* p. 164.

[9] René Fülop-Miller, *The Power and Secret of the Jesuits,* p. 208.

[10] Henri Bernard, S.J., *Aux Portes de la Chine,* p. 42.

[11] *Ibid.,* p. 49.

[12] The little volume entitled *Avisi particolari del aumento cheiddiodi alla Chiesa catholica* ... is a meager and superficial composition of information which, according to the author, was obtained from the most reliable sources.

There is a copy of the work in the British Museum (No. 4767*b*. 22 under "China"). It is very rare.

[13] According to Mendoça, Spanish missionaries from Manila visited the mainland in 1575, 1579, and 1582 but were forced to withdraw. Their failure may have been due in part to Portuguese opposition from Macao. The Portuguese, at any rate, accused the members of the 1579 group of being spies and thus hastened their ejection from the empire (Bernard, *op. cit.*, p. 131).

[14] J. Nieuhoff, *An Embassy . . . to the emperor of China* (Eng. trans., 2d ed.; London, 1673), p. 31. Perhaps the best account of the early history of Macao is to be found in Montalta de Jésus, *Historic Macao*. The first half of the seventeenth century was the "golden age" of Macao. According to Montalto de Jésus there was scarcely a street without a church and the city "well deserved its appellation of Holy City" (*ibid.*, p. 48). Among the many churches was the beautiful cathedral of Saint Paul, a notable example of neoclassic ecclesiastical architecture. The church was destroyed by fire in 1835. At the beginning of the seventeenth century there were about one thousand Portuguese in Macao out of a population of five thousand (*ibid.*, p. 50).

[15] In 1575 Gregory XIII had established the episcopal see of Macao. In 1595 the king of Portugal, wishing to keep out the Spaniards coming from the Philippines, had decreed that only two religious orders—the Jesuits and the Franciscans—should have establishments in the city, but this decree seems to have been ignored. (*Ibid.*, p. 44.)

NOTES TO CHAPTER IV

Ricci, the Pioneer

[1] It is certain that the missionaries did not at first get much encouragement from Macao. In a letter to Cardinal Acquaviva in Rome (published in the *Opere storiche del P. Matteo Ricci,* Vol. II) Ricci states that for some time Ruggieri had been suffering greatly from lack of sympathy on the part of his fellow priests. Semedo (*Imperio de la China* [French translation, 1667]) states that there were no fewer than fifty-four persecutions from the time Ricci left Macao until he reached Nanking.

[2] *Ibid.*, p. 253.

[3] Bernard, *Aux Portes de la Chine*, p. 249.

[4] Ricci, *Opere storiche*, II, 35.

[5] Writing to the general of the order in 1598, Longobardi emphasizes their need for many books. He asks for the Bible "strongly and curiously bound" in several languages, for texts of the Church Fathers, and for "images and the simplest pictures expressing the mysteries of the Faith" (*Nouveaux advis du royaume de la Chine*, p. 48).

[6] Letter of November 30, 1584, to Acquaviva (Ricci, *op. cit.*, II, 51).

[7] Havret, *La Stèle chrétienne de Si-ngan-fou*, p. 12, note.

[8] The identification of Cambaluc (or Khanbaliq) with Peking and of Cathay with China came slowly. Ricci himself at first thought that Nanking

was the city described by Marco Polo as Cambaluc. When in the south, the Jesuit priest talked with merchants who had made the trans-Asian journey; as a result he began to suspect the identity of the two cities. He wrote to Europe, expounding his theory. Partly as a result of the letter, Benedict Goës made his remarkable journey from India to Kansu (see Wessels, *Early Jesuit Travellers in Central Asia*). When Ricci, in Peking, received news of Goës' arrival at Suchow, Kansu, he felt that the identity of the two places was finally established.

⁹ Ricci's superior, Valignani, had also realized the necessity of direct contact with Peking. On the advice, probably, of Ricci he had sent Ruggieri, who was getting too old for active service, to Rome with the object of inducing the Pope to send an embassy to Wan Li's court. Ricci prepared a letter in Chinese and Latin which the Pope was to send to the viceroy of Kwangtung and to the emperor. This letter may still be seen in the archives in Rome. Shortly after Ruggieri arrived, however, Pope Sixtus died, and the suggestion was not carried out. Ruggieri died in Italy some nine years later (Bernard, *Aux Portes de la Chine*, p. 275).

¹⁰ The Jesuits gave to their converts a foreign name, as is the practice sometimes in Christian missions today. Thus Hsü Kuang-ch'i was named Paul, and Li Chih-tsao, Léon. The Chinese priests were given a foreign surname.

¹¹ Ricci gave seven reasons for his success with the officials at Nanchang: (1) their curiosity to see the learned foreigner; (2) the reputation he had acquired of possessing the secrets of alchemy; (3) his venerable appearance; (4) their curiosity to see the foreign curios, books, and instruments; (5) Ricci's skill in mathematics and cosmology; (6) their curiosity over his theories regarding memory training; and (7) their eagerness to hear him discourse on religious matters (*Opere storiche*, II, 184).

¹² Semedo, *op. cit.*, p. 255.

¹³ From a translation of the document appearing in the *Chinese Repository*, X, 401.

¹⁴ Huc, *Le Christianisme en Chine, en Tartarie et au Thibet*, II, 179. Chinese records seem to suggest that Ricci met the emperor face to face and that he was the first foreigner to be granted this privilege. This may have happened later.

¹⁵ *Ibid.*, p. 162.

¹⁶ *Lettres édifiantes*, XXV, Preface, p. vii. The references, here and elsewhere, to this work are to the eighteenth-century Mérigot edition.

¹⁷ This point of view has been thoroughly developed by Father Henri Bernard in his recent work, *Le Père Matthieu Ricci et la société chinoise*.

¹⁸ In addition to Ricci, the following Jesuits were buried at the Chala cemetery: Jean Terrenz, Jacques Rho, F. Mendez, Christophor, Longobardi, D. Coronatus, De Sequeira, A. de Magalhaens, L. Buglio, F. Verbiest, F. Simoci, Ch. Dolzé, L. Pernon, Fr. Frapperie, and De Brossia (Thomas, *La Mission de Pékin*, p. 83).

¹⁹ Hsü's daughter, baptized Candida, was the outstanding figure of these early days. Married at sixteen and widowed at thirty, she spent the rest of her

life in promoting the welfare of the religion she had adopted. She is said to have erected, at her own expense, thirty-nine churches in different provinces and to have printed one hundred and thirty books written by the missionaries. She died at the age of seventy-three.

NOTES TO CHAPTER V

CHRISTIANITY UNDER THE MINGS

[1] Adam Schall von Bell (T'ang Jo-wang) was born at Cologne in 1591. He went to China with Trigault in 1622, going first to Peking. In 1627 he was sent to Sianfu and later to Hangchow. He returned to the capital in 1630 and succeeded Longobardi (who died in 1654 at the age of ninety-five) as head of the mission in 1640.

[2] Ferdinand Verbiest (Nan-hwei-jen), born at Pitthem near Courtraî, Belgium, October 9, 1623, studied at Bruges and Louvain. He entered his novitiate in 1641 and for five years taught rhetoric and the humanities. He then completed his studies at Rome and in Spain. Embarking for China in 1657, he reached Macao in 1659. He spent ten months in the mission in Shensi and was called to the capital in May, 1660. He had therefore spent twenty-eight years working at the court when he died on January 28, 1688.

[3] It is to be noted that, although the Jesuit missions were considered primarily a Portuguese enterprise, the majority of the greatest missionaries were not of that nation. Ricci was Italian, Schall was a German, while Verbiest was a native of Belgium.

[4] It is related that, when the rebel Li Tzu-ch'eng had caused the last of the Ming emperors at Peking to commit suicide, among the sycophants who came to render fawning homage to the new monarch were the astrologers, who begged for the privilege of making a new calendar.

[5] Semedo, *Imperio de la China,* p. 131.

[6] Notably Fathers Brancati, Smogolenski, and Gravina.

[7] Vaeth, *Johann Adam Schall von Bell,* p. 286.

[8] Pierre Bayle, *Pensées diverses sur la comète,* Amsterdam, 1682.

[9] Vaeth, *loc. cit.*

[10] Pfister, "Parennin" in *Notices biographiques et bibliographiques,* I, 510.

[11] The hostile historian of the Jesuits, Abbé Guettée, writing about the middle of the nineteenth century, repeats this charge. He cites the title of the calendar: *Nouvelles règles d'un calendrier ou almanach conformément à l'astrologie de l'Europe, par le maître Jean Adam, astrologue du roi* to show that the Jesuit aided and abetted idolatrous superstition (Guettée, *Histoire des Jésuites,* II, 87).

[12] Their title was *ch'ing t'ien chien chien cheng.* In addition to a director there were two European assessors in the bureau. Among other privileges, the director had the right to address the throne directly, a right which the missionaries used on several occasions to good advantage.

[13] *Mémoires concernant les Chinois,* IX, 95.

[14] Semedo, *op. cit.*, Part I, chap. xxi.

[15] Cordier, *Histoire générale de la Chine,* III, 78. Texeira was killed later in a fight with the Manchus, and there is reason to believe that the Chinese on this occasion did make use of the foreign guns.

[16] Vaeth, *op. cit.*, p. 111.

[17] At Ch'ing Lung Chiao, outside the western wall of Peking, there was, until 1900, a tombstone of a Portuguese, thought to be that of Correa. The inscription told of his coming to Peking in 1624. In 1621 the city of Macao had sent three cannon as a gift to the emperor but, after killing one of the Portuguese who brought them, these guns were sent to the northern borders to frighten the Manchus. Until recently, at least, there could be seen at the Nankou Pass in the Great Wall cannon of this kind, probably cast under Portuguese direction about 1631. Bland and Backhouse (*Annals of the Court of Peking,* p. 95) say that Jesuit cannon were used successfully at Ping Yang in Shansi and at Marco Polo's city of Yangchow.

[18] Cordier, *Histoire de la Chine,* III, 83. Bland and Backhouse (p. 91) say that of a population estimated at over a million scarcely one-tenth escaped.

[19] Bland and Backhouse, pp. 119–120.

[20] An English translation of the letter was published by E. H. Parker in the *Contemporary Review,* January, 1912. The first translation appeared in Kircher's *China Illustrata.*

[21] See Chabrié, *Michel Boym,* pp. 191–202.

[22] Vaeth, p. 151.

[23] Bland and Backhouse, p. 90.

[24] For an account of the adventures of these two missionaries see Pfister, "Magalhaens" in *Notices biographiques.*

[25] Martin Martini, *Histoire de la guerre des Tartares* (Paris, 1654), p. 131.

[26] Vaeth, p. 146.

[27] The annual letter of 1637 speaks of eighteen converts in the palace. By 1642 there were fifty

NOTES TO CHAPTER VI

SCHALL AND VERBIEST

[1] In 1645 Schall made friends with the king of Korea, who was visiting Peking, and advised him concerning the compiling of astronomical data in the Hermit Kingdom.

[2] See above, pp. 6–7.

[3] It was built in European style, modified to suit Chinese tastes, in the form of a Latin cross, with four lateral chapels. This was the *Nan T'ang,* or "Southern Church." It was burned in 1775 and later rebuilt.

[4] See chap. vi.

[5] Vaeth, *Adam Schall von Bell,* p. 192.

[6] After the emperor's death there grew up a persistent legend to the effect that Shun Chih had not died but had retired to a monastery on the Sacred

Mountain Wu T'ai Shan. According to the story, the funeral was a fake one carried out for purposes of state. The legend was later shifted to the temple of T'ien T'ai Shan in the Western Hills. Today a visitor to this temple is shown an image with a gilded face, garbed in imperial robes, which, the abbot insists, is the mummified remains of Shun Chih. This legend has been examined and discredited by the late Sir Reginald F. Johnston ("The Romance of an Emperor," *New China Review,* Vol. II).

[7] H. Bosmans, S.J., "Ferdinand Verbiest," *Revue des questions scientifiques,* XXI, 222.

[8] Vaeth, p. 296

[9] *Ibid.,* p. 297

[10] The veteran missionary had been suffering from a paralytic stroke since the twentieth of April, 1664.

[11] Schall was accused of (1) preaching Christ crucified, (2) baptizing annually two or three hundred converts, (3) claiming that the emperor had accepted Christianity, (4) preaching that Adam was created of God and was the father of the human race, (5) seducing the people by the preaching of repentance and by the administration of baptism and anointing, (6) preaching that Heaven (*T'ien*) is the seat of God and not God himself, (7) forbidding the worship of ancestors, (8) holding, four times a year, suspicious meetings with Christians and collecting money from them and lastly (9), having suspicious relations with the Portuguese at Macao.

[12] At any rate these are the figures given by the Jesuit historian De Mailla (*Histoire générale de la Chine,* XI, 88), who claims to have taken them from Chinese records

[13] Vaeth, p. 170.

[14] The story, spread in Peking and later in Europe, was to the effect that Schall had had an affair with a Chinese woman, from which had resulted a son. The explanation given by the supporters of Schall is simple and logical: At the suggestion of his friends, the missionary had adopted the son of a trusted and faithful servant. This adopted "grandson" had (according to Chinese custom) many of the rights of a real son. It was felt that Schall trusted the boy's father too much, and the jealousy of some of the priests undoubtedly added zest to the report that the boy was Schall's natural child. One can imagine that the missionary's frequent intolerance of his confreres' lack of intelligence gained him enemies by whom the story was credited and spread.

[15] The growth of the mission can be judged by the figures compiled by the Jesuits. In 1663 Schall had 13,000 Christians in his congregation. Verbiest says there were about ten thousand conversions annually (Vaeth, p. 217).

[16] Verbiest had come to the Orient with Martini and fourteen other Jesuits, who were permitted by imperial patent to enter the empire.

[17] Cordier, *Histoire générale de la Chine,* III, 266.

[18] De Mailla, XI, 62.

[19] The following were the Jesuit directors of the bureau: Schall (1630–1666), Verbiest (1673–1688), Grimaldi (1688–1712), Ignatius Kogler (1716–1746), Hallerstein (1746–1774), Da Rocha (1774–1781). Kogler's assessor was Andrew Pe-

reyra and Hallerstein's assessor was Anthony Gogeisl. Gogeisl was a learned and modest Jesuit, who collaborated with Kogler in the compilation of astronomical tables and who invented an improved quadrant.

None of these was Portuguese (Pereyra was a Portuguese by nationality, but of English blood). It was, however, the Portuguese mission which controlled the office of director. When the French Jesuits came, although several of them were skilled in astronomy, none of their number obtained the coveted post. They had, however, an observatory of their own, with instruments given by Louis XIV. In 1755, there were four observatories in the capital: the imperial bureau, the French Jesuit observatory, that of the Portuguese college, and another at the Portuguese residence of Saint Joseph. (Rochemonteix, *Amiot*, p. 53. See also P. L. van Hee, "Les Jésuites mandarins," *Revue d'histoire des missions* [March, 1931], pp. 287 *et seq*.)

[20] Huc, *Le Christianisme en Chine*, III, 72. That the position of the Jesuits at the bureau was never entirely secure is shown by the fact that as late as 1680 the foreign scholars were bitterly criticized in connection with an eclipse which had been foretold in the calendar (Bosmans, p. 388).

[21] *Ibid.*, p. 382. According to this writer, Verbiest reached the zenith of his influence in 1687.

[22] Already, in 1634, Schall and Rho had suggested some such task. In that year they presented to the Ming emperor a model in wood of a great astronomical machine. No permanent copy of this model seems to have been made. Verbiest's instruments were evidently made after the model of Tycho Brahe's instruments, the circle being divided into 360 instead of 365 degrees and each degree into six parts. In 1900, the Germans seized three of these instruments, and for a score of years they rested in the imperial grounds at Potsdam. They were returned to China, in 1920, under the terms of the Versailles Treaty.

NOTES TO CHAPTER VII

THE GROWING POWER OF THE JESUITS

[1] Huc, *Le Christianisme in Chine*, III, 91. In 1674 Verbiest made 132 large brass "bombardes" of different kinds, which were sent to Chinese generals fighting the rebels in various provinces; in 1680 he made some three hundred smaller ones, together with eight large cannon, decorated with dragons, for the emperor's tent.

[2] Navarrete, in his *Tratados,* attacked Verbiest for his cannon-making activities. Verbiest defended himself in a *Responsum Apologeticum* in 1681.

[3] Bosmans, "Ferdinand Verbiest," p. 258.

[4] Verbiest, *Lettre ... écrite de la cour de Pékin.*

[5] Louis Lecomte, S. J., *Nouveaux Mémoires sur la Chine*, I, 68.

[6] See chap. xiv, "Persecution and Progress."

[7] This Congregation (*Sacra Congregatio Christiano nomini propaganda*) was created by Pope Clement VIII in 1597, but it was not fully organized until 1622 when Gregory XV gave it its present form. It is the department of the

pontifical administration charged with the spreading of Catholicism and with the regulation of ecclesiastical affairs in non-Catholic countries.

[8] This institution was established between 1658 and 1663 by the bishops mentioned. A seminary for the training of priests was founded in 1663 and the organization has continued to flourish to the present time. It is not an order but a "Congregation." There are no vows but only a common purpose, approved by the Pope, of evangelization. The affairs of the Congregation are supervised by the directors of the seminary in Paris.

[9] The subsequent history of Christianity in that country was similar to that of the Faith in China. The Jesuits affiliated themselves with the liberal party at court and endeavored to gain an opportunity for Christianity through the teaching of Western science. They interfered a great deal in politics. Finally, the regime came to an end, in 1688, through a revolution in the palace, which upset all their plans and nullified their efforts.

[10] Lecomte, *op. cit.*, Vol. I

[11] Later the company ran into financial difficulties. In 1719 it was merged with other companies into the *Compagnie des Indes,* which was finally dissolved in April, 1770

[12] Of these only five were called to Peking: Parnon (who died shortly after his arrival), Régis, Parennin, D'Entrecolles, and Foucquet.

[13] Cordier, *Histoire générale de la Chine,* III, 256.

[14] H. Dudgeon, "Russian Ecclesiastical Mission," *Chinese Recorder,* III, 321.

[15] E. T. Williams, *A Short History of China,* p. 233.

[16] Du Halde's account is repeated in De Mailla's *Histoire,* XII, 61–108. For an account of the negotiations see Cordier, *Histoire,* Vol. III, *passim,* also Cahen, *Relations de la Russie avec la Chine,* chap. i. J. F. Baddeley, *Russia, Mongolia, China* contains firsthand accounts of the Russian embassies.

[17] Du Halde, *Description de la Chine,* IV, 189 *et seq.*

[18] The Russians assert that the Jesuits from the start tried to get control of the negotiations, for they protested against the attempt of the Russians to talk directly, in Mongolian, to the Chinese delegates (Cahen, p. 47).

[19] *Ibid.,* p. 49.

[20] Cordier, *Histoire générale de la Chine,* III, 274.

NOTES TO CHAPTER VIII

THE GOLDEN DAYS OF THE MISSION

[1] Charles le Gobien, S.J., *Histoire de l'Edit de l'Empereur de la Chine,* pp. 83–84. See also Lecomte, *Nouveaux Mémoires,* II, 437.

[2] De Mailla, *Histoire générale de la Chine,* XI, 171. It was probably the successful treatment of the malady by the Jesuits which aroused the interest of the monarch in Western medicine, and particularly in anatomy. The priests were ordered to establish a laboratory in the palace. Gerbillon and Bouvet, and later Parennin, gathered equipment and instructed K'ang Hsi in the rudiments of the science.

[3] The following description of the new building, taken from the *Lettres édifiantes* (XVII, 5–8), gives an idea of its proportions and architecture:

"In the front was a large court, some forty feet wide, by fifty feet long. On one side of this court was a big room fifty feet in length, for the use of converts; on the other side a similar hall for the reception of guests. In the latter room were placed portraits of Louis XIV, princes of the royal family of France, of the king of Spain, the king of England and other sovereigns, together with beautiful musical instruments and scientific apparatus. There were also finely engraved picture books which proclaimed to the visitors the pomp and splendor of the court of France.

"The cathedral at the end of this court was seventy-five feet long, thirty-three feet wide and thirty feet high. The building in the interior was arranged on two architectural levels, each level having sixteen half-columns covered with green lacquer. The pedestals of the lower level were made of marble; those of the upper were gilded as were also the capitals, filets and cornices, the frieze and the architrave. The upper level was pierced with twelve large windows, six on each side, in the form of an arch, which lighted the church perfectly.

"The entire ceiling, divided into three parts, was painted. The middle represented an open dome of rich architecture. Here were columns of painted marble which supported an arcade surmounted by a fine balustrade of a beautiful design, with flower vases placed at regular intervals. Above was to be seen God the Father seated in the midst of a group of angels and holding the world in his hands.

"On the two sides of the dome were two ovals the paintings of which were very attractive. The *retable* was a continuation of the architecture of the church, in perspective. The altar was well proportioned and, when bearing the rich presents from the king [Louis XIV], appeared truly to be an altar erected by a king for the King of Kings."

One of the most significant decorations of the building from the Chinese point of view was the inscription, carved in marble, above the main entrance. It read: "The Temple of the Lord of Heaven, built by order of the emperor" (*Chih Chien T'ien Chu T'ang*). This inscription gave to the building a sort of official status.

[4] *Ibid.*, XVIII, 6.

[5] This was the third church in Peking, the first having been built in 1650. The first church was the Nan T'ang (called, at first, the Hsi T'ang). It was built on ground given to Ricci by the emperor Wan Li. The title was reaffirmed by Shun Chih. It was enlarged and its architecture was Westernized by Schall in 1650. Severely damaged by the earthquakes of 1720 and 1730, it was restored by Thomas Pereyra in 1743. It was destroyed by fire in 1775 but was rebuilt by funds supplied by the emperor Ch'ien Lung.

The second church, the Tung T'ang, was built on land given to the Jesuits by K'ang Hsi in 1653. The first structure was built in 1655 and it was known as the St. Joseph Mission. This first church was replaced in 1721, when Father Fridelli became superior, by an edifice of which Brother Moggi was the architect. The decorations were done by Castiglione. The Russian ambassador, who visited the first Tung T'ang in 1694 describes it as a fine building in the Italian style and mentions particularly the celestial and terrestrial globes, each a fathom high, standing under separate roofs in the entrance court, and an organ of considerable size constructed by Father Pereyra (Baddeley, *Russia, Mongolia, China,* II, 429). The Nan T'ang and the Tung T'ang were Portuguese residences.

The third church, the Pei T'ang, was the residence of the French Jesuits. Built on ground given the French priests by K'ang Hsi in 1693, it was completed early in 1700. The building was decorated by Brother de Belleville and adorned with gifts from Louis XIV. Father Jartoux has left a good description of the church (letter to De Fontaney, August 20, 1704, published in the *Lettres édifiantes*). It was 70 feet long, 33 feet wide and 30 feet high. The building was consecrated on December 9, 1703 (see Thomas, *La Mission de Pékin,* pp. 116–118). In the days of persecution under Tao Kuang (1820–1850) the church was sold for five thousand taels. It was restored by treaty in 1860 but, since the empress dowager needed the site for her new palace, the location was changed, in 1885, and the present Pei T'ang was built in 1888, immediately inside the Hsi Hua Men of the Imperial City. It was the site of a heroic and successful defense against the Boxers in 1900.

The fourth mission in the capital was the Hsi T'ang, known as the Italian church since it housed the representatives of the Propaganda. Established in 1723 by Father Pedrini, it was the only non-Jesuit establishment in the capital before the nineteenth century.

In other places, notably at Fuchow and Canton, handsome structures were erected toward the end of the seventeenth century.

[6] In 1701 Fathers de Brossia and Gollet went to Ningpo and started to build a church there. They were prevented by the viceroy who appealed for support to the Board of Rites (*Li Pu*). The board interpreted the sense of the imperial edict as permitting the building. (De Mailla, XI, 306.)

[7] Huc, *Le Christianisme en Chine,* III, 389–392, gives a translation of K'ang Hsi's political testament

[8] *Lettres édifiantes,* XVI, 392.

[9] In the year 1751, for example, the number of adults and children of Christian parents baptized in Peking was 122 whereas the number of exposed children receiving baptism was 2423. According to the Jesuit writer 97 per cent of the exposed children were females (*ibid.,* XXIII, 562).

NOTES TO CHAPTER IX

The Rites Controversy: The Principles

[1] De Groot in his *Sectarianism and Religious Persecution in China* denies this theory and asserts that Confucianism has persecuted other cults, but the tolerant nature of Chinese religious thought is maintained by most scholars.

[2] The Noachide theory was bitterly opposed by members of the Missions

Etrangères—and one can readily see why. It was an indirect attack on the doctrine of the Chosen People, on the authority of Abraham, Moses, and the Prophets and—more important still—on the doctrine of the Redemption.

³ Of these men Foucquet was the most ardent in support of his theories, since his ideas were the most extreme. Of a subtle and inquiring mind, this priest had the gift of original thinking which often resulted in disagreements with his confreres. His radicalism soon made him *persona non grata* with them and he was sent back to Europe. Here he continued his campaign for the acceptance of his views. Guettée (*Histoire des Jésuites*, II, 133) implies that he ended by joining the ranks of those attacking the Jesuit policies in China. There is no doubt that in certain matters he was a rebel and the order had no place for rebels. His Christian zeal was rewarded, however, and he was made titular bishop of Eleutheropolis in 1725.

⁴ The writer of the anti-Jesuit *Anecdotes sur l'état de la religion dans la Chine* refers to Pereyra as a man "dur et inflexible, aussi agréable à sa Majesté qu'il était odieux à tous les missionaires qui n'étaient pas jésuites et aux jésuites qui n'étaient pas venus par la voie de Portugal."

⁵ *Lettre à Madame de Lionne sur la Libelle des Jésuites contre l'évêque de Rosalie, son fils,* Rome (1701).

⁶ W. A. P. Martin, "The Worship of Ancestors, a Plea for Toleration," *Record of the General Conference of Protestant Missionaries of China held at Shanghai, May 7–20, 1890* (Shanghai, 1890), p. 619.

NOTES TO CHAPTER X

THE RITES CONTROVERSY: THE DEVELOPMENT OF THE QUARREL

¹ Translated into French by Mgr. de Cicé with the title *Traité sur quelques points de la religion chinôise* (Paris, 1701). The French translation was included, with notes, in the edition of the works of Leibnitz published in Geneva in 1768 (Pfister, *Notices biographiques,* I, 65).

² Colombel, Auguste, S.J., *Histoire de la mission du Kiangnan (s.l.n.d.),* vol. 1, bk. iii.

³ "Quaesita missionariorum Chinae." As early as 1638 a conference had been held in the Philippines by Jesuits, Dominicans, and Franciscans. This probably influenced the bishop to appeal to Rome.

⁴ Colombel, *op. cit.,* vol. 2, bk. v, chap. 4.

⁵ These *quaesita* are to be found in the *Apologie des Dominicains* among the "Documenta Controversiam Missionariorum Apostolicorum Imperii Sinicii," pp. 3–19.

⁶ *Ibid.,* pp. 19–20.

⁷ On October 15, 1648, Morales wrote from the Philippines to Rome accusing the Jesuits of ignoring the papal decree and even of denying its authenticity (Chabrié, *Michel Boym,* p. 171).

⁸ "Documenta Controversiam Missionariorum," *Apologie des Dominicains,* pp. 21–28.

⁹ *Ibid.,* pp. 130–132.

¹⁰ Among the questions addressed to the Holy See was the following: "Whether in regard to the frailty of the people it could be tolerated for the present that Christian magistrates (*gubernatores*) carry a Cross hidden ... and secretly worship that, while they are in outward form and appearance worshipping the idol" (Jenkins, *The Jesuits in China,* p. 19, quoting from Bettilinelli, *Memorie storiche,* V, 8)

¹¹ J. Brucker, "Ricci" in *Catholic Encyclopedia.*

¹² The work was in two volumes. Only the first was widely circulated. The British Museum possesses what is probably the only copy of the second volume in existence outside the archives at Rome. A tome of 668 pages, this volume omits none of the multitudinous charges against the Society. Some of the most valuable pages of the first volume deal with Chinese manners and customs. Navarrete evidently knew the people better than many of his fellow Dominicans, and his keen observations lend much weight to his arguments. The general scope of the work shows that by this time the Rites controversy had become merged in the larger question of missionary aims and procedure. The *Tratados,* although highly partial, stands out preëminently in the literature of the quarrel.

¹³ A vicar apostolic usually holds the title of bishop of an extinct see. He is generally sent to a district which has not been organized as a diocese or is given jurisdiction where, for some special reason, it is found advisable to have a special representative of Rome.

¹⁴ For details of the Maigrot injunction see Thomas, *La Mission de Pékin,* pp. 166–170. For the Latin text see "Documenta Controversiam Missionariorum," pp. 178–185.

¹⁵ Pfister, *Notices biographiques,* I, 394.

¹⁶ *Lettre de MM. des Missions Étrangères au Pape sur les idolâtries et les superstitions chinoises.* This open letter is dated Brussels, 1700. It seems that Brisacier, the head of the mission, sought the advice of Bishop Bossuet and of Archbishops de Noailles of Paris and le Tellier of Rheims. They advised him to publish the letter without the usual "approbation," thinking that Jesuit influence at court would make it impossible to obtain the authorization.

¹⁷ *Réflexions générales sur la lettre qui parut sous le nom des MM. du séminaire des Missions Étrangères.*

¹⁸ *Journal historique des assemblées tenues en Sorbonne pour condamner les "Mémoires de la Chine,"* cited by C. Jourdain, *Histoire de l'Université de Paris au XVIIᵉ et au XVIIIᵉ siècles,* II, 67.

¹⁹ The condemned statements in the *Mémoires* are as follows:

1. "Le peuple de la Chine a conservé près de deux mille ans la connaissance du véritable Dieu, et l'honore d'une manière qui peut servir d'exemple et d'instruction même aux chrétiens" (*Mémoires* [first ed.], II, 141).

2. "Si la Judée avait l'avantage de consacrer un Temple à Dieu plus riche et plus magnifique, sanctifié même par la présence et par les prières du Rédempteur, ce n'est pas une petite gloire à la Chine d'avoir sacrifié au Créateur dans le plus ancien temple de l'Univers" (*ibid.,* II, 134–135).

3. A series of quotations from the classics to show that the people of China had a system of morals of a high order and had been led by rulers of great wisdom and nobility, whose virtue must have been inspired by God. These assertions brought the stern reproof: "Falsa est, temeraria, scandalosa, impia, Verbo Dei contraria, haeretica, Christianae Fidei et Religionis eversiva, virtutem Passionis Christi et Crucis ejus evacuans."

4. An assertion that the emperor of China cannot look upon the Christian religion as a foreign one since the ancient religion of the empire adored the same God and recognized Him as Lord of Heaven and Earth. This statement also incurred the censure: "Haec proposita est falsa, temeraria, scandalosa et erronea."

[20] De Mailla, *Histoire générale de la Chine,* XI, 303.

[21] Colombel, *op. cit.,* pp. 527–529.

[22] The Jesuit apologists claim that the tactics of their opponents drove the missionaries to appeal to the judgment of the emperor (B. Lefevre, "Thomas de Namur," *Biographie nationale de l'Académie de la Belgique.*

[23] Fénelon's letter is to be found in the *Œuvres complètes* (1843 ed.), IV, 101. Bossuet's answer is given in his *Seconde Instruction pastorale sur les Promesses de Jésus Christ à son Eglise.* In a letter to Brisacier, Fénelon says that his reply can be summed up as follows: "Le moins qu'on puisse attendre d'un pape pieux, ferme et éclairé, c'est qu'il ne voudra pour aucune considération humaine ni prolonger le scandale ni tolérer un seul moment l'idolâtrie, si elle est bien prouvée" (letter of October 5, 1702).

NOTES TO CHAPTER XI

The Rites Controversy: The De Tournon Legation

[1] Jenkins, *The Jesuits in China,* p. 39.

[2] *Ibid.,* p. 34. Jenkins quotes from Cardinal Albano's *Life of Clement XI.*

[3] The main source of the history of the legation is Bettilinelli, *Memorie storiche dell' Eminentiss. Mgr. Cardinale di Tournon* . . . , an eight-volume work published in Venice in 1761.

[4] *Ibid.,* I, 25.

[5] *Ibid.,* VIII, 15. See also *Lettres édifiantes,* XXVI, 300

[6] Huc, *Le Christianisme en Chine,* III, 275.

[7] Gonzales de Saint-Pierre, *Relation abrégée de la nouvelle persecution de la Chine jusqu'à la mort du Cardinal de Tournon.*

[8] Jenkins, *op. cit.* (quoting from the *Memorie storiche,* II, 39). The taei was not, as Jenkins suggests, worth four pounds but rather about three or four shillings, or something less than an American dollar, at the time Jenkins was writing.

[9] Brucker, "Ricci," *Encyclopedia Britannica.* The account of the interview is to be found in the *Extrait de la Relation de Pékin le 30 octobre, 1706, touchant l'entretien qu'eut Mgr. Maigrot . . . avec l'empereur de la Chine* (MS Bibliothèque Nationale, fonds fr. 9093).

[10] *Memorie storiche,* III, 69.

[11] For a French translation of the mandate see Thomas, *La Mission de Pékin,* pp. 204–205.

[12] The legate, before leaving Peking, had taken from Barros and Beauvoilliers their title of apostolic missionary. This was probably one of the chief reasons for the bishop's anger. Bishop Favier, a veteran of recent Catholic missions in China, praises De Tournon for taking upon himself the onus of the hostile decision, thus leaving the hands of Rome free to take any subsequent action it might think fit (Favier, *Péking,* p. 172).

[13] Guettée, *Histoire des Jésuites,* II, 122.

[14] Writing to the governor of Manila, April 26, 1710, the cardinal says, "Un enlèvement ne serait nullement de mon goût et je n'y consentirais jamais. Je ne suis pas encore las le l'exercice de mon ministère" (*Nouvelles de la Chine reçues à Rome par voye d'Espagne*).

[15] *Memorie storiche,* I, 317–319.

[16] For example, see Guettée, II, 121, note.

[17] Jenkins suggests (*op. cit.,* p. 47) that De Tournon's illness was a form of cholera, but asserts later (*ibid.,* p. 60) that the legate was subject to epilepsy.

[18] Notably by Father Antoine Thomas in a letter published in the *Lettres édifiantes,* XXVI, 295 *et seq.* Guettée cites also (*op. cit.,* II, 121, note) a letter in the Roman archives from Father Killian Stumpf refuting the charge of poisoning.

[19] The leaders of the opposition to the legate were Pereyra, Grimaldi, Stumpf, and, to a lesser extent, Gerbillon in Peking, and Ozorio at Macao. Of the last-named, Father Angelita, one of the legate's staff, writes: "One hundred thousand deaths would not suffice to cancel the tenth part of the iniquities committed by Father Ozorio" (Jenkins, p. 51, note).

[20] *Ibid.,* p. 101.

NOTES TO CHAPTER XII

The Rites Controversy: The End of the Quarrel

[1] For a complete translation of the bull see Thomas, *Mission de Pékin,* pp. 243–251.

[2] Mosheim, *Authentic Memoirs of the Christian Church in China* (Eng. trans., London, 1750).

[3] "Memoirs of Father Ripa during the Thirteen Years' Residence at the Court of Peking" (London, 1844). The book is part of a longer work in Italian. Father Ripa left China in 1723 and founded in Naples a training school for Chinese neophytes.

[4] On his accession, the emperor Yung Cheng, whose tutor Pedrini had been, set the priest at liberty and, when Pedrini died in 1746, the emperor granted him posthumous honors.

[5] *Anecdotes sur l'état de la religion dans la Chine,* IV, 316 *et seq.* See also Thomas, *op. cit.,* pp. 259 *et seq.*

[6] *Anecdotes,* IV, 58.

[7] It is interesting to note that the emperor's reply involved, in effect, a condemnation of what was later called extraterritoriality, the system of local autonomy by foreigners in certain restricted districts which still prevails at Shanghai, Tientsin, and elsewhere in China.

[8] Soulié de Morant, *L'Epopée des Jésuites en Chine,* p. 174.

[9] *Ibid.,* p. 179.

[10] *Les Jésuites convaincus d'obstination à permettre l'Idolâtrie dans la Chine* (Paris, 1744).

[11] Guettée, *Histoire des Jésuites,* II, 134.

[12] Soulié de Morant, p. 200.

[13] Thomas, p. 372. This work contains a French translation of the whole document.

[14] *Ibid.,* p. 373.

[15] The full text of the decree of December, 1938, is as follows. The translation is from the official *Acta Sedis Romanae* published in *The Tablet* (London, January 20, 1940), p. 59.

"It is a matter of common knowledge that some ceremonies common in the Orient, though in earlier times connected with rites of a religious nature, have at the present time, owing to changes in customs and ideas in the course of centuries, no more than mere civil significance of filial respect for ancestors, of patriotic sentiment or of social amenity. Hence in conformity with Canon 22 and with the approval of the late Pope Pius XI of blessed memory, this Sacred Congregation in the course of 1935 and 1936 established for the Ordinaries of Manchuria and of the Japanese empire, new norms more in harmony with actual conditions at the present day.

"A short time ago, in their general session, on December 4th, 1938, Their Eminences the Cardinals of the Sacred Congregation of Propaganda deliberated whether an analogous procedure ought not to be adopted also for other localities where it was clear that similar changes in circumstances had taken place with the lapse of time. After weighing carefully the arguments on both sides, and consulting men of prudence and experience, these Eminent Fathers determined upon the following declarations:

"1. Inasmuch as the Chinese Government has repeatedly and explicitly proclaimed that all are free to profess the religion they prefer, and that it is foreign to its intentions to legislate or issue decrees concerning religious matters, and that consequently ceremonies performed or ordered by the public authorities in honour of Confucius do not take place with intent to offer religious worship, but solely for the purpose of promoting and expressing the honour due to a great man, and proper regard for tradition; it is licit for Catholics to be present at commemorative functions held before a likeness or tablet of Confucius in Confucian monuments or schools.

"2. Hence it is not to be considered illicit, particularly if the authorities should order it, to place in Catholic schools a likeness of Confucius, or even a tablet inscribed with his name, or to bow before such. Where scandal may be feared, the right intention of Catholics should be made clear.

"3. It is to be tolerated that Catholic functionaries and students assist, if ordered to do so, at public ceremonies which bear some semblance of super-stition, provided that, in accordance with Canon 1258, they remain passive and participate only in such outward marks of respect as may be regarded as purely civil in character, after declaring their intention as above, whenever this may seem necessary in order to avoid misinterpretation of their actions.

"4. Inclinations of the head, and other signs of civil respect in presence of the dead or before their images, or even before a tablet inscribed simply with the name of the defunct, are also to be regarded as licit and proper.

"Furthermore, in consideration of the fact that the oath on Chinese Rites, demanded of all priests 'in the Chinese Empire and other Kingdoms and Provinces bounding or adjacent to them' of July 11th, 1742, is not entirely consonant with recent norms laid down by this Sacred Convention; and in consideration, moreover, of the fact that this same oath is today wholly super-fluous as a disciplinary measure, because, as is well known, the old controver-sies regarding Chinese Rites have died down and the missionaries and other priests have no need to be forced by oath to render prompt and filial obedience to the Holy See: the same Eminent Fathers have decided that the obligation of taking this oath wherever customary in China or elsewhere, should be dispensed with, although all the other prescriptions of Pope Benedict XIV, in so far as they have not been changed by later instructions, are to remain in force, notably the prohibition to discuss the Chinese Rites.

"When these views of the Eminent Fathers were referred to his Holiness Pope Piux XII by the undersigned Cardinal Prefect of this Sacred Congrega-tion, in an audience on December 7th, His Holiness deigned to approve and ratify them in every respect.

"Given at Rome ... on the 8th day of December, 1938.

"PIETRO CARDINAL FUMASONI BIONDI, PREFECT
'Celsus Constantini"

[18] Guettée asserts that the opposition of the Jesuits to the papal commands continued until the dissolution of the Society. Mgr. de Souza, the Jesuit Bishop of Peking, wrote to the Holy See in 1744 complaining that he had been accused of remissness in enforcing the terms of the bull. Rome answered with the stern statement that the best form of self-justification was the real enforcement of the papal order. Mgr. Gouvea, as late as 1785, accused the Jesuits of having continued their struggle against the bull (Thomas, p. 378).

NOTES TO CHAPTER XIII

THE DECLINE OF THE MISSION

[1] For a list of the most influential of the sons of K'ang Hsi see Bland and Backhouse, *Annals and Memoirs of the Court of Peking*, pp. 245–247.

[2] For an account of the conspiracy see Bland and Backhouse, chaps. xi-xii. There is considerable doubt whether Father Morao was guilty. The only for-

eign work which supports the accusation is *Anecdotes sur l'état de la religion dans la Chine,* which is bitterly hostile to the Jesuits.

[3] Letters of July 20, 1725, August 20, 1726, and September 26, 1727, *Lettres édifiantes,* Vol. XX.

[4] Bland and Backhouse, p. 270: "In his domestic life, as in his relations with his Ministers and Court, he has written himself down, without possibility of doubt, as a suspicious, querulous and savagely vindictive individual."

[5] De Mailla, *Histoire de la Chine,* XI, 392, note.

[6] The so-called Sacred Edict was issued by K'ang Hsi in 1691. It contained sixteen moral maxims for the guidance of the people. The emperor gave orders for it to be read aloud throughout the empire on the first and fifteenth day of each month. It has always been highly esteemed by the Chinese. In 1724 Yung Cheng had one hundred of the best scholars write commentaries on the maxims, and from these the sixteen best were chosen to be printed with the edict. In the section dealing with false sects or heterodoxy is the following comment: "So, too, those Western doctrines which teach the worship of the Lord of Heaven (*T'ien Chu*) are also uncanonical. However, because the missionaries understood mathematics the State employed them. It is important for the people to know this" (Giles, *Gems of Chinese Literature,* p. 227).

[7] Already, in 1662, the king of Portugal had attempted to intercede for his subjects at Macao, but the results obtained from the action were so bad that the people of Macao begged him not to repeat the experiment. Metello's embassy cost Macao 30,000 taels.

[8] Soulié de Morant, *L'Epopée des Jésuites français en Chine,* p. 205.

[9] There were in 1736 ten French priests in the capital, besides those of other nationalities. They were: D'Entrecolles, Régis, De Mailla, Gaubil, De la Charme, Chassier, Boussel, Fourreau, and the superior, Parennin. There were, in all, twenty-two Jesuits in Peking. Of the Portuguese, Pinheiro was superior and Pereyra was vice-provincial (*Lettres édifiantes,* XXII, 106).

[10] *Ibid.,* XXIII, 154.

[11] Dominique Parennin was born September 1, 1665, near Besançon; he studied at Lyons and began his novitiate at Avignon. He took final orders in 1693, arriving in China in 1699. He was chosen superior of the French mission in 1723 and later became procureur. He died in Peking on September 29, 1741.

[12] Voltaire, *Siècle de Louis XIV,* chap. xxxix.

[13] Huc, *Le Christianisme en Chine,* IV, 87. Pfister (*Notices biographiques,* p. 512) gives a list of his principal works. Father Chalier wrote an eloquent eulogy of Parennin which was published in the *Lettres édifiantes,* XXII, 385 *et seq.*

[14] Pelliot, "La Peinture et la gravure européennes en Chine au temps de M. Ricci," *T'oung Pao,* Vol. XX.

[15] Pelliot, "Les Conquêtes de l'Empereur de la Chine," *ibid.* For an account of Attiret's work see *Lettres édifiantes,* XXIII, 33 *et seq.,* also Pfister, *op. cit.,* pp. 787–793.

[16] *Lettres édifiantes,* XXIV, 491 *et seq.* See also Pfister, pp. 830–832.

[17] Pfister, p. 972. Panzi arrived in Peking in 1773 to succeed Castiglione, who had died in 1766, and Attiret, who had died in 1768. He was one of the last surviving members of the mission, dying about 1812.

[18] A fairly complete list of Castiglione's paintings has been published by J. C. Ferguson in the *China Journal of Sciences and Arts,* Vol. XII (January 24, 1930). In the same journal is a reproduction of the "Hundred Horses."

Laurence Binyon's *Les Peintures chinoises dans les collections d'Angleterre* contains several paintings showing Jesuit influence, notably Plates LXIII and LXIIIa. J. C. Ferguson's *Chinese Art* contains a reproduction of a portrait of Ch'ien Lung by Castiglione and Wang Tai. The Paris Musée Guimet has another of Ch'ien Lung and his court by Castiglione as well as other painting by the same Jesuit painter. For years a curious painting of one of Ch'ien Lung's court ladies clad in Italian armor was to be seen at the National Museum in Peking. For an account of Castiglione's work see Huc, *op. cit.,* IV, 71–72 and Pfister, *op. cit.,* pp. 635–640.

[19] An interesting commentary on the increasing importance of Chinese relations with Russia.

[20] For a list of the writings of Gaubil see Pfister, pp. 676–693.

[21] For an account of the Yuan Ming Yuan see Malone, *History of the Peking Summer Palaces.*

[22] The last plate arrived in China in 1775. Altogether two hundred copies were printed from the plates in France. The whole work cost the astonishing sum of 204,000 taels. For a list of the engravings see Pelliot, *Les Conquêtes de l'empereur de la Chine.*

[23] Rochemonteix, *Joseph Amiot.* See also Cordier, "La Suppression des Jésuites et les derniers jours de la Mission à Pékin," *T'oung Pao,* Vols. XVII–XVIII.

[24] Rochemonteix, *op. cit.,* p. 332.

[25] *Ibid.,* p. 420.

[26] Letter to his sister, cited by Rochemonteix, p. 428.

[27] Poirot was the last of the French Jesuits in Peking. He died in 1814.

NOTES TO CHAPTER XIV

PERSECUTION AND PROGRESS

[1] Latourette, *Christian Missions in China,* pp. 103–104. A. C. Moule (*New China Review,* IV, 450–456) gives an account of the persecution taken from Chinese records.

[2] Huc, *Le Christianisme en Chine,* III, 193.

[3] *Ibid.,* p. 205

[4] *Ibid.,* IV, 19.

[5] *Ibid.,* pp. 22–39. See also, Brucker, "La Mission de Chine de 1722 à 1735," *Revue des questions historiques,* XXIX, 491–532.

[6] This system was a great drain, financially, on the resources of the mission.

Gaubil, writing in 1728, declares: "We have exhausted ourselves in furnishing the funds necessary for the safety of missionaries in hiding ... and if our two new Fathers [La Charme and Challier, who had just arrived at Canton] do not bring the help we have asked for I do not know how we shall continue to exist" (*ibid.*, p. 513).

[7] *Lettres édifiantes*, XXI, 237.

[8] *Ibid.*, XXII, 400.

[9] *Ibid.*, p. 434.

[10] The books were returned later by the officials with the sole comment: "Unless one were a holy man (*Shêng jen*) it would be difficult to obey this law."

[11] Huc, *op. cit.*, IV, 78.

[12] *Ibid.*, pp. 109–110.

[13] *Ibid.*, p. 116.

[14] *Ibid.*, p. 122.

[15] *Lettres édifiantes*, XXIII, 25.

[16] Latourette, *op. cit.*, p. 163.

[17] By his final defeat of the Eleuths in 1760 Ch'ien Lung had brought to successful conclusion a long war which rendered him master of the entire region of the T'ien Shan (Cordier, *Histoire générale de la Chine*, III, 346–349).

[18] *Lettres édifiantes*, XXIII, 217.

[19] *Ibid.*, p. 412.

[20] Huc, IV, 176.

[21] *Lettres édifiantes*, XXIV, 151 et seq.

[22] Huc, IV, 184–191.

[23] *Ibid.*, II, 258.

[24] Semedo, *Histoire Universelle de la Chine*, p. 303.

[25] Huc, II, 290.

[26] Thomas (*La Mission de Pékin*, p. 298) gives the following figures for the personnel of the missions in the middle of the seventeenth century: Jesuits, 41 residences, 159 churches; Dominicans, 2 residences, 21 churches; Franciscans, 1 residence, 3 churches. Havret (*Le Stèle chrétienne de Si-ngan-fou*, p. 97) says that in 1636 there were 40,000 in Shantung, Shansi, Shensi, Chihli, Honan, Chekiang, Kiangsi, Kiangnan, and Fukien.

[27] Thomas, p. 397. See also Brucker, *Catholic Encyclopedia* (New York, 1912), XIII, 522.

[28] In addition to these totals, the Dominicans claimed 3400 converts for the period 1650–1664, and the Franciscans 3571 for 1633–1660, making a grand total of 261,951. See Thomas, p. 397. The catalogue of Father Gama, however, gives only 110,000 for the year 1663 (*ibid.*, p. 398). Father Gaubil wrote in 1726: "Je ne crois pas qu'en Chine et en Tartarie il y ait plus de 300,000 chrétiens" (Crétineau-Joly, *Histoire de la Compagnie de Jésus*, V, 59). De Mailla, writing two years earlier (October 16, 1724), had given the same figures. Obviously, these figures were dictated by the spirit of enthusiasm rather than by knowledge of the facts. The catalogue of the archives of the order gives the following

figures for the number of priests: thirteen in 1610; thirteen in 1621; eighteen in 1626; twenty-four in 1630; twenty-five in 1642; eighteen in 1650. See Thomas, *op. cit.,* p. 401.

[29] Members of the Dominican order had landed in the empire in 1593, 1596, 1621, 1635, 1636, 1638, and 1640. See Latourette, *op. cit.,* p. 101.

[30] *Ibid.,* p. 110.

[31] Gregory Lopez (*Lo*) was baptized at sixteen (1626) by the Franciscan Father Sainte-Marie. He studied at Manila and entered the Dominican order, being ordained in 1656. He worked chiefly in Fukien. Named Bishop of Basileus or Basilinopolis, January 4, 1674, he at first refused the honor but later accepted and was consecrated at Canton, April 8, 1685, as vicar apostolic of Nanking, with the administration of the provinces of Chihli, Shantung, Shansi, Honan, Shensi, and the kingdom of Korea. He died at Nanking, February 27, 1691. See De Moidrey, *La Hiérarchie catholique en Chine,* p. 22.

[32] Latourette, p. 118.

[33] *Ibid.,* p. 127.

[34] In 1695 there were 75 priests in China including 38 Jesuits, 9 Spanish Dominicans, 5 Spanish Augustinians, and 4 Franciscans. In 1751 there were 59 Jesuits, 29 Franciscans, 8 Dominicans, 6 Augustinians, 15 secular priests— 117 in all. From 1694 to 1705 there was an addition of 88 priests to the Jesuit order alone.

[35] Hukuang comprised the two provinces of Hunan and Hupeh, but they were not separated until later.

[36] Latourette (p. 129) cites these figures but warns that they are to be taken only as a maximum. They were possibly very much less.

[37] According to Jesuit figures, the mission in Nanking province numbered 60,000 by the middle of the century. In Peking alone there were 50,000 Christians. In 1741 Gaubil reported 100,000 Christians in Chihli province, where the number of baptized infants amounted annually to 1500—as compared with 3,000 before the persecution. During the period of famine in Szechuan the priests baptized 30,000 of these foundlings.

[38] Latourette, p. 162.

[39] Thomas, p. 403.

[40] Latourette, p. 168.

[41] In this whole period there were in China a total of 454 Jesuits, of whom 66 were lay brothers. Of the total, 153 were Portuguese, 96 French, 81 Chinese (of whom only 50 were professed priests), and the remainder were divided among twelve other nationalities. See De Moidrey, *op. cit.,* p. 187.

NOTES TO CHAPTER XV

PRIESTS AND COURTIERS

[1] According to Yule (*Cathay and the Way Thither,* I, cxl) the same saying is to be found in the travel accounts of Nicolò Conti, Clavijo, and Josaphat Barbaro, as well as of Haytoun.

[2] Sonnerat, *Supplément au voyage dans les Indes Orientales* (Paris, 1782), quoted by Chabrié, *Michel Boym,* p. 35.

[3] Chabrié, p. 44.

[4] Schall, Parennin, and others owed not a little of their influence in their later years to their venerable appearance.

[5] Parennin's letter of September 28, 1735. See *Lettres édifiantes,* XXII, 146. An interesting commentary on the Chinese official attitude is to be found in the following passage from the annals of the Ming dynasty. Speaking of Ricci's famous map, the chronicle says: "His [Ricci's] words were vague, confused and unreliable, but since a native has penetrated to China there is no doubt that his country [Italy] really exists."

[6] A. C. Moule, "The First Arrival of the Jesuits at the Capital of China," *New China Review,* IV, 455.

[7] Letter of September 28, 1735, *Lettres édifiantes,* XXII, 134.

[8] *Ibid.,* p. 147.

[9] *Lettre d'un missionaire de la Cie. de Jésus écrite de la Chine à M* ... Even as late as the end of the nineteenth century this love of clocks as ornaments persisted with the Chinese. The apartments of the late empress-dowager, Tzu Hsi, were literally filled with timepieces of all descriptions, valued not as clocks but as *objets d'art*

[10] Bosmans, "Ferdinand Verbiest," p. 232.

[11] *Ibid.,* p. 217

[12] Guettée, *Histoire des Jésuites,* II, 86.

[13] E. T. Williams, *Short History of China,* p. 227.

[14] See pp. 196–197 of the present work.

[15] Ripa says: "He supposed himself to be an excellent musician and a still better mathematician but, though he had a taste for science and other acquirements in general, he knew nothing of music and scarcely understood the five elements of mathematics."

[16] Brucker, "La Mission de Chine de 1722 à 1735," *Revue des questions historiques,* XXIX, 503. Wang Yu-fo, writer of the well-known amplification of the edict, made the following note concerning Christianity: "... Even the sect of the Lord of Heaven (*T'ien chu chiao*), who talk about heaven and prate about earth, and of things without shadow and without substance, their religion is unsound and corrupt ... You should not on any account believe them [the foreign missionaries]. The Law is very rigorous against all these left-hand-road and side-door sects." See *Chinese Repository,* I, 308.

[17] Lecomte, *Nouveaux Mémoires,* I, 68. It is interesting to compare this description with that given by Evart Isbrand Ides, the Russian envoy to Peking in 1669, who says: "The monarch was then fifty. His mien was very agreeable. He had large black eyes and his nose was somewhat raised. He had a small black moustache and very little or no beard on the lower part of the face. He was much pitted with small-pox and of medium stature ... His hair was plaited into one lock and hung behind. He had no gold or jewels about him." See Ides, *Three Years of Travel Overland from Moscow to China* (London, 1706).

[18] *Lettres édifiantes,* XIX, 258.

[19] Du Halde, *Description,* III, 151.

[20] Several facts make the comparison justifiable. Louis and K'ang Hsi both succeeded to the throne at an early age and both at first ruled through regents. Both took up the responsibilities of kingship as young men and reigned long and gloriously. Their reigns were almost contemporaneous (Louis XIV, 1643–1715; K'ang Hsi, 1662–1722). Both were great patrons of arts and letters.

[21] De Mailla, *Histoire générale de la Chine,* Vol. XI.

[22] Father Ripa (*Memoirs,* pp. 28–29) gives the following picture of K'ang Hsi: "I saw him several times about the gardens but never on foot. He was always carried in a sedan chair, surrounded by crowds of concubines, all walking and smiling. Sometimes he would sit in a high chair in the form of a throne with eunuchs standing around him and, watching a favorable moment, he would suddenly throw among the ladies grouped around him on carpets of felt artificial snakes, toads and other loathsome reptiles in order to enjoy the pleasure of watching them scamper away on their crippled feet. At other times he would send some of his ladies to gather filberts and fruits on the neighbouring hills and, pretending to be craving for some, he would urge on the poor lamed creatures with noisy exclamations, until some fell to the ground, when he would indulge in a hearty laugh ... Whether he was in the country or in Peking he saw no other company but his ladies and his eunuchs." This account is evidently dictated by malice. The reference to the bound feet of the concubines is almost certainly inaccurate since the Manchu court women did not bind their feet; also, it was contrary to Manchu imperial law and custom to have Chinese women in the imperial household.

[23] *Lettres édifiantes,* XXII, 389.

[24] Du Halde, IV, 95.

[25] Duméril, "L'Influence des Jésuites sur le mouvement des idées ... ," *Mémoires de l'Académie de Dijon* (1874), pp. 1–33.

[26] *Lettres édifiantes,* XXIV, III.

[27] *Ibid.,* p. 237.

[28] MS, Bibliothèque Nationale, fonds français 17240, f. 89.

[29] *Ibid.*

[30] *Lettres édifiantes,* XXIII, 177.

[31] *Ibid.,* pp. 302 *et seq.*

[32] Father Amiot gives the following account of his presentation to the emperor in 1752: "In one of the courts of the palace the three Jesuits placed themselves in line with their faces turned towards the emperor's apartments. They prostrated themselves gravely in a profound and respectful silence. Twice they touched the earth with their foreheads. They then rose and repeated the ceremony a second and then a third time" (*ibid.,* p. 162).

[33] E. T. Williams, *op. cit.,* p. 243.

[34] J. Nieuhoff, *An Embassy from the East India Company ...* (English translation; London, 1673), pp. 299–317. Internal evidence seems to show that the letter was written by Father Magalhaens.

[35] *Ibid.,* p. 306.

[36] *Ibid.*, p. 309.

[37] "Father Adam" claims that the "atheistic" practices of the Dutch visitors scandalized the Chinese Catholics and did much harm to Catholic propaganda (*ibid.,* p. 304).

[38] However, when Father Avril tried to get permission from the tsar to proceed to Peking by way of Siberia, his request was refused. In his account of his travels he claims that Grimaldi always mistrusted the Russians, fearing that the latter, if once they entered the country, would do harm to the fortunes of Christianity through their boorishness and ignorance. It is probable that Avril's disappointment at the tsar's refusal colored his views. See Avril, *Voyage en divers états,* Préface.

[39] For an interesting account of Spathary's relations with the Jesuits see J. F. Baddeley, *Russia, Mongolia, China,* Vol. II, *passim.*

[40] Gowen and Hall, *An Outline History of China,* p. 201.

[41] H. Dudgeon, "Russian Ecclesiastical Mission," *Chinese Recorder,* Vols. III–IV, *passim.*

[42] Sanchez seems to have been the "stormy petrel" of the Jesuit mission at this time. A man of excessive but misguided fervor, he greatly embarrassed his colleagues in China. If he represents the attitude of the Philippine Jesuits (as well as the Philippine Catholics in general) toward China, it is not surprising that the general of the order forbade the Jesuit superior in the Islands to allow any more of their number to go to China. See Bernard, *Aux Portes de la Chine,* pp. 248–250.

[43] It was probably on account of his apparently francophile tendencies that Verbiest was deprived of his rank as rector of the mission by the Portuguese visitor to China; the post was given to Pereyra. See Bosmans, *op. cit.,* p. 457.

[44] Gonzales de Saint-Pierre, *Relation de la nouvelle persecution,* p. 217.

NOTES TO CHAPTER XVI

JESUIT SINOPHILE LITERATURE OF THE SEVENTEENTH CENTURY

[1] Juan Gonzales de Mendoça, *Historia de las cosas mas notables, ritos, y costumbres del gran reyno de la China* ... . Four other Spanish editions of this work appeared in the sixteenth century, and six editions in Italian. Besides these there were six French editions, those of 1589 (translated by Luc de la Porte), 1600, 1604 (Lyons), 1604 (Rouen), 1606 (Geneva), and 1606 (Lyons); a Latin edition (Frankfort, 1589); a German edition (1589); and an English edition by R. Parkes (1589–1590). The last-named is the basis for the Hakluyt edition entitled, *The History of the Great and Mighty Kingdom of China and the Situation thereof ... edited by Sir George Staunton Bart....* (London, 1853).

[2] *Ibid.* (Hakluyt ed.), I, 56.

[3] Trigault, *De Christiano Expeditione apud Sinas.* A French translation was published in Lille, 1617, and in Paris, 1618.

[4] Nicolas Trigault, born March 3, 1577, at Douai, studied at Tournai and

Lille and taught rhetoric at Ghent. He arrived in China in 1611 and was sent to Rome a year later to obtain recruits for the mission. He returned in 1618 and remained until his death in 1628, working chiefly at Nanking, Hangchow, and Sianfu. In the last-named city he founded an important mission; also one in Shansi.

[5] Trigault, *op. cit.* (1615 ed.), p. 3.

[6] Alvarez Semedo, *Imperio de la China* (Madrid, 1642). French editions of Semedo's book appeared in 1642 (Paris) and 1667 (Lyons); a Latin edition, in 1645. Semedo, a native of Portugal, was born in 1585. He arrived in Nanking in 1613, worked at Hangchow, Kia T'ing, Shanghai, and Sianfu. He was the first European to see the Nestorian tablet at Sianfu. He visited Rome 1642–1644 and spent the last years of his life at Canton, dying in 1658.

[7] Athanasius Kircher, *China monumentis qua sacris qua profanis, illustrata* (Amsterdam, 1667; 2d ed., Amsterdam, 1672); French edition, *La Chine illustrée,* translated by d'Alquié (Amsterdam, 1670). Kircher also published a translation of the Nestorian monument in his *Prodromus Coptus sive Aegypticus* in 1635.

[8] Navarrete, *Tratados historicos, politicos, ethicos y religiosos de la Monarchía de China* (Madrid, 1676).

[9] For an account of the nature and influence of the imaginary or extraordinary voyage see the three volumes by Geoffroy Atkinson cited in the Bibliography.

[10] A. H. Rowbotham, "La Mothe le Vayer's *Vertu des Payens* and Eighteenth-Century Cosmopolitanism," *Modern Language Notes,* January, 1938.

[11] Louis Lecomte, S.J., *Nouveaux Mémoires sur l'état présent de la Chine* (Paris, 1696). An English edition was published in London and a German edition at Leipzig in 1699.

[12] Philippe Couplet, ed., *Confucius Sinarum Philosophus* (Paris, 1687).

[13] *La Science des Chinois ou le livre de Cum-fu-çu, traduit mot par mot de la langue chinoise par le P. Intorcetta* (Paris, 1673).

[14] *Sinensis imperii libri classici sex . . . e sinico idiomate in latinum traducti a Francisco Noël.* The work contained the Ta Hsueh, Lun Yu, Chung Yung, and Meng Tze.

[15] Virgile Pinot, *La Chine et la formation de l'esprit philosophique en France, 1640–1740* (Paris, 1932), pp. 347–367.

[16] Published in Vossius, *Variarum observationum liber* (London, 1685).

[17] Baruzi, *Leibnitz et l'organisation religieuse de la terre.*

[18] Adolph Reichwein, *China and Europe,* p. 80.

[19] Franz Rudolf Merkel, *G. W. von Leibniz und die China-Mission.*

[20] Christian Wolff, *De Sinarum philosophia practica.* The work was published in 1722 with the title *De Sapientia Sinarum,* and again in Frankfurt in 1726, with copious notes based on the works of Intorcetta, Couplet, and Noël. It was translated into French by J. H. Formey and published in the work *La Belle Wolfienne* from which the English edition, *The Real Happiness of a People* (London, 1750), was copied.

[21] The novelistic literature of Germany during this period also felt the in-

fluence of the Sinophile movement. The widely read *Simplicissimus* of Grimmelshausen contains pages on China inspired by the narrative of Fernand Mendez Pinto. Hagdorn's *Aeyquan* (1670) includes the story of the last of the Mings, taken from Martini's work. In Hoppel's *Asiatischer Onogombo*, the emperor Shun Chih is represented as a wandering knight. The priest Gasser's *Aussförderung* is an exemplary novel with a utopian China as its background. The whole of the baroque movement of the latter part of the century is closely allied with the growing spirit of Sinomania. See Eduard Horst von Tscharner, "China in der Deutschen Dichtung," *Sinica,* XII (1937).

[22] Matthew Tindal, *Christianity as Old as Creation* (2d ed.; London, 1731), p. 314. Other deistic writers, for example Shaftsbury, may have been indirectly influenced by the Chinese vogue, though there is little evidence to prove this.

[23] See Pinot, *op. cit.,* pp. 328 *et seq.*

[24] In the Mérigot edition the China letters are to be found in Vols. XVI–XXVI. The letters appeared in groups in the course of the eighteenth century. There were many translations. Cordier notes a German edition of 1728, an English edition of 1743, and one of 1767. There were several editions in the nineteenth century. A revised and enlarged edition appeared in 1838–1843.

[25] Du Halde, *Description géographique, historique, chronologique et physique de l'empire de la Chine et de la Tartarie chinoise* (4 vols. in 4to; Paris, 1735), with an atlas of 42 maps. A second edition was published at La Haye, 1736. An English translation by Brooks appeared the same year in London, and there was also a second edition, translated by Edward Cave in 1738–1741. For an account of the work see Lin Yian Tsouan, *Essai sur le Père Duhalde et sa description de la Chine* (Fribourg, 1937).

[26] The *Mémoires* were published at intervals between 1777 and 1814. They are almost entirely the work of the last group of Jesuits at Peking.

[27] Cordier, *La Chine en France au XVIIIᵉ siècle.*

[28] Belevitch-Stankevitch, *Le Goût chinois en France au temps de Louis XIV.* See also Reichwein, *op. cit., passim.*

[29] E. von Erdberg, *Chinese Influence on European Garden Structures.*

[30] Sir William Temple, "Essay Upon the Gardens of Epicurus," written in 1685 and published (1692) in his *Essays.* See also his essay, "Upon Heroick Virtue," for his ideas on China.

[31] *Lettres édifiantes,* XXII, 496 *et seq.*

[32] The Chinese garden was an attempt to reproduce, in miniature, within the somewhat narrow confines of the walled "park," the illusion of the hills, valleys, and streams of nature itself. One of the most enlightening interpretations of the spirit which dominates Chinese garden architecture is to be found in Florence Ayscough's *A Chinese Mirror.* Dr. Ayscough has included in her study a translation of the famous description of the making of a garden in the classic Chinese novel *Hung Lou Meng* ("Dream of the Red Chamber").

[33] A. O. Lovejoy, *The Chinese Origin of a Romanticism.*

[34] John Evelyn notes in his diary in 1664 that "one Tomson, a Jesuit, showed me such a rich collection of rarities ... brought to London by the East India ships ... as in my life I have not seen. ...."

NOTES TO CHAPTER XVII

THE JESUITS AS INTERPRETERS OF THE CULTURES OF EAST AND WEST

[1] Martin Martini, *Sinicae historiae decas prima res a gentis origine ad Christum natum* (Munich, 1658).

[2] Antoine Gaubil, *Histoire de Gentchiscan et de la dynastie des Mongous* (Paris, 1739). De Visdelou had written a *Histoire de la Grande Tartarie* which was published in Herbelot's *Bibliothèque Orientale.*

[3] *Le Chou King traduit et annoté* was written about 1739 and published in Paris in 1770, edited by De Guignes.

[4] Prémare, *Recherches sur les temps antérieurs à ceux dont parle le Chou King.*

[5] Gaubil, *Histoire de la grande dynastie des Thang,* published in Vols. XV and XVI of the *Mémoires.*

[6] D'Orleans, *Histoire des deux conquérants Tartares qui ont subjugué la Chine.*

[7] Joachim Bouvet, *Portrait historique de l'empereur de la Chine*

[8] Le Gobien, *Histoire de l'édit de l'empereur de la Chine en faveur de la religion chrétienne.*

[9] De Mailla, *Histoire générale de la Chine,* edited by Abbé Grosier. An Italian edition appeared about the same time.

[10] C. R. Beazley, *The Dawn of Modern Geography.*

[11] For an account of Ricci's map see Henri Bernard, *Les Etapes de la cartographie scientifique pour la Chine.* The map and its accompanying text have been discussed by Kenneth Ch'en in the *Journal of the American Oriental Society* (1939) LIX, 325-359.

[12] "Vraiment," says the Sinologue Chavannes, "si l'on compare les cartes de fantaisie des anciens Grecs et Romains avec les cartes relevées sur place par les Chinois, on est obligé de reconnaître encore une fois sur ce point comme sur tant d'autres la superiorité de la race jaune sur la race blanche" (quoted by Bernard, *Les Etapes de la cartographie,* p. 429).

[13] Martini, *Novus Atlas Sinensis.* The work included 17 maps and 171 pages of text.

[14] After the province of Chihli had been mapped, Régis and Cardoso surveyed Shantung; and a group including Jartoux, Cardelli, and an Augustinian named Bonjour went north to survey the country of the Kalkas, a task which took a year to complete. Cardoso and De Tartre mapped Shansi, Shensi, Kiangsi, Kwangsi, and Kwangtung, while De Mailla and Hinderer were surveying Honan, Kiangnan, Kiangsu, Chekiang, and Fukien. In 1715 Bonjour, Fridelli, and Régis made maps of Szechuan and Yunnan and later of the provinces of Hukuang and Kweichow.

[15] Bernard, *Les Etapes de la cartographie,* p. 460.

[16] The Jesuits in China were apparently dissatisfied with the D'Anville maps, and it is true that the French engraver took some liberties with his originals.

[17] This map, of which a hundred copies were made, was of considerable service later to geographers in their researches in Central Asia. See Bernard, *Les Etapes de la cartographie*, p. 475.

In 1756 Ch'ien Lung sent a group of Chinese geographers, including Fathers da Rocha and d'Espinha, to chart the region of Chungkar in Central Asia, but their maps have apparently been lost.

[18] Verbiest, *Astronomia Europœa sub Imperatore Tartaro-Sinico Cam Hy* (Dillingen, 1687).

[19] Chabrié, *Michel Boym*, pp. 235–248.

[20] *Lettres édifiantes*, XXI, 5 *et seq*. It was William Harris in his *De Peste cui accessit descriptio inoculationis variolarum* (London, 1721) who first directed attention to the Chinese treatment.

[21] The standard work on Chinese agriculture, *Nung Cheng Chüan Shu*, was written by the most distinguished of the Jesuit converts, Hsü Kuang-ch'i. See Maverick, "Hsü Kuang-ch'i, a Chinese Authority on Agriculture," *Agricultural History*, XIV, 143–160.

[22] The first work in linguistics was a little volume by the Augustinian Martin da Rada, entitled *Arte y Vocabulario de la lengua China*, based on the dialect of Ch'üan Chou. See Bernard, *Aux Portes de la Chine*, p. 105, note. Of the early dictionaries mention should be made of a Chinese-Italian work, compiled by the Franciscan Charles de Castorano, and a Chinese-Latin dictionary by the Franciscan Basil of Cremona (which Klaproth claimed was the best of its kind in his day). Prémare collaborated with Hervieu in a Chinese-Latin dictionary of which Fourmont later made use.

[23] Henri Bernard, "Galilée et les Jésuites de la Mission d'Orient," *Revue des questions scientifiques* (1937), p. 362. Verbiest was the author of the first Manchu grammar, *Elementa Linguae tartaricae*, which was reprinted in Thevenot's *Voyages* (Paris, 1696), II, 4.

[24] *Ibid.*, p. 375.

[25] According to Wylie, *Notes on Chinese Literature* (from which most of these facts concerning Jesuit books in Chinese are taken), the *Chien Ping I Shuo*, written by De Ursis in 1611, was based upon a tacit acceptance of the Ptolemaic system. The greater part of the early Jesuit contribution in the field of astronomy is summed up in two compendious works, the *Hsin Fa Süan Shu*, a collection of a hundred books compiled under the Ming dynasty by Longobardi, Terrenz, Schall, Rho, and others, with the aid of Chinese converts, and the *T'ien Hsiao Ch'u Han Ch'i Pien*, a collection in thirty volumes of ten treatises of the early Jesuit missionaries. The former adheres to the Ptolemaic system, as does also the *Leih Hsiang K'ao Ching*, which appeared in 1713. It must not be forgotten that the works of Copernicus remained on the Index until the beginning of the nineteenth century.

[26] The first Chinese work to use logarithms was the *T'ien Pu Chen Yüan*, a treatise on the calculation of eclipses by the Jesuit pupil Hsueh Feng-tso. This writer was also the author of *T'ien Hsueh Hui T'ung*, an attempt to reconcile Chinese and European conceptions of astronomy. Both works appeared about 1650. Among other books in allied fields may be mentioned a

treatise by Terrenz on mechanics, with fifty plates describing the use of foreign machines; a work on field glasses by Schall, entitled *Yuan Ching Shuo,* and one on hydraulic machinery, *T'ai Hsi Shui Fa,* by De Ursis.

[27] An exception to this rule is to be found in Vagnoni's life of the Virgin Mary, *Sheng Mu Hsing Shih,* a work filled with the mystical and miraculous. Latourette cites a treatise on God by Father Prémare, which was later used and admired by Protestant missionaries. This was probably the *De Deo et divinis attributis* inserted in the *Notitia linguae sinicae.* Pfister (*Notices biographiques,* p. 523) claims this was written not by Prémare but by one of his fellow priests. Among the works later translated by the Jesuits were Thomas à Kempis' *Imitation of Christ,* the *Summa Theologiae* of St. Thomas Aquinas and Loyola's *Exercises* (Latourette, *Christian Missions in China,* p. 189).

[28] *Chi Ko Ta Ch'uan.*

[29] *Er Shih Wu Yen.*

[30] *Hsi Kuo Chi Fa.*

[31] *Chiao Yu Lun.*

[32] *Chi Jên Shih Pien.*

[33] Wylie asserts that most of Aleni's works were still in circulation at the end of the last century.

[34] J. C. Ferguson, *Chinese Painting,* pp. 179–184.

NOTES TO CHAPTER XVIII

JESUIT SOURCES OF THE RÊVE CHINOIS OF THE AGE OF ENLIGHTENMENT

[1] Voltaire, *Relation du banissement des Jésuites de la Chine* (1768).

[2] Montesquieu, *Lettres Persanes.*

[3] Cited by Lovejoy in *Chinese Origin of a Romanticism.*

[4] Richard Walter, *A Voyage Around the World ... by George Anson.*

[5] In Germany, as well as in France, the influence of Jesuit literature on China can be readily traced in the belles-lettres of the time. The Rococo movement in Germany, slightly different in its manifestations from the French movement, was greatly influenced by Chinese modes. Many of the great minds of Germany were Sinophile.

[6] Carcassonne, "La Chine dans l'*Esprit des lois,*" *Revue de l'histoire littéraire de la France* (April-June, 1924).

[7] Voltaire, *Essai sur l'Histoire générale et sur les Mœurs et l'Esprit des Nations ...* (1756).

[8] Voltaire, *Le Siècle de Louis XIV* (1751).

[9] A. H. Rowbotham, "Voltaire, Sinophile," *PMLA,* XLVII (1932), 4.

[10] De Silhouette, *Idée générale du gouvernement et de la morale des Chinois.*

[11] Pierre Poivre, *Voyage d'un Philosophe.*

[12] François Quesnay, "Le Despotisme de la Chine," published in the *Ephémérides du Citoyen.* The theories put forward by Dr. François Quesnay were elaborated by his disciple, Mercier de la Rivière, in a brochure entitled *La*

Vie naturelle et essentielle des sociétés politiques, appearing in the same year (1676). Both works were attacked by the liberal philosopher Mably. Voltaire satirized the Physiocrats and their theories in his tale, *L'Homme aux quarante écus.* See Pinot, "Les Physiocrates et la Chine au XVIII⁶ siècle," *Revue d'histoire moderne et contemporaine,* VIII (1907); also L. A. Maverick, "Chinese Influence on the Physiocrats," *Economic History,* February, 1938.

[13] Turgot, *Réflexions sur la Formation et la Distribution des Richesses* (Paris, 1766).

Ko (Kao Lei-se) and Yang (Yang Teh-wang) returned to Peking in 1766 with an annual pension of twelve hundred livres from the king of France. Ko was for a time a priest of the Hukuang mission. He died in 1780, probably in Peking. Yang worked in Kiangsi. In 1777 he became procureur of the French mission at Canton. Arrested in Kiangsi during a period of persecution in 1787, he probably died as he was being taken to Peking (Pfister, *Notices biographiques,* pp. 922–923). See Cordier, *La Chine en France au XVIII⁶ siècle.*

[14] Grimm *et al., Correspondance littéraire* (1785).

[15] Cordier, "Les Correspondants de Bertin," *T'oung Pao,* XVIII, 309.

[16] Condorcet, *Esquisse d'un tableau historique des progrès de l'esprit humain* (1793).

NOTES TO CHAPTER XIX

The Achievements of the Jesuit Mission in China

[1] Since this work was written, the author has had the opportunity of examining the recent book of Professor Teggart, entitled "Rome and China," which suggests a new technique for solving the historical problems involved in relations between East and West. Basing his theories on a survey of the period from B.C. 58 to A.D. 187, Professor Teggart shows that "wars in Europe were preceded invariably by the outbreak of war either on the eastern frontier of the Roman empire or in the 'Western regions' of the Chinese" and he finds that the barbarian outbreaks were consequent upon wars in the T'ien Shan or the Roman East. He concludes that "the comparison of histories is necessary for a comprehension of what actually happened within the borders of any national state." The work is, in effect, a plea for the extension of the spirit of cosmopolitanism to the study of history.

[2] The famous modern Chinese scholar Liang Ch'i-ch'ao claims that the Jesuit missionaries provided the Chinese with a new and better logical method, but other Chinese scholars, Dr. Hu Shih for example, dispute this (Latourette, *Christian Missions in China,* p. 196, note). In general, modern Chinese scholars agree that the Jesuit contribution to the culture of the empire was negligible.

BIBLIOGRAPHY

BIBLIOGRAPHY

ALEXANDRE, NOËL. *Apologie des Dominicains Missionaires de la Chine ou Réponse au Livre du Père Le Tellier, Jésuite, intitulé* Défense des nouveaux chrétiens; *et à* L'Eclaircissement *du P. Le Gobien de la même Compagnie sur les honneurs que les Chinois rendent à Confucius et aux Morts par un Religieux ... de l'Ordre de S. Dominique.* Cologne, 1699.

An important anti-Jesuit contribution to the Rites controversy. The second edition (Cologne, 1700) contains the Latin version of the most important documents of the controversy before 1700.

———. *Conformité des cérémonies chinoises avec l'idolâtrie grecque et romaine ... par un religieux, docteur et professeur en théologie.* Cologne.

An interesting example of the use of parallelism in eighteenth-century philosophical thought. Anti-Jesuit.

ALLAN, C. WILFRED. *The Jesuits at the Court of Peking.* Shanghai, 1936.

A short, popular review of the subject.

Anecdotes sur l'état de la religion dans la Chine, ou Relation de M. le Cardinal de Tournon, écrite par lui-même. Paris, 1733–1742.

A virulent attack on the Jesuit policies in China and on the treatment of the De Tournon legation in particular. Anti-Jesuit.

ANSON, GEORGE. See WALTER, RICHARD.

ANVILLE, D', ———. *Nouvel Atlas de la Chine, de la Tartarie chinoise et du Thibet.* Paris, 1737.

Contains the maps drawn by the Jesuit cartographers.

Apologie des Dominicains. ... See ALEXANDRE, NOËL.

ARGENS, D', BOYER. *Lettres chinoises.* 5 vols. La Haye, 1739–1740.

An important example, by a French philosopher, of the use of Chinese philosophy as a vehicle for the expression of skeptical thought.

ARNAULD, ANTOINE. *Lettre d'un théologien contre la* Défense des nouveaux chrétiens.

———. *La Morale pratique des Jésuites.* 7 vols. Cologne, 1669–1694.

A violent condemnation of Jesuit policies and methods by the famous Jansenist leader. Volume VI is a reply to Le Tellier's *Défense.* It contains a list of the documents of the Rites Controversy up to 1692.

ASSEMANI, ———. *Bibliotheca orientalis* (1717).

ATKINSON, GEOFFROY. *The Extraordinary Voyage in French Literature before 1700.* New York, 1920.

———. *The Extraordinary Voyage in French Literature from 1700 to 1720.* New York, 1922.

ATKINSON, GEOFFROY (*Continued*)
————. *Les Relations de voyage au XVIIIe siècle et l'évolution des idées*. Paris, *s.d.*

These three works deal with the relation between the literature of imaginary voyages and the growth of cosmopolitanism in eighteenth-century France. The last volume has a number of illuminating pages on the influence of Chinese thought.

AURICH, URSULA. *China im Spiegel der deutschen Literatur des 18. Jahrhunderts*. Germanische Studien, No. 169.

A brief review of Sinophilism in eighteenth-century German literature.

AVITY, D', ————. *Les Estats, Empires et Principautez du monde*. Omer, 1614.

AVRIL, PÈRE. *Voyages aux divers états d'Europe et d'Asie entrepris pour découvrir un nouveau chemin à la Chine*. Paris, 1692.

AYSCOUGH, FLORENCE. *A Chinese Mirror*. New York, 1925.

Contains an illuminating description of Chinese gardens and an interpretation of the psychology which underlies Chinese garden architecture.

BACKER, AUGUSTIN and ALOYS DE, and SOMMERVOGEL, CARLOS. *Bibliothèque des écrivains de la Compagnie de Jésus*. II vols. Bruxelles, 1890–1932.

The standard bibliography of the writings of members of the Society.

BÄCKER, LOUIS DE. *L'Extrême-Orient au Moyen Age*. Paris, 1877.

BACKHOUSE, E. *See* BLAND, J. O. P.

BADDELEY, J. F. "Father Matteo Ricci's Chinese World Maps," *Geogr. Jour.* (London), L:255 *et seq.*

————. *Russia, Mongolia, China ... A Record of the Relations between them from the Beginning of the Seventeenth Century to the Death of Tsar Alexei Mikhailovich*. 2 vols. London, 1921.

A history of Sino-Russian relations in the seventeenth and eighteenth centuries described chiefly through the personal accounts of the Russian envoys

BARTOLI, DANIELLO. *Dell' Istoria della Compagnia di Gesù. La Cina, terza parte dell'Asia*. Rome, 1663.

BARUZI, JEAN. *Leibnitz et l'organisation religieuse de la terre*. Paris, 1907.

A scholarly account of Leibnitz' dream of a universal religion. Part I, chap. iii deals with Leibnitz' relations with the Jesuits.

BAUDIER, MICHEL. *Histoire de la Cour du roy de la Chine*. Paris, 1624.

An early popular account of Chinese government.

BEAZLEY, C. RAYMOND. *The Dawn of Modern Geography*. London, 1906.

————. *John and Sebastian Cabot*. New York, 1898.

————. *Prince Henry the Navigator*. New York, 1904.

————. *The Texts and Versions of John de Plano Carpini and William de Rubruquis*. London, 1903.

The Latin texts with English translations and a valuable introduction.

BELEVITCH-STANKEVITCH, H. *Le Goût chinois en France au temps de Louis XIV.* Paris, 1910.

The best work dealing with Chinese influence on arts and decorations in France during the *siècle d'or.* Good illustrations.

BELL, JOHN. *Travels from Saint Petersburg in Russia to Divers Parts of Asia.* Glasgow, 1763.

Contains a translation of the *Journal* of Lawrence Lange. Bell's work was reprinted in Pinkerton's *Voyages.*

BENEDETTO, LUIGI F. *Marco Polo, "Il Milione," prima edizione integrale.* Florence, 1928.

A recent critical edition of the text of the original French version, with notes and index. Long introduction discussing the manuscripts of the classic. Illustrated with reproductions from the manuscript.

BERNARD, HENRI, S.J. *L'Apport scientifique du Père Ricci à la Chine.* Peiping, 1935; English translation by E. C. Werner, Peiping, 1935.

————. "L'Art chrétien en Chine au temps du P. Mathieu Ricci," *Revue d'histoire des missions,* XII (1935):199–229.

The author shows that Ricci did not try to orientalize Western religious art in using it for propaganda purposes.

————. *Aux Portes de la Chine. Les Missionaires du XVIᵉ siècle, 1514–1588.* Tientsin, 1933.

A well-documented account of the history of the China mission before Ricci arrived in Peking.

————. *Les Etapes de la cartographie scientifique pour la Chine et les pays voisins depuis le XVIᵉ jusqu'à la fin du XVIIIᵉ siècle.* Monumenta Serica; Peking, 1938.

————. "Etudes sur l'humanisme chrétien en Chine à la fin des Ming," *Nankai Social and Economic Quarterly,* IX (1936):1–3.

————. "Galilée et les Jésuites de la mission d'Orient," *Revue des questions scientifiques* (1937).

A review of the Jesuit missionaries' work as astronomers.

————. *Le Père Matthieu Ricci et la société chinoise de son temps (1552–1610).* 2 vols. Tientsin, 1937.

A scholarly interpretation of the work of the Jesuit pioneer. The most illuminating book on Ricci and his Chinese environment.

————. "Whence the Philosophical Movement at the Close of the Ming Dynasty," *Bulletin of the Catholic University of Peking* (1931), No. 8.

BETTILINELLI, GIUSEPPI. *Memorie storiche dell' Eminentiss. Mgr. Cardinale di Tournon esposte con monumenti vari e autentici.* 8 vols. Venice, 1761–1762.

The most complete *apologia* of the De Tournon legation.

BLAND, J. O. P., and BACKHOUSE, E. *Annals and Memoirs of the Court of Peking.* 2d ed.; London, 1913.

> With material taken (without citations) chiefly from Chinese documents, this work is a valuable and highly readable account of the last of the Mings and of the Ch'ing dynasty. The absence of citations detracts from the scholarly value of the book.

BOEHMER, H. *Die Jesuiten.* Leipzig, 1921; French translation by Monod, Paris, 1930.

BOSMANS, H. "Ferdinand Verbiest, Directeur de l'Observatoire de Pékin (1623–1688)," *Revue des questions scientifiques,* 3ᵉ série, Vol. XXI, pp. 195–273, 325–464.

> The best source available for information concerning this Jesuit priest.

BOUVET, JOACHIM, S.J. *L'Estat présent de la Chine en Figures.* Paris, 1697.

―――. *Portrait historique de l'Empereur de la Chine.* Paris, 1697.

> A valuable contemporary description of K'ang Hsi written by one of the court Jesuits.

BOYM, MICHEL. *Briefve Relation ... de la Chine.* Paris, 1654.

> An account of Christianity in the family of the last Ming Pretender.

―――. *Flora sinensis, ou Traité des fleurs, des fruits, des plantes et des animaux particuliers de la Chine.* Vienna, 1656.

> The first European work on Chinese botany, this book contains twenty-three sketches of flora and fauna, with Chinese names. It was included, with the *Briefve Relation,* in Thevenot's *Voyages* (1663–1672).

―――. *Clavis medica ad Chinarum doctrinam de pulsibus.*

> Published by Andreas Cleyer in 1682 with the title, *Specimen medicinae sinicae.*

BRAAM, ANDRÉ EVERARD VAN. *An Authentic Account of the Embassy of the Dutch East Indies to the Court of the Emperor of China in the years 1794 and 1795 taken from the journals of van Braam,* translated by L. E. Mercan de Saint Méry. London, 1798.

BRAND, ADAM. *Relation du Voyage de M Evart Isbrand [Ides], Envoyé de Sa Majesté Czarienne à l'Empereur de la Chine en 1693, 1694, par le sieur Adam Brand.* Amsterdam, 1699.

> A valuable account of the fourth Russian embassy to Peking.

BRÉHIER, L. *L'Eglise et l'Orient au Moyen Âge.* Paris, 1921.

BRETSCHNEIDER, E. *History of European Botanical Discoveries in China.* London, 1898.

―――. *Mediaeval Researches from Eastern Asiatic Sources.* London, 1910.

BROU, A., S.J. "Le Père Matthieu Ricci, fondateur des missions de la Chine," *Etudes,* Paris, 1910.

―――. *Saint François Xavier.* Paris, 1922.

> A standard work on the great Jesuit missionary

BRUCKER, JOSEPH, S.J. "La Chine et l'Extrême-Orient d'après les travaux historiques du Père A. Gaubil," *Revue des questions historiques* (1885).

———. "La Mission de Chine de 1722 à 1735," *Revue des questions historiques*, Vol. XXIX.
> Detailed and well-documented account of the Jesuit mission during the reign of Yung Cheng.

BUDGE, SIR E. WALLIS. *The Monks of Kublai Khan, Emperor of China.* London, 1928.
> A recent translation of the history of Mar Yaballaha III, containing Prayer and Preface omitted by Montgomery, with introduction and good illustrations. Bibliography.

Bulletin of the Catholic University of Peking. Peking, 1926–1930.
> Contains some excellent articles dealing with different phases of the history of Christianity in China. No longer published. It has been supplanted by the Monumenta Serica.

BUSHELL, S. W. *Chinese Art.* London, 1910.

CAHEN, GASTON. *Histoire des relations de la Russie avec la Chine sous Pierre le Grand (1689–1730).* Paris, 1912.
> An account of Sino-Russian relations of this period with excerpts taken from Russian and other documents.

CAMPBELL, T. J. *The Jesuits, 1534–1721.* London, 1921.
> A somewhat uncritical treatment of the subject.

CARCASSONNE, E. "La Chine dans l'*Esprit des lois*," *Revue d'histoire littéraire de la France,* April–June, 1924.

CARUS, PAUL. *The Nestorian Monument.* Chicago, 1909.
> Contains A. Wylie's translation of the tablet.

Catalogus Patrum ac Fratrum e Societate Jesu qui a Morte S. Fr. Xaverii ad annum MDCCCLXXII Evangelio Christi Propagando in Sinis adlaboraverunt. Shanghai, 1873.

Catholic Encyclopedia. New York, 1907–1914. "Ricci," "China," etc.

CHABOT, J. B. *Histoire du Patriarche Mar Jabalaha III et du moine Rabban Çauma.* Paris, 1895.

CHABRIÉ, ROBERT, S.J. *Michel Boym, Jésuite polonais et la fin des Ming (1646–1662).* Paris, 1933.
> Deals chiefly with the Ming Pretender and his Jesuit advisers. A well-documented work. Bibliography.

CHAMBERS, SIR WILLIAM. *A Dissertation on Oriental Gardening.* London, 1772.
> The first important European work on Chinese gardens, written by the architect of Kew Gardens, who had himself visited China.

CHANG TIEN-TSÊ. *Sino-Portuguese Trade from 1514 to 1644.* Leyden, 1934.

CH'EN, KENNETH. "Matteo Ricci's Contribution to, and Influence on, Geographical Knowledge in China," *Journal of the American Oriental Society* (1939), pp. 325–359.
   A detailed discussion of the text accompanying the map and of its influence on subsequent Chinese scholarship in this field.

CHEN KUO-CHEN. *Les Religieux missionaires en Chine aux XVIIe et XVIIIe siècles, leur rôle comme intermédiaires entre les deux civilisations orientale et occidentale.* Paris, 1936.
   A doctoral thesis, which the author has not had the opportunity to examine.

CHEN SHOU-YI. "Sino-European Cultural Contacts since the Discovery of the Sea Route," *Nankai Social and Economic Quarterly,* April, 1935.

Chinese Recorder and Missionary Journal, The. Shanghai, 1868——.
   A Protestant missionary journal containing (particularly in the earlier numbers) some articles of value.

Chinese Repository, The. Canton, 1832–1851.
   Published by the first generation of Protestant missionaries, it sets a high standard for missionary Sinological studies. Even today some of its articles can be read with much profit.

CLOUGHERTY, DOM FRANCIS. "The Franciscan Contemporaries of Marco Polo," *Bulletin of the Catholic University of Peking,* No. 5 (1928), pp. 37–60.

COEDÈS, G. *Textes des auteurs grecs et latins relatifs à l'Extrême-Orient.* Paris, 1910
   A collection of the references to the Orient by classical writers, with critical comments

COLOMBEL, AUGUSTE M. *Histoire de la mission de Kiangnan.* 5 vols. Shanghai, 1895–1905.
   A planograph copy published in limited edition. Though often unreliable, the work contains much interesting information, taken chiefly from the documents in the Siccawei library.

CONDORCET, ANTOINE N. DE. *Esquisse d'un tableau historique des progrès de l'esprit humain.* Paris, 1793.
   The epitome of the French eighteenth-century vision of human perfectibility.

CORDIER, HENRI. "L'Arrivèe des Portuguais en Chine," *T'oung Pao,* série 2, vol. xii.

———. *Bibliotheca Sinica, dictionnaire bibliographique des ouvrages relatifs à l'empire chinois.* Paris, 1904–1908; Supplément, 1924.
   The standard bibliographical work on China. Part I, sec. ix deals with Christianity in China. For bibliography of Term and Rites controversies see cols. 869–926, 1279–1294, 3125–3126, 3132–3133, 3580–3600, 3768–3769. Part II deals with foreigners in China and Part III with foreign relations of the Chinese.

———. *La Chine en France au XVIII° siècle.* Paris, 1910.

———. "Le Christianisme en Chine et en Asie Centrale sous les Mongols," *T'oung Pao,* série 2, vol. xviii.

———. "Les Correspondants de Bertin," *T'oung Pao,* série 2, vol. xviii.
Valuable article dealing with Sino-French cultural relations in the eighteenth century.

———. "Documents pour servir à l'histoire ecclesiastique de l'Extrême-Orient," *Revue de l'Extrême-Orient,* vol. iii.

———. *Essai d'une bibliographie des ouvrages publiés en Chine par les Européens au XVII° et au XVIII° siècles.* Paris, 1883.

———. *La France en Chine au XVIII° siècle.* Paris, 1883.

———. *Histoire générale de la Chine et de ses relations avec les pays étrangers.* 4 vols. Paris, 1920.
A concise, highly factual summary of the subject. Vol. III deals with the Jesuit period. An excellent reference work.

———. *Mélanges d'histoire et de géographie orientales.* Paris, 1914–1923.

———. *Ser Marco Polo. See* YULE.

———. *La Suppression de la Compagnie de Jésus et les derniers jours de la mission de Péking.* Leyden, 1918.
Covers the same material as the work of Rochemonteix.

———. *Les Voyages en Asie au XIV° siècle du bienheureux frère Odoric de Pordenone.* Paris, 1891.
The outstanding critical edition of Odoric's travels, with valuable introduction and notes.

COULING, S. *Encyclopedia Sinica.* London, 1917.
A one-volume encyclopedic work containing many short articles on Protestant and Catholic missions and missionaries. Despite age and numerous errors it is still a highly useful volume.

COUPLET, PHILIPPE, ed. *Catalogus Patrum Societatis Jésus ... ab anno 1581 ad 1681.* Paris, 1686.

———. *Confucius Sinarum Philosophus sive scientia sinensis latine exposita, studio et opera Prosperi Intorcetta.* Paris, 1687.

CRÉTINEAU-JOLY, J., S.J. *Histoire religieuse, politique et littéraire de la Compagnie de Jésus.* 6 vols. Paris, 1844–1846.
Though outdated, this work is still probably the best on the subject written from the Jesuit point of view. For China material see Vol. III, chap. iii and Vol. V, chap. i.

CROS, P. L., S.J. *Saint François de Xavier, sa vie et ses lettres.* 3 vols. Paris, 1900.

CRUZ, GASPARD DA. *Tractado em que contam muito por estenso as Cousas da China.* Evora, 1569.
The first missionary book on China.

CURTIN, JEREMIAH. *The Mongols.* Boston, 1908
  A highly readable work, though not so well documented as Howorth.

DAHLMANN, JOSEPH. *Die Thomas Legende.* Fribourg, 1912.

Défense des nouveaux chrétiens ... See LE TELLIER.

DE GROOT, J. J. M. *Sectarianism and Religious Persecution in China. A Page in the History of Religion.* 2 vols. Amsterdam, 1903–1904.
  A work associating the development of religious sects in China with periods of political revolt.

DEHAISNES, CHRÉTIEN. *Vie du P. Nicolas Trigault de la Compagnie de Jésus.* Douai, 1864.

DELLON, GABRIEL. *Voyage de M. Dellon avec sa Relation de l'Inquisition de Goa.* 3 vols. Cologne, 1709–1711.

DOUGLAS, R. K. *The Life of Genghis-Khan.* London, 1877.

DUDGEON, H. "Russian Ecclesiastical Mission," *Chinese Recorder,* Vol. III, pp. 143–146, 273–280, 319–322, 337–345 and Vol. IV, pp. 12–17, 35–40, 68–74, 96–99, 186–192, 206–214, 227–231.
  From the fifth article on the title reads: "Sketch of Russian Intercourse with, and the Greek Church in, China."

DU HALDE, J. B., S.J. *Description géographique, historique, chronologique et physique de l'empire de la Chine et de la Tartarie chinoise.* 4 vols. Paris, 1735.

DU JARRIC, PÈRE. *Histoire des choses plus mémorables advenues ez Indes.* 3 vols. Bordeaux, 1608–1614.

———. *Thesauris Rerum Indicarum.* Paris, 1615.

DUMÉRIL, A. "Influence des Jésuites considérés comme missionaires sur le mouvement des idées au XVIIIᵉ siècle," *Mémoires de l'Académie de Dijon* (1874), pp. 1–33.

DUNYN-SZPOT, THOMAS I., S.J. "Collectanea historiae sinensis ab anno 1641 ad an. 1700 ex variis documentis in Archivio Societatis." 2 vols.
  An unpublished document not consulted by the author.

———. "Sinarum historia." 2 vols.
  A condensed version of the "Collectanea," also unpublished.

ENGEMANN, WALTER. *Voltaire und China, ein Beitrag zur Geschichte der Völkerkunde und zur Geschichte der Geschichtsschreibung sowie zu ihren gegenzeitigen Beziehungen.* Leipzig, 1932.
  Doctoral dissertation. Not as formidable as the title indicates. A work on the relation of Voltaire's Sinomania to his philosophy of history.

Ephémérides du Citoyen. Paris, 1767.
  The most important general publication of the Physiocrat school.

ERDBERG, E. VON. *Chinese Influence on European Garden Structures*. Harvard University Press: Cambridge, 1938.
Profusely illustrated scholarly treatment of the subject.

FARIA Y SOUSA, MANUEL DE. *Imperio de la China*. Madrid, 1642.

FARJENEL, FERNAND. "Voltaire et les Chinois," *Revue Hebdomadaire*, August 6, 1910.

FAVIER, MGR. *Péking, histoire et description*. Lille, 1900.

FERGUSON, DONALD. "Letters of Portuguese Captives in Canton Written in 1534 and 1536," *Indian Antiquary*, XXX:421–451, 467–491; XXXI:10–32, 53–65.
Highly valuable documents concerning the early Sino-Portuguese relations.

FERGUSON, JOHN C. *Chinese Painting*. Chicago, 1927.

FEUILLET DE CONCHES, M. F. "Les Peintres européens et les peintres chinois," *Revue Contemporaine* (1856), Vol. XXV.

FORMEY, J. H. *La Belle Wolfienne*. La Haye, 1741.

FOUCQUET, JEAN-FRANÇOIS, S.J. *Dissertation pour prouver la conformité de la chronologie des Chinois avec celle des Chrétiens*. Paris, 1728.
An important contribution by the most radical of the Figurist group of Jesuit missionaries.

FOUQUERAY, H., S.J. *Histoire de la Compagnie de Jésus en France*.
The standard work on the subject.

FRÉRET, NICOLAS. "De l'Antiquité et de la Certitude de la Chronologie chinoise," *Mémoires de l'Académie des Inscriptions et Belles-lettres* (1736), Vol. X.
A contribution to the chronology controversy by one of the most brilliant French scholars of the eighteenth century.

FÜLOP-MILLER, RENÉ. *The Power and Secret of the Jesuits*. New York, 1930.
A popular but thorough review of Jesuit history. Impartial and interesting. Good bibliography.

GAILLARD, LOUIS, S.J. *Croix et swastika en Chine*. Variétés sinologiques, No. 3. 2d ed.; Shanghai, 1904.

GAUBIL, ANTOINE, S.J. *Histoire abrégée de l'astronomie chinoise*.
Published in Souciet's *Observations*.

———. *Histoire de Gentchiscan et de toute la dynastie des Mongous ses successeurs, conquérants de la Chine*. Paris, 1739.

———. *Histoire de la grande Dynastie des Thang*. In the *Mémoires concernant les Chinois*, Vols. XVI and XVII.

———. *Traité de la chronologie chinoise*. Paris, 1814.

GAZIER, GEORGES. *Un Artiste comtois à la cour de Chine au XVIIIe siècle: le Frère Attiret (1702–1768).* Besançon, 1912.

————. *Histoire générale du mouvement janséniste depuis ses origines jusqu'à nos jours.* Paris, 1922.

GHERARDINI, GIOVANNI. *Relation du Voyage à la Chine sur le vaisseau «l'Amphitrite» en l'année 1698.* Paris, 1700.

GILES, HERBERT. *Gems of Chinese Literature.* (2d ed.; Shanghai, 1923).

GONZALES DE MENDOÇA. *See* MENDOÇA.

GONZALES DE SAINT-PIERRE. *See* SAINT-PIERRE.

GOTO, SOUÉO. "Les premiers Echanges de civilisation entre l'Extrême-Orient et l'Occident dans les temps moderns," *Revue de littérature comparée,* September, 1925.

GOWEN, H. H., and HALL, J. W. *An Outline History of China.* New York, 1927.

GRANET, M. *La Religion des Chinois.* Paris, 1922.
    An important interpretation of Chinese religion by one of the greatest of the French Orientalists.

GRESLON, ADRIEN. *Histoire de la Chine sous la domination des Tartares.* Paris, 1671.

GRIMM, MALCHIOR, DIDEROT, *et al. Correspondance littéraire, philosophique et critique ... depuis 1753 à 1790.* Paris, 1829.

GROUSSET, R. *Histoire de l'Asie.* Paris, 1922.

GUÉRIN, J. *La Chinoiserie en Europe au XVIIIe siècle.* Paris, 1911.

GUETTÉE, ABBÉ RENÉ. *Histoire des Jésuites composée sur des documents authentiques en partie inédits.* Paris, 1858.
    An unsympathetic account of the history of the Society, partial and often unreliable.

GUYON, ABBÉ. *Histoire des Indes Orientales ancienne et moderne.* Paris, 1744.

GUZMAN, LUIS DE. *Historia de las missiones que han hecho los religiosos de la Compania de Jesus ... en la India Orientale y en los reynos de la China y Japon.* Alcalà, 1601.
    An important early work.

HARRIS, WILLIAM. *De Peste cui accessit descriptio inoculationis variolarum.* London, 1721.
    Containing an account of the Chinese method of inoculating for smallpox.

HAVRET, H., S.J. *La Stèle chrétienne de Si-ngan-fou.* Variétés sinologiques, Nos. 7, 12, 20. Shanghai, 1895–1902.
    Contains a translation of the Nestorian monument together with many valuable notes concerning Jesuit missions and missionaries.

HEE, P. L. VAN. *Ferdinand Verbiest, écrivain chinois.* Bruges, 1913.

HELLER, J. E. *Das Nestorianische Denkmal in Singanfu* (1897).

HERBELOT, J. *Bibliothèque Orientale.* La Haye, 1778–1779.

HERING, H. W. "A Study of Roman Catholic Missions in China, 1692–1744," *New China Review* (1921), Vol. III.
> A brief, popular review of the golden days of the mission.

HIBBERT, ELOISE T. *K'ang Hsi, Emperor of China.* London, 1940.
> The American edition bears the title, *Jesuit Adventures in China During the Reign of K'ang Hsi* (New York, 1941).

HIRTH, F. *China and the Roman Orient.* Shanghai, 1885.

Histoire de ce qui s'est passé au royaume de la Chine en l'année 1624. Tirée des lettres écrites et adressées au R. P. Matio Vitelleschi, Général de la Cie. de Jésus. Trad. de l'Italien. Paris, 1629.

Historia cultus sinensium seu varia scripta. Cologne, 1700.

HOWORTH, SIR HENRY. *History of the Mongols.* 3 vols. London, 1876–1888; supplement, 1927.
> The most scholarly and critical work on the subject in English.

HUC, ABBÉ E. *Le Christianisme en Chine, en Tartarie et au Thibet.* 4 vols. Paris, 1857.
> The best general history of the subject from the Catholic viewpoint. Composed by a non-Jesuit Catholic, it is on the whole objective and impartial. It is written in a popular rather than critical manner, and its weakness is its lack of notes and bibliography.

HUDSON, G. F. *Europe and China, a Survey of Their Relations from Earliest Times to 1800.* London, 1931.
> A scholarly and valuable general account of Sino-European relations.

HUONDER, ANTON. *Deutsche Jesuiten-Missionäre des 17. und 18. Jahrhunderts.* Freiburg, 1899.

INTORCETTA, PROSPER, S.J. *See* COUPLET.

JENKINS, R. C. *The Jesuits in China.* London, 1894.
> Deals exclusively with the De Tournon mission.

Jésuites convaincus d'obstination à permettre l'Idolâtrie dans la Chine, Les (1744).
> A typical anti-Jesuit contribution to the Rites controversy. Its authorship is attributed to Abbé Villiers.

JOURDAIN, C. *Histoire de l'Université de Paris au XVII⁰ et au XVIII⁰ siècles.* Paris, 1888.
> Contains a short account of the Lecomte affair.

Journal historique des Assemblées tenues en Sorbonne pour condamner les Mémoires de la Chine. Paris, 1700.

The best "official" account of the Lecomte controversy, containing the decisions of the Faculty of Paris.

KIRCHER, ATHANASIUS, S.J. *Prodromus Coptus sive Ægypticus.* Rome, 1636.

―――. *China monumentis qua sacris qua profanis, illustrata.* Amsterdam, 1672.

Contains one of the first translations of the Nestorian monument. Particularly interesting for its illustrations.

KLAPROTH, J. H. *Mémoires relatifs à l'Asie.* Paris, 1824.

LA CROIX, PÉTIS DE. *Histoire du Grand Genghizcan, Premier Empereur des anciens Mogols, trad. de plusieurs auteurs orientaux et des voyageurs européens.* Paris, 1710.

A widely read work, though written from secondary sources.

LAMB, HAROLD. *Genghis Kahn, the Emperor of All Men.* New York, 1927.

―――. *The March of the Barbarians.* New York, 1940.

An excellent, popular general history of the Mongols. Good bibliography.

LANSON, GUSTAVE. "Formation et développement de l'esprit philosophique au XVIII⁰ siècle. Influence de l'Orient et de l'Extrême-Orient." *Revue des Cours et Conférences,* Paris, March, 1909.

A masterly synthesis of the subject by a great French critic.

LA PEYRÈRE. *Prae Adamitae sive exercitatis . . . systema theologicum ex Prae Adamitarum hypothese* (1651).

An interesting contribution to the seventeenth-century controversy over chronology.

LA SERVIÈRE, J. DE, S.J. *Les anciennes missions de la Cie. de Jésus en Chine (1552–1814).* Shanghai, 1923.

LATOURETTE, KENNETH S. *A History of Christian Missions in China.* New York, 1929.

The standard work on the subject. Well documented with important bibliography. Chapters vi–x deal with the Jesuit period. Subsequent chapters deal with nineteenth-century missions in China.

LECOMTE, LOUIS, S.J. *Nouveaux Mémoires sur l'état présent de la Chine.* Paris, 1696. 2 vols.

―――. *Eclaircissements sur la dénonciation faite à N.S.P. le Pape des* Nouveaux Mémoires de la Chine *composez par le P. Louis Lecomte de la Cie. de Jésus.* Paris, 1700.

LE FAVRE, ―――, S.J. *De Sinensium ritibus politicis acta.* Paris, 1700.

Describes the Jesuit position on the Chinese Rites.

Bibliography

LEFEVRE, B., S.J. "Antoine Thomas de Namur" in the *Biographie Nationale,* Brussels.
   The best biographical account of this important Jesuit missionary.

LE GENTIL. *Nouveau Voyage autour du monde ... avec une description de l'Empire de la Chine.* 3 vols. Amsterdam, 1730–1731.

LE GOBIEN, CHARLES, S.J. *Histoire de l'Edit de l'Empereur de la Chine en faveur de la Religion chrétienne avec un éclaircissement sur les honneurs que les Chinois rendent à Confucius et aux morts.* Paris, 1698.

LEIBNITZ, G. W. VON. *Novissima Sinica. Historia Nostri Temporis Ilustratura. In quibus de Christianismo publica nunc primum auctoritate propagato missa in Europam relatio exhibetur, deque favore scientiarum Europaearum ac moribus gentes et ipsius praesertim Monarchae, tum et de bello Sinensium cum Moscis ac pace constituta multa hactenus ignota explicantur* (1697).

LE TELLIER, MICHEL, S.J. *Défense des nouveaux chrétiens et des missionaires de la Chine, du Japon et des Indes contre* La Morale pratique des Jésuites *et* L'Esprit *de M. Arnauld.* Paris, 1696.
   A widely read and important document of the Rites controversy.

Lettre à Mme de Lionne sur la libelle des Jésuites contre l'évêque de Rosalie, son Fils. Rome, 1701.

Lettre de MM. des Missions Etrangères au Pape sur les Idolâtries et les Superstitions chinoises. Bruxelles, 1700.
   Pamphlet attacking the Jesuit policies.

Lettre de M. l'Abbé de Lionne, évêque de Rosalie ... à M. Charmot, Directeur des Missions Etrangères de Paris. Canton, 1700.

Lettres édifiantes et curieuses écrites des Missions Etrangères. 26 vols. Mérigot ed.; Paris, 1780–1783.
   For various translations and editions see p. 255 of the present work, and notes.

LIN, YIAN-TSOUAN. *Essai sur le père Duhalde et sa description de la Chine.* Fribourg, 1937.
   Dissertation. Unimportant, though it contains some interesting comments.

LJUNGSTEDT, ANDREW. *An Historical Sketch of the Portuguese Settlement in China.* Boston, 1836.
   Though out of date this is still a valuable reference for the history of the Portuguese in China and particularly at Macao.

MADROLLE, C. *Les Premiers Voyages des Français à la Chine de 1698 à 1719.* Paris, 1901.
   An account of the attempt made by the French to establish commercial relations with China in the seventeenth and eighteenth centuries.

MAGAILLANS. *See* MAGALHAENS.

MAGALHAENS, GABRIEL. *Doze Excellencias da China.* Madrid, 1668; French translation, *Nouvelle Relation de la Chine,* Paris, 1670.

A widely read book dealing with the early days of the mission.

MAILLA, JOSEPH DE MOYRIAC DE, S.J. *Histoire générale de la Chine ou Annales de cet Empire trad. du Tong-Kien-Kang-Mou.* 13 vols. Paris, 1777–1785.

The first general history of China in a European language. The first part is a translation of the Chinese text named. The history of the seventeenth and eighteenth centuries was written by De Mailla himself.

MAIRAN, DORTOUS DE. *Lettres au Père Parennin contenant diverses questions sur la Chine.* Paris, 1770.

A noteworthy document illustrating Sino-French cultural relations.

MALEBRANCHE, NICOLAS DE. *Entretiens d'un philosophe chrétien et d'un chinois sur la Nature de Dieu.* Paris, 1708.

MALONE, CARROLL B. *History of the Peking Summer Palaces under the Ch'ing Dynasty.* Illinois Studies in the Social Sciences, Vol. XIX. Urbana, 1934.

The best description of the Yuan Ming Yuan and the palaces of the Western Hills of Peking, taken chiefly from Chinese sources. Chap. vi deals with European influence on architecture during Ch'ien Lung's reign.

MARTINI, MARTIN, S.J. *De Bello Tartarico in Sinis.* Rome, 1654.

Published in French with the title, *Histoire de la guerre des Tartares contre la Chine,* at the end of Semedo's work (Paris, 1654 and 1657; Lyons, 1667).

———. *Novus Atlas Sinensis.* Amsterdam, 1651.

———. *Sinicae historiae decas prima Res a gentis origine ad Christum natum.* Munich, 1658.

MARTINO, PIERRE. *L'Orient dans la littérature française au XVIIᵉ et au XVIIIᵉ siècles.* Paris, 1906.

The best account of the purely literary influences of the China cult during this period.

MASPERO, GEORGES. *La Chine.* Paris, 1906.

MAVERICK, LEWIS A. "Chinese Influences on the Physiocrats," *Economic History,* February, 1938.

———. "Hsü Kuang-ch'i, a Chinese Authority on Agriculture," *Agricultural History* (October, 1940), XIV:143–160.

———. "A Possible Source of Spinoza's Doctrine," *Revue de Littérature comparée,* July–September, 1939, pp. 417–428.

Spinoza's thought may have been influenced by the description of Chinese religion in Bernhard Varen's *Descriptio Regni Japoniae.*

McGOVERN, WILLIAM M. *The Early Empires of Central Asia.* University of North Carolina Press, 1939.

Bibliography

Mémoires concernant l'histoire, les sciences, les arts, les mœurs, les usages, etc. des Chinois. Par les Missionaires de Pékin. 17 vols. Paris, 1777–1814.

Mémoires de la Congrégation de la Mission [Lazaristes] en Chine. 3 vols. Paris, 1911–1912.

MENDOÇA, JUAN GONZALES DE. *Historia de las cosas mas notables, ritos, y costumbres del gran reyno de la China.* Rome, 1585.

The best English edition, edited by Staunton, is in the Hakluyt series. The title of this and of the French and Italian editions, *The History . . . of China,* is misleading.

MENDOZA. *See* MENDOÇA.

MERKEL, FRANZ RUDOLF. *G. W. von Leibniz und die China-Mission, eine Untersuchung über die Anfänge der protestantischen Missionbewegung.* Leipzig, 1920.

A well-documented account of Leibnitz' Sinophilism and of his interest in foreign missions. The work includes some interesting pages on Leibnitz' correspondence with English scholars and with Francke.

MEZZABARBA, GEORGE AMBROSE DE. *Journal de Voyage.* In the *Anecdotes . . . de la religion dans la Chine,* Vol. IV, *q.v.*

MINGANA, A. *The Early Spread of Christianity in Central Asia and the Far East.* London, 1925.

Reprinted from the *Bulletin of the John Rylands Library* (Manchester, 1925), IX: 297–371. The most scholarly account of Nestorianism in the Orient.

MOIDREY, J. DE, S.J. *La Hiérachie catholique en Chine, en Corée et au Thibet (1307–1914).* Variétés sinologiques, No. 38. Shanghai, 1914.

A standard work on the personnel and stations of Catholic missions in the Far East.

MONTALTO DE JÉSUS, C.A. *Historic Macao.* Hongkong, 1902.

A prejudiced and often inaccurate but still valuable work on the development of the Portuguese center in China.

MONTANUS, A. *Atlas Chinensis, Being a Second Part of a Relation of Remarkable Passages in two Embassies for the East Indies Co. . . . to Kouchi Emperor of China . . . with a more exact Geographical Description of the Empire of China . . . collected out of several writings and journals by Arnoldus Montanus. Englished by John Ogilby.* London, 1671.

A general description of China taken from the records of the Dutch embassies of 1661 and 1664 and from Jesuit sources. Interesting illustrations.

MONTESQUIEU, CHARLES DE SECONDAT, BARON DE. *Lettres persanes.* Paris, 1721.

MONTGOMERY, JAMES A. *The History of Yaballaha III, Nestorian Patriarch and of his Vicar Bar Sauma, Mongol Ambassador at the End of the Thirteenth Century.* New York, 1927.

A translation of the Bedjan document with notes supplementing those of Chabot and with an illuminating introduction.

Monumenta Serica. Peking, 1935――――.

> A series of monographs published by the Catholic University of Peking, dealing with various aspects of Sinological studies, particularly with the Catholic missions and missionaries in China.

MORANT, SOULIÉ DE. *L'Epopée des Jésuites français en Chine*. Paris, 1928.

> A short, popular account of the French Jesuit mission.

MORSE, H. B., and MacNAIR, H. F. *Far Eastern International Relations*. Boston–New York, 1931.

MOSHEIM, J. L. *Historia Tartarorum Ecclesiastica*. Helmstedt, 1741; English translation, *Authentic Memoirs of the Christian Church in China*, London, 1750.

MOULE, A. C. *Christians in China before the year 1550*. London, 1930.

> The most recent and the most readable general account of pre-Jesuit Christian missions in eastern Asia with lengthy citations from the documents, valuable illustrations, and chronological index.

――――. "Documents Relating to the Mission of the Minor Friars to China in the Thirteenth and Fourteenth Centuries," *Journal of the Royal Asiatic Society* (1914), pp. 533-599.

――――. "The First Arrival of the Jesuits at the Capital of China," *New China Review*, Vol. IV.

――――. "Notices of Christianity in China Extracted from Marco Polo," *Journal of the Royal Asiatic Society, North Branch* (1937), Vol. XLVI.

MOULE, G. E. "Early Chinese Testimony to Matteo Ricci," *Chinese Recorder* (1889), XX:81–83.

> Translation of passages from a Chinese document of 1688.

MOURRET, ABBÉ FERNAND. *Histoire générale de l'Eglise*. Vol. VI. Paris, 1914–1919.

NAVARRETE, DOMINIQUE. *Tratados historicos, politicos, ethicos y religiosos de la Monarchía de China*. Madrid, 1676.

> For description of work see text, p. 247.

NEWTON, A. P., et al. *The Great Age of Discovery*. London, 1932.

NIEUHOFF, JOHN. *An Embassy from the East India Company of the United Provinces to the grand Tartar Cham emperor of China by ... Peter de Goyer and Jacob de Keyzer ... also an epistle of Father John Adam [Schall?] ... Englished and set forth by John Ogilby*. 2d ed.; London, 1673.

> An account of the Dutch embassy of 1655. See pp. 299–317 for a translation of Schall's letter. Pages 319–431 reproduce a large part of Kircher's *China Illustrata*. The work is reprinted in Pinkerton's and in Churchill's *Voyages*.

NÖEL, FRANÇOIS. *Sinensis imperii libri classici sex ... e sinico idiomate in latinum traducti a Francisco Nöel*. Prague, 1711.

> One of the pioneer translations of the Chinese classics. See text, p. 250.

NORBERT (ABBÉ PLATEL). *Mémoires historiques présentés au souverain pontife Benoit XIV sur les Missions des Indes Orientales.* 4 vols. Luques, 1745.
A violently anti-Jesuit work written by an ex-Capuchin (later Abbé Platel). The work contains Angelita's account of the De Tournon legation.

Nouveaux advis du royaume de la Chine. 1598.

Nouvelles de la Chine reçues à Rome par voye d'Espagne (1740).

OGILBY, JOHN. *See* NIEUHOFF and MONTANUS.

OHSSON, D', BARON. *Historie des Mongols depuis Tchinguiz-Khan jusqu'à Timour Bey ou Tamerlan.* 4 vols. La Haye and Amsterdam, 1834–1835.
Probably more accurate than Howorth. Taken from original sources.

ONCKEN, F. *Œuvres économiques et philosophiques de François Quesnay.* Francfort, 1888.
The best edition of the works of the Physiocrat leader.

OPPÉ, A. P. "Chinese and English Landscape Painting," *English* (London), I:115–124.

ORLEANS, D', PÈRE, S.J. *Histoire des deux conquérants Tartares qui ont subjugué la Chine.* Paris, 1688; English edition (Hakluyt), 1854.

O'TOOLE, G. B. "Random Notes on Early Christianity in China," *Bulletin of the Catholic University of Peking,* No. 3 (1927), pp. 31–39.

———. "John of Montecorvino," *Bulletin of the Catholic University of Peking,* No. 6 (1929), pp. 13–53.

PALAFOX Y MENDOÇA, JUAN DE. *Historia de la Conquista de la China par el Tartaro.* Paris, 1670.

PALLU, FRANÇOIS. *Relation abrégée des missions et des voyages des évêques français envoyés aux royaumes de la Chine, Cochin-Chine, Tonkin et Siam,* 2d ed.; Paris, 1682.

PARENNIN, DOMINIQUE, S.J. *Lettres d'un missionaire à Péking concernant diverses questions sur la Chine.* Paris, 1782.
Parennin's noteworthy correspondence with Dortous de Mairan.

PASTOR, LUDWIG VON. *History of the Popes from the Close of the Middle Ages.* London, 1891–1940.

PAUTHIER, G. *L'Inscription Syro-Chinoise de Si-ngan-fou.* Paris, 1858.

———. *Le Livre de Marco Polo, citoyen de Venise.* Paris, 1865.
Though displaced by more modern studies this edition is still valuable as a reference work.

PAUTHIER, G., et BAZIN. *La Chine ancienne et moderne.* Paris, 1853.

PELLIOT, PAUL. "Chrétiens d'Asie Centrale et d'Extrême-Orient," *T'oung Pao*, 1914.
An illuminating article by the greatest of modern Sinologists.

————. "Les Mongols et la Papauté," *Revue de l'Orient Chrétien*, 1924.

PEZRON, PÈRE. *Défense de l'Antiquité des Tems*. Paris, 1691.
An important document in the controversy over chronology in the seventeenth century.

PFISTER, LOUIS, S.J. *Notices biographiques et bibliographiques sur les Jésuites de l'ancienne Mission de Chine (1552–1773)*. 2 vols. Variétés sinologiques, Nos. 59–60; Shanghai, 1932, 1934.
An invaluable reference work. Contains the lives and the writings of all the Jesuits of the China mission together with much additional material. The biographical material abounds in interesting facts concerning missions and missionaries. Bibliography and index.

PINOT, VIRGILE. *La Chine et la formation de l'esprit philosophique en France (1640–1740)*. Paris, 1932.
The most critical study of the influence of China on French thought up to 1740. The account of Chinese influence on European ideas of chronology is outstanding. Bibliographies. The death of the author prevented the writing of a second volume which would have brought the study up to the end of the century.

————. *Documents inédits, 1685–1740*. Paris, 1932.

————. "Les Physiocrates et la Chine au XVIIIᵉ siècle," *Revue d'histoire moderne et contemporaine*, Vol. VIII (1907).

PINTO, FERNAND MENDEZ. *Adventures and Voyages of Fernand Mendez Pinto, a Portugal, during his Travels in the Kingdoms of Ethiopia, China, etc.* London, 1653 (original Portuguese edition, 1614).
Highly unreliable in many respects, this work is nevertheless an interesting and valuable link between the medieval accounts and the later Jesuit literature.

PLATEL, ABBÉ. *See* NORBERT.

POIVRE, PIERRE. *Voyage d'un Philosophe ou Observations sur les Mœurs et les Arts des peuples de l'Afrique, de l'Asie et de l'Amérique*, Paris, 1768; English edition, 1769.
A small work which influenced the Physiocrats in France.

PRÉVOST, ABBÉ. *Histoire générale des Voyages*. Paris, 1746–1761.
Reproduces several of the Jesuit works on China.

"Projet des Jésuites pour envoyer des missionaires mathématiciens en Chine," MS Bibliothèque Nationale fonds français 17240.

QUATREMÈRE, E. M. *Histoire des Mongols de la Perse ... par Raschid-ud-din traduite, accompagnée de notes*. Paris, 1836.
A critical edition by one of the most fascinating of medieval historians.

Réflexions générales sur la lettre qui parut sous le nom des MM. du séminaire des Missions Etrangères (s.l.n.d.).
A document of the Rites controversy.

REICHWEIN, ADOLPH. *China und Europa.* Berlin, 1923; English edition, *China and Europe: Intellectual and Artistic Contacts in the Eighteenth Century,* translated by J. C. Powell. London–New York, 1925.
An excellent short review of the subject.

Relazione delle cose piu notable scritte en gli anni 1619, 1620, 1621 dalla China al P. Mutio Vitelleschi, Preposito generale delle Compagnia di Giesu. Rome, 1624; French edition, Paris, 1629.

RÉMUSAT, ABEL. *Mélanges Asiatiques.* Paris, 1825.

————. *Nouveaux Mélanges Asiatiques.* Paris, 1829.

Revue de l'Extrême-Orient, publiée sous la direction de M. Henri Cordier. Paris, 1882–1887.

RHODES, ALEXANDRE DE, S.J. *Sommaire de divers voyages et missions apostoliques du R.P.D. de Rhodes à la Chine et aux autres royaumes d'Orient avec son retour de Chine à Rome l'année 1618 jusqu'à l'année 1633.* Paris, 1653.

RICCI, MATTEO. *Opere storiche del P. Matteo Ricci,* edited by Pietro Tacchi-Venturi, S.J. Macerata, 1911.
The standard reference work on Ricci based on documents in the Roman archives of the Society; important as a reference work but not without its weaknesses. A new edition is in course of preparation with Father Paschal d'Elia, S.J., as co-editor.

RIPA, M. *Memoirs of Father Ripa during Thirteen Years' Residence at the Court of Peking.* London, 1844.
A very readable little book with an anti-Jesuit bias. The work consists of excerpts from his *Storia della Fondatione della Congregatione del Collegio di Cinese* (Naples, 1832).

RIVIÈRE, ERNEST. *Corrections et additions à la Bibliographie ... de Bäcker.* Toulouse, 1911. *See* BÄCKER and SOMMERVOGEL.

ROCHEMONTEIX, CAMILLE DE, S.J. *Joseph Amiot et les derniers survivants de la mission française de Pékin, 1750–1795.* Paris, 1915.
A well-documented account of the last days of the Peking mission.

ROCKHILL, W. W. *The Journeys of William of Rubruck ... and of John of Pian de Carpini.* Hakluyt Society, 1900.
One of the best editions of the accounts of these two medieval travelers.

ROHRBACHER, R. F. *Histoire universelle de L'Eglise Catholique.* 12 vols. Paris-Lyons, 1872.

ROSS, JOHN. *The Manchus or the Reigning Dynasty of China, Their Rise and Progress.* London, 1880.

ROUGEMONT, FRANCISCO DE, S.J. *Historia Tartaro-Sinica.* London, 1673.

ROWBOTHAM, ARNOLD H. "Voltaire, Sinophile," *Proceedings of the Modern Language Association of America* (1932), XLVII:4.

SAEKI, P. Y. *The Nestorian Monument in China*. London, 1916.
A translation of the inscription with a valuable introduction.

———. *The Nestorian Documents and Relics in China*. Tokyo, 1937.
The latest and most thorough scholarly examination of records of Nestorianism in
China including the Hsianfu tablet and other relics and manuscripts, with copious
illustrations. For translation of the Hsianfu tablet see chap. ii.

SAINT-PIERRE, FRANÇOIS GONZALES DE. *Relation abrégée de la nouvelle persecution de la Chine jusqu'à la mort du Cardinal de Tournon*. Paris, 1714.
An account of the De Tournon legation hostile to the Jesuits.

SAINT-PRIEST, A. DE. *Histoire de la Chute des Jésuites au XVIII° siècle*. Paris,
1846.

SEE, HENRI. *Les Idées politiques en France au XVIII° siècle*. Paris, 1920.

SEMEDO, ALVAREZ, S.J. *Imperio de la China y Cultura Evangelica en el por los
Religiosos de la Compania de Jésus sacado de las noticias de Padre Alvaro
Semedo*. Madrid, 1641; English edition, *A History of the Great and Re-
nowned Monarchy of China,* London, 1655. For description see text, p. 246,
and notes.

SERVITO, V. *Giornale della Legazione della China che incomincia dalla 23
Settembre 1720, scritto de Padre Viani Servito, Confessori di Monsignor
Patriarca nella tempo delle sua Legazione*.
A sympathetic account of the Mezzabarba legation.

SILHOUETTE, ETIENNE DE. *Idée générale du gouvernement et de la morale des
Chinois, tirée particulièrement des Ouvrages de Confucius par M. D.*———.
Paris, 1920.
Important because of its influence on the Physiocrats.

SÖDERBLOM, NATHAN. *Das Werden des Gottesglaubens. Untersuchungen
über die Aufänge der Religion*. Leipzig, 1916.
The author asserts that the controversy over the Term question inspired the increased usage of the term "Heaven" for "God in Heaven" in Christian countries.

SOMMERVOGEL, CARLOS. *See* BACKER, AUGUSTIN and ALOYS DE, and SOM-
MERVOGEL, CARLOS.

SONNERAT, ———. *Voyage aux Indes Orientales et à la Chine*. Paris, 1782.

———. *Supplément au voyage dans les Indes Orientales*. Paris, 1783.

SOUCIET, ———, S.J. *Observations mathematiques, astronomiques, géographi-
ques ... aux Indes et à la Chine par les pères de la Cie de Jésus*. 3 vols. Paris,
1729–1732.

SOUÉO, GOTO. *See* GOTO.

SOULIER, GUSTAVE. *Les Influences orientales dans la peinture toscane*. Paris,
1920.

SPIZELIUS, TH. *De re literaria sinensium commentarius.* Lugd. Batav., 1660.

STAUNTON, SIR GEORGE, ed. *The History of the Great and Mighty Kingdom of China.* Hakluyt Society: London, 1853. *See* MENDOÇA.

STEINMETZ, A. *History of the Jesuits.* 3 vols. London, 1848.

STEWART, J. *Nestorian Missionary Enterprise: The Story of a Church on Fire.* Edinburgh, 1928.
A readable though uncritical account of Nestorianism.

SYKES, SIR PERCY. *A History of Exploration from the Earliest Times to the Present Day.* New York, 1934.
Chapter xviii deals with the penetration of China and Tibet in the seventeenth and eighteenth centuries.

————. *The Quest for Cathay.* London, 1936.
A well-written popular account of the medieval travelers, with useful reproductions of old maps.

TACCHI-VENTURI, PIETRO. *See* RICCI.

TACHARD, GUY, S.J. *Voyage de Siam des Pères Jésuites envoyés par le Roi aux Indes et à la Chine.* Paris, 1686.
An account of the voyage of the first French Jesuit group.

TCHANG TSONG-MING. *Voltaire et la Chine.* April, 1930.
French doctoral thesis.

TEGGART, FREDERICK J. *Rome and China, A Study of Correlations in Historical Events.* University of California Press, Berkeley, 1939.
For a discussion of Professor Teggart's study see note 1 to chap. xix, p. 336 of the present work.

THIERSANT, DABRY DE. *Le Catholicisme en Chine au VIIIᵉ siècle de notre ère avec une nouvelle traduction de l'inscription de Syngan-fou.* Paris, 1877.

THOMAS, A. *Histoire de la mission de Pékin depuis ses origines jusqu'à l'arrivée des Lazaristes.* Paris, 1923.
A general review of the subject, particularly of the Rites controversy. Unsympathetic to the Jesuits, in spite of the author's claim of impartiality. No index or bibliography.

TINDAL, MATTHEW. *Christianity as Old as Creation or the Gospel a Republication of the Religion of Nature.* London, 1730.

TING, TCHAO-TS'ING. *Les Descriptions de la Chine par les Français (1650–1750).* Paris, 1928.
Deals with the Jesuit attempts to interpret Chinese culture. Author thinks missionaries were poor Sinologists.

T'oung Pao, Archives pour servir à l'étude de l'histoire des langues, de la géographie et de l'ethnographie de l'Asie Orientale. Leiden, 1890——.
The most scholarly periodical of Chinese studies. Invaluable for students of Far Eastern culture.

TRIGAULT, NICOLAS, S.J. *De Christiano Expeditione apud Sinas suscepta ab Soc. Jesu ex P. Matthieu Ricci ejusdem Soc. Commentariis . . . Auctore Paul Nicolio Trigaultio Belga ex eadem Soc.* Amsterdam, 1615.
See pp. 245–246 of present work and notes.

TSCHARNER, EDUARD HORST VON. "China in der deutschen Dichtung," *Sinica* (1937), Vol. XII.
A brief account of Sinomania in Germany of the seventeenth and eighteenth centuries.

TURGOT, A. R. J. *Réflexions sur la Formation et la Distribution des Richesses.* Paris, 1766.

VAETH, ALFONS, S.J. *Johann Adam Schall von Bell, S.J., Missionar in China, Kaiserlicher Astronome und Ratgeber am Hofe von Peking, 1592–1666. Ein Lebens und Zeitbild.* Köln, 1933.
A long and detailed account of the life and works of the Jesuit missionary. Invaluable for reference.

VERBIEST, FERDINAND, S.J. *Astronomia Europœa sub Imperatore Tartaro-Sinico Cam Hy, appellato ex umbra in lucem revocata a R.P. Ferdinand Verbiest.* Dillingen, 1687.

———. *Lettre écrite de la cour de Pékin sur un voyage que l'empereur de la Chine a fait dans la Tartarie occidentale.* Paris, 1684.

VLADIMIRTSOV, B. YA. *The Life of Ghinghis Khan.* English translation, London, 1930.

VOLTAIRE, FRANÇOIS MARIE AROUET. *Œuvres complètes.* Moland, ed. Paris, 1877–1885.

VOSSIUS, ISAAC. *Isaaci Vossii variarum observationum liber.* London, 1685.

WADDING, LUKE. *Scriptores Ordinis Minorum.* Rome, 1806.

WALTER, RICHARD. *A Voyage around the World in the years MDCCXL. I. II. III. IV. by George Anson . . . compiled by Richard Walter.* London, 1748.

WERNER, E. C. *Matteo Ricci's Scientific Contribution to China. Peiping, 1935. See* BERNARD, HENRI.

WESSELS, C., S.J. *Early Jesuit Travellers in Central Asia, 1603–1721.* The Hague, 1924.
Contains an account of Goës' overland journey from India to China.

WIEGER, L., S.J. *Textes historiques: Histoire politique de la Chine depuis l'origine.* Sienhsien–Paris, 1922–1923.

WILLIAMS, E. T. *China Yesterday and Today.* New York, 1923.

———. *A Short History of China,* New York, 1928.

WYLIE, A. *Notes on Chinese Literature.* Shanghai, 1901.
A highly valuable bibliographical work.

———. *Chinese Researches.* Shanghai, 1897.

YIAN TSOUAN LIN. *See* LIN.

YING-KI, IGNATIUS. "The Last Emperor of the Ming Dynasty and Catholicity," *Bulletin of the Catholic University of Peking,* No. 1 (1926), pp. 23–28.

YOHANNON, A. *The Death of a Nation or the Ever-Persecuted Nestorian or Assyrian Christians.* New York, 1916.
    A short and superficial summary of the fortunes of the Nestorian Church up to the present time.

YULE, SIR HENRY. *The Book of Ser Marco Polo.* 3 vols. Rev. ed. by Henri Cordier; London, 1921.
    As revised by Cordier, the work remains the peerless critical edition of this great masterpiece of travel literature.

————. *Cathay and the Way Thither, Being a Collection of Mediaeval Notices of China.* 4 vols. New edition by Henri Cordier, Hakluyt Society; London, 1913–1916.
    A translation of the accounts of the medieval travelers, including Odoric of Pordenone, John of Montecorvino, the Archbishop of Soltania, Rashid-ud-din, Pegolotti, John of Marignolli, Ibn Batuta, and Benedict Goës, preceded by a two-hundred-page preliminary essay. Copious notes. The most convenient and scholarly single work on the subject.

INDEX

INDEX

Index

DATF